THE POPE

The Pope

His Mission and His Task

Gerhard Cardinal Müller

Translated by Brian McNeil

The Catholic University of America Press
Washington, D.C.
2021

Originally published as
Gerhard Ludwig Müller, *Der Papst. Sendung und Auftrag*

The present text is the translation of an abridgement
made by Cardinal Müller of the original work.

The paper used in this publication
meets the minimum requirements of
American National Standards for Information Science—
Permanence of Paper for Printed Library Materials,
ANSI Z39.48-1984.

Library of Congress Cataloging-in-Publication Data

Names: Müller, Gerhard Ludwig author | McNeil, Brian, translator
Title: The Pope: His Mission and His Task / Gerhard Ludwig Müller
Translated by Brian McNeil.
Other titles: Papst. English
Description: Washington, DC : The Catholic University of America, 2021.
Includes bibliographical references and index.
Identifiers: LCCN 2021035710 (print) | LCCN 2021035711 (ebook)
ISBN 9780813234694 (paperback) | ISBN 9780813234700 (ebook)
Subjects: LCSH: Papacy | Petrine office | Papacy and Christian union | Popes–Primacy.
Classification: LCC BX1805 .M85513 2021 (print) | LCC BX1805 (ebook) |
DDC 262/.13--dc23
LC record available at https://lccn.loc.gov/2021035710
LC ebook record available at https://lccn.loc.gov/2021035711

Printed in the United States.
Book design by Burt&Burt
Interior set with Minion Pro and Meta Pro

With gratitude
to
Lois and Carl Davis
whose generosity
made this publication possible

Contents

Translator's Note

Biblical texts are quoted from *The Holy Bible, Revised Standard Version, Second Catholic Edition,* San Francisco: Ignatius Press, 2006.

Texts of the Second Vatican Council are quoted from *The Documents of Vatican II, With Notes and Index, Vatican Translation,* Strathfeld NSW and Staten Island, N.Y.: St Paul's, 2009.

Other documents of the magisterium of the Catholic Church are quoted from the official Vatican English texts. Available at www.vatican.va

I wish to emphasize that the use of masculine terms ("his," "he," etc.) is dictated exclusively by stylistic concerns.

Preface

In the contemporary religious, moral, cultural, and political crisis, which has no parallel in world history hitherto, all the hopes and fears of humankind come together in Rome, the center of the worldwide Catholic Church, as in a burning glass.

The Church does not close her eyes to this. She knows that she can be the Church of Christ only if she is the "Church for others" (Dietrich Bonhoeffer).

The Second Vatican Council summarized the fellowship in solidarity of the people of God with the whole of humanity in the celebrated words:

> The joys and the hopes, the griefs and the anxieties of the men of this age, especially those who are poor or in any way afflicted, these are the joys and hopes, the griefs and anxieties of the followers of Christ. Indeed, nothing genuinely human fails to raise an echo in their hearts. For theirs is a community composed of men. United in Christ, they are led by the Holy Spirit in their journey to the Kingdom of their Father and they have welcomed the news of salvation which is meant for every man. That is why this community realizes that it is truly linked with mankind and its history by the deepest of bonds (*Gaudium et spes* 1).

All the popes since then have been guided in their saving ministry, which was entrusted to them by Christ, by the idea of the solidarity of the Catholic Church with the whole of humanity. Pope Francis is the first universal shepherd of the Church who contributes to the Petrine ministry the mentality and experience of a Latin American and is thus able to add to the intention of the council a new dimension in its realization.

Peter, the rock, will inevitably always be also a stumbling block, because the Word of God must be proclaimed, whether people want to hear it or not (see 2 Tm 4:2).

But the pope is also a bearer of hope for Christianity and for the world, because it is to him that the words of the Son of God apply: "You and Peter, and on this rock I will build my Church, and the gates of Hades shall not prevail against it. I will give you the keys of the kingdom of heaven" (Mt 16:18–19). The pope is recognized by many persons of good will as the highest moral authority, even by those who do not belong to the Christian community. He is a sign both of the orientation of the human being to the truth of God and for the dignity that the human being cannot lose. He is a sign of peace and of social justice in the family of peoples.

In 2017, the year of remembrance of the Reformation of 1517, but also moved by grief over the division of Western Christianity, many Christians who are not yet in full communion with the successor of Peter yearn for an ecumenical form of the papacy, so that we may make progress towards the visible unity of the Church that is the will of her divine Founder.

In order to fulfill the task given him by Christ, the Holy Father needs the skilled and committed sharing in his concern on the part of the College of Cardinals, who together with him represent the Roman church, the mother and teacher of all the churches. The congregations of cardinals of the Roman church, which were founded in the early modern period, are the present-day form of the synodal participation of the Roman church in the Petrine ministry; in the early centuries, this was exercised by the Roman synods, which were extremely important for the universal Church, and later on by the College of Cardinals as a whole.

The Congregation for the Doctrine of the Faith has a special function in the exercise of the papal magisterium. It shares in the teaching office of the pope and supports him in all questions of the doctrine of faith and of morals, acting in accordance with the task entrusted to it. The teaching ministry of the pope is the *raison d'être* and the very core of his mission: Christ "instituted in him a permanent and visible source and foundation of unity of faith and communion" (*Lumen gentium* 18). The Congregation for the Doctrine of the Faith has twenty-five members or fathers, the cardinals and bishops from every part of the world who are personally appointed by the pope. Its task is to promote the Catholic faith everywhere in the Church and to protect it against reductions or falsifications. The cardinal prefect bears the responsibility for the entire activity of the congregation immediately and personally vis-à-vis the pope, the father and teacher of the universal Church who is called by Christ.

In view of the importance of the successor of Peter for the Church of God in today's world, I should like to bring together my experiences and observations, as well as reflections and references about the origin, the essence, and the mission of the successor of Peter, to form an overall picture. I do so from my perspective as theologian, bishop, and prefect of the Roman congregation which is intimately united to the teaching office of the pope.

I have deliberately avoided the title *papacy*, in order to emphasize the precedence of the person before the institution. According to the Catholic faith, Christ made Simon, a simple fisher from the Lake of Gennesaret, as the first of a long line of his successors, the rock on which he would build his Church. Peter's ministry continues to exist, even when the persons who carry it out succeed one another in the course of time. But Christ, the Head of the Church, personally appoints the bishop of Rome, whom he entrusts with Peter's mission. The persons change, but the task remains the same. The pope's primary task is the serve the unity and communion of the Church with God and to bear testimony with his living and his dying to "Christ, the Son of the living God" (Mt 16:16). Together with all the shepherds of the Church, Peter is "a witness of the sufferings of Christ as well as a partaker in the glory that is to be revealed" (1 Pt 5:1). The pope has no political office that would be concerned with power in the world or prestige among human beings. His criterion and model is the "good shepherd, who lays down his life for the sheep" (Jn 10:11). And this good shepherd is Jesus himself, who confirms three times the commission he entrusts to Simon Peter when he says: "Pasture MY sheep!" (Jn 21:15).

The pope and the cardinals who assist him fraternally in the governance of the universal Church, and all the shepherds of the Church, should let themselves be taken hold of by the apostolic zeal of Saint Paul, who together with Peter is the fundament of the church of Rome. The apostle of the Gentiles summarizes the spirituality and ethos of "God's fellow-workers" (2 Cor 6:1) in the following words:

> We put no obstacle in any one's way, so that no fault may be found with our ministry, but as servants of God we commend ourselves in every way: through great endurance, in afflictions, hardships, [...] labors, [...] by kindness, the Holy Spirit, genuine love, truthful speech, and the power of God; with the weapons of righteousness for the right hand and for the left; in honor and dishonor, in ill repute and good repute (2 Cor 6:3–10).

Rome, on the Solemnity of the Chair of Saint Peter the Apostle, 2017

Gerhard Cardinal Müller
Prefect of the Congregation for the Doctrine of the Faith

Abbreviations

AUGUSTINE OF HIPPO

Civ.	*De civitate Dei* (CCSL 47-48)
Conf.	*Confessionum libri XIII* (CCSL 27)
Serm.	*Sermones* (PL 38-39)
Tract. in ev. Ioh.	*Tractatus in evangelium Iohannis* (CCSL 36)

CYPRIAN OF CARTHAGE

Domin. or.	*De dominica oratione* (CCSL 3A)
Eccl. unit.	*De ecclesia unitate* (CCSL 3)
Ep.	*Epistulae* (CSEL 3/2)

DIETRICH BONHOEFFER

DBW	*Dietrich Bonhoeffer werke*

EUSEBIUS OF CAESAREA

Hist. eccl.	*Historia ecclesiastica* (GCS 9)

GELASIUS I

Ep.	*Epistulae*

GREGORY THE GREAT

Ep.	*Epistulae* (CSEL 140-140A)

IGNATIUS OF ANTIOCH

Ep. ad Rom.	*Epistula ad Romanos* (PG 5)
Ep. ad Smyrn.	*Epistula ad Smyrnaeanos* (PG 5)

IRENAEUS OF LYONS

Adv. haer.	*Adversus haereses* (PG 7)

JEROME

Adv. Iovin.	*Adversus Iovinianum* (PL 23)

JUSTINIAN I

Cod. Just.	*Codex Justiniani*

LEO THE GREAT

Ep.	*Epistulae*
Serm.	*Sermones*

MARTIN LUTHER

WA	*Weimarer ausgabe*

OPTATUS OF MILEVIS

C. Parmen.	*Contra Parmenianum donatistam* (CSEL 26)

SERIES

ACO	*Acta Conciliorum Oecumenicorum*
DBW	*Dietrich Bonhoeffer werke*
DThC	*Dictionnaire de Théologie Catholique*
WA	*Weimarer ausgabe* (Martin Luther)

TERTULLIAN

Praescr.	*De praescriptione haereticorum*

THOMAS AQUINAS

Com. ad Rom.	*Commentarium ad Romanos*
Com. ad Gal.	*Commentarium ad Galatas*
De ver.	*Quaestio Disputata de Veritate*
Ev. Jo.	*Super Evangelium Joannis Lectura*
Ev. Matt.	*Super Evangelium Matthaei Lectura*
S.th.	*Summa Theologiae*

VATICAN DOCUMENTS

AG	*Ad gentes*
CCC	*Catechism of the Catholic Church*
CIC	*Codex Iuris Canonici*
CD	*Christus Dominus*
DH	*Denzinger, Enchiridion symbolorum*
DV	*Dei verbum*
GS	*Gaudium et spes*
LG	*Lumen gentium*
OE	*Orientalium Ecclesiarum*
OT	*Optatam totius*
PO	*Presbyterorum ordinis*
UR	*Unitatis redintegratio*

The Pope

His Mission and His Task

I

The Popes in the Story of My Life

1. THE EMERGENCE OF MY RELIGIOUS CONVICTIONS

THANKS TO MY FAITH IN JESUS CHRIST and to life in the Church, my relationship to the Roman pope already had positive connotations, even before I could begin my academic studies of the biblical basis, the testimonies of tradition, the definitions by the magisterium, the controversies with the Orthodox Churches and Reformation Protestantism about the papacy, and the challenges in the modern and postmodern periods. It was not abstractions and theories but living persons and witnesses to the faith who laid the foundations of my relationship to the Catholic Church, and thereby also to the papacy, and who left their mark on the ideas I had about these matters.

Credere means "to believe"—not in the sense of having an opinion on this or that important question, but *believing* in the theological sense, which denotes the relationship to God who addresses me personally in the word of his revelation. *Credere* comes from *cor dare.* Believing in God means giving my own heart to the One who has opened his heart to me. For me, believing means that I place all my hope, in my living and in my dying, in the God and Father of Jesus Christ. I am deeply moved when I pray: "The Lord is my shepherd, I shall not want.... Surely goodness and mercy shall follow me all the days of my life; and I shall dwell in the house of the Lord forever" (Ps 23:1, 6).

Faith in God does not exist without a love for him that surpasses all created things, and the love of neighbor as oneself, since he has created me, and all my dear friends, and all those whom I revere, in his own image and likeness (Gn 1:28). Faith is not merely an intellectual insight into questions about religion and the Church. It is significant for salvation only when it is active in love (Gal 5:6) and when all the sadness of time fades away in the joy of eternity.

God liberates and sanctifies the human being. He brings him into the state of sanctifying grace, giving him a share in his own being and life, and filling him with his own goodness and truth. God makes us his own sons and daughters. This divine childhood is bestowed on us through grace and through justifying faith in hope and love (*fides caritate formata*).

Faith belongs to a different category than the knowledge of the things of the world. It surpasses participation in social and media networks, and this means that it is not in the least to be dismissed as a deficient form of knowledge and information. In the words of Dietrich Bonhoeffer (1906–1945), God is neither a working hypothesis nor a gap-filler for questions of the natural sciences that have not yet been cleared up.[1] The faith that is put into practice by the reason and by the assent of the free will in the power of the Spirit of God is the highest form of knowledge that exists under the conditions of our earthly existence; it will be surpassed only in "seeing God face to face" (1 Cor 13:12) in eternity. In faith, the relationship of the created person and of human society to the triune God succeeds and turns out well. Salvation takes place therein, because it is a matter, not of insight into a state of affairs, but of a participation in God's inner knowledge in the Word and in his relationship to his own self as love in the *koinonia* of the Father and the Son and the Holy Spirit. Accordingly, the contents of the faith signify knowledge and acceptance of his salvific will through his salvific action in history. In faith in God, the disciple of Christ trusts *formaliter* in the truthfulness of God (*veracitas Dei*). This was made possible for the disciple on the basis of the testimony of the God who speaks to us through Jesus Christ, the *verbum incarnatum*, the eternal WORD of the Father, who took our flesh from the Virgin Mary. This means that the Son of God is not only our Lord but also our brother, because he became like us human beings (Heb 2:14). Christ's testimony to the Father is mediated to us in its individual contents in the confession of the Church in the articles of the creed.[2]

1 Dietrich Bonhoeffer, *DBW*, vol. 8, *Widerstand und Ergebung: Briefe auf dem Gefängnis aus der Haft* (Munich: Chr. Kaiser, 1970), 415.

2 Thomas Aquinas, *De ver.* 14.8.

The "I" of my personal faith in God is maternally (so to speak) conceived, borne, brought into the world, and nourished by the Church. The "I believe in God" is taken up and enveloped by the "We believe in God." I am liberated from the tortured isolation in the solitary confinement of my ego to the glory of the children of God in the Church, the family and community of the believers. The Church does not stand over against me as an institution. On the contrary, I belong to it as the limbs of a body form with its head a unity and a community of life. Vis-à-vis God, the Church is the virgin (*virgo*) who receives the Word in faith; vis-à-vis us, the Church is the mother (*mater*) who bestows the divine life on us in faith.

The Church has never meant an anonymous institution for me, something as unattainable as justice in Kafka's *Castle*. The papacy always had a human face from my childhood down to my present-day ministry as Prefect of the Roman Congregation for the Doctrine of the Faith, a human face that represented this foundation by Christ.

The papacy is not an objective and impersonal institution. Rather, it is a sequence of persons who accomplish their mission, which the exalted Lord confers on them individually. Each pope, as the successor of Peter, has a name in which he appears before us in his specific individuality. The person is antecedent to the institution and makes the abiding task and mission of Peter visible and alive. Christianity is not a sum total of dogmatic propositions and ethical principles that I would have to drag laboriously through life in a heavy rucksack. Its content becomes light, bearable, and sustainable in personal faith and in the community of the Church *in via*. And I know that what I bear, and what bears me, is Christ himself. He is the water of life (Jn 4:14) that refreshes me, and he is the bread that strengthens me and keeps me alive (Jn 6:48).

Christian existence takes place in following Christ, whose yoke is easy and whose burden is light (Mt 11:30), because everything is borne in love for him. In this way, the community of those who walk with him gives help and stimulus. The Church exists in persons in their relationship to Christ, both in one's fellow Christians and also specifically in the messengers of Jesus and the witnesses to the Gospel, the apostles, bishops, and priests "to the ends of the earth" (Acts 1:8; Mt 28:20).

This is why I begin by looking at the seven popes during the span of my life up to now. I would like to make clear in this way my religious convictions and my rootedness in the Catholic faith on the basis of God and Christ and the Church.

2.
MY CATHOLIC CHILDHOOD AND YOUTH
Pius XII (1939–1958)

ON THE DAY I WAS BORN, the feast of Pope Saint Sylvester I (r. 314–335) in 1947, Pius XII (1939–1958) had already experienced war, Italian Fascism, and the Nazi period. At that period, he had to confront the atheistic threat to Christianity in the East and the intensifying secularism in the West. When I began school, and during my preparation for First Communion, we heard who the pope was, and above all that we, the Catholic Christians, venerated him as the successor of Peter, the prince of the apostles, and thus as the Vicar of Christ on earth. The pope embodied in his person the unity of the pilgrim Church on earth.

One day—it was on October 9, 1958—my sister Antonia (1940–2010), who was graduating from high school and thus was in my eyes the highest authority of knowledge, rushed into my room and cried out: "Have you already heard it? The pope has died."

At that moment, I was most moved by the idea that the pope was now in heaven with Christ. The concept of "pope" was linked to God, Christ, and the Church. As I understood it, the word "dying" had something to do with heaven. After death, our soul comes to God, and then we hope in the resurrection of the flesh to eternal life, and the resurrection of all the dead for the final judgment. In a child's imagination, the office is virtually identical with the person of the office bearer. For us, Pius XII was simply "the" pope, the successor of Saint Peter, the highest authority in all questions of faith, just as for me at that time Albert Stohr (1890–1961) was the bishop of Mainz, and we simply could not imagine any other parish priest than our own Philipp Heinrich Lambert (1896–1960). My first home pastor was the very embodiment of a priest who was zealous for souls; his heart belonged entirely to the poor and the sick and, especially after 1945, also to the German prisoners of war in the camps around Mainz. In his profoundly religious attitude and his social involvement, he was for me the first and the most impressive expression of a "shepherd of souls."

Pius XII is the pope of my childhood, and he was regarded simply as the embodiment and the criterion of what "Catholic" meant.

As a child of parents who were believers, I received the grace of growing into a life based on faith in God, the origin and the goal of life, and of making this faith more and more something that belonged to me internally. Faith did not spring from an internal subjective experience that then found a secondary expression, as the rationalist philosophy of religion would have us believe. On the contrary, "faith comes from what is heard, and what is heard comes by the preaching of Christ" (Rom 10:17), which was entrusted to the apostles and to the entire Church to be proclaimed. Faith comes from the outside, from hearing and learning and living together with the community of believers in the family, the kindergarten, and the youth group, in the parish community, in the school class and the Church as a whole. In praying and singing, the youthful spirit joins in the melody and harmony of the praise of God, and experiences Jesus, his mother Mary, and the apostles as immediately close in the biblical story. And in the catechism, the child's spirit finds nourishment and acquires clear ideas about God, Christ, and the Church.

I grew into faith in Christ, so to speak. It is impossible to understand my internal development and my intellectual-moral life without faith in God and love for the Church of Christ. The objective tradition of the Church, as this has found expression in sacred scripture, in the creeds, in the solemn liturgy, and in the dogmatic decisions of the magisterium, is what one learns; and even an educated non-Christian can and ought to be well informed about this.

But how does the external confession of the Church, the content of the faith, enter into the spirit and understanding of the person, so that a young person or an adult catechumen who hears the human word externally can make this word his own in such a way that he hears in it the Word of God, and recognizes and acknowledges Christ himself as his internal teacher? The apostles "Paul, Silvanus, and Timothy" address their community in Thessalonica and attest the inseparable co-operation between God's grace and the Church's proclamation: "And we also thank God constantly for this, that when you received the word of God which you heard from us, you accepted it not as the word of men but as what it really is, the word of God, which is at work in you believers" (1 Thes 2:13).

The external and objective tradition of the Church must become internal and subjective tradition, like a bubbling spring from which the Christian personality draws "the water of eternal life" (Jn 4:14). God communicates his word through the Church, so that we may enter into an immediate relationship to God through the virtues of faith, hope, and love that are infused in us by the Holy Spirit. But immediacy to God does not discard integration into the community of salvation in the way that a satellite discards its rocket engine once it has reached its orbit.

Immediacy to God is always mediated through the humanity of Christ and the ecclesial-sacramental form of Christ's community. Personal immediacy to God and the ecclesial-sacramental mediation belong together because of the divine-human unity of Christ, the revealer and mediator of salvation.

This is in accordance with our physical nature and our constitution as beings made for community, beings who need the ecclesial mediation of revelation. Only in this way can I enter into the personal relationship to God, both in his Word that he addresses to me and in his salvific action on my behalf.

The important Tübingen theologian Johann Adam Möhler (1796–1838) expressed the reciprocal relationship between objective and subjective tradition, between external-ecclesial mediation and internal-Christological immediacy to God, as follows:

> What is tradition? The specific sense [*Sinn*] that is present in the Church and propagates itself through the Church's education. But this cannot be thought of without its content; on the contrary, it is by means of and through its content that it has taken shape, so that it can be called a perfected sense. Tradition is the word that continuously lives in the hearts of believers. The exposition of sacred scripture is entrusted to this sense as a total sense.[3]

The Christian education attains its goal when it awakens in the members of the Church the *supernaturalis sensus fidei fidelium,* the supernatural sense of the faith (cf. LG 12). The identity of the Catholic believer is constituted by the sense (*sentire cum ecclesia*) of the inherent connection between God and Church, of Christ as Head and body, and of the real activity of grace in the sacred signs instituted by Christ.

Through his love and the gift of his life on the Cross, Christ has acquired the Church as his own body, which he "loves and does not hate, but nourishes and cherishes, that he might sanctify her, having cleansed her by the washing of water with the word" (Eph 5:26). The personal immediacy to God, who has known me and has destined me beforehand "to share in the being and the form of his Son" (Rom 8:29), and the sacramental mediation of salvation through the Church (Mt 28:19) and sharing in the Church's life indicate what is distinctly Catholic. In my youth, one often heard in sermons the words of Saint Cyprian of Carthage (ca. 200–258): "The one who does not have the Church as his mother can no longer have God as his Father," and I grasped at once the inseparability of the relationship to God and the community of the Church.[4]

When I received the divine childhood through baptism and was incorporated into the Church, the body of Christ, and was led at the age of nine

3 Johann Adam Möhler, *Symbolik oder Darstellung der dogmatischen Gegensätze des Katholiken und der Protestanten nach ihren öffentlichen Bekenntnisschriften*, ed. J. R. Geiselmann (Cologne: Hegner, 1958), §38.

4 Cyprian of Carthage, *Eccl. unit.* 6.

to the encounter with Christ in the sacraments of penance (confession) and First Communion, my elders and priests understood these at that time—as I myself understood them when I was mature—not merely as rites of socialization. Tertullian, the great North African patristic writer (ca. 160–220), put it as follows: "Christ called himself Truth, not custom."[5] I experienced the inner encounter with Jesus, whom I love, as an integration into the divine life of the Father, the Son, and the Holy Spirit, an integration that sustains my person. This is the relationship to God as his creature and his child, the indwelling of the Trinity in the soul, in accordance with Jesus's words: "If anyone loves me, he will keep my word, and my Father will love him, and we will come to him and make our home with him" (Jn 14:23). Faith was not imposed by our parents' authority in the manner of an indoctrination that steered us from the outside. It was sown gently in the heart, and thus I never felt that my freedom was under threat.

The dichotomy between authority and freedom has brought some people shipwreck, but the dichotomy does not exist where "there is planting and watering, but the growth is entrusted to God" (cf. 1 Cor 3:6–7). Later, as a religious teacher in school and a preacher, I was often asked what I myself thought. "It is of course clear that you know the teaching of the Church," I was told, "and that you are obliged to support it in an official context, but what do you personally think?" This question was posed in private, away from the public sphere. But my answer was always: If one believes that God's revelation and his history with us human beings is preserved in its totality in the Church's creed, and that there is no private and secret access to God that could bypass Christ and the Church, how is it possible for me to believe any differently than the Church believes? That would mean making myself higher than God.

My mother awakened love for Jesus in me at a tender age. This love did not get stuck in sentimentality, and it did not infantilize me. Love kindled in my inner eye a light that continued to shine over the whole of my life.

"Jesus, I live for you; Jesus, I die for you; Jesus, I am yours in death and in life" (cf. Rom 14:8). This was my first prayer. Every evening, my brother Günter and I prayed like this before we went to sleep. The cross, with Jesus nailed to it, hung over my bed—the visible proof that Jesus truly laid down his life for me and for us, *pro me et pro nobis*. The thought that I am God's creature and his child, called to eternal life, fills my heart and mind down to the present day with astonishment and admiration (as one could say, adapting a phrase of Kant). What was communicated to us was the certainty that God is well disposed towards us and ultimately leads all things to the good

5 Tertullian, *De virginibus velandis*, I.1.

(cf. Rom 8:28). "Begin with God and end with God—that is the finest life": this was another prayer that expresses a child's primal trust in God.

Prayer also included the daily examination of conscience in the evening, before falling asleep. The recognition that the existence of free will means that I am obliged to accept responsibility for my conduct was the best preparation for the sacrament of penance, which I received later on. As is well known, this has three steps: the repentance of the heart, the oral explicit confession of sins, and the reparation in good works—these are followed by God's forgiveness in the absolution. A good examination of conscience does not lead to fear and trembling before the strict God who judges. Since God is the forgiving Father precisely in his judgment, the reference to the personal judgment on each person after death, and to the Last Judgment on the whole of humankind at the end of history, leads rather to shock at myself—for I have separated myself from loving God above all else and loving my neighbor, either by transgressing the commandments of God or through a lack of good works. "There is no fear in love, but perfect love casts out fear. For fear has to do with punishment, and he who fears is not perfected in love" (1 Jn 4:18).

In the preparation for confession, I look at myself and submit myself to the judgment of God's love. My conscience becomes "torment and hell" for me only if I suppress my sins and errors in order to justify myself. It is only the unatoned-for sin, which I want to suppress through self-justification, that leads to hatred of God and contempt for his Church. But if I humbly recognize my sins and repent of them, God's mercy becomes an invitation to the prodigal son to return home to the Father's house (cf. Lk 15:11–32). In religious education, it is intellectually and psychologically important to draw a careful distinction between the everyday (or venial) sins and the grave sins that lead to the "spiritual death of the soul" (cf. 1 Jn 5:16). Scruples and self-doubts are a lack of love and of trust in God, who is always the God of the ever-greater love that forgives—not the God of the vengeance that leads one to fear and to run away from him.

I can be certain of his forgiveness and grace, not when I look at myself, but when I look to God and to the affection he shows me in Jesus Christ. This means that I am set free from sin and can venerate God and serve human beings with a happy conscience: "The one who has faith can be certain of the omnipotence and the mercy of God."[6] Faith is motivated by the gracious God who truly transforms us from enemies and slaves into friends and children of God.[7] "So you also must consider yourselves dead to sin and alive to God in Christ Jesus" (Rom 6:11).

6 Thomas Aquinas, *S.th.* I-I q18 a4 ad 2.

7 Rom 5:10; 6:20; 8:14.

It may indeed be the case that ancient pagan authors such as Lucretius and Epicurus, or the atheistic-rationalistic critique of religion in the eighteenth and nineteenth centuries, or Freud's depth psychology derived religion or the belief in gods from the so-called primitive human being's fear in face of the powers of nature or from unprocessed emotions. In my recollection of my early childhood and in my reflection as a scholar, belief in the God of love in Jesus Christ does not have its genesis in mental conditions and dynamics. The analogy to the human emotions is valid in relation not to the powers of nature and to the blows of fate in our temporal existence but to the child's trust in the father to whom he owes the origin and the support of his life, and thus to the parents, the ancestors, and the brothers and sisters in the family of God that takes the path of Christ as a pilgrim Church until the end of time, when "the holy city, new Jerusalem, comes down out of heaven from God, prepared as a bride adorned for her husband, and the dwelling of God is with men" (Rv 21:2–3a).

Against the psychology of religion that derives Christianity from the shattering experience of the contingency of all that is earthly, the pain of being doomed to die, or the fear of the powers of nature that cannot be dominated by technology and of the blind blows of fate, it is only God's consolations and promises that help: "For you did not receive the spirit of slavery to fall back into fear, but you have received the Spirit of sonship, in whom we cry: Abba, Father" (Rom 8:15).

Our faith is not born of wishes and illusions. It is no abstract idea, nor an ideal of the pure reason that is unsupported by experience. On the contrary, it has a real foundation—namely, God's salvific action in the midst of the world and of history. Job, the suffering righteous man, confesses: "I know that my Redeemer lives" (Jb 19:25). One who—like Jesus—has taken such pains upon himself for my sake is right and makes me righteous; I can entrust myself to him in living and in dying. No one who subsequently attempted, in the name of the self-enlightened reason in the philosophical salons, with a blind belief in progress and an apparently objective science, to convince me of the intellectual inferiority of Christianity or of its "medieval parochialism" (I quote here the polemical formulae that are not in fact *arguments*) was ever able to dislodge the primal experience of God as love.

Behind the hollow and lofty façade of free thought lies so much arrogance and cynicism that it would be impossible to find a genuine friend among its representatives. A good friend is nothing but well-meaning towards me. He does not want merely to win me as a comrade who shares his own worldview and thus confirms him. If all that existed was this short life, and its meaning consisted only of enjoyment, why should I lay it down, if not in the name of the one who has given us life in fullness and who says to us: "Greater love has no man than this, that a man lay down his life for his friends" (Jn 15:13)? For down to the present day, none of the prominent representatives of the ancient pagan and modern anti-Christian ideologies has accepted to give his life for mine. Nor has any of them even remotely the power to overcome, now and forever, my finitude, my suffering and my death, and the transience of all those whom I love. God, who handed over his only Son for us out of love for us, and whom we love above all things, was and is the most real reality in and above the world. God, from whom we come and who is our goal: this is the certainty implanted in both the heart and the understanding, the certainty that gives firm support and discloses the meaning of life.

When I look back on the slow maturing of my religious consciousness and its ever-deeper rooting in the mystery of Christ, I can put a name to what I owe to the grace of God and not merely to happy circumstances. I know not only *what* I believe but also *whom* I believe. This is how Paul, as "preacher, apostle, and teacher of the Gospel" appointed by Christ, interpreted the adversities of his mission: "That is why I suffer as I do. But I am not ashamed, for I know whom I have believed, and I am sure that he is able to guard until that Day what has been entrusted to me" (2 Tm 1:12). And I hear, from those who were my own teachers and pastors, the commission that he gave to his pupil and successor in the apostolic ministry: "Follow the pattern of the sound words which you have heard from me, in the faith and love which are in Christ Jesus; guard the truth that has been entrusted to you by the Holy Spirit who dwells within us" (2 Tm 1:13–14).

In the solemn liturgy of the eucharistic sacrifice, and in the silent adoration of the Lord in the Blessed Sacrament, and in the solemn splendor of the feast of Corpus Christi, the heart gains so great an experience of the true presence of Christ that all trust in God is sustained by Christ and all love for God and for one's neighbor is kindled ever anew. This closeness to God gives support to the whole of one's life and lets the paschal Alleluia resound ever anew in the heart. This is the recognition that Jesus was not merely an important human being who lived two thousand years ago and is now dead, someone whom we remember in historical terms, a model who can give us moral strength. No:

> He is eternally alive in his Church, and makes this vivid to the sensuous human being, in a manner appropriate to the senses, in the sacrament of the altar. In the proclamation of his Word, he is the perennial teacher; in baptism, he unceasingly grants admission into his fellowship, in the sacrament of penance he forgives the penitent sinner, he strengthens the adolescent in confirmation with the power of his Spirit, he inspires in bridegroom

> and bride a higher view of the state of marriage, he unites himself most intimately under the forms of the bread and wine with all who sigh for eternal life, he consoles the dying in the anointing, and in the ordination of priests he installs the organs through which he brings all this about in an activity that never wearies.[8]

Not even a child's faith lacks understanding. That which is irrational can never become rational in the course of time. As far back as I can remember, I had always a sense of the categorically different truth content of the biblical history and the doctrines of the faith, on the one hand, and the fairytales and legends and adventure stories, on the other hand. These certainly provided much food for a child's imagination, but we were always told afterwards that a fairytale was only a fairytale, and hence not realistically true. We read of John the Baptist: "The child grew and became strong in spirit" (Lk 1:80). As children, we were always impressed by the fact that the same was related about Jesus, as he grew up in his family in Nazareth: "The child grew and became strong, filled with wisdom; and the favor of God was upon him" (Lk 2:40). When intellectual and existential difficulties in my faith and my life occurred, my principle was always to seek the reasons for this not in the revelation of God or in the teaching of the Church but in my still-imperfect knowledge, which could be overcome by a deeper study and a more intensive prayer for better insight. For it is the *person* that, with the aid of prevenient grace, enters through his or her reason and free will into a relation to the personal God in faith. It is only through faith that the reason comes to its goal, which is the knowledge of the truth—and God in person is the truth. Revelation leads to the truth, because God makes himself known as the truth in his Word and his Spirit. Accordingly, the truth of faith is not an insight that I myself achieve into the structure of created material and non-material realities but the insight of love that exists in a relationship between *persons*. The truth of faith is not about how things are in material terms. It is a personal relationship, and therefore infinitely superior to all such expertise.

The objections of the reason put forward by materialistic and atheistic philosophy, which either dispute the existence of God or agnostically maintain the impossibility of proving God's existence (as, for example, in the Kantian critical philosophy), were unable to shake my faith in the living, personal God or to call into question my conviction that the existence of God can be justified rationally. This is because these arguments are ultimately and fundamentally incapable of calling into question the presuppositions of the rational conviction of the existence of God and of the comprehensive relat-

8 Möhler, *Symbolik,* §34.

edness to HIM of all that exists. The militant atheists make things too easy for themselves, when they deny that believers have a critical understanding. There is indeed no way back to the Ptolemaic conception of the world, but that is a matter of empirical knowledge; this particular picture of the world was never the object of faith in God the creator. Similarly, superseded or modern pictures of the world produced by the scientific reason have nothing at all to do with God's revelation as the salvation and truth of the human being. What does faith in God have to do with one particular stage of the knowledge of nature?

It is indeed true that there is no way back behind the consciousness of the problem in Kant's critique of knowledge. But this does not mean that it is impossible for a new form of epistemological realism, schooled in this critique, to be developed—a form that would make possible theology as a science. This is why it is necessary to enter into the debate with these objections rationally and argumentatively, in order to attain clarity about the metaphysical foundation of theology. Theology's object is the revealed faith: this is its specific character in contradistinction to all the other empirical and transcendental sciences. But the principle of theology is not faith but the reason that constitutes all the sciences and links them together (*ratio fide illustrata*). This is why theology is possible at and has a completely justified place at the university, as the science of the contents of faith, because the principle of the university is knowledge—not ignorance (for example, in relation to the science of the Christian confession of faith, and to all its literary and historical manifestations).

Nihilism, which Nietzsche called "the uncanniest of all guests," and thereby moral relativism, wait before every door and cannot be dismissed as long as the mystery of being is not accepted as love, and love is not accepted as the mystery of God. Reason is incapable of acting *ab extra* as a corrective to faith. Faith is indeed borne up by grace, but in itself it is already an act of the mind in the understanding and the will. Faith and reason are not related to each other in the manner of the irrational and the rational: faith in God is rational, because God is reason, and the yearning for love is never frustrated, because God is love. In faith, there occurs a "worship of God in accordance with reason," a *rationabile obsequium* (Rom 12:1). When Paul bore witness to the Christian kerygma before King Agrippa II of Judea (r. 50–70) and Porcius Festus, the Roman governor in Syria from 60 to 62, he defended himself against his accusers in these words: "That the Christ must suffer, and that, by being the first to rise from the dead, he would proclaim light both to the people and to the Gentiles" (Acts 26:23). When Festus exclaimed: "Paul, you are mad; your great learning is turning you mad," Paul replied: "I am not mad, most excellent Festus, but I am speaking the sober truth" (Acts 26:25).

This is faith's ability to enter into a rational dialogue in which it brings its deeper reason and its greater plausibility into play against the denial of faith.

Since my parents at home, the nuns in the kindergarten, and our priests in the parish and the school had introduced me mystagogically into the encounter with the personal God in reverence for him and in love for him, I was also immune against a theopanistic or pantheistic dissolution of the understanding of God. What the philosophical doctrine of God calls personal reality discloses itself in revelation, so that we can understand the Trinitarian life of the three divine Persons as relationships to each other that do not dissolve the unity of God but allow this unity to emerge, in its unfathomable depth, as a communion in love. This is why I can say "you" to God dialogically and address him through the Son in the Holy Spirit as "Abba, Father!" (Rom 8:14–17; Gal 4:4–7). And the Son of God himself taught his disciples to pray to God in these words: "*Our Father* who art in heaven, hallowed be thy name. Thy kingdom come. Thy will be done on earth as it is in heaven. Give us this day our daily bread; and forgive us our trespasses as we forgive those who trespass against us. And lead us not into temptation, but deliver us from evil" (Mt 6:9–14; Lk 11:2–4).

I find the naturalistic and rationalistic interpretation of the world similarly unconvincing. It is true that the individual feels small and insignificant in the immeasurable cosmic processes and in the ocean of historical events and sequences. The infinite spaces and times cannot be grasped by any imagination, and in the inexhaustible richness of evolution, the individual living being must feel lost like a drop in the ocean. All this may make him inclined to worship the creation in its power and glory, instead of the creator, or to capitulate before the tragedy of finitude, or else to revolt against the unknown power that does not prevent the suffering of creatures. The discrepancy between the apparent endlessness of the world and the tininess of the individual makes it seem obvious that one should seek redemption in the return of individuality into the eternal cycle of nature or into the indifference of nirvana. No one has ever expressed more deeply than Saint Augustine (354–430) the fundamental Christian definition of the human being as a creature of the God who accepts us and redeems us. He begins the confession of his life as follows:

> You are great, O Lord, and supremely worthy of praise; great is your might, and there is no end to your wisdom. And a human being wishes to praise you, a tiny part of your creation, a human being who finds the burden of his mortality hard to bear, and who finds the testimony of his sin hard to bear, as well as the testimony that you resist the proud. And yet the human being, who is himself a part of your creation, wishes to praise you. You

> prompt him to seek his delight in praising you, because you have made us for yourself, and our heart is restless until it comes to rest in you.[9]

God as personal-relational love in the communion of Father, Son, and Spirit is not an anthropomorphic illustration of the nothingness that annihilates; nor is he the infantile downsizing of the inconceivably impersonal oneness of all that exists. The person-reality of God is the unfathomable mystery of truth and of love that is not invented by us, nor constructed as a projection. It is that which makes me a person who can accord with and reply in spirit and love to the mystery of being and of life. It is not I who make the infinite God a person through my finite thinking. Rather, by thinking of me, God makes me the finite person who is thus able to reply to his call to me. The very fact of thinking about being and putting words to the question about the origin and goal of all that exists makes the human being qualitatively, infinitely superior to the entire quantity of matter and of biological life. God is life because he is the communion of Father, Son, and Spirit. A God who was not personal would swallow us up, just as the cold, indifferent sea swallows up the individual swimmer, and the universe lets the disconnected astronaut disappear, never to be seen again.

In his *Pensées,* the French mathematician, physicist, and philosopher Blaise Pascal (1623–1662) vividly expresses the human being's existential experience of nothingness and his qualitative difference from all sub-intellectual being as follows:

> It is thinking that constitutes the greatness of the human being. Only a reed, the most fragile thing in the world, but a reed that thinks [...], if the universe were to destroy him, the human being would nevertheless be more noble than that which destroys him, for he knows that he dies, and he knows the superior power that the universe has over him; but the universe knows nothing of this. Our whole dignity consists therefore in thinking. It is by thinking that we must elevate ourselves; not in relation to space and time, which we can never truly unlock. Let us therefore endeavor to think correctly: this is the foundation of morality.[10]

Accordingly, I am grateful to those who introduced me to faith in God, and to the community of believers, for the personal relationship to God in truth and love that constitutes the very essence of the religious act. "For such the Father seeks to worship him. God is spirit, and those who worship him must worship in spirit and truth" (Jn 4:23–24).

9 Augustine, *Conf.* 1.1.

10 Pascal, *Pensées,* frag. 346–347.

I was not cheated of God in my childhood and my youth, and I regard this as both a grace and as something that obligates me. If only parents today could find words to answer the deepest questions of their children! Mystagogy into the mystery of Christ is the noblest realization of the shared priesthood of all believers on the part of parents towards the children whom God entrusts to their care.

The answer to the introductory question of the catechism in elementary school, which satisfied my mind as a child and an adolescent (and that can indeed be enriched in the course of life, but not surpassed), was: "We are on earth in order to know God, to love him, to serve him, and one day to live eternally with him."[11]

This is exactly what the Second Vatican Council says in the Pastoral Constitution *Gaudium et spes*. The human being experiences dramatically the dichotomy between the brutal experience of finitude and the unlimited yearning for fulfillment, a yearning that infinitely transcends the possibilities of the transient world. Neither the theoretical nor the practical Marxism; the liberal faith in progress that reckons on redemption through the technological-scientific domination of the world; a nihilism that may be experienced tragically or endured heroically—none of these is capable of doing justice to the basic existential questions: "What is man? What is this sense of sorrow, of evil, of death?" (GS 10). These questions determine the finite-infinite being of the human person, so that it is only in the mystery of Christ that light is shed on the mystery of the human person, and solutions can be found to the great challenges that face humanity in the present day and in the future, for time and for eternity. "The Church firmly believes that Christ, who died and was raised up for all, can through His Spirit offer man the light and the strength to measure up to his supreme destiny. [...] She likewise holds that in her most benign Lord and Master can be found the key, the focal point and the goal of man, as well as of all human history" (GS 10).

The piety into which we four children of a Catholic family, two girls and two boys, grew, and the instruction in the faith that we received in school and parish had (to put it in theological terms) a theocentric and Christocentric orientation, but it also had a warm, feminine-Marian keynote. The mystery of Catholic piety, with its Marian character, is that the true and the good do not contradict the beautiful: on the contrary, it is in the beautiful that they shine out. This is how the Second Vatican Council concludes its teaching about the essence and the mission of the Church of Christ: "In the interim just as the Mother of Jesus, glorified in body and soul in heaven, is the image and beginning of the Church as it is to be perfected in the world to come, so

11 *Katholischer Katechismus der Bistümer Deutschlands* (Freiburg: Herder, 1955), 4.

too does she shine forth on earth, until the day of the Lord shall come [cf. 2 Pt 3:10], as a sign of sure hope and solace to the people of God during its sojourn on earth" (LG 68). We Catholics pray with the words spoken by the angel Gabriel to Mary and with Elizabeth's greeting, venerating every day "the mother of the Lord" (Lk 1:43) in the Ave Maria: "Hail, Mary, full of grace, the Lord is with thee. Blessed art thou among women, and blessed is the fruit of thy womb, JESUS. Holy Mary, Mother of God, pray for us sinners now and at the hour of our death. Amen." With the Lord's Prayer, it forms the core of the rosary prayer, in which the mysteries of the life, suffering, death, and Resurrection of Mary's divine Son are contemplated in the spirit of Mary.

We had respect and trust in regard to the sisters and teachers in the kindergarten, to the teachers in school, to the priests, the bishops, and the pope, but a "child-friendly" veneration of persons was explicitly avoided, since our faith was in the triune God, the Creator, Redeemer, and Reconciler. The apostles and missionaries of Christ are only witnesses to the message of salvation, in which they, like us, believe; they are not the content and the motivation of faith in God and in the saving work of his Son. Precisely as witnesses, however, they bear such a high responsibility for planting trust in God and deep love for Christ in the hearts of those entrusted to their care, who are meant to mature and grow not only bodily, but intellectually, morally, and religiously. For the goal of religious education "is love that issues from a pure heart and a good conscience and sincere faith" (1 Tm 1:5). The intellectual and spiritual life of young Christians depends lastingly on its development, in a positive or a negative sense, from the credibility of the first witnesses in family, parish, and school. Looking back, I can avow, full of gratitude, that my parents, teachers, and pastors did "not cheat me of God" (in Albert Biesinger's phrase). With Paul, I profess: "I thank God whom I serve with a clear conscience, as did my fathers" (2 Tm 1:3).

A relationship to Christ and to his Church that is constructed only on feelings and on a mechanical imitation of external customs easily falls into its opposite. A carping criticism of the Church, and indeed a destructive hatred of Christianity, are often nourished by an unsuccessful mystagogy. In such cases, the Christian religion was unfortunately imposed only externally, with the doctrine, cult, and constitution of the Church (dogmas, liturgy, canon law), and was misunderstood as conditions that human beings must meet if they are to obtain anything from God. This is the idea of grace as a reward for good conduct; where there is bad conduct, this leads to a kind of "withdrawal of affection" by God in his relation to the sinner. In reality, the doctrine that the Church communicates, the sacramental liturgy, and the apostolic ministry lead only, as media of grace, to the encounter with God here on earth in faith and then in heaven to the vision of God face to face.

The apostles are God's fellow workers. All that they can do in God's field is to plant and to water; it is God alone who bestows growth (1 Cor 3:6): "Unless the Lord builds the house, those who build it labor in vain" (Ps 127:1). An introduction into the mystery of God's love cannot consist in indoctrination or a moral coercion to a mere presence at Mass when these are detached from the development of a personal relationship to God and from friendship with Jesus. If faith is not planted in the heart as a relationship to the living God that sustains everything, the adult mind emancipates itself from "the child's faith," dismissing this as a supposed preliminary stage to a scientific worldview and a self-determined, autonomous "adult" view of the drama of one's own existence between the tragedies and the comedies in this world. At most, there remains the yearning for the lost faith of one's childhood and for a nostalgic return to it on one's deathbed, instead of a profound and inner reconciliation with God. Similarly, an uncritical veneration of the pope can tip over into hatred of the Church or become an anti-Roman sentiment that destroys the joy in faith when the adult Christian experiences the human—indeed, the all too human—element that is present even in the persons who are (and ought to be) one's models in faith. This is the pool that nourishes the denunciatory literary exposés that have such a long history.

Faith is preserved in the various ages of one's life story and remains the same because it is oriented to the living God and to the person of Jesus Christ. For faith is not based on wavering feelings. It is the recognition of God, and hence the love of him above all created things. Faith is preserved in life with the aid of grace. And love for God ought to become perfect through our taking our cross upon ourselves. But faith can also become more mature; it can even pass through the wildernesses of doubt and the wretchedness of sin and come anew to the well of the living water (Jn 4:11), since it is God himself in his revelation who remains the foundation and the motivation of our believing. We must not make him dependent on the perfection or the shortcomings of those who mediate him. In his commentary on the Letter to the Romans, Saint Thomas Aquinas explains the relationship between faith as infused grace and as an external hearing of the words of those who proclaim it:

> Two things are required for faith: first, the inclining of the heart to faith, and this comes, not from hearing, but from the gift of grace; secondly, the definition on the part of the object of faith, and this comes from hearing. This is why Cornelius, who had a heart that inclined to faith, nevertheless still needed Peter to be sent to him, in order to define for him more precisely what was to be believed.[12]

12 Thomas Aquinas, *Com. ad Rom.* 10.17, lcct 2.

The immediacy of the believer to God and the mediation of faith through the hierarchical-sacramental Church are two sides of one and the same coin. They determine each other reciprocally, albeit under the primacy of the divine initiative. It is here that we see the specific character of the Catholic understanding of the Church, which begins with the inseparability of God and man in Christ. The consequence of the Incarnation is that the Church cannot be split into an inner, invisible communion of grace with God and a sacramental mediation in the visible apostolic Church. And this is related to the constitution of the human being as an intellectual-physical and historical-social unity:

> Accordingly, it is obvious that although the Church consists of human beings, it is not merely human. On the contrary, just as in Christ the divine and the human can indeed be distinguished, but are both linked to form a unity, so he continues in undivided wholeness in the Church. The Church, his abiding manifestation, is at one and the same time divine and human, it is the unity of the two. It is he who works, hidden in the Church in earthly and human forms; this is why it has a divine and a human aspect that are not divorced from each other. This means that the divine cannot be separated from the human, nor the human from the divine. But this also means that these two aspects exchange their predicates: if the divine is the living Christ, and his Spirit in the Church is that which is infallible, then that which is human is also infallible and unerring, because the divine does not in the least exist for us without the human; the human does not possess this quality *per se,* but as the organ and as the manifestation of the divine. This shows us *how* it *was possible* for something so great, important, and significant to be entrusted to human beings.[13]

The understanding of the faith (*fides quaerens intellectum*) can be grasped reflexively in greater depth, because it is of its very nature a participation in the divine act of knowing (in the internal Word of God, in which his being is realized in the relation of the three divine persons, in the Logos who was with God and who is God). Although every human being is called to the knowledge and love of God, and the understanding of the faith (*intellectus fidei*) can never replace, exhaust, or make superfluous the hearing of the faith (*auditus fidei*), the intellectual communication and the argumentative presentation of the revealed faith in academic theology are necessary tasks of the Church, which belong essentially to the proclamation and exposition of the faith (cf. 1 Pt 3:15). This also concerns the authentic explanation of the doctrine of the faith by the popes as Peter's successors.

13 Möhler, *Symbolik,* §36.

The story of Peter moved me already in kindergarten and in the school, when the passages about him in the Gospels and the Acts of the Apostles were read in worship. He had denied Jesus three times, and after he had professed his love for Jesus the risen Lord three times, he was given the unique commission: "Feed my sheep and lambs!" No one other than the pope in Rome was his successor.

When we were learning how to serve Mass, we saw in the reception room in the rectory a picture of Pius XII that kindled our reverence: he was kneeling on a prie-dieu with his hands folded in prayer. This taught me that even the pope confesses how small he is before the eternal and almighty God, the Creator of heaven and earth. In prayer, he beseeches God's grace and assistance. He lifts up his eyes to HIM who hears us. We can trust in God. God hears our prayers and leads us safely to salvation, even when we in the present moment think that our cross is too heavy. The pope, who leads the Church in prayer, and the Church are a community en route, a community of faith and of prayer. The universal pastor of the Church is at the service of the only true "pastor and bishop of your souls" (1 Pt 2:25)[14]—these are the religious images of the pope that left an imprint on a child's mind.

It is inevitable that mockers dismiss such a photograph as an artificial pose. But they are led to such insinuations by their prejudice with regard to the person in question. All portraits and passport photographs are in some way or other an artificial pose, but even so, they display the character of a person. And what I later read in the texts of Pius XII and in serious scholarship about him only served to confirm the deep impression made in my early years.

Faith in Jesus Christ is consolidated in the light of the life stories of convinced Christians. When I was about twelve years old, I discovered in the house of my aunt, Anna Müller (1907–1987), the book by William Hünermann *Brennendes Feuer* ["Burning Fire," 1954] about Pope Pius X (1903–1914), and I felt a vivid empathy with this exemplary pastor-pope. His motto was "To restore all things in Christ." I experienced in all the priests of my young years the apostolic zeal for the house of God that is expressed in these words. My godfather, Ludwig Andres (1906–1976), had the celebrated history of the popes by Ludwig Pastor (1854–1928) on his bookshelves; I inherited it after his death and studied large sections of it. It was said in our family that my great-granduncle Wilhelm Müller (1843–1917), an ornamental carpenter and organist, went with two friends on a pilgrimage to Rome on foot, and was received in a private audience by Leo XIII (1878–1903), the great pope of Catholic social doctrine. In its obituary, the *Mainzer Jour-*

14 cf. 1 Clement 61:3.

nal called him a humble pilgrim to Rome who did not conceal his simple origins: "And yet, there were surely few in the group of pilgrims who had read more about Italy and eternal Rome than this modest artisan. In him, we lose a man who inherited his faithful Catholic sentiments from doughty parents and preserved them unalloyed throughout his long life."[15] This was always understood in our whole family tradition as proof of the fidelity to the Church and of the devotion to the pope that can be traced back through written testimonies and the culture of memory back to the time of Napoleon (1769–1821). Jakob Müller (1798–1884), the grandfather of my grandfather Peter Müller (1877–1960), is said to have seen the emperor of the French as he fled through Mainz after losing the Battle of the Nations near Leipzig in 1813.

One childhood memory also leads to Pope Benedict XV (1914–1922). When the First World War (1914–1918) broke out, my father Martin (1905–1990) was nine years old, and his sister Anna ten. They often told us children how they saw, day after day and week after week, the lines of very young soldiers marching past our house on the Paris Alley on their way to France, to the western front—and so many of them never returned when the troops retreated in 1918. Instead of the radiant youth, they saw lines of misery and men marked by the horror of the war. When I was a child, I heard the generation of my grandfathers talk about the battles of Verdun, Fort Douaumont, and in Champagne or Flanders, or Poland and Russia.

Later on, I read the autobiography *Als wär's ein Stück von mir: Horen der Freundschaft* ["As if It Was a Piece of Me: Hours of Friendship," 1966] by Carl Zuckmayer (1896–1977), a writer who came from Nackenheim, close to my own hometown. Here, he processes his memories of the First World War. As a child and an adolescent, one cannot yet fully appreciate the horror and madness that is linked to the experiences of war in the two generations of our grandfathers and fathers. Karl Geyer (1922–1942), my mother's brother who was always opposed to Hitler, paid with his life at the age of twenty for the greatest criminal of German history.

It was said in our family circles that Pope Benedict XV, with his attempt to mediate peace in 1917, was the only one to oppose the meaninglessness of the war. However, Prussian generals like Erich Ludendorff (1865–1937), later for a time a comrade-in-arms of Hitler (1889–1945), were hostile to Catholicism and wagered everything on total victory—and lost everything. Their attitude was: "We are not going to let a pope dictate peace to us." This was fresh in people's memory, because the oppression and misery of the French occupation of Germany west of the Rhine (1918–1930) was a very present reality until the death of my father's generation. The question of war guilt

15 *Mainzer Journal*, December 31, 1917.

ought to look not only at the outbreak of the war but also at the criminal failure to put an end to it. Who takes responsibility for the millions of human lives that were sacrificed by both sides to the idol of "victorious peace"? We were accustomed from childhood onward to the idea that the papal office had something to do with the peace of the nations and that this office occupied a neutral position above the parties. We remembered the attempts by Pius X and Pius XII to prevent the outbreak of war in 1914 and 1939.

The memory of the struggle for the freedom of the Church from the state in the German *Kulturkampf* (1871–1878) was linked to pride at our great bishop of Mainz, Wilhelm Emmanuel Freiherr von Ketteler (1811–1877), who bravely defended the independence of the Catholic Church against liberalism and the idea of a state church. His social teaching made him doubtless the most prominent German bishop in the nineteenth century. In the convent of the Sisters of Divine Providence in my hometown, Finthen, there is a memorial stone at the entrance to the convent church that recalls him as the founder of this community; this meant that I knew about him in my earliest childhood. The social market economy on the basis of Catholic social doctrine is the answer to the destructive economic systems of the Manchester capitalism that was interested only in profit without a just distribution, and of the socialism that was interested only in redistribution without production. The decisive point is the orientation to the Christian image of the human being, which takes its starting point in his or her dignity. Personality, subsidiarity, and the societal obligation incumbent on property are essential principles for the creation of a just social order.

From time immemorial, my family was politically rooted in the tradition of the Center Party and was immune to the shawms of National Socialism. My mother, Lioba Müller, née Straub (1912–1999), who was a young woman of twenty at the beginning of Hitler's barbarism, had not had an academic education, but she was convinced that Hitler was a mischief-maker because "he screamed in such a terrible and inhuman way." This was not only good common sense; it was the sensitivity to the faith on the part of the people of God, which allowed many people to sense from the outset the abyss into which the godless ideology, so hostile to human beings, would lead us. And my father saved the child of a Jewish classmate in November 1938, when a fanatical Nazi wanted to throw the child out of a widow.

In addition to my own personal recollections, my parents and grandparents told me about something they themselves remembered—namely Pope Pius XI's encyclical *Mit brennender Sorge* ["With burning concern"] of March 14, 1937 about the situation of the Catholic Church in the German Reich, in which he unambiguously and sternly rejects the Nazi ideology from the standpoint of the Christian faith. I found a copy of it in my early years in high school, and I was impressed by its honest and courageous language. After explaining the inherent connection between the faith in the one and true and personal God, in the true divinity and humanity of Christ, and the faith in the visible Church as "the pillar and bulwark of the truth" (1 Tm 3:15), Pope Pius XI, as the highest guarantor of the natural moral law that is accessible to every human being in virtue of his reason, made the following declaration against ethical relativism and subjectivism:

> It is on faith in God, preserved pure and stainless, that man's morality is based. All efforts to remove from under morality and the moral order the granite foundation of faith and to substitute for it the shifting sands of human regulations, sooner or later lead these individuals or societies to moral degradation. The fool who has said in his heart "there is no God" goes straight to moral corruption (Ps 13:1), and the number of these fools who today are out to sever morality from religion, is legion. They either do not see or refuse to see that the banishment of confessional Christianity, i.e., the clear and precise notion of Christianity, from teaching and education, from the organization of social and political life, spells spiritual spoliation and degradation. No coercive power of the State, no purely human ideal, however noble and lofty it be, will ever be able to make shift of the supreme and decisive impulses generated by faith in God and Christ. If the man, who is called to the hard sacrifice of his own ego to the common good, loses the support of the eternal and the divine, that comforting and consoling faith in a God who rewards all good and punishes all evil, then the result of the majority will be, not the acceptance, but the refusal of their duty. The conscientious observation of the ten commandments of God and the precepts of the Church (which are nothing but practical specifications of rules of the Gospels) is for every one an unrivaled school of personal discipline, moral education and formation of character, a school that is exacting, but not to excess. A merciful God, who as Legislator, says—Thou must!—also gives by His grace the power to will and to do. To let forces of moral formation of such efficacy lie fallow, or to exclude them positively from public education, would spell religious under-feeding of a nation. To hand over the moral law to man's subjective opinion, which changes with the times, instead of anchoring it in the holy will of the eternal God and His commandments, is to open wide every door to the forces of destruction. The resulting dereliction of the eternal principles of an objective morality, which educates conscience and ennobles every department and organization of life, is a sin against the destiny of a nation, a sin whose bitter fruit will poison future generations.[16]

16 Pius XI, Encyclical Letter *Mit brennender Sorge* (March 14, 1937), 29.

When we learned how to serve Mass at the age of nine in the 1950s, we already realized that our Catholic faith was different from the faith of our Protestant classmates, because we acknowledged the pope as the supreme pastor of the Church and the father and teacher of Christendom, while the others rejected him. The Protestants referred to the bad popes. Later on, I often heard it said: "Your faith is medieval; we Protestants are free in our thinking and follow our consciences, and you let the pope tell you everything that you have to believe." I then heard that the main thing in the Catholic Church was power, and that there was too much external splendor; this was said by people who were at a distance from the Church (and there were many of them even at that time). People mentioned the golden telephone of the pope and the luxurious life that the princes of the Church led, despite the fact that there were so many poor people. I was told that the Church had always been an ally of the rich and the powerful. Celibacy was completely unacceptable; the priests had their mistresses in secret. It was much better that Protestant pastors were married and took care of their families; and the advantage was that they knew something about marriage and children.

Our priests and parents did not call into question the existence of bad priests and bishops, but they pointed out that this had happened long ago, and that we had had holy popes in recent years. Besides this, one must always draw a distinction between the office and the person. Where there are human beings, we often find the all-too-human element, even in priests and the highest ranks of the clergy. We did not go to church because of our parish priest, nor did we stay away in order to annoy him, still less in order to punish him. The parish priest, and even the pope himself, had to go to confession. This teaching about the discrepancy between the ideal and reality has always remained with me. Later, in religion classes, we were impressed by the reply of Cardinal Ercole Consalvi (1757–1824), the Secretary of State under Pope Pius VII (1800–1823), to Napoleon when the Emperor asked in 1801, "Are you aware, Your Eminence, that I can destroy the Church at any time?" Consalvi answered: "Are you aware, Your Majesty, that not even we priests have managed to do so in the course of eighteen hundred years?"

Napoleon belonged to the past, as far as we were concerned, but Jesus, the Church's Lord, is present reality in the Mass. We were taught that the sacrifice of the Mass is nothing other than the unique sacrifice of the Cross in its sacramental re-presentation. And in my earliest years, I learned this formulation: after the consecration, Christ himself under the species of bread and wine is "truly, genuinely, and essentially present"—not merely present in terms of our memory. At that time, of course, I did not yet know that this was defined by the Council of Trent in 1551, and that the doctrine of transubstantiation, the change of the substance of the bread and wine into the substance of the flesh and blood of Christ, went back to the decree *Caput firmiter* of the Fourth Lateran Council in 1215, which had declared it to be a binding doctrine of the faith.

When the gospel of Peter's confession of Jesus as Messiah and the promise to him of primacy was read, Simon Peter's words to Jesus, "You are the Christ, the Son of the living God," had a power of conviction that took hold of my innermost being. This is the truth, nothing can be truer! And when Jesus asked the twelve, "Will you also go away?", the same Peter replied: "Lord, to whom shall we go? You have the words of eternal life; and we have believed, and have come to know, that you are the Holy One of God" (Jn 6:68–69). At that instant, I heard Jesus ask me if I wanted to part company with him, internally and externally, or to remain with HIM and with the pilgrim Church. No other answer than Peter's has ever occurred to me, down to the present day. I have often renewed my baptismal covenant in a well-known German hymn: "My baptismal covenant shall always stand fast; I will listen to the Church, which shall always see that I am a believer and follow her teachings. Thanks be to the Lord who has called me out of grace into his Church: I will never deviate from her." I hope, with the grace of God, to remain true until death to my baptismal promise, to which my parents and godparents lent their lips at my baptism.

Jesus's promise to Peter, "You are Peter, and on this rock I will build my Church, and the gates of Hades shall not prevail against it," was every bit as plausible and convincing to me as the fact that Jesus is truly the Word of God that has become flesh (Jn 1:14). The construction of the visible Church, which as the body of Christ forms a vital unity with its Head, is precisely a consequence of the Incarnation and its abiding physical presence in the world.

Heinrich Schlier (1900–1978), a scripture scholar who was originally a Protestant, defines "that which is abidingly Catholic" as follows:

> God has taken a concrete decision that goes to the uttermost limit in Jesus Christ and in his history. This decision of God has entered into the definite word and sign that are entrusted to a definite ministry in order that God's decision can be made present. It brings about separation and decision in the definite faith, in love and in hope. In this way, the Church is founded as the location of his decision, and the Church penetrates the dimension of that which belongs to the world. When the world is affected by such a decision, it rises up against it and thereby reflects that decision back.[17]

17 Heinrich Schlier, *Exegetische Aufsätze und Vorträge*, vol. 3, *Das Ende der Zeit* (Freiburg: Herder, 1971), 320. [Translator's note: The play on words in the German text between *Entscheidung* ("decision") and *entschieden* ("definite") cannot be reproduced exactly in English].

This description of the Catholic understanding of salvation and the Church simply expresses reflexively what was transmitted holistically in a Catholic education and passed into the flesh and blood of my Catholic sense of the faith.

I can still remember the reform of the liturgy of Holy Week and the Easter Vigil that was encouraged by Pius XII in 1956, because there was a great deal of uncertainty in the sacristy about the changes to the order of the liturgy. Later, I became fully conscious of the importance that this pope had for liturgical reform with his encyclical *Mediator Dei* (1947), and for the development of ecclesiology with his encyclical *Mystici corporis* (1943), which paved the way for *Lumen gentium,* the Constitution on the Church of the Second Vatican Council, in 1964. The sense of the Church, the receptivity to the mystery of the Church, in which the vital unity with God is really and truly mediated, is closely linked with the sacred and divine liturgy (the name that Eastern theology so appositely gives to the Eucharist). In the course of the Church's year, from Advent to Christmas, from Lent to the celebration of the Passion and the Resurrection, the Christmas and Easter mystery of the redemption becomes present, so that we can are completely taken up into it in faith and love. We encounter Christ here in his divinity and his humanity, just as the apostles once encountered him and drew close to him. Together with the ever-broader knowledge of the whole of the Bible in the readings at Mass and in scriptural instruction in school, the inner participation in the liturgy with all one's senses awakens the inner sense and is the best spiritual introduction to God, to his glorification, and to our experience of salvation.

There is scarcely any more beautiful description of something that even a young Christian can already experience mystically than the affirmation of the Second Vatican Council in the Constitution on the Liturgy:

> For the liturgy, "through which the work of our redemption is accomplished," most of all in the divine sacrifice of the Eucharist, is the outstanding means whereby the faithful may express in their lives, and manifest to others, the mystery of Christ and the real nature of the true Church. It is of the essence of the Church that she be both human and divine, visible and yet invisibly equipped, eager to act and yet intent on contemplation, present in this world and yet not at home in it; and she is all these things in such wise that in her the human is directed and subordinated to the divine, the visible likewise to the invisible, action to contemplation, and this present world to that city yet to come, which we seek. While the liturgy daily builds up those who are within into a holy temple of the Lord, into a dwelling place for God in the Spirit, to the mature measure of the fullness of Christ, at the same time it marvelously strengthens their power to preach Christ,

> and thus shows forth the Church to those who are outside as a sign lifted up among the nations under which the scattered children of God may be gathered together, until there is one sheepfold and one shepherd (SC 2).

In the aftermath of Hochhuth's play *Der Stellvertreter* (1963), we sixteen-year-old high school students discussed passionately whether a public protest against the genocide of the Jews would have stopped Hitler and his henchmen. Our history and religion teachers at the Willigis High School in Mainz discussed in detail the true story of the Nazi rule, the genocide of the Jews, and also the bases of this ideology in a worldview marked by racism and biologism that despised human beings, and they dealt with these matters very competently; I still have the history textbooks. My attitude to the hypothetical question whether a public accusation by Pius XII would have stopped the extermination machine of the Nazis is that the pope was caught in an insoluble dilemma, where both options were equally false. The reaction to the pastoral letter of the Dutch bishops against the persecution of the Dutch Jews in 1942 showed what the Nazis were capable of. I found it simply outrageous and scandalous to insinuate that the pope kept silent out of indifference, or even approval, of the cruel fate that met millions of persons in the most dreadful crime of human history, and to explain this silence with a reference to traditional Christian anti-Judaism.

I learned recently that Pius XII ordered rooms in the building of the Congregation for the Doctrine of the Faith to be used as hiding places for Jewish Romans. This connection with the pope of my childhood filled me with gratitude.

Pope Saint John XXIII (1958–1963)

THE CONSCIOUSNESS OF AN ADOLESCENT between the ages of eleven and sixteen is naturally much broader and more capable of forming a judgment than in the case of a child, whose memories and deep experiences are strongly formed by the narratives and the interpretations of adults. When puberty comes, the child faces the great test of maturity. Changing from a boy to a man is a huge challenge, and ultimately an achievement—although it leads to gratitude to others, rather than to pride at one's own self. But let me encourage everyone who enters this stage of his life: It is good to hold firm! God affirms you, and it is good to accept this affirmation with the whole of your life!

The television that made its way into more and more households in my youth had decreased the optical and the experienced distance from Rome. The changed style of the papacy could be recognized directly through many articles in church magazines, and it was discussed privately and publicly. Good Pope John simplified the ceremonial that seemed so old-fashioned, and he appeared to be less remote from everyday life. The pope visited prisoners. He was no longer "the prisoner in the Vatican," but went on pilgrimages to Loreto and Assisi. He relaxed many a difficult situation with his natural wit. The most important event of recent church history, the Second Vatican Council (1962–1965), was his initiative. We young Catholics were impressed by the solemn, almost endless procession of the conciliar fathers from everywhere in the world at the opening on October 11, 1962, which we watched on the television in the rectory. Here, one could watch church history. An illustrated book called *Überall bist du zu Hause* ["You are at home everywhere"] influenced my idea of the universality of the Church. Priests from Africa who visited and helped out in the parish in the summer were interesting dialogue partners for us, and they greatly expanded the horizon of our experiences. What a feeling it was to see the words of Jesus made visible in our own days: "Go into all the world and preach the gospel to the whole creation. He who believes and is baptized will be saved" (Mk 16:15).

Just as people from all languages and regions had come together at the first Christian feast of Pentecost (Acts 2:1–42) and were united by the Holy Spirit to form a universal community, so too the Church of the present day, which encompassed all the peoples, was visible to our own eyes: "After this I looked, and behold, a great multitude which no man could number, from every nation, from all tribes and peoples and tongues" (Rv 7:9). A Catholic feels that he or she belongs to the one family of God: "We have one God and Father, one Lord; we are one body and one spirit through the one baptism; we are united by one faith, one hope and vocation; and through love, we can bear and support one another, keep peace with one another, and thus preserve the unity of the Spirit" (cf. Eph 4:1–6). Racist sentiments or cultural feelings of superiority or inferiority are essentially foreign and repulsive to a truly Catholic mentality. The family solidarity includes all "those who sat about Jesus" (Mk 3:34), all those of whom the Lord said: "Whoever does the will of my Father in heaven is my brother, and sister, and mother" (Mt 12:50). All "those who hear the word of God and do it" (Lk 8:21) belong to Jesus's true relatives. Every conflict among human beings is a conflict among brothers and sisters, and no war between the nations is ever anything other than fratricide. The diplomatic initiative of John XXIII and his urgent prayer to God to prevent the nuclear war that threatened during the Cuba crisis in 1962 was the exercise of his supreme responsibility as the Vicar of Christ for peace and the good of humanity. In this dramatic moment, he was the conscience of the world. That was how I and many other young Catholics already understood it, when we were fifteen years old.

At that time, I read at least some excerpts from the encyclical *Pacem in terris* (1963). Its program of an aggiornamento of the Church found a positive echo everywhere. What John XXIII meant was the opposite of a secularization of the Church or a lessening of the demands entailed by following the crucified and risen Lord. The materialism and consumerism of Western prosperity were already casting their shadows. A great acknowledgment of the cultural achievements and the social work of the Church, and little personal following of Christ—that was the atmosphere at the beginning of the 1960s. When I graduated from high school in June 1967, Dr. Jakob Bergmann (1900–1982), a learned retired priest in our parish of Saint Martin in Mainz-Finthen, gave me a copy of the *Imitation of Christ* by Thomas à Kempis. He wrote a dedication in Greek: the words of Paul that have accompanied my path as a Christian and a priest down to the present day: "For me, to live is Christ" (Phil 1:21).

Later, after I entered the seminary in Mainz on October 10, 1967, I was impressed by reading the spiritual journal of John XXIII. This did not justify the polarization of the Church into a conservative and a progressive wing, which was beginning at that time; on the contrary, it helped to overcome it. It was at this time that I first became aware of the tension between the faithful transmission of the deposit of the faith and its modern presentation, although the ideological ditch between parties in the Church that fought each other vehemently became unmistakable only with the Catholic Conference (*Katholikentag*) in Essen in 1968 and the hostile reaction to Paul VI's encyclical *Humanae vitae*. One was inextricably faced on every question with the decision to let oneself be mocked as close to the pope or praised as critical of the pope. In some people, Catholicism took on pathological traits. "Progressive" or "conservative" became the defining labels of what was Catholic—although the Catholic faith ought to overcome the party spirit.

Henri De Lubac (1896–1991), later a cardinal, helped me with his book *Die Kirche: Eine Betrachtung*, which was published in German by Hans Urs von Balthasar (1905–1988) in 1968, to find my own path beyond the destructive dichotomy of conservatism (integralism) and progressivism (modernism). These attitudes are unfruitful and harmful because, instead of emphasizing one important element in the totality, they break it out of the totality. This is due to the confusion of the faith that comes from hearing the divine Word with an ideology that they have thought up for themselves—and that is nothing other than a gnostic self-redemption.

As Cardinal Prefect of the Congregation for the Doctrine of the Faith, I took part, on Divine Mercy Sunday 2014, in the canonization of John XXIII (together with John Paul II) on Saint Peter's Square, and I asked him to pray to our heavenly Father for unity within the Church. It was in the reign of John XXIII that the idea—already signaled in my earliest childhood—became ever more mature: I ought to study theology and serve the Church one day as a priest, if God wished to call me. Perhaps every future priest is, like Paul, "called" to be an apostle before he "was born and called through his grace" (Gal 1:15). For my generation, Pope Saint John XXIII was a convincing embodiment of the successor of Peter, who recognized the signs of the times and showed the Church the way, humbly and surely.

I could not, however, say that the pope was the role model for my priestly vocation. The decisive men were the pastors whom I directly experienced. They were spiritual models with their apostolic zeal. One must be cautious about evaluating a pontificate in terms of the rising or falling numbers of vocations; what counts is the clearly seen closeness to the Christian and priestly life. It is with the family and the parish community, and in a very special way the priests, that the experience of being called becomes concrete and is then translated into the personal "yes" to the call. But it is only in sacred ordination that one truly becomes a priest, shepherd, and teacher in the Church of God through the laying on of hands and the consecration by the bishop. That which God objectively entrusts to one must, however, prove true subjectively in one's life. I can gratefully bear witness, with my own experience of the path, to what the Second Vatican Council states in its decree about the education of priests:

> The duty of fostering vocations pertains to the whole Christian community, which should exercise it above all by a fully Christian life. The principal contributors to this are the families which, animated by the spirit of faith and love and by the sense of duty, become a kind of initial seminary, and the parishes in whose rich life the young people take part. Teachers and all those who are in any way in charge of the training of boys and young men, especially Catholic associations, should carefully guide the young people entrusted to them so that these will recognize and freely accept a divine vocation. All priests especially are to manifest an apostolic zeal in fostering vocations and are to attract the interest of youths to the priesthood by their own life lived in a humble and industrious manner and in a happy spirit as well as by mutual priestly charity and fraternal sharing of labor (OT 2).

I look back with pleasure here on the conversations I had with a Protestant student of theology who had rented a room in our house, which was fairly close to the University of Mainz, and who was training to become a Protestant pastor. Naturally, we spoke of the controversial questions, which were especially acute in the understanding of the Church, of the sacraments, of the sacramental priesthood, and of the relationship between scripture, apostolic tradition, and the magisterium. He was not a little impressed by the religious interest of a seventeen- or eighteen-year-old high school student. We discussed the differences in the understanding of original sin and whether human nature was wholly corrupt or only wounded; we spoke of what the justification of the sinner is, and how this takes place. This also involved the questions about the formal and material Protestant principles of *sola scriptura, sola gratia, sola fides,* and *solus Christus*—or as we would have to say, in Catholic terms, scripture *and* tradition, grace *and* nature, faith *and* good works, and finally, Christ *and* the Church. When I think back to the religion classes in school, to the sacramental catechesis and to the communication of the faith in sermons and lectures, I am amazed at the level of knowledge and the surety of judgment that the human spirit can acquire at an early age, provided that it gets the right nourishment in childhood and adolescence.

When I remember the children's Bible in elementary school and the school Bible we had in high school, it is astonishing how much knowledge of the sacred scriptures of Old and New Testaments one could already have when leaving school to begin studying theology. We were also familiar with the systematic knowledge of the faith in all the principal themes of the question of God, Christology, and the understanding of the Church and of the fundamental mysteries of revelation, as well as the objections by the criticism of religion and the basic philosophical questions and the tension vis-à-vis the natural-scientific and historical worldview.

When I look, half a century later, at the textbook, *The Catholic Faith: God—Christ—Church,* I am still astonished to see what a lively consciousness of the problems we had towards the end of our school years.[18] I was at high school from 1958 to 1967. The theodicy question of Gottfried Wilhelm Leibniz (1646–1716) and the controversy about grace between Thomists and Molinists (about the relationship between grace and freedom) belonged to the educational canon, as did the parable of the ring in Lessing's *Nathan der Weise* ["Nathan the Wise"] and the theory of projection in Feuerbach's *Das Wesen des Christentums* ["The Essence of Christianity," 1841] and the reduction of the biblical tradition about Christ to the productive imagination of "the sage who unintentionally wrote poetry" in David Friedrich Strauss's *Das Leben Jesu, kritisch bearbeitet* ["The Life of Jesus, critically examined," 1835–36]. We also knew Ernest Renan's (1823–1892) thesis of the community that had turned the human being Jesus into a god in the evolution of its consciousness of faith. I had my first encounter with Protestant Christianity

18 Herman Schneller, *Der katholische Glaube: Gott—Christus—Kirche*, 5th ed. (Munich: Kösel, 1962).

on this level with our Protestant theological student. Later, of course, I came to grapple with the origin, the history, and the great representatives of the Reformation Christian faith. The doctrine of the sacraments in Bonhoeffer's understanding of "religionless Christianity" was the topic of my doctoral dissertation in 1977. After my postdoctoral dissertation in dogmatics and the history of dogma, on the theme of the communion and the veneration of the saints, in 1986, I was considered suited to lead the Ecumenical Commission of the German Bishops' Conference and the Protestant-Catholic Contact Discussion Group in Germany and to lead the delegation of the German Bishops' Conference to the Russian Orthodox Church.

My youthful encounter with this student of Protestant theology, who doubtless went on to become a good pastor, remains in my memory, because the Christocentrism of Protestant theology and piety fascinated me. I was suspicious from then onwards, thanks to the encounter with Protestant Christians who lived their faith in a serious manner, of the confessional polemic that was widespread at that time and that sought to demonstrate one's own superiority by disparaging the other party. During my high school and university years, I regularly heard works by Johann Sebastian Bach, whom Nathan Söderblom called "the fifth evangelist," in the Protestant Christ Church and in Saint John's Church in Mainz: His *Christmas Oratorio* and his *Saint Matthew* and *Saint John Passions* are regarded as a "musical expression" of Reformed theology and spirituality. The Reformed *Soli Deo gloria* ("To God alone be glory") that he set at the head of many of his works seemed to me even then not so very far distant from the motto of Saint Ignatius of Loyola (1491–1556), the founder of the Jesuits, *omnia ad Dei maiorem gloriam* ("Everything to the greater glory of God"). Many years after its publication, I read a book by Friedrich Richter, a Protestant pastor who converted to Catholicism, *Martin Luther und Ignatius von Loyola: Repräsentanten zweier Geisteswelten* ["Martin Luther and Ignatius of Loyola: Representatives of two intellectual worlds," Stuttgart 1954]. This work confirmed the impression of my youth that this consistently theocentric orientation of Christianity can prepare the way for the unity of all Christians in the one Church.

I experienced the same thing when my two sisters married into Protestant families. The parents-in-law of my sister Hildegard (1937–2000) were convinced Protestant Christians, who impressed me greatly in their piety with its authentically Reformation character. The question of the religious education of the children of a mixed marriage was still a very painful experience at the end of the 1950s precisely for those families who took their faith very seriously. From what I experienced at that time, I drew the conclusion, not that indifference lessens the scandal of the division among Christians, but that only the path to full fellowship in the one Church can heal the wounds of schism. The unity in faith in the triune God, who attests his care for us throughout the entire history of salvation and brings it to fulfillment in Jesus Christ, his Son; and the unity of the Church on the basis of baptism, prayer, faith, hope, and love—all these inner and visible elements of construction of the Christian life and of the Church could be perceived in these conversations and contacts. And I could see how unnatural the divisions among Christians were, since they are already united in their roots through the confession of faith and baptism. I realized later that at that same time, the Second Vatican Council expressed on the level of the magisterium, in the Decree on Ecumenism (November 21, 1964), what I had found expressed in our dialogues, as far as my youthful understanding could grasp it.

At any rate, these conversations opened for me a door onto the ecumenical movement, with the goal of presenting even the classical controversial questions (including that of the papacy) in such a way that, without abandoning their substance, they could at least be understandable for non-Catholic Christians too, who would not see them as the antithesis of the essential core of their own faith.

3.
THEOLOGICAL STUDIES, DOCTORATE, AND ORDINATION TO THE PRIESTHOOD
Pope Saint Paul VI (1963–1978)

John XXIII was the pope of my early youth. His successor was completely familiar and present to me reflexively, in his activity in the magisterium and in Church reform, in my time as a high school and university student and in the period of my doctoral studies. I was keenly aware of the council discussions, as these were mediated in newspaper articles and lectures, as well as in discussions in religion classes.

It was during his pontificate that I entered the seminary in Mainz on October 10, 1967. It has rich traditions; it suffices to recall Romano Guardini (1885–1968), one of its most celebrated alumni. When I wrote to the revered Auxiliary Bishop Josef Maria Reuss (1906–1985), who had confirmed me a few years previously, it was no mere customary formula but the expression of my full conviction when I said: "After mature reflection, I am now convinced that I am called by Jesus, the high priest of the new covenant, to serve his Church as a priest."

It goes without saying that I did not understand the Catholic priesthood in a secularized sense, nor did I reduce the priest to a sort of functionary of a religious-social association, which was a false interpretation of the council that was widespread and that did great harm to the Church and to the theological-spiritual identity of thousands of priests and seminarians. Thanks to all the exemplary priests whom I had encountered in the parish and the school, and thanks to what I had read on this topic up to then, I had no need to cobble together my own image of the priest, or to allow self-appointed progressive theologians to pluck apart the classic image of the priest.

The best orientation even today is provided by the Second Vatican Council in its Decree on the Ministry and Life of Priests, which was promulgated in 1965: "Priests by sacred ordination and mission which they receive from the bishops are promoted to the service of Christ the Teacher, Priest and King. They share in his ministry, a ministry whereby the Church here on earth is unceasingly built up into the People of God, the Body of Christ and the Temple of the Holy Spirit" (PO 1).

An argument against the unbiblical sacerdotalization and clericalization of the priestly ministry and against the ontologization of the sacramental character and the cultic narrowing-down of the Catholic priesthood, which was allegedly caused by the Council of Trent, was taken over uncritically from Reformation and liberal theology. It ran as follows: Jesus himself was a "layman," because he was not a member of the Temple priesthood. Scripture never calls the apostles "priests" in scripture in contradistinction to the "common priesthood" (that is, to the description of the Church as the priestly and kingly people of God, 1 Pt 2:5, 9; Rv 1:6). Accordingly, a sacramental priesthood is a contradiction of the categorical abolition of all pre-Christian priesthood which, if we take seriously what the Letter to the Hebrews says, is the consequence of the unique high priesthood of Jesus Christ. Here too, however, we have nothing more than a play on the ambiguity of concepts. And many people let themselves be led astray. For it is, of course, correct that Christ was not a "priest" in the sense of the Levitical priesthood, still less a "minister of a sacrificial cult" in the pagan sense. The foundation of Christ's high priesthood and his unique role as mediator of salvation in the new covenant, with the sacrificial laying down of his life (Heb 9:11–14) that reconciles sinners to God (2 Cor 5:19), is his divine sonship. As God, he was able (!) to reconcile us to himself, and as man, he was able to reconcile us (!) to himself. Thereby, thanks to his divine nature, he is our redeemer. And by means of his human nature, he brought about this new and eternal communion of life with God (1 Tm 2:4–5).

Through their ordination and mission, the apostles and their successors, the bishops with their presbyters (priests), share in Christ's work of salvation by sanctifying, guiding, and teaching the people of God:

> The office of priests, since it is connected with the episcopal order, also, in its own degree, shares the authority by which Christ builds up, sanctifies and rules his Body. Wherefore the priesthood, while indeed it presupposes the sacraments of Christian initiation, is conferred by that special sacrament; through it priests, by the anointing of the Holy Spirit, are signed with a special character and are conformed to Christ the Priest in such a way that they can act in the person of Christ the Head (PO 2).

The unity, and the distinctiveness, of the common priesthood of all the baptized (1 Pt 2:5, 9) and the ordained priesthood of the pastors of the Church under Christ, the supreme pastor and bishop (1 Pt 2:25; 5:4) and the one who presides in word and teaching (1 Tm 5:17, 22), comes from the fact that they share in the priesthood of Christ, but in an essentially different way (cf. LG 10). Thomas Aquinas expresses this with regard to the celebration and participation in the Eucharist:

> This sacrament is of such dignity that it is celebrated only in the person of Christ. But what is done, by anyone at all, in the person of someone else must take place by means of the authority that that "someone else" has granted. And just as Christ grants the baptized person the authority to receive this sacrament, so too the authority to consecrate this sacrament in the person of Christ is bestowed on the priest when he is ordained. [...] The sacramental power lies in many things, not only in one alone. [...] This is why the power to consecrate lies not only in the words themselves, but also in the power that is transmitted to the priest at his consecration and ordination. [...] The righteous layperson is united to Christ in a spiritual union through faith and love, but not through the sacramental authority.[19]

During my study and my activity as a teacher of theology, the sixteen documents of the Second Vatican Council that were promulgated under Pope Paul VI were naturally primary witnesses to the Church's consciousness of faith in the modern world, which is characterized by natural science and technology. These texts must be read in the context of the challenge that the Christian faith and life met in the intellectual and cultural context. Paul VI suffered greatly under the lack of understanding that extreme conservative and progressive groups had for him; this went as far as a malicious gloating because of the encyclical *Humanae vitae* (1968), which had a prophetic character that is being recognized only today. Some blamed the council itself for the crisis of faith that was obvious to everyone after the council, while others held that the reforms of the council had not been implemented with sufficient radicality. In reality, it was precisely an ideological interpreta-

19 Thomas Aquinas, *S.th.* III q82 a 1.

tion of the council that split the Church into "council skeptics" and "council enthusiasts." Instead of the hoped-for renewed Pentecost, what came was a confused babble of languages.

The interpretation of the conciliar documents has its starting point in the revelation that has been made once and for all in Jesus Christ and in the testimony of the apostles, and that is faithfully preserved by the magisterium of the bishops with and under the pope. The revelation "which is written or orally handed down is transmitted in its entirety through the legitimate succession of bishops and especially in the care of the Roman Pontiff himself, and which under the guiding light of the Spirit of truth is religiously preserved and faithfully expounded in the Church. [...] But a new public revelation they do not accept as pertaining to the divine deposit of faith (*divinum fidei depositum*)" (LG 25).

The expectation or the fear that an ecumenical council would bring about a breach with tradition is not only heretical with regard to one single question; it would also unhinge the entirety of the supernatural revelation and its historical mediation through the Church. There can only be a "hermeneutic of reform and of continuity" (to use Benedict XVI's phrase). Otherwise, the Church would secularize itself and dissolve itself—for there would be no reason to belong to an association of ideologues who cast the mantle of the Holy Spirit over their own poor and arrogant thinking. The magisterium, and especially an ecumenical council, can neither create a new Church nor abolish an old Church. Unlike the hermeneutic of a breach, the hermeneutic of continuity does not take its starting point *outside*, so that the observer could reduce the content to his own formal standpoint. The hermeneutic of reform and of continuity is nothing other than the hermeneutic of faith, with its substantial content and the formal teaching authority of the Church. In the same supernatural faith with which the revelation is accepted, it is also expounded in the Church's consciousness of the faith through the power of the Holy Spirit. The Church is founded on revelation, not on the magisterium, which is itself a part of Christ's salvific work and is responsible for its faithful exposition and preservation. The appropriate hermeneutical key to the understanding of scripture and tradition, and of the definitions of the magisterium in doctrines of faith and morals, is not an a priori mental or psychological tying oneself to a conservative or progressive ideology, but the faith in God's self-communication as truth and grace: "The obedience of faith is to be given to God who reveals, an obedience by which man commits his whole self freely to God, offering the full submission of intellect and will to God who reveals" (DV 5), and this differs from an ideology that claims power over the search for truth, and the moral conscience of human beings, every bit as much as heaven differs from hell.

Among Pope Paul VI's apostolic exhortations, I was particularly impressed by *Evangelii nuntiandi,* while the encyclicals *Ecclesiam suam* (1964), about the path of the Church in the present time, and *Mysterium fidei* (1965), about the Eucharist as the center of the Church, remain in my memory, in addition to *Populorum progressio* (1967) and the encyclical *Sacerdotalis caelibatus* (1967), which was much discussed in my first years in the seminary.

The remembrance of Paul VI is linked to my path through life, since I was able to complete my doctoral dissertation on the topic of "Church and Sacraments in the Religionless Christianity of Dietrich Bonhoeffer" in Freiburg im Breisgau in 1977 under Professor Karl Lehmann. On February 11, 1978, the year in which the saintly pope died, I was ordained to the priesthood in Mainz through the laying on of hands of my bishop, the learned Cardinal Hermann Volk (1903–1988). While I was at a summer camp with 120 young people from my first parish, Saint Nicholas in Klein-Krotzenburg in the Diocese of Mainz, we learned on August 6 that the pope had died. 1978 took its place in church history as the year of three popes. During the reign of Paul VI, I studied theology and took my doctorate under Karl Lehmann in Freiburg. I am grateful to all my academic teachers, since academic theology is and remains the basis of all fruitful activity in preaching and pastoral work. As a representative of all the professors who supported me during my study, or whose writings have left their mark on my own thinking, I should like to pay tribute here to my most important academic teacher, to whom I dedicated a little memorial in the *Mainzer Allgemeine Zeitung* on the occasion of his eightieth birthday on May 16, 2016.

Karl Cardinal Lehmann as Academic Teacher

To honor Cardinal Lehmann on his eightieth birthday sounds in Mainz like bringing owls to Athens—for what do we expect, when one cardinal sings the praises of another cardinal? But perhaps this is an opportunity to draw attention to a less well-known aspect of his lifework. It is time for those whom he supported academically to thank him in full public view. Professor Dr. Dr. Karl Lehmann was professor of dogmatics, the history of dogma, and ecumenical theology from 1968 to 1983, first in Mainz and then in Freiburg im Breisgau. His significance for the Church and for society is based not only on his popularity but also on his great achievements for the Diocese of Mainz as bishop and on his exceptional commitment to the universal Church as cardinal. Let me mention only a few points. While he was professor of theology in Freiburg, he was a member of the top-level International Theological Commission in Rome. One of its profound studies of the "theology of liberation," which was the object of vehement discussion at that period, was largely the work of Karl Lehmann. As bishop and cardinal, he was for a long time a member of the Congregation for the Doctrine of the Faith, which advises and supports the pope in carrying out his universal ministry of teacher and pastor.

Many people probably do not know of his exceptional commitment to his students who wrote their diploma, doctoral, and postdoctoral dissertations under him. These three stages of an academic qualification after one has finished the normal course of study can be roughly compared to a professional training that finishes with the apprentice's examination, leading to the higher qualifications: first to the test piece, and then to the master craftsman's diploma.

A professor of theology at the university has to hold lectures and seminars for the students. But it is also his duty to offer them themes for the diploma dissertation, to identify special academic abilities, and then to propose to some of them a theme for a doctoral dissertation. And he can then encourage suitable persons who have already taken their doctorate to write a postdoctoral dissertation and thus gain the entitlement to teach and do research at a college or university as lecturers and professors.

Professor Karl Lehmann always had an alert eye for those who had academic interests. If one wanted to submit one's diploma dissertation in the tenth semester, one had to find the topic, the academic field, and the professor already in the seventh semester. When the young Professor Lehmann was appointed at the age of thirty-two to the professorship of dogmatics (that is, of "systematic theology" in contradistinction to the biblical and historical disciplines of theology), many students in the early semesters, who were not yet required by the plan of studies to hear lectures in dogmatics, filled his lecture halls—and I was one of them. We young students were fascinated by his comprehensive erudition in theology, but also in philosophy and in the biblical basis he gave to the doctrine of the faith. In style and methodology, everything was new. As in his great teacher, Karl Rahner, SJ (1904–1984), his reflections began with the questions of the human being, which were then discussed in the light of revelation. The Second Vatican Council had set theology on a new course: starting from the human being, in order to lead him or her to God. In an age of secularized thinking, one cannot tackle the crisis of faith with one's starting point in the simple fact of revelation. Theology must first accept human beings with their questions and doubts, and then lead them to the theme of God. In the Pastoral Constitution On the Church in the Modern World, we read:

> In the face of the modern development of the world, the number constantly swells of the people who raise the most basic questions or recognize them with a new sharpness: what is man? What is this sense of sorrow, of evil, of death, which continues to exist despite so much progress? What purpose have these victories purchased at so high a cost? What can man offer to society, what can he expect from it? What follows this earthly life? The Church firmly believes that Christ, who died and was raised up for all, can through His Spirit offer man the light and the strength to measure up to his supreme destiny (GS 10).

One who carefully studies Karl Lehmann's publications will recognize the extraordinary width of his interests, as well as their concentrated orientation to the fundamental philosophical and theological questions about human existence. I know of scarcely any scholars who are as capable as Lehmann of familiarizing themselves so precisely with completely different academic fields and defining the thematic connections in the interdisciplinary dialogue.

In a lecture on "Penance and the sacrament of confession," Professor Lehmann mentioned the Protestant theologian Dietrich Bonhoeffer, who was executed on Hitler's orders in the last days of the war because he had been a member of the resistance to the Nazi regime. Bonhoeffer was interesting because he attributed the same great significance to confession for pastoral work in the Protestant Church then as Pope Francis does to confession today, when he repeatedly emphasizes the connection between God's mercy and the human experience of sin and the possibility of reconciliation with God and with the Church. When Bonhoeffer was in Rome in 1924, he was deeply impressed by the long lines of people before the confessionals in Saint Peter's. He grasped that in addition to the sermon, which can only be addressed to people in general, individual pastoral care in confession and in dialogue is also necessary—at that time, a revolutionary idea in Protestant Christianity, and today, sadly, an idea that is almost forgotten within Catholicism. When he ran a seminary for preachers in the Confessing Church at the period when Christians were discriminated and persecuted under the Nazi regime, he studied intensively the connection between confession and the Lord's Supper from biblical, theological, and pastoral perspectives.

Professor Lehmann once proposed to the students who were present that if anyone was interested in Protestant theology, he should think of taking "Bonhoeffer and confession" as the theme of a diploma dissertation. I volunteered, and I was subsequently able to submit a voluminous doctoral dissertation about Bonhoeffer under Karl Lehmann in Freiburg. He examined very intensively the first outlines and plans, and many others have told me that he did the same for them. I always admired how he had such detailed knowledge that he could recommend out of his memory even highly obscure secondary literature. He had many students who wrote their doctoral and postdoctoral dissertations, and he enjoyed the justified reputation of being one of the best academic supervisors. His motto was that one should never say or write anything, or form any judgment, without first having become conscious of the problem at stake; for otherwise, one could fail to do justice to the standards of academic discussion. Apart from the very varied contents and topics of the monographs for the doctoral or professorial dissertations in his branches of "dogmatics, history of dogma, and ecumenical theology," all his academic pupils share the same scientific method: the elaboration of an appropriate consciousness of the problem as the presupposition that permits one to formulate a thesis.

I may permit himself, in the name of all his pupils, to say a heartfelt word of thanks to our former teacher in theology, the bishop of Mainz, Karl Cardinal Lehmann, for the academic part of his outstanding life's work and for the careful and committed supervision of the qualifying dissertations. What remains of a professor are not only his writings but also the efforts he has invested in his pupils. Accordingly, I should like to recommend to today's academic teachers the man whose birthday we are celebrating, as a model for the supervision of academic studies.

Pope John Paul I (1978)

His pontificate lasted only thirty-three days, but it was no mere episode. In the television age, it was easy for him to open the hearts of many millions of people with his smile. He abandoned many customs of the court ceremonial that had become anachronisms. The unusual double name was intended as a direct link to his two predecessors and to guard against the modern bad habit of playing one pope off against another in terms of one's own ideological preferences. *Illustrissimi,* his letters to famous personalities including Pinocchio, was soon known in Catholic circles everywhere. And when he once spoke of God as Father and also as a Mother, this was not an obeisance before feminism: it was a pointer to the biblical teaching about the mercy of God, who loves us just as a mother holds her child to her heart and caresses it.

When I celebrated Mass in the parish church on September 29, 1978, a notice was placed on the altar to inform me that John Paul I had died. I could not believe this—I thought there was a mistake in the notice, and it was only afterwards that I realized the truth of the disturbing news. Many people both inside and outside the Church were shocked by the sudden death of a good shepherd on whom so many had pinned their hopes immediately after his election.

Il sorriso di Dio, his "smile of God," remains an inheritance for the Church, which has the task of proclaiming "the appearing of the goodness and loving kindness of God our Savior" (Ti 3:4) with joyfulness and a smile.

4. ASSISTANT PASTOR, PROFESSOR, BISHOP

Pope Saint John Paul II (1978–2005)

After a pastoral ministry as assistant pastor in parishes in my home diocese of Mainz for four years, I was sent to Freiburg to Professor Karl Lehmann to finish my postdoctoral dissertation, which I published in 1986 under the title of *Gemeinschaft und Verehrung der Heiligen* ["Communion and Veneration of the Saints"].

During this period, I was often glad to help out in the pastoral work in the Parish of Saint Blaise in Zähringen, where I lived. Sixteen years later, I did so every day in the Parish of the Sufferings of Christ in Munich while I was a professor at the Ludwig Maximilian University. The unity of theology and pastoral work, of thinking and praying, has always been important to me—not only out of a personal interest but also because the world of faith cannot be broken down into a theoretical and a practical dimension. Christ in his person is inseparably both truth and life. A professor of dogmatics must hold lectures and seminars for students; he must supervise doctoral and postdoctoral dissertations. Theology is the science of the profession and of the praxis of the Christian faith. The central themes of systematic theology are dealt with in the so-called treatises: theological epistemology, theological anthropology, the doctrine of creation, Christology and soteriology, pneumatology and the doctrine of grace, the doctrine of God and Trinitarian doctrine, ecclesiology, the doctrine of the sacraments, Mariology, and eschatology. I published a textbook entitled *Katholische Dogmatik: Für Studium und Praxis der Theologie* as the fruit of my lectures.[20] Work at a theological faculty is intellectually fulfilling, but it also presents a pastoral challenge when the students and doctoral students are seen as young people who deserve personal attention and care in their professional search and their intellectual orientation.

20 Gerhard Ludwig Müller, *Katholische Dogmatik: Für Studium und Praxis der Theologie* [Catholic Dogmatics for the Study and Practice of Theology] (Freiburg: Herder, 1995).

Most of my work as an assistant pastor, teacher of religion, and university professor took place in the reign of one of the most important popes of recent centuries. He appointed me bishop of Regensburg on October 1, 2002, and I was ordained on the feast of Christ the King by Friedrich Cardinal Wetter, the archbishop of Munich and Freising (r. 1982–2007); the other consecrators were Karl Cardinal Lehmann, my predecessor in the see of Saint Wolfgang, Bishop Manfred Müller (1926–2015), and Auxiliary Bishop Vinzenz Guggenberger (1929–2012), who was at that time the diocesan administrator. Unlike the popes of my youth and my time as a theological student, I later came to know this pope personally. I can still remember vividly how he went out onto the loggia of Saint Peter's after his election and cried out to the assembled people of God: "*Non avete paura*—have no fear!"

Everyone sensed that these words were spoken out of a profound trust in Jesus Christ, an unshakable awareness that the grace of God is stronger than the wickedness of human beings and the adversities of life.

He lost his mother when he was a child, and his brother died soon afterwards; his father died at the beginning of the Second World War. He had no close family, but he had good, open relationships with his friends and he was full of confidence as he looked to the future. He experienced the cruel occupation of his Polish homeland by neighboring Germany and the merciless oppression of his people under the Nazi rule. He saw what people without God, people blinded by a racist ideology, are capable of inflicting on their fellow human beings in the persecution and the killing of the Polish and European Jews in Auschwitz, which is close to Wadowice, where he was born, and to Cracow, the headquarters of Hitler's so-called governor general and vicegerent, Hans Frank (1900–1946).

One mad despot was followed by another. Stalin (1878–1953) and Hitler (1889–1945) regarded themselves as lords over the life and death of their subjects. The Gulag archipelago, Katyn, and Auschwitz are stigmas that remain forever linked to their names. For Hitler's and Stalin's henchmen, the Christian faith and the Church were the greatest obstacle to the establishment of their totalitarian rule over human beings—since God's rule means the establishment of freedom and life. The rule of human beings over each other leads, not to paradise on earth, but to the hell of absolute evil.

As archbishop of Cracow, Karol Wojtyła successfully resisted the attempt by the communist party to create a city without God in Nova Huta by preventing the construction of a church—against the will of the Catholic majority (1977). This already gives a glimpse of the deepest conviction of the man who would later be pope: the human being can develop in freedom and love only when he allows God to live with him. The Church must remain the visible sign among the peoples that Jesus Christ remains with us until the end of the world. The decisive error that underlies the immanentism of rationalist and empiricist philosophy, and subsequently also of the nihilistic anthropology of social Darwinism, is its failure to recognize the spiritual nature of the human being. This leads to the celebrated recognition of the "dialectic of the Enlightenment" (Max Horkheimer and Theodor W. Adorno). One who denies the essential difference between animal and human being abolishes the absolute difference between truth and falsehood, and between good and evil. This is why all the ideologues of the twentieth century held that they could deduce from the subhuman nature, the realm of the wild instincts and unrestrained passion, the law of the right of the stronger, which they elevated (in contradiction of their own agnosticism) to a metaphysical principle. Even in the animal realm more is involved than naked survival, eating or being eaten. Even in the beasts of prey that follow only their instinct, there exists an altruism that takes care of the brood and protects their own group. But the life of the human being is spirit and thus self-transcendence towards the truth and that which is good per se, as the goal of the act of knowing and willing. If human beings take up weapons against each other, this is not based on animal instincts, "on our animal inheritance," or on our DNA; it is generated by a clear calculation and is thus a contradiction of the spirit. The reason is always oriented to knowledge, and the free will is always oriented to love and to the gift of self.

In all these naturalistic worldviews there breathes the negative spirit of the dualism between spirit and nature, of the antagonism between high ideals and blunt instincts. The philosophy of the modern period is located in the dialectic between an idealistic monism that wants to elevate the bodily-mental nature into pure spirit, and a materialistic monism that is willing to acknowledge the spirit only as an epiphenomenon of matter, and that underestimates the spirit with devastating consequences. In reality, there exists in the human being a substantial unity between spirit and body, which is sustained by his person, which is capable of transcendence towards other persons, and can ultimately open itself for communion with the triune God.

The destructive tendency does not come from our animal instincts or from what remains of the animal nature. And evolution, with the principle of the survival of the stronger and the one who is well adapted, does not excuse war and the crimes against humanity. Of his nature, the human person is a being of communion and friendship: the good desires to make the gift of itself, and that is why it opposes the evil. No, the evil thoughts and deeds have their origin in the broken nature that was created good by God but was wounded through the free act of opposition to God, and that cannot extract itself from the swamp of egoism and insensitivity—for that, it needs the aid of grace. The doctrine of the primal state in the grace of "righteousness and holiness" (Lk 1:75) and of original sin is the best insurance against the naturalism that fails to recognize the destiny of the human being and wants to reduce him to an animal. The Darwinian principle of the "survival of the fittest" and the false inference from this that right is on the side of the stronger cannot be transposed to the morality and ethics of persons who have a spiritual-ethical constitution. John Paul II experienced in his own person, and in the body of the Polish people, the application of social Darwinism in the countries that were under National Socialist and communist rule, and he recognized the murderous consequence to which this led. This social Darwinism is not an error of the intellect but a crime against the spirit. The alternative, a counterculture to death and a civilization of life, was not simply a beautiful formulation. On the contrary, John Paul II had recognized that love is the only route out of the self-annihilation of the human race.

His important collaboration in the writing of the Pastoral Constitution *Gaudium et spes* on "The Church in the Modern World" (1965) already points forward to the program of his future pontificate. There is an inherent correlation between Christology and anthropology: "The truth is that only in the mystery of the incarnate Word does the mystery of man take on light. For Adam, the first man, was a figure of him who was to come—namely, Christ the Lord. Christ, the final Adam, by the revelation of the mystery of the Father and His love, fully reveals man to himself and makes his supreme calling clear" (GS 22).

When Archbishop Wojtyła was called to be the universal pastor and teacher of the Church, and thus to be Peter's successor, on October 16, 1978, the human race was in a precarious situation both politically and militarily. The Cold War of the superpowers with their systems of alliances had brought humanity more than once to the brink of a nuclear war. And it seemed that nothing could stop the victory of the communist ideology. The West was able to resist the military might of the Soviet Union thanks to its capitalistic economic system and its advances in military technology, but it had nothing in intellectual and moral terms with which it could counter dialectic materialism, because the West itself had rushed headlong into the abyss of consumerist materialism and nihilism, and it could not pull itself out with the rope of moral relativism. The Western liberal atheism and the ideological state atheism in the twentieth century both held that by denying God they could elevate the human being to be his own creator and redeemer. For Karl Marx (1818–1883) and Vladimir Ilyich Lenin (1870–1924), religion was the opium of the people or for the people, something that would distract people from their hopeless conditions by giving them the hope of an imaginary life beyond death. Every reference to transcendence and every remembrance of Christianity must be expunged from the memory of the human race, in order that the human being might find his goal in purely immanent terms in the paradise of the consumption of material and cultural goods. This, however, is a futile endeavor, since finite and transient goods do not correspond to the infinite striving of the human being.

What Henri De Lubac called "humanism without God" inevitably failed as a philosophical and societal project, and ended in the greatest barbarism of human history, in a humanism without human beings, the absolute inhumanity or the madness of a trans- and posthumanism. It was only out of the springs of faith in the God who is the foundation of our dignity, and who has given us a supernatural calling, that a deeper renewal and a hopeful orientation to the future were possible.

Joy in Christ, versus the hopelessness of materialism—this was the key to a new society. In an interview in 1995, looking back on the first seventeen years of the pontificate of John Paul II, the then Cardinal Prefect of the Congregation for the Doctrine of the Faith, Joseph Ratzinger, summarized the theme of this pontificate, on the basis of the encyclical *Redemptor hominis*:

> As already became clear in the first encyclical of the Holy Father, his great theme is the human being. He is concerned about the redemption of the human being, that is to say, about his liberation from alienations, from oppression and a lack of freedom; he wants the human being to be righteous and to discover his truth, his own self. The pope is convinced that the human being can find his truth, the truth itself, only in Christ. In other words, the human being needs the encounter with Christ in order to be "redeemed." "Throw open the doors for Christ and do not be afraid of him!" That is what he said in his first sermon as pope in 1978, and these words are his real program. Everything else is a consequence of this.[21]

My pastoral work in the parishes in which I served, and my work in theological teaching and scholarship, likewise had their place in this epochal struggle between human failure without God or success with God. The question was: Will the dechristianization of Europe and of the world continue until human identity is finally dissolved, or is there a new encounter with Christ and his Gospel?

I came to know John Paul II personally. From 1998 to 2003, I was a member of the International Theological Commission, which published two important studies under the leadership of Cardinal Ratzinger: one about the pope's request for forgiveness of the transgressions in church history in 2000,

21 Gerhard Ludwig Müller, interview, *Kirchenzeitung für das Erzbistum Köln*, no. 21.3 (May 26, 1995). Previously published in full in KNA Basisdienst, May 15, 1995.

the Holy Year of the Incarnation of Christ, and one about the history and theology of the diaconate. I was also appointed an expert for two synods of bishops. The second special assembly of the Synod for Europe (1999) had as its theme "Jesus Christ, who lives in his Church—source of hope for Europe," and the tenth ordinary general assembly of the synod in 2001 studied the theme of "The bishop as servant of the Gospel of Jesus Christ for the hope of the world."

I was able to experience the pope close at hand during the celebration of Mass in the private chapel of the Apostolic Palace and also when I was invited with a small group to lunch with him. He was authentic as a human being and convincing as a Christian. He did not revel populistically in the splendor of his office, nor did he display a false modesty. It is precisely the acceptance of oneself, the knowledge that life with its opportunities and challenges is a grace and a gift, that makes it possible to collaborate with one's talents and charisms in building up the kingdom of God and to put oneself at the service of Christ for human beings. He was able to fulfill the threefold commission to Peter to pasture the sheep and lambs of the Lord only because his strength was nourished by the assurance of love for Jesus. In the suffering that he bore with a heroic configuration to the pains of the crucified Lord until his death on the eve of Divine Mercy Sunday, the "sense of faith" of the people of God discerned his complete assimilation to Christ in suffering, cross and resurrection, which extinguishes all sins and errors (LG 16). When he sought for the last time to raise his hand with a great effort to give the blessing at the window of the Apostolic Palace, he was visibly marked by pains and by the powerlessness of his approaching death. I thought then of Paul's words: "That I may know him and the power of his resurrection, and may share his sufferings, becoming like him in his death, that if possible I may attain the resurrection from the dead" (Phil 3:10–11).

The essential character of the Petrine ministry becomes visible not only in his authority for the universal Church, but also when the pope, like Peter, presents himself as "a witness of the sufferings of Christ as well as a partaker in the glory that is to be revealed" (1 Pt 5:1). Death for one who follows Jesus is not a fall into meaninglessness, but—as the Lord promises Peter—"the glorification of God" (Jn 21:19) The shout *Santo subito!* ("Make him a saint at once!") from the lips of millions of the faithful was a confirmation of this knowledge by the Holy Spirit. Saints are models on the path of following Christ. They help us in our service of the kingdom of God, when we unite ourselves to them in prayer to the Father through Christ, the Lord and Pastor of his Church.

On the feast of Saint Anne in 2014, at the close of the great pilgrimage week in Sulzbach-Rosenberg, I preached about the canonization of these two great popes before a congregation of thousands of the faithful. On Divine Mercy Sunday, April 27, 2014, Pope Francis canonized two of his predecessors in the Petrine ministry in the presence of one and a half million of the faithful on Saint Peter's Square. In my sermon, I spoke about John XXIII and John Paul II:

> They were two courageous men, filled with the inner freedom of the Holy Spirit, and they bore witness to the Church and to the world of the goodness of God and of his mercy.
>
> These two popes did not live in a far distant past. They were men of the twentieth century, and the older ones among us knew them personally. And even the younger ones can easily get to know the story of their lives and read their writings. All they need to do is click on their names on the internet, where they will find solid information. Films and other media give easy access to the persons of these popes and to what they achieved in their lives. For us, however, as believing Christians, it is even more important to know that the key to other people—to their dignity and to their importance after their death—cannot be the picture that we reconstruct of them with the aid of the historical sciences. What matters is the picture that God has of us. What matters is that we, who are created in God's image and likeness, allow the image of Christ to come to expression in us. We could compare our path as human beings to liquid wax that is imprinted by the configuration to the suffering and the Resurrection of the Lord. This is how we become the seal of the Spirit of God. Christians ought to be an authenticated letter of recommendation from God, a living invitation to all who are still far from the kingdom of God, but who are moved in their hearts by the longing for God. At the beginning and at the end, it is the Spirit of God who authenticates us and makes us credible witnesses of the kindness and mercy of God.
>
> The two new saints did not begin their lives as popes. Our path with God began already with the predestination and the choice by grace before we were conceived in our mother's womb. When our historical and real existence as creatures of God in time and space begins, we are already surrounded by the love of the Father for the Son in the Holy Spirit.
>
> It is not as if a blind chance thrusts us out like a spaceship into empty infinity, and then someone unexpectedly comes by and catches us again. On the contrary, we come forth from the love of God the Father, the Son, and the Holy Spirit. Our beginning in time has its origin before time in God's eternity. God works in everything for good, because we are called in accordance with his eternal plan. Before we know anything about it, God

has already destined us to share in the being and the form of his Son, as we have heard today in the Letter to the Romans (Rom 8:29).

In the course of our lifetime, we encounter Christ, the Son of God, who has realized God's plan of salvation in history. Through faith in him, we have peace and reconciliation with God, and the prospect of being brought to perfection in the love and mercy of God: "And those whom he predestined he also called; and those whom he called he also justified; and those whom he justified he also glorified" (Rom 8:30).

When we run our course through life, we are held, led, and borne up from birth to death by his grace and his closeness. This is why we do not boast of ourselves. We do not contemplate our own reflection in the vain and transitory madness of ambition and hubris. The two saints show us how the Christian copes with all challenges, efforts, blows of fate, and the ups and downs of life in inner serenity, with trust in God and unwearying love. They show us how we draw closer to God in all this, and how at the end, God's grace wins the victory over sin, death, and the devil.

The apostle says openly: "We know that in everything God works for good with those who love him" (Rom 8:28). The two holy popes came from poor backgrounds. The young Karol Wojtyła lost his mother when he was only nine years old, and he had only just grown to adulthood when his father died, at the beginning of the despotism that Hitler inflicted on Poland, our neighboring land. Both saints were involved in the terrible chaos of war as young men, and then in the ministry of priest and bishop. Both were witnesses who suffered under the atheistic regime of Stalinism and National Socialism and the appalling genocide of the Jews and the murderous persecution of all who did not fit the ideological schema of races and social classes. There is no space here to speak in detail of their great importance for church history, for the convocation of the Second Vatican Council and for its subsequent reception; we can only recall it briefly. The great guiding principle of both pontificates was the attempt at aggiornamento, at the actualization of the doctrine of the faith, achieving the new culture of an inner synthesis of the Gospel of Christ with the state of knowledge and the conditions of life in the industrialized, globalized, and digitalized world of today and tomorrow. The inalienable dignity of every human being, his or her freedom in conscience and in responsible activity in society, in culture and science, in work and leisure, consists in his or her existence as a person. There are no exceptions: no human being exists as a goal for another human being. On the contrary, every human being exists for his or her own sake in view of God, who is the origin and the goal of all being. The goal of human life is to find the fulfillment of its meaning in the love of the triune God, in communion with all those who have taken the path of faith in love until the end.

John Paul II put it as follows: The Church's path is the human being; but *not* the human being left to his own resources, the human being exposed to his own arbitrariness and to that of others, but the human being who has his center in God. After the despotism of Napoleon had devastated the Church in Germany two hundred years ago, Johann Michael Sailer, the great bishop of Regensburg, began the work of reconstruction with the essential summary of our profession of faith: "God in Christ: the salvation of the world, the future of the human being."

John XXIII and John Paul II were not canonized for profane reasons—for what we might call reasons of propaganda—in the way that worldly organizations glorify their leaders. A holy pope understands himself as a humble servant of the Church of his Lord. He is inspired by the love of the Good Shepherd and cares like a father for the well-being of the children of God, so that they may come to God their Father and recognize to what hope, to what freedom and glory of the children of God, they are called. As successors to the ministry of Saint Peter, they orient and concentrate the entire Church on the God-Man, the one mediator between the one God and the many human beings. When the disciples are asked: "What do you think of the Son of Man?", Peter confesses in every one of his successors, until the return of the Lord: "You are the Christ, the Son of the living God!" (Mt 16:16). The Christian veneration of the saints means that we take our place in their fellowship and thank God through Christ for all grace, love, and mercy. In view of the many witnesses to the faith and martyrs in salvation history, the author of the Letter to the Hebrews writes: "Therefore, since we are surrounded by so great a cloud of witnesses, let us also lay aside every weight, and sin which clings so closely, and let us run with perseverance the race that is set before us, looking to Jesus the pioneer and perfecter of our faith, who for the joy that was set before him endured the cross, despising the shame, and is seated at the right hand of the throne of God" (Heb 12:1-3).

Saint John XXIII and Saint John Paul II, you holy popes—pray with us to God, and pray for us to God for "perseverance," so that we too may not lose in this "race," but may "have faith and keep our souls" (Heb 9:39). Amen.

My Encounter with Gustavo Gutiérrez

Over a space of fifteen years, I regularly visited Peru and other countries in Latin America during the months when I had no lectures to deliver in

Munich. In addition to guest lectures at a number of universities and seminaries, I also worked in the parishes of Lares and Choquecancha in the Archdiocese of Cuzco. It was a completely new experience to share daily life with people in the Andes and to work for them in pastoral care and catechesis. A decisively important experience for me was getting to know personally the father of liberation theology and becoming his friend. Later on, we wrote several books together, for which Pope Francis supplied the foreword. At the beginning of my activity as Prefect of the Congregation for the Doctrine of the Faith, it was possible to clear up some misunderstandings that had arisen in the wake of the two declarations by the congregation (*Libertatis nuntius,* 1984; *Libertatis conscientia,* 1986). In 2008, the Pontifical Catholic University of Lima awarded me an honorary doctorate, and I expressed my thanks in the following statement:

> This is why the theology of liberation is linked for me with a face: that of Gustavo Gutiérrez. I was one of several theologians from Germany and Austria who took part in a course on this subject at the invitation of José Sayer, who is currently the head of [the Catholic aid organization] Misereor. The course took place in the Institute Bartolomé de Las Casas, which even then was well known. At that time, I had been teaching dogmatics for two years at the Ludwig Maximilian University in Munich.

Seminar on Liberation Theology in Lima

Thanks to the seminar under the leadership of Gustavo Gutiérrez, there occurred in me a shift from academic reflection on a new theological conception to experience with persons for whom this theology had been developed. This reversal of the sequence from theory to praxis, in the direction of the three-step model of "seeing—judging—acting," was decisive for my own theological development.

We who took part in the seminar were fully loaded up with a great deal of knowledge about the origin and the development of liberation theology, and our discussions concentrated primarily on the analysis of the situation—an analysis that was accused of an excessively naïve proximity to Marxism. We were familiar with the statements of the Latin American bishops' conference at Medellín and Puebla, and the debate centered on whether the intention was to turn Christianity into a kind of political program of redemption that would tolerate (under certain circumstances) even revolutionary violence against persons and things. Some regarded liberation theology with suspicion; others invoked it to legitimate terrorist violence in the service of the just revolution.

The first thing that Gustavo taught us was the important insight that what is involved here is theology—not politics. He made clear the distinction between liberation theology and Catholic social ethics on the lines of the great social encyclicals of the popes. While social ethics is based on the natural law and wants to ensure a justly organized society by means of the principles of personality, subsidiarity, and solidarity, the theology of liberation is a practical and theoretical program that helps us to understand and to change the world, history, and society in the light of the supernatural self-revelation of God as redeemer and liberator of human beings.

How can one speak of God in view of the suffering of human beings, of the poor who cannot give their children any bread to eat, who have no entitlement to medical care, who have no access to schooling, who are excluded from societal and cultural life, who are marginalized and are felt to be a burden and a threat to the lifestyle of a few rich persons?

And these poor persons are not an anonymous mass: each of them has a face. How can I—as a Christian (whether priest or layperson)—speak kerygmatically or as an academic theologian of God and of his Son who became a human being for us and died for us on the Cross out of love, how can I bear witness to him, if my desire is, not to erect a theological edifice alongside those that already exist, but to say from face to face to the specific poor person who stands before me: "God loves you, and your dignity, which cannot be lost, is grounded in God"? How can the biblical insight be experienced concretely in the individual and societal life of human beings, if human rights have their genesis in the creation of the human being in God's image and likeness?

My visit to Peru in 1988 brought not only the seminar with Gustavo Gutiérrez, where I realized the genuinely theological approach of liberation theology, but also the living encounter with the poor about whom we had spoken. We lived for a time together with the people in the slums of Lima and then also with the campesinos of the Parish of Diego Irrarázaval at Lake Titicaca. Since then, I have been in Peru and other Latin American countries more than fifteen times, often for several months during the semester vacations in Germany. My work with theological courses, above all in the seminaries in Cuzco, Lima, Callao, and other places, was always joined to long weeks of pastoral work in the Andes communities, especially in Lares in the Archdiocese of Cuzco. Here, faces became names for me, and many became my personal friends—an experience of the worldwide communion in the love of God and of neighbor that must be the very essence of the Catholic Church. Later on, as a bishop, I had the profound joy of administering the sacrament of confirmation in the Archdiocese of Cuzco in 2003 to young people whose parents I had known for a long time, and whom I myself had baptized.

This is why I do not speak abstractly and theoretically about liberation theology—and certainly not in an ideological manner, as if I wanted to commend myself to a progressive wing of the Church as a kindred spirit. Nor am I afraid that this could be interpreted as a lack of orthodoxy. Whichever way one looks at it, the theology of Gustavo Gutiérrez is orthodox because it is orthopractical, and it teaches us what we must do because it has its source in the true faith.

His book *Beber en su proprio pozo* (English: *We Drink from Our Own Wells*) clearly shows that the theology of liberation is based on a deep spirituality. It is rooted in the following of Jesus, in the encounter with God in prayer, in participation in the life of the poor and the oppressed, and in the readiness to join in their cry for the freedom and glory of the children of God, to take part in their struggle for an end to exploitation and oppression, their struggle for human rights to be respected and for all to be able to share on equal terms in cultural and political life in a democracy where they do not experience themselves as foreigners in their own land. They want to see that Church and state are willing to give us a home to live in and a guarantee of spiritual and civic freedom. The goal is the introduction and accompaniment of a dynamic process that seeks to free people from cultural and political dependency.

Bartolomé de Las Casas as Model

Just as Gustavo gives liberation theology a face in our time with his person, his spiritual testimony, his commitment to the poor, and his magnificent reflection, so too he has brought close to us in an impressive way the figure of Bartolomé de Las Casas. Unlike his acquaintance Columbus, he did not discover a country in the sixteenth century and lay claim to it for the Spanish crown; what he discovered was the injustice of the oppression and degradation of the local population. He desired to lay claim to human beings for the kingdom of God, in which there cannot be masters and slaves, but only brothers and sisters with equal rights.

Las Casas came as an adventurer and soldier of fortune to the West Indies, as he supposed: to the continent discovered by Columbus that we call America today. From the perspective of the "discoverers" of America, this was a land of which one could take possession for kings, a land where no laws protected its natural resources or its people, and thus a land that was utterly exposed to the grasp of those who aimed at a boundless self-enrichment. Las Casas was initially involved in the entire system that deprived people of liberty and exploited them.

Ultimately, he recognized in the face of the tormented the face of Christ, and he became an eloquent advocate and champion of the oppressed peoples in their own country, America. This was also linked to the return to the original meaning of Christian mission. Jesus had sent his disciples out into the world to proclaim the Gospel of redemption and liberation to every human being. In this sense, mission as the encounter from person to person in the name of Jesus is the absolute opposite of a form of colonialism and imperialism or proselytism that is merely garbed in a religious mantle. One cannot conquer countries for Christ and subjugate their populations as subjects of a state that has some kind of "Christian" character.

On the contrary, the proclamation by the authorized messengers of Christ essentially demands the free acceptance of the faith. It is in this way that there arises a worldwide network of disciples of Jesus who are a fellowship of brothers and sisters in accordance with his will and are thus the visible Church of God in the world. People contribute their own historical background and their cultural identity to this process and let themselves be reshaped by the Spirit of God into a higher common identity, that is to say, in the recognition that we are children of God, called to lead an exemplary life, destined to be perfected in the future that belongs to God. The Church can thus be in Christ the sacrament of the salvation of the world. It serves as a sign and instrument of the intimate union of human beings with God and of the unity of the peoples (cf. LG 1).

In his account of the destruction of the West Indian lands (*Brevísima relación de la destrucción de las Indias occidentales*), Las Casas identifies the real reason for the tremendous injustice that the conquerors from Spain inflicted on those whom they encountered on their journeys of exploration.

He writes of these men, who were Christian in name but not in conduct: "The sole and true basic reason why the Christians murdered and wiped out such a vast number of innocent human beings was simply that they sought to get hold of their gold."[22]

Gustavo Gutiérrez has summed up the liberating path taken by Las Casas as the alternative of "God or gold."[23]

This is the liberating path that Jesus lays down in the Gospel: "One cannot serve two masters, God and Mammon." In another passage, the basic attitude of the Christian existence is affirmed by means of a negative: "The love of money is the root of all evils" (1 Tm 6:10).

22 Bartolomé de Las Casas, *Kurzgefasster Bericht von der Verwüstung der westindischen Länder*, trans. Hans Magnus Enzensberger (Frankfurt: Insel, 1981), 13.

23 Gustavo Gutiérrez, *Dios o el oro en las Indias: Siglo XVI* (Lima: Instituto Bartolemé de las Casas, 1989).

The One in Whom We Trust—He is Truly Our God

Today, we Christians of the twenty-first century, as well as the humanists of every hue, are proud that we have abandoned a Eurocentric colonialism and imperialism. But in our righteous indignation at the cruelties involved in the conquest of America and Africa and India, and in the humiliation of China, we do not always escape the risk of lulling ourselves in the moralistic certainty that if we had lived in the sixteenth century, we would certainly have stood with Las Casas on the side of God against the exploiters on the side of gold. It is, of course, true that the historical circumstances of that time are not directly comparable to today's globalized world.

However, the basic alternatives between the option for money and power, on the one hand, and for God and love, on the other hand, remain for each individual and for all fellowships and societies and states and associations of states. Even today, entire continents like Africa and South America are marginalized. A small percentage of the world's population share the resources among themselves and are thus immediately responsible for the premature deaths of millions of children and the catastrophic situations in which most of the world's population lives.

The Disgrace of Our Times: Neoliberal Capitalism

When the Soviet Union collapsed, many hoped for an end to liberation theology, which they saw as close to Marxist liberation movements.

In reality, liberation theology, if correctly understood on the basis of what it seeks to do, is the best response in praxis and in theory to the Marxist criticism of religion. A comprehensive view of God as the one who creates, redeems, and perfects the human being makes us aware of the dualistic trap into which it was hoped Christianity would fall. There is no alternative between well-being in this life and salvation in the life to come, between grace and human activity, between commitment in the Church and criticism and active shaping in the world. Orientation to God and shaping the world, love of God and love of neighbor, are two sides of the same coin. Christians are surpassed by no one when human rights and dignity are at stake, when at one and the same time they criticize both the structural sin of an unjust political system and individual human irresponsibility.

At the presentation of the first volume of the collected writings of Pope Benedict XVI on the "Theology of the liturgy," which I edit for the publisher Herder, one speaker mentioned the fine sentence: "When the monks grew careless about the praise of God, the soup for the poor also became thinner."

The praise of God summons us to take responsibility for the world, and the commitment to social justice, peace, and freedom, the preservation of nature as the basis of physical and social life, are all grounded in God's creative and redemptive activity.

After the collapse of communism, many thought that paradise on earth was now to be set up by means of an unbridled capitalism. Left to themselves, the self-regulatory powers of the market on a global scale would lead to prosperity for all, or at least for most people. The reality is otherwise.

It was not the apparently omnipotent powers of the market that caused today's world financial crisis, but human beings acting out of sheer greed. And once again, it is the poor, and the poorest of the poor, who will pick up the tab—with their life and their health, with a premature death, and with all the opportunities that God gave them but that they have missed.

In the past, the representatives of neoliberalism defended their view of the human being by saying that one cannot rule the world with the Sermon on the Mount. They failed to take into account that Jesus is not concerned about ruling the world. He wants the human being to rule himself and to be free from greed, so that he can be a human being for others.

It is claimed that the Church understands nothing of economics and capitalism. If we are absolutely determined to be altruistic, we can carry out social work for the victims of capitalism.

The Church is permitted to work in hospitals and in hospices for the dying—but not to proclaim any ethics for Wall Street. The faceless expression of neoliberalist capitalism includes the vulture funds. Speculators devoid of conscience have specialized in business ventures with the debts of entire countries. If a country finds it difficult to pay, the "vultures" buy up the original sum at a huge deduction on the original sum and then demand the payment of a much higher sum with interest and compound interest. It is thus an easy task to bring a country into poverty once and for all. At the close of the 1990s, Peru in particular fell victim to an "investment strategy" that meant that an investment of eleven million dollars brought a return of fifty-eight million. The consequences this has for human beings, for children, for the elderly and the sick, indeed for the entire societal structure of a country, are approved and accepted. Pure profit is the only goal.

This makes terribly clear the whole drama of a world, of an economic market, with no binding moral regulations. The greed for gold and money is even today the reason for the destruction of moral values that have a power to benefit the human being—a power that comes from the only source that leads the human being to his or her own humanity and that truly makes one's fellow human being one's neighbor.

Racism and paternalism, a society that disintegrates into upper and lower classes and therefore functions on the principle of the right of the stronger, and that dissolves its own self, remain incompatible with our spirituality and the profession of our Christian faith.

After decades of terror and counter-terror in Peru, at the cost of many thousands of innocent persons—and precisely of the poor indigenous population—the Truth and Reconciliation Commission has been set up under the leadership of Professor Salomón Lerner. The extent of the brutality that comes to light is horrifying. The only possibility is a new start with a development that leads to a socially just society in which the state guarantees human rights. But a spirituality of human rights is also needed. The individual must make the innermost concern of his personality the consciousness of the responsibility of the human being before God, and the spirit of brotherhood in the depths of the conscience, because only in this way can a limit be put to the greed for money and power that is the source of all evils. If one does not seek to create justice and reconciliation for one's own self, but rather receives this as a gift of God and as a structure of life for oneself and for everyone else, it is possible for thankfulness to grow in our hearts—the thankfulness that allows me to lead a human existence on behalf of others, as the highest measure of the *humanum* and of the developmental possibilities of every single individual in the splendor of God's love. *Deus caritas est*: this is the goal and the means of the liberation and the perfection of the human being in the direction of the triune God.

In Peru, I encountered two Christians who symbolize the people's yearning to experience the inalienable dignity of the human being. Saint Rose of Lima and Saint Martin de Porres have become my dear friends, in whom the goals of liberation and redemption shine forth in their ultimate form.

I should like to conclude these reflections with a prayer to Saint Rose and Saint Martin.

May they protect the Church and the people of Peru with their prayer to the heavenly Father and Creator that he may reveal to us his Son as the mediator of the hope of a transformation of the world in the direction of the goal that the Spirit of Pentecost shows us: "Fear came upon every soul; and many wonders and signs were done through the apostles. And all who believed were together and had all things in common; and they sold their possessions and goods and distributed them to all, as any had need. And day by day, attending the temple together and breaking bread in their homes, they partook of food with glad and generous hearts, praising God and having favor with all the people. And the Lord added to their number day by day those who were being saved" (Acts 2:43–47).[24]

5.
CARDINAL PREFECT OF THE CONGREGATION FOR THE DOCTRINE OF THE FAITH
Pope Benedict XVI (2005–2013)

On April 19, 2005, the Catholic world heard the moving news from the loggia of Saint Peter's in Rome: *Annuntio vobis gaudium magnum. Habemus Papam: Eminentissimum ac Reverendissimum Dominum, Dominum Josephum Sanctae Romanae Ecclesiae Cardinalem Ratzinger!* The pontificate of Benedict XVI lasted almost eight years, until February 28, 2013.

I was already familiar with Joseph Ratzinger from the beginning of my student days. His book *Introduction to Christianity* made a very profound impression on me in the first semesters of my theological studies in 1968.[25] It offered an existential approach to the person of Christ. Faith as a relationship to the person of Jesus and faith in God in his working in salvation history, faith as act and as content, were presented here as a unity that is founded in God himself; it is not in the least a construction of human thought at some later period. This is because the Church's faith has its origin in the word of revelation. Since the Word of God is itself substantially God and has taken on our flesh in the WORD of the Father, the obedience of the Son unto death on the Cross is the foundation and the core of the confession made by the community of disciples. Since we are sons and daughters of God in the Son of the Father, our faith, which follows the obedience of Christ unto his expiatory death on the Cross, is a participation in the Trinitarian life of God. Through the Word that became flesh, we take part in the dialogue of the Father with the Son and in their communion in the Holy Spirit. The creed of the Church, which we join in speaking at our baptism, is not in the least a summary and synthesis of all the important statements and theological interpretations that have been made in the course of church history. In the baptismal confession, the disciple of Jesus opens himself to receive the self-communication of God as truth and life that took place once and for all, and that is an abiding presence in the confession of the Church's faith: "And thus God, who spoke of old, uninterruptedly converses with the bride of His beloved Son; and the Holy Spirit, through whom the living voice of the

24 Gerhard Ludwig Müller, "Theologie der Befreiung: Marx die Grundlage entziehen," *Rheinische Merkur*, no. 11.24, March 13, 2009.

25 Joseph Ratzinger, *Introduction to Christianity*, trans. J. R. Foster (London: Burns & Oates, 1969). Originally published as *Einführung in das Christentum: Bekenntnis—Taufe—Nachfolge* (Munich: Kösel Verlag, 1968).

Gospel resounds in the Church, and through her, in the world, leads unto all truth those who believe and makes the word of Christ dwell abundantly in them (cf. Col 3:16)" (DV 8).

My spiritual life and my theological thinking were enriched by new horizons because Joseph Ratzinger discussed the intellectual situation of the times, and also the crisis of faith, in the broad context of the tradition of the church fathers and the great theological figures of the nineteenth and twentieth centuries, thereby also illuminating the ecclesial character of faith, which is essential for the Christian profession of faith. With Erich Przywara (1889–1972), Gustav Siewerth (1903–1963), Karl Rahner (1904–1984), Hans Urs von Balthasar (1905–1988), Jean Daniélou (1905–1974), Henri De Lubac (1896–1991), Yves Congar (1904–1995), and Louis Bouyer (1913–2004), he was one of those Christian thinkers of whom I have read almost everything I could get my hands on. Later, I also came to know him better as a person, when he was the President of the International Theological Commission, to which I belonged from 1998 to 2003. After he became pope, the idea of publishing his collected works arose, and he gave me the task of editing the sixteen volumes published by Herder. In order to realize this great project, I founded in 2007, during my time as bishop of Regensburg (2002–2012), the "Pope Benedict XVI Institute."

In May 2012, I was asked to come to Rome for an audience in which the pope revealed his intention to appoint me as Prefect of the Congregation for the Doctrine of the Faith, of which I had been a member since 2007. This office entails a great responsibility in immediate collaboration with the magisterium of the pope. But one who accepts this charge must also accept that all the arrows of anti-Catholic resentment from outside the Church and of anti-Roman feeling within the Church will be aimed at him. With the authority bestowed on it by the pope, the congregation has the task of promoting and protecting the Catholic faith. As a child and a young man, but also as a student of theology and as a university professor, I could never have imagined that I would one day serve the Church in this way. But it is not secular reasonings about career and influence and "power," with the possibility of enforcing one's own favorite ideas, that lead one to accept such an offer but rather the readiness to support the pope in the carrying out of his mission. For the successor of Saint Peter, this mission can be nothing other than a service, and he draws on the aid of the congregations in this work, since he knows that he is not the lord of the Church, nor the teacher of believers in his own name. He teaches, guides, and sanctifies the Church in the humble imitation of his Lord and in his name. As the vicar of the true Shepherd and Teacher, he is the one who goes ahead of the whole flock of Christ, representing in his own person its unity in the revealed truth and in the fellowship of grace with God. Through his word and example, he trains it in the perfect obedience of Christ to the heavenly Father.

One important characteristic of the pontificate of Benedict XVI was his exceptional theological giftedness. I do not mean simply the way in which a person is marked by his activity as a professor but rather the stamp impressed upon the most important themes of the doctrine of the faith by the high originality of his theology. What applies to every Christian in general applies in a special way to the popes: the various charisms are given by the Spirit of God in order to benefit others (1 Cor 12:7). This is how the whole body grows towards Christ, its Head, when all its members work together, in order to become the perfect human being: "The body makes bodily growth and upbuilds itself in love" (Eph 4:16). The one who has received the gift of teaching is to teach—"in accordance with the faith" (Rom 12:7), with the *analogia fidei.* As the successors of the apostles, the bishops are appointed by the exalted Lord "as pastors and teachers, to equip the saints for the work of ministry, for building up the body of Christ" (Eph 4:12).

This analogy of faith, the insight into the inherent connection between the revealed truth and the goal of salvation for every human being, is based on the analogy of being—that is to say, on the capacity even of the created finite reason to grasp the truth, when this reason recognizes, in the real existence of the world, the *esse, verum, et bonum* (being, the true, and the good). The human being is capable of understanding in the principles that sustain the created world the grammatical rules with which the divine reason has founded the creation and given it its structure. The creation is the mirror and similitude of the reason and the love of God. Thanks to the *analogia entis,* theology, as the science of the revealed faith, is possible in accordance with the *analogia fidei.*

Theological knowledge is not a servant of the intellectual curiosity that mirrors its own self in the closed circle of a few specialists and delights in its own intelligence. Without the continuous exchanges with theology, as it has been elaborated by the biblical writers, the church fathers, and the great theologians of the Middle Ages and the modern period in the various schools, the magisterium could not do justice to its responsible task. This is because the Church's magisterium bears witness to the revealed faith of the Church in the profession of faith, in the *auditus fidei,* while its intellectual and linguistic presentation takes place rationally and conceptually, in the *intellectus fidei.* In this way, the inherent rationality of the entire content of the faith, the *depositum fidei,* shines forth in theological reflection and bears fruit in preaching and in pastoral care.

In its authority as an authentic witness to what has been revealed, and thanks to the assistance of the promised Holy Spirit, the magisterium is doubtless superior to academic theology; but it makes use of this academic theology out of an inherent necessity. The pope and the bishops can teach completely and without falsification, and present as that which is to be believed, only that which—and all that which—is contained in the historical revelation of God. With regard to its linguistic and intellectual form, however, "the Roman Pontiff and the bishops by fitting means diligently strive to inquire properly into that revelation and to give apt expression to its contents; but a new public revelation they do not accept as pertaining to the divine deposit of faith" (LG 25). Unlike Peter and the other apostles, the pope and the bishops are not personal bearers of revelation, nor do they receive any inspiration like the authors of the sacred scriptures. Rather, they are bound to the testimony of the Word of God in sacred scripture and in the apostolic tradition. However, they enjoy the assistance of the Holy Spirit (*assistentia Spiritus Sancti*) when they faithfully hand on the faith in their teaching office.

Peter himself, in his circular letter to many communities, his "encyclical," had already summoned the Christians, and especially the priests and bishops, to "make a defense" (*apo-logia*) to everyone who asks about the "*logos* of hope" that is in them (1 Pt 3:15) through their faith in Christ the Lord, the "shepherd and bishop of your souls" (1 Pt 2:25).

One great concern of the theologian Joseph Ratzinger, but also of the Prefect of the Congregation for the Doctrine of the Faith and of Pope Benedict XVI in the varied responsibilities he held, was to demonstrate the inherent connection between faith as hearing and faith as understanding, between *auditus* and *intellectus fidei*. Faith is not measured here (as in the rationalist concept of the reason, which is reduced to the question of practicability) by means of a criterion that remains external to it; nor is it subjected here to a criterion of truth that is alien to it. One cannot carry out theology, philosophy, and the historical and social sciences *more geometrico*. It is not a matter of numbers and things but of persons and of the Spirit in the Word. Instead, faith, which means enlightenment by the light of Christ (*lumen fidei*), is rational per se, in accordance with the Logos of God. It is a *rationabile obsequium* (Rom 12:1). The task of academic theology is to mediate between the knowledge of God in faith and the knowledge of the world through the natural reason (*lumen naturale*), as this is presented in the natural and human sciences. In this way, there is generated in the reflexive consciousness of faith a synthesis between the knowledge of God from revelation and the theoretical and practical knowledge of the world.

One cannot, of course, reduce the overall impact of his pontificate and its fruitfulness for the Church—of which God alone, in any case, is the judge—to one single benefit. However, the theological elaboration of the inherent unity and the mutual compenetration of faith and reason is surely an aspect that bestows a particular splendor on the pontificate of Benedict XVI. Faith and reason do not set boundaries to each other, nor are they mutually exclusive. On the contrary, they are at the service of the perfecting of the human being in God and in his Word, which took on our flesh, and in his Spirit, which reveals the deepest being and life of God: God is love (1 Jn 4:8, 12), which was the theme of his first encyclical, *Deus caritas est*. Only God's truth can set the human being free (Jn 8:32) and can liberate our contemporaries from the systemic constraints of the ideologies of self-redemption and of the dictatorship of relativism. The name "relativism" stands here for the abolition of truth as the content and the goal of all human intellectual work. In his celebrated "Biglietto Speech" on May 12, 1879 in Rome, Cardinal Newman had described the same reality, under the term "liberalism," as a characteristic of secularization; in Joseph Ratzinger, "liberalism" is called "relativism."

Saint John Henry Newman affirmed on that occasion:

> Liberalism in religion is the doctrine that there is no positive truth in religion, but that one creed is as good as another, and this is the teaching which is gaining substance and force daily. It is inconsistent with the recognition of any religion, as *true*. It teaches that all are to be tolerated, for all are matters of opinion. Revealed religion is not a truth, but a sentiment and a taste; not an objective fact, not miraculous; and it is the right of each individual to make it say just what strikes his fancy. Devotion is not necessarily founded on faith. Men may go to Protestant Churches, and to Catholic, may get good from both and belong to neither. They may fraternize together in spiritual thoughts and feelings, without having any views at all of doctrine in common or seeing the need of them. Since, then, religion is so personal a peculiarity and so private a possession, we must of necessity ignore it in the intercourse of man with man.[26]

That is to say, "we must of necessity ignore it," in the state, society, science, and the public sphere.[27]

It can certainly be affirmed that Benedict XVI was one of the truly great theologians on the chair of Peter. In the long line of his predecessors, the obvious comparison is with Pope Benedict XIV (1740–1758), the outstanding eighteenth-century scholar. One may also recall Pope Leo the Great (r. 440–461), who formulated the insight that was to prove decisive for the

26 John Henry Newman, "Biglietto Speech," in *Addresses to Cardinal Newman with His Replies*, ed. W. P. Neville (London: Longmans, Green, and Co., 1905), 64–65.

27 See Gerhard Ludwig Müller, *John Henry Newman* (Augsburg: Sankt Ulrich, 2010), 59–62.

Christological profession of faith of the Council of Chalcedon (451). This pope also offers the most fully developed theology of the Petrine ministry in the early centuries of the Church. When his letter to Patriarch Flavian of Constantinople was read aloud at the Fourth Ecumenical Council, the conciliar fathers cried out: "Peter has spoken through Leo!" Similarly, the fathers of the Third Council of Constantinople (680–81), which condemned Monothelitism, welcomed the letter of Pope Agatho and cried out: "Peter has spoken through Agatho!" And we read in a synodal letter of the archbishops who took part at this council: "We entrust what is to be done to you, as the one who presides in the first chair of the universal Church, which stands on the firm rock of the faith."[28] In the long years of his academic activity as professor of fundamental theology and dogmatics, Benedict XVI elaborated his own body of theological work, which gives him a place among the most important theologians of the twentieth and twenty-first centuries. For more than fifty years, the name of Joseph Ratzinger has stood for an original approach to systematic theology as a whole. His writings unite the academic insights of theology with the living form of faith. As a science that has its genuine place within the Church, theology can show us the special definition of the human being as God's creature and his image.

In his scholarly works, Benedict XVI was always able to draw on his admirable knowledge of the history of theology and of dogmas, and he has communicated this in such a way that God's vision for the human being—the vision that is the basis of everything—shines forth. This became accessible to many people through Joseph Ratzinger's use of words and language. Complex matters are not presented in a complex way that makes it impossible for people in general to grasp them; instead, they are made transparent, so that their inherent simplicity can be seen. The central point is always that God wants to speak to every person, and that his Word becomes the light that enlightens everyone (cf. Jn 1:9).

Faith and Reason

Let me recall only one of the many trail-blazing theological discourses of the pope. In his lecture at the University of Regensburg on September 12, 2006, he once again highlighted the inherent connection between faith and reason. Neither reason nor faith can be thought of independently of the other; only in this interconnection can their true definition be identi-

28 See Erich Caspar, *Geschichte des Papsttums von den Anfängen bis zur Höhe der Weltherrschaft* (Tübingen: J. C. B. Mohr, 1933; Munster: Stenderhoff, 1985), 2:604–605. Citation refers to the Tubingen edition.

fied. Reason and faith are protected from dangerous pathologies by their reciprocal correction and purification. Benedict XVI picks up here the great tradition of the theological sciences that can be seen, in the total structure of the university, as the element that binds everything together.

He echoes John Paul II's encyclical *Fides et ratio* when he speaks of dramatic developments in European intellectual life. A voluntaristic image of God had developed in nominalism. In order to make God inaccessible to our philosophical reason, God is thought of as pure will, which the human being must accept in blind obedience, without any possibility of comprehending it rationally. Vis-à-vis this God, it was necessary for the human being to declare his autonomy, in order to guarantee his freedom. As the philosopher Hans Blumenberg puts it in *Die Legitimität der Neuzeit*, "the theological absolutism" provoked a "human self-assertion."[29] One of the roots of the atheism (whether without God or against God) in the modern period is a faulty theological development. If the primordial and original sin is interpreted as the total corruption of the orientation of the reason and the will to God, the grace of justification is and remains external; for it does not transform the human being into the image of God if there is no inherent, sanctifying grace. In that case, the relationship between the divine and the human, between nature and grace, is one of dialectical contradiction: they do not become compatible. But grace and revelation abolish the sinful contradiction, so that justification brings about not only sanctification as the raising up to the supernatural relationship to God, but also the healing of the *humanum* in its created nature. The revealed truth perfects reason, just as the will finds its goal in the communion of nuptial love between God and the human being. If, however, God himself is reason and will, Word and Spirit, then there is no antithesis between the knowledge of God and the understanding of the world, between nature and grace, or between reason and freedom. Rather, these can be seen to be the expression of the personal fellowship between God and the human being in Jesus Christ, the God-Man. God is not the human being's rival but the fulfillment of all the seeking for truth and for the perfecting of the human being in freedom as love and sacrifice, as gift of self and service.

This happy union between the mission of the pope as universal teacher of the faith and the theological thinking Joseph Ratzinger can be seen at its most convincing in his trilogy *Jesus of Nazareth.*

29 Hans Blumenberg, *Die Legitimität der Neuzeit* (Frankfurt: Suhrkamp, 1966).

The Figure of Jesus of Nazareth

As the successor of Peter, the pope professes the revealed truth that Jesus of Nazareth, the Messiah, is the Son of the living God, a truth that surpasses the natural reason. Thanks to his lifelong study of the question about Jesus in historical-critical exegesis, the theologian Ratzinger possesses the intellectual instruments that allow him to present convincingly the consistency and the inherent truth of the identity of the "Jesus of history" with the "Christ of faith," the divine Word who became flesh, and to communicate this intellectually. In other words, he can display the unity of the believing reason and the rational faith.

The book about Jesus is the culmination of Joseph Ratzinger's lifework. His three volumes about Jesus have prompted a long-lasting discussion about Jesus of Nazareth, whom Christians profess as the universal bringer of salvation and the only mediator between God and human beings. In this individual human being, Jesus of Nazareth, God has made the historical coinciding of the divine revelation and the human handing over of oneself to the Father a concrete event in an eschatological, that is to say, a definitive and irreversible, manner. With the Church, therefore, we profess that Jesus is the Christ, in whom the historical presence of God's salvation can be experienced by the human being. HE is the one who realizes the will of the Father and wishes to lead everyone on the path to the knowledge of the truth (cf. 1 Tm 2:4–5).

In the New Testament writings, we find the articulation, in the living faith of the disciples, of the confession of the apostolic Church, which came into being in the encounter with Jesus of Nazareth as a historical person, with the words of his proclamation of the kingdom of God, and in the experience of his death and his Resurrection from the dead. In the event of Jesus's Resurrection from the dead on Easter morning, and in the light of God's self-revelation in his Son, the believer encounters a person who is both his creator and the one who brings him to perfection: Jesus Christ is the Lord whom we confess in faith, the Lord and the Head of his Church, the firstborn from the dead, the head of the entire creation (Col 1:18). "The God and Father of our Lord Jesus Christ set forth his purpose in Christ as a plan for the fullness of time, to unite all things in him, things in heaven and things on earth" (Eph 1:3, 9–10).

The epilogue to the Gospel of John explains the reason for its composition and for the entire ecclesial testimony to the faith in scripture and in the Church's tradition, in order to counter every attempt to read the Gospel as a purely historical biography that is limited to events that can be recorded in an external manner and to the psychological and social repercussions of such a biography. What is involved here is the event that takes place between the heavenly Father and his Son, Jesus of Nazareth. The biblical testimonies are a "Gospel," an account of everything that happened to Jesus in the light of his self-revelation as the Son of God and the universal mediator of salvation. The Catholic doctrine of faith has its origin in the ecclesial catechesis, not in philosophical speculation, although it makes use of philosophy and enters into a fruitful dialogue with it. The facts of history can be ascertained by historical methods. But only faith in the Holy Spirit opens up the access to the mystery of his person in his eternal and his temporal relation to his heavenly Father. The project of writing down the teaching of the apostles, "who from the beginning were eyewitnesses and ministers of the word" (Lk 1:2; Acts 6:2), and whose tradition lives in the Church's profession of faith, did not intend to offer a mere information about a human being. On the contrary, the Gospels and the Letters of the apostles were written "that you may believe that Jesus is the Christ, the Son of God, and that believing you may have life in his name" (Jn 20:30–31).

When we look at the six decades of intense spiritual and academic penetration of the themes of Christology in the theological work of Joseph Ratzinger, we see the continuity of his thinking. The long wrestling with the figure of Jesus, which he himself formulates in the first volume of the trilogy, can be traced throughout his writings. From the very outset, he asks the question: "Who is this Jesus of Nazareth?"—for human beings, for the world?

He resolutely opposes a skeptical attitude that does not trust that God would definitely reveal himself; and he is acutely sensitive to the various ideological reductionisms that want to take human beings captive in this area.

With the clarity that has its source in the Church's profession of faith, he elaborates, on the basis of the historical evidence and of the "Gospel of Jesus Christ, the Son of God" (Mk 1:1) in the earliest ecclesial tradition, a total way of seeing Jesus of Nazareth that is an invitation to the reader to reflect further. On the basis of the formulations of the Christological dogmas that are consolidated in the course of history and were defined in the great ecumenical councils of Nicaea and Chalcedon, Joseph Ratzinger unfolds his approaches to Christology and to the totality of Catholic theology. A systematic overview is now accessible in the sixteen volumes of his collected works.

"You are the Messiah, the Son of the living God!"

Ultimately, the human being finds his or her definitive fulfillment in looking at the crucified and risen Lord Jesus, "whom God made our wisdom, our righteousness and sanctification and redemption" (1 Cor 1:30), and "in whom are hidden all the treasures of wisdom and knowledge" (Col 2:3).

Until the return of Christ, Peter unites the many disciples and the entire Church in the profession of the one faith: You are Christ, the Son of the living God.

This is the perennial mission of the papacy for the Church and for all human beings. This is the abiding bequest of the pontificate of Benedict XVI, even beyond February 28, 2013, when considerations of his age led him to renounce the exercise of the Petrine ministry and to place in the hands of the cardinals of the Holy Roman Church the election of a new successor of Peter.

Pope Francis (2013–Feliciter Regnans)

Jorge Bergoglio, the archbishop of Buenos Aires (born on December 17, 1936), emerged from the conclave on March 13, 2013 as Pope Francis. His character and his life experience are very different from those of his predecessors, with their European conditioning. The first pope from Latin America has placed the poor, the suffering, and those excluded on the periphery at the center of his pontificate. In his Apostolic Exhortation *Evangelii gaudium* and the two encyclicals *Lumen fidei* and *Laudato si'*, as well as in the Post-Synodal Exhortation *Amoris Laetitia* on marriage and the family, we can see his intention of building bridges to reach even those who are alienated and distant, and indeed, even those who are hostile. The ideological conflicts between conservatives and liberals that paralyze the Church's life and mission are to be overcome. He repeatedly warns against a worldly lifestyle on the part of Christians and against an assimilation of the Church to the world, as if the Church of God were only one spiritual-humanitarian aid organization among many others.

In the Holy Year of Mercy (2016), we are to pass through the holy door, which symbolizes Christ, into the temple of the Holy Spirit, into the fellowship of life with God. God's readiness to forgive cannot be confused with the "cheap grace" against which Dietrich Bonhoeffer warned. Pope Francis's theological concern is expressed in very impressive terms in the following words from *Evangelii gaudium*:

> For the Church, the option for the poor is primarily a theological category rather than a cultural, sociological, political or philosophical one. God shows the poor "his first mercy." This divine preference has consequences for the faith life of all Christians, since we are called to have "this mind … which was in Jesus Christ" (Phil 2:5). Inspired by this, the Church has made an option for the poor. […] This is why I want a Church which is poor and for the poor. They have much to teach us. Not only do they share in the *sensus fidei*, but in their difficulties they know the suffering Christ.

> We need to let ourselves be evangelized by them. The new evangelization is an invitation to acknowledge the saving power at work in their lives and to put them at the center of the Church's pilgrim way. [...] The poor person, when loved, "is esteemed as of great value," and this is what makes the authentic option for the poor differ from any other ideology, from any attempt to exploit the poor for one's own personal or political interest. [...] Only this will ensure that "in every Christian community the poor feel at home. Would not this approach be the greatest and most effective presentation of the good news of the kingdom?"[30]

Pope Francis was only doing justice to his mission to be the conscience of the world as the advocate of humaneness when he traveled to the island of Lesbos, a focal point of the European refugee crisis. No politician, and no opinion leader, had the courage and the strength to make the tragedy of the refugees, thousands of whom drown wretchedly in the Mediterranean, the topic of European politics. The pope criticizes very openly a capitalism of the old, brutal "Manchester" style as a power "that kills." He consistently denounces every war as fratricide in the human family. In the past, Pope John Paul II was laughed at for being insufficiently in tune with realpolitik when he warned against the American military adventure in Iraq. The negative consequences, with the spread of terrorist groups that appeal to Islam in the Middle East and Africa, have only served to confirm that one cannot infringe the natural law and go unpunished. It may be possible for a short time employ military might to halt evil, but it is only with the good that we can overcome the evil. Only love is stronger than death and hatred.

On September 21, 2013, Pope Francis confirmed me as the Prefect of the Congregation for the Doctrine of the Faith. On February 22, 2014, the Solemnity of Saint Peter's Chair, he received me in a solemn consistory into the College of Cardinals and bestowed on me the titular church of Sant'Agnese in Agone.

At the Synod of Bishops on the theme of marriage in 2015, I made the following contribution:

> In the act of creation, God gives a participation in his being, in his truth, and in his goodness. This finds its highest expression in the creation of the human being, as a person with his or her spiritual-bodily nature. The relationship of the human being to the transcendent and personal God is reflected in the personal and polar relatedness of human beings as man and woman. This is why marriage is not only a practical affair that serves

30 Francis, Apostolic Exhortation *Evangelii gaudium* (Nov. 24, 2013), 198–99.

a purpose, something purely secular—as it were, only a human ideal. On the contrary, it is an indestructible reality established by God. Since they are the image of God, the marriage between man and woman, already in primordial times, is the similitude of the inner fullness of life of God *qua* love. As a sign of grace, it is an instrument that helps the human being to attain his supernatural goal in God. In the light of the eschatological self-revelation of God in the Word made flesh (Jn 1:14) and in the Holy Spirit who is poured out over all flesh (Acts 2:27), the human being is *imago trinitatis* not only as a person, but also in the *communio* of marriage. The Church is the Church of the triune God because through Christ, its head, it is drawn into the reciprocal relations of the divine Persons. The indissoluble union between Christ as Head and the Church as the body—the body that the Church is in its members—is the foundation of the Church as the sacrament of the salvation of the world. All the seven sacraments are rooted here. The specific character of the sacrament of marriage is that the marital existence of husband and wife, which is integral to the grammar of the creation, shares in, and depicts, Christ's unconditional love and his unreserved gift of self for the Church (LG 11).

Marriage as a sacrament is a perfect analogy of Christ's loving gift of self on the Cross, through which he won for himself the Church as bride. Accordingly, the marriage of baptized persons depicts the covenant of God with human beings. The meaning of marriage in the natural and in the sacramental order, which encompasses all the individual goods of marriage (*bonum fidei, bonum prolis, et bonum sacramenti*), is the sanctification of the marriage partners on their shared path towards eternal life in God. The analogical relationship Christ-Church and husband-wife is not a metaphor used solely in an illustrative and moral sense. This is because the sacraments cannot be an incomplete and imperfect participation in the mystery of salvation. What is involved here is the substance of marriage as a sacrament (*res sacramenti*). What is signified is also realized.

> Christian spouses, in virtue of the sacrament of Matrimony, whereby they signify and partake of the mystery of that unity and fruitful love which exists between Christ and His Church (cf. Eph 5:32), help each other to attain holiness in their married life and in the rearing and education of their children. By reason of their state and rank in life they have their own special gift among the people of God (cf. 1 Cor 7:7).
>
> From the wedlock of Christians there comes the family, in which new citizens of human society are born, who by the grace of the Holy Spirit received in baptism are made children of God,

> thus perpetuating the people of God through the centuries. The family is, so to speak, the domestic church. In it parents should, by their word and example, be the first preachers of the faith to their children; they should encourage them in the vocation which is proper to each of them, fostering with special care vocation to a sacred state (LG 11).

The added value of sacramental marriage in relation to the natural marriage that belongs to the order of creation consists in sanctification, and concretely in the increase in justifying grace.[31] Accordingly, marriage is not in the least a human ideal at which many people aim, without ever attaining it fully, or indeed without attaining it at all, thanks to human frailty—with the consequence that a second and a third chance to succeed in married happiness must be possible. There is an erroneous opinion that God, as creator, is responsible for the weakness of human beings, and that he therefore owes them (to so speak) a second chance.

Marriage comes about by means of a consecration. In other words, it communicates, increases, and specifies justifying and sanctifying grace, and gives a share in the new creation, the kingdom of God (*ex opere operato*). It is thus something other than a blessing of persons that contains only a grace to aid them (*ex opere operantis*). The indissolubility of marriage and the other goods of marriage belong to it essentially and intrinsically. Since it is God himself who has bound the Christian marriage partners together on the basis of the "yes" that they have spoken freely, they have become one flesh in Christ. And this is why marriage is also inherently indissoluble. Not even the highest Church authority could encroach upon the "substance of a sacrament."[32] The Church accepted, and still accepts, grave disadvantages, rather than dissolve one single valid sacramental marriage. This has also happened in conflicts with Christian potentates, as in the splitting-off of the Catholic Church in England from Rome through Henry VIII of England. On this point, the Church must obey God rather than human beings. It must not sacrifice the truth of the Gospel, which transcends the insight of the natural reason, to a purely human calculation. Cardinal John Fisher (1469–1535), the bishop of Rochester, and the great humanist and Lord Chancellor of England, Thomas More (1478–1535), are the martyrs of the indissolubility of marriage and of the pope as the universal pastor of the Church—against the absolutism of earthly power and the idea of national churches, which diametrically contradicts the essence of the Catholic Church of Christ.

31 Council of Trent, "Proemium to Decree on the Sacraments," DH 1600.

32 Council of Trent, "21st Session 1562," DH 1728.

Human frailty—or, to put it in correct theological terminology, concupiscence as a tendency towards sin that remains even after baptism—must not serve as a pretext to relativize the commandments of God and the obligation to lead a Christian life that flows from the sacraments. It is an inconvertible Catholic doctrine that one who is justified in Christ can, with the help of grace, fulfill the commandments of the Decalogue and the ethical requirements that flow from the sacraments.[33] His configuration to the crucified and risen Lord in baptism and confirmation has made him capable of bearing his cross. No Christian is exempt from this in the vicissitudes of life, and this applies undoubtedly to marriage and family life too. God's mercy cannot generally be interpreted to mean that he closes his eyes to sin. And here, specifically, this cannot be interpreted as giving permission to a second marriage-like relationship when, according to human criteria, living together in marriage has become intolerable or boring. Legal separation is an emergency solution; but there is no legitimate second marriage as long as one's marriage partner lives. God shows his mercy to the sufferer, the one who is weak, and the sinner by not withholding the aid of grace to the one who humbly prays for it. The Christian is able to pass through even deep valleys of suffering, and to set his entire hope of redemption beyond the boundaries of time, in God himself.

The Church must remain faithful to God's word in scripture and tradition and in the binding exposition by the magisterium, for otherwise it incurs guilt with regard to the salvation of souls. In Christ, the Teacher of the truth and the Good Shepherd, the doctrine and the life of his Church are inseparable. If it were to offer the sacraments of penance and the Eucharist only in order not to disturb people's feeling that they belong to the Church, but without drawing attention to the need to overcome the objective obstacle to the reception of the sacrament, it would lull people in a false certainty of salvation. God alone sees people's hearts, and he alone pronounces the final judgment about each individual. But the Church must stick to the path of the sacramental mediation of salvation. The sacrament of penance does not exist in order to tell people that they ought not to have a consciousness of sin, but in order to arouse repentance in them, with the intention of leading a better life, in order that their guilt may truly be expunged through absolution. The absolution is a genuine forgiveness of sin, not merely a declaration that God closes his eyes to sin. The wounds are not covered up by the divine physician, but are healed in their depth, since "he has borne our sickness and carried our pains, [and] with his stripes we are healed" (Is 53:4–5).

33 Council of Trent, "Decree on Justification, canon 18," DH 1568.

6.
A GRATEFUL LOOK BACK

WHEN I LOOK BACK AT MY PATH OF FAITH together with the Church, which is linked to the pontificates of the last seven popes, I can only be thankful to God with all my heart and ask him to assist me in the future too, in order that I may bring my path to its fulfillment in him. "Begin with God, and end with God: that is the finest life." That is how we learned to pray as children.

My path in the Church led me from my hometown, Mainz-Finthen, to the seminary and the theological faculty in Mainz, and then, after ordination to the priesthood and ministry as an assistant pastor in parishes of the diocese, via my doctoral and postdoctoral studies in Freiburg to the Ludwig Maximilian University in Munich, where I taught dogmatics for sixteen years. After ten years as bishop of Regensburg, God directed my path to Rome at the side of the pope, whose universal magisterium is structurally supported and shared by the Congregation for the Doctrine of the Faith. In his successors, the bishops of Rome, Peter exercises the primacy of teaching, of governing, and of sanctifying that was entrusted to him for the universal Church "until the end of the world" (Mt 28:20). Number 48 of *Pastor bonus,* the Apostolic Constitution on the Roman Curia, states: "The proper duty of the Congregation for the Doctrine of the Faith is to promote and safeguard the doctrine on faith and morals in the whole Catholic world; so it has competence in things that touch this matter in any way"[34]

No one—not even in the Church—is spared disappointments, even with regard to persons to whom one owes a debt of gratitude and persons to whom one has given support. It is doubtless due only to grace, and to a healthy emotional and intellectual introduction to the faith, that I can look back on my path of faith from child to young man, from theology student to dogmatics professor, from priest to bishop, and finally to the Prefect of the Roman Congregation for the Doctrine of the Faith, and apply to myself too the words of Saint Basil the Great (330–379):

> Although we ought otherwise to weep over our conduct, I dare at least to boast in the Lord on this one point: that I never had erroneous views about God, or thought differently and later deviated from my original intention. On the contrary, I kept safe in myself the idea of God that I received as a child from my blessed mother and grandmother, an idea that was subsequently enriched. As I grew to maturity, I did not exchange one view for another. Instead, I perfected the rudiments that they had imparted to me.

34 John Paul II, Apostolic Constitution *Pastor Bonus* (June 28, 1988), 48.

> As a seed grows, it is initially small and then becomes larger, but it remains identical to itself and does not alter its nature but is perfected in its growth. So too, I believe, the identical knowledge has only developed and been perfected in me. The knowledge that I have today has not taken the place of the knowledge I had in the past.[35]

7.
IN SAINT PETER'S BASILICA IN ROME

ONE ELEMENT OF THE MINISTRY OF THE CARDINALS in Rome is the concelebration of the liturgy with the Holy Father on great feast days. Those familiar with art history may perhaps be reminded of the concept of "architecture of domination" when they catch sight of Saint Peter's Basilica. And a puritanically minded Christian may be irritated by the contrast to the simplicity of the apostles. He might say that the fisher from the Sea of Galilee would "never have dreamed" that such a huge palace, like that of a Roman emperor, would be built above his grave. But it is not a question of external effects that are meant to dazzle the simple people with a splendor that passes away. The Council of Trent (1562) justified the solemn ceremonies, symbols, liturgical garments, and hence also the artistic construction of churches, which the Church had introduced in its maternal care, by appealing to the sensuous nature of the human being, whom these things serve as means of salvation, "in order to rise up to the contemplation of the divine things and to be moved by the sublimity of the sacrifice of Christ and of the Church."[36]

It is the greatness of the faith that is reflected in the highest possible attempt to depict it. The Church celebrates Christ's triumph over sin—not the victory over the Church's enemies. The Christian spirit of forgiveness led Pius VII, who was terribly humiliated by Napoleon, to plead consistently on behalf of the emperor and his family when they were imprisoned on Saint Helena. Christian triumphalism rightly celebrates God's victory over evil, sin, death, hatred, and the fear of nothingness. Whenever the faithful come together to pray and celebrate the Eucharist, whether in a splendid basilica or in a very simple chapel on the banks of the Amazon, the entire Church calls out, in the midst of earthly tribulations and persecutions, with the words of the protomartyr Stephen. He was filled with the Holy Spirit and looked up to heaven, to the glory of God, and said: "I see the heavens opened, and the

35 Basil, *Letters*, 67.3.

36 Council of Trent, "Decree on the Sacrifice of the Mass, ch. 5," DH 1746, 1757.

Son of Man standing at the right hand of God" (Acts 7:56). One who lifts up his eyes to the heights above the sepulcher of the first martyr of papal history, the apostle Peter, above the baldachin erected by Gian Lorenzo Bernini (1598–1680), finds the words with which Jesus established the primacy of the Roman bishops and of the "Roman Church, the mother and teacher of all the Churches."[37]

In the frieze that runs around the cruciform interior of Saint Peter's Basilica, in Greek and in Latin, we can read the words of promise with which Jesus entrusted the universal office of pastor and teacher to the apostle Simon Peter:

You are Peter, and on this rock I will build my Church,
and the gates of Hades shall not prevail against it.
I will give you the keys of the kingdom of heaven,
and whatever you bind on earth shall be bound in heaven.

Feed my lambs, tend my sheep, feed my sheep!

I have prayed for you
that your faith may not fail;
and when you have turned again,
strengthen your brethren!

His successors on the chair of Peter fulfill this mission in the power of this promise. And in the cupola above the crossing around the altar with its baldachin that rises up majestically above the grave of the prince of the apostles, we find the words of Saint Cyprian about the prince of the apostles and his chair in the principal church of Christendom: *Ad Petri cathedram atque ad ecclesiam principalem, unde unitas sacerdotalis exorta est.*[38] This is Saint Peter's service of the unity of the faith and the fellowship of the faith of the Church: "One body and one spirit, just as you were called to the one hope that belongs to your call, one Lord, one faith (*una fides*), one baptism, one God and Father of us all, who is above all and through all and in all" (Eph 4:4–6).

From the Roman *Sedes Sancti Petri,* the one faith radiates out into the world. Here is the origin of the unity of the priesthood:

37 DH 1749.

38 Cyprian of Carthage, *Ep.* 59.14. ("To the chair of Peter and to the principal church, from which the unity of the priesthood has its origin"). See Graeme W. Clarke, trans., *The Letters of Cyprian of Carthage*, 4 vols., Ancient Christian Writers 43, 44, 46, 47 (New York: Newman Press, 1983–1989). [Note: Some earlier translations follow a different numbering system for the *Letters* than the one used in this book.]

HINC UNA FIDES MUNDO REFULGET
HINC SACERDOTII UNITAS EXORITUR

When the community gathers around the altar, it knows that Christ is really present in the eucharistic sacrifice, the same Christ who also announced to Peter that he would suffer a bloody martyrdom through which "he would glorify God" (Jn 21:19). There can be no reasonable doubt that Saint Peter shed his blood in Rome as "a witness of the sufferings of Christ as well as a partaker in the glory that is to be revealed" (1 Pt 5:1).[39] And this is why, in the apostolic tradition, the church of Rome with its bishop and head is honored with the same primacy within the fellowship of the local churches that Peter by analogy held among the apostles in the apostolic period—the primacy that was bestowed on him by Christ himself, the Lord and Head of the Church.

On the solemnity of Saints Peter and Paul, the choir of the Sistine Chapel sings the hymn *O Roma felix* in the Basilica of Saint Peter. On that day, the entire Catholic Church throughout the world prays in these words:

O happy Rome!
The death of the princes of the apostles
has decorated you with the purple of their blood.
Their great life—
not your glory and your power—gives you preeminence
over all the cities of the world.

Doorkeeper of heaven, Peter, the key-bearer,
Apostle of the nations, Paul, who calls the Gentiles:
lamps who give light to the universe,
you have borne witness to the faith—
one on the cross, the other by the sword.

Divine Trinity, Father, Son and Holy Spirit,
hear the praise we dedicate to your greatness,
since the memory of your witnesses gives us joy.
Give us, like them, one day the throne of bliss.
Amen.

39 See Christian Gnilka, Stefan Heid, and Rainer Riesner, *La morte e il sepolcro di Pietro* (Vatican City: Libreria editrice Vaticana, 2014).

II

The Papacy as a Fact of History and of Revelation

1. THAT WHICH IS DEFINITIVE IN HISTORY

THE LIGHT OF CHRIST did not flare up briefly only once, two thousand years ago. On the contrary, it has shed light on the Church for two millennia, and it will not cease to do so until the Last Day. The risen Christ assures the apostles and their successors of his presence: "I am with you always, to the close of the age" (Mt 28:20). The revelation is unique, and its fullness in Jesus Christ is unsurpassable. This is why there is no end to the deeper penetration into the mystery, and to the certain knowledge of the Word of God in the Church's consciousness of faith, in its synchronous and its diachronic unfolding. This is because:

> This tradition which comes from the Apostles develops in the Church with the help of the Holy Spirit. For there is a growth in the understanding of the realities and the words which have been handed down. This happens through the contemplation and study made by believers, who treasure these things in their hearts (cf. Lk 2:19, 51) through a penetrating understanding of the spiritual realities which they experience, and through the preaching of those who have received through Episcopal succession the sure gift of truth. For as the centuries succeed one another, the Church constantly moves forward toward the fullness of divine truth until the words of God reach their complete fulfillment in her. [...]

> Thus God, who spoke of old, uninterruptedly converses with the bride of His beloved Son; and the Holy Spirit, through whom the living voice of the Gospel resounds in the Church, and through her, in the world, leads into all truth those who believe and makes the word of Christ dwell abundantly in them (cf. Col 3:16) (DV 8).

The following reflections do not intend to offer a history of the individual pontificates and of the institution of the papacy that are the objects of the study of church history. Nor is my theme here the development in the history of theology in a narrower sense, down to the formulation of the dogma of the infallibility and of the jurisdictional primacy of the pope in the Dogmatic Constitution *Pastor aeternus* of the First Vatican Council.

A basic knowledge of the history of the papacy and of the development of the idea of primacy must, however, be assumed, in order to relativize the kind of stereotypes and platitudes that one often encounters both in the populist anti-Roman polemic and in the excessively enthusiastic apologists for the pope.[1]

A divine institution with two hundred and sixty-six officeholders from Saint Peter down to the present day cannot remain untouched by the drama of history. The changes of epoch, the concrete circumstances and crises, as well as the personalities of the popes make the papacy a distinctive phenomenon in the history of the world and of the Church. A believer sees the Church and the papacy as something instituted by God; but this is certainly compatible with a sober look at the light and shadow in church history, in their antithesis and in their nuances. Indeed, this is demanded by the nature of the matter.[2] A mature faith is able to give a spiritual interpretation not only of one's own sufferings but also of the pilgrim people of God on the right and wrong paths it has taken—in the light of faith in Christ who is present in the servant form of his Church.

It is a question here of the theological and spiritual profile of the highest ministry for the Church and for the world, which the Head of the Church has entrusted to Saint Peter and his successors.

1 See, e.g., August Franzen and Remigius Bäumer, *Papstgeschichte: Das Petrusamt in seiner Idee und in seiner geschichtlichen Verwirklichung in der Kirche* (Freiburg: Verlag Herder, 1974); Martin Greschat, ed., *Das Papsttum*, 2 vols. (Stuttgart: W. Kohlhammer, 1984–1985); Gerhard B. Winkler, *Das Papsttum: Entwicklung der Amtsgewalt von der Antike bis zur Gegenwart* (Innsbruck: Tyrolia, 2002); Klaus Herbers, *Geschichte des Papsttums im Mittelalter* (Darmstadt: WBG, 2012).

2 See Walter Brandmüller, *Licht und Schatten: Kirchengeschichte zwischen Glaube, Fakten und Legenden* (Augsburg: Sankt-Ulrich-Verl, 2007).

2.
SECULAR AND THEOLOGICAL PAPAL HISTORY

NOT EVEN LIBERAL HISTORIOGRAPHY, which regards the primacy of the Roman church merely as a human creation or a chance product of historical constellations and therefore thinks that it can or must deconstruct it sociologically and politically, can escape the fascination of a two-thousand-year-old tradition. Even in purely inner-worldly terms, the papacy, from Simon Bar-Jona from Bethsaida down to Jorge Bergoglio from Buenos Aires, is the most interesting phenomenon of secular history too. Academic church history plays the important role of mediator between a wholly secular historiography and a systematic-theological view, for it is here that the object one wishes to grasp theologically—namely, the Church—is analyzed with the instruments of historical science. Before studying the development of a historical phenomenon, one must study the essence of the object involved and the self-understanding of its representatives. And here, one must distinguish between the element that determines its essence and the secondary attendant phenomena.

One can, of course, note—from a purely phenomenological perspective—that it was only in the sixth century that the official titles were consolidated, so that (for example) the bishop of Rome was called "pope" (*papa—father*); this was originally the designation of every bishop and priest, and its meaning is preserved in the address "Holy Father";[3] even today, in many languages all priests are addressed as "Father." An active exercise of a universal primacy of jurisdiction is attested only in the fourth century, with Pope Damasus I (r. 366–384), when the letters sent by the bishops of Rome to their colleagues in the episcopal office adopted the decretal style. This period also saw the development of technical terms that sought to describe the specific character of the Petrine ministry: *primatus, principatus, cathedra Petri, Sancta* or *Apostolica sedes, sollicitudo omnium ecclesiarum, plenitudo potestatis, prima sedes a nemine iudicatur,* and so on. This, however, does not mean that the papacy slowly evolved out of a secular claim to power that forced its way up onto the peak of a universal spiritual governance of the world in the Middle Ages. Both with and without the later specifically papal titles and the style of the papal office, the bishop of Rome has from the very beginning held a responsibility for the entire Church and for its unity

3 We are indebted to Pierre Battifol for comprehensive studies of the development of the official titles of the popes: *Cathedra Petri: Études d'Histoire ancienne de l'Église* (Paris: Cerf, 1938), 83–195.

in faith in Christ. This is more extensive than the responsibility that he bears as bishop of Rome for those who belong to his own diocese.

The historical phenomenon of the papacy, which is the object of secular historical research, has a substance of divine right that is anchored in the constitution of the Church: it is the office of the bishop of the Roman church, to which, by divine providence, Saint Peter's universal office as pastor and teacher has passed over. The pope and bishop of Rome receives his universal pastoral office from Christ for the Church; but he does not receive it through the Church. This is the object of the supernatural faith with which a Catholic sees the Church in its origin and in its historical realization.

Everything has come into being in history, but not everything has its origin in the causality of the created realities that have appeared in history, including the causality of human freedom. The Church of God owes its existence to the working of God. It has a divine mission that is carried out through human beings empowered by Christ. This is why everything it does in history can also be the object of secular historiography. But the historical-critical method on its own can neither demonstrate nor refute the origin and the essence of the Church in the universal will to salvation, and its task as the universal sacrament of salvation in Christ.

Independently of the question of faith, therefore, the Catholic Church, with the primacy of the pope, is also a fact of world history. The history of the Church is a mighty historical phenomenon that must be explained and understood, even if one does not share its self-understanding in terms of the theology of revelation. This is the basic assumption both of the secular historian Leopold von Ranke (1795–1886), who had been brought up as a Protestant, with his grandiose "History of the Roman Popes," and of Horst Fuhrmann (1926–2011) in his history of the popes "From Peter to John Paul II."[4] We should also mention the impressive results of the researches by Erich Caspar (1879–1935) and Johannes Haller (1865–1947).[5] The methodological difference is due to the differing understandings of the Church, which inevitably led to a differing evaluation of the historical development and of the traces it has left in written and monumental documents.

Church historiography looks at the Church with the theological and the historical eye. This applies both to the history of dogma and to the real-

4 Leopold von Ranke, *Die römischen Päpste: In den letzten vier Jahrhunderten,* 6th ed. (Leipzig: Dunker and Humblot, 1874); Horst Fuhrmann, *Die Päpste: Von Petrus zu Johannes Paul II.,* 3rd ed. (Munich: C. H. Beck, 1998); 4th updated and expanded edition with a new title (*Von Petrus zu Benedikt XVI*), Munich 2012.

5 Erich Caspar, *Geschichte des Papsttums von den Anfängen bis zur Höhe der Weltherrschaft* (Tübingen: J. C. B. Mohr, 1930–1933; Munster: Stenderhoff, 1985); Johannes Haller, *Das Papsttum: Idee und Wirklichkeit,* 5 vols. (Stuttgart: Port Verlag, 1950–53).

life history of the papacy. The mystery of the Church can be grasped only in faith—namely, that it is both established by God and inseparably also a human reality, as a part of universal history:

> Thus the Church, at once "a visible association and a spiritual community" (LG 8), goes forward together with humanity and experiences the same earthly lot which the world does. She serves as a leaven and as a kind of soul for human society as it is to be renewed in Christ and transformed into God's family. That the earthly and the heavenly city penetrate each other is a fact accessible to faith alone; it remains a mystery of human history, which sin will keep in great disarray until the splendor of God's sons is fully revealed. Pursuing the saving purpose which is proper to her, the Church does not only communicate divine life to men but in some way casts the reflected light of that life over the entire earth, most of all by its healing and elevating impact on the dignity of the person, by the way in which it strengthens the seams of human society and imbues the everyday activity of men with a deeper meaning and importance. Thus through her individual members and her whole community, the Church believes she can contribute greatly toward making the family of man and its history more human (GS 40).

3.
THE PAPACY—SEEN IN THE HERMENEUTIC OF FAITH

An investigation of the papacy from political and sociological perspectives, in the context of the history of ideas, and even from a standpoint critical of ideology, is thus legitimate and necessary, if we are to have a complete overview. *Nevertheless, the theological category is the precisely appropriate approach.* It is only from this perspective that a synthesis between a theological and a historical view becomes possible, since the Church is of its nature a supernatural reality that can be adequately known only in the light of God's self-revelation in Jesus Christ (Jn 1:9), who is "the way, the truth, and the life" (Jn 14:6). In the phenomenon that can be perceived historically and empirically, God's will for his Church and for its supernatural mission is expressed and is understood in the light of faith. The divine institution of the Church, of the episcopal ministry, and of the papacy is a part of the revelation that must be accepted with a supernatural faith that is relevant for salvation. All this is not in the least an externally imposed structure of a religious community, a structure that could be changed and that must be acknowledged, in practical and pragmatic terms, merely as a sensible regulation of life in common within the Church.

This applies both to the theological tractate of ecclesiology and to the theological discipline of church and papal history. Helpful works here are Ludwig von Pastor's *Geschichte der Päpste*, or Franz Xaver Seppelt's comprehensive study; for the modern period, I refer to Georg Schwaiger's monograph.[6] The sources for the history of the papacy have been edited in an exemplary manner by the Protestant church historians Carl Mirbt and Kurt Aland.[7] In recent editions, these scholarly works offer an improved knowledge, which is the presupposition of an ecumenical rapprochement in the understanding of the papacy.

4.
THE PAPACY IN THE CLASH OF IMAGES OF THE CHURCH

THE COMPREHENSIVE HERMENEUTIC OF REVELATION AND FAITH, of the essence and the form of the Church, also determines the differing evaluation of one and the same historical documents in the Protestant-Catholic controversy about the papacy.

An understanding of the Church that completely deviated from the Catholic faith, because it was essentially spiritualist and Donatist, led already in John Wycliffe (1320–1384) and Jan Hus (ca. 1369–1415) to a negative evaluation of the papacy as an ecclesiastical institution—and not merely to a negative evaluation of some of its representatives. The criticism of the Church in the *Defensor pacis* by Marsilius of Padua (ca. 1280–1343) has, in reality, already abandoned the terrain of the theology of revelation. The Church, which is wholly exposed to the *raison d'état*, is apparently subject to the sovereignty of the people, but is, in reality, subjugated to the absolutist princes; this Church no longer has any connection with the Church of which God is the sovereign and Christ the founder.

One must, however, understand the rift in the hearts of men like Wycliffe, Hus, and Luther. Originally, they wanted not a Church with a spiritualist makeup but a reform of the concretely existing Church in the spirit of the Gospel. In their eyes, they were condemning the worldly princes of

6 Ludwig von Pastor, *Geschichte der Päpste seit dem Ausgang des Mittelalters*, 16 vols. (Freiburg: Herder, 1886–1933); Franz Xaver Seppelt, *Geschichte der Päpste*, 5 vols. (Munich: Kösel, 1954–1956); Georg Schwaiger, *Papsttum und Päpste im 20. Jahrhundert: Von Leo XIII. zu Johannes Paul II.* (Munich: Kösel, 1954–1956).

7 Carl Mirbt and Kurt Aland, *Quellen zur Geschichte des Papsttums und des römischen Katholizismus*, 6th rev. ed. (Tübingen: J. C. B. Mohr, 1972).

the Church for holding a false concept of the Church. They believed that the Church's teaching authority was being used or abused both in order to justify deplorable situations that were obvious to everybody, as (for example) in the Avignon papacy, and in order to oppose every radical renewal of the Church *in capite et membris.* If the prelates of the Church had set themselves at the vanguard of the spiritual reform, or if they had led the way with their good example, this rift might never have broken open. Popes and bishops are not entitled to appeal merely to their authority (which is, of course, bestowed on them by God). They must also be models for their flocks (1 Pt 5:4). The Church's leading representatives had their share in the blame for the crisis of its credibility in the fourteenth and fifteenth centuries.

For Martin Luther (1483–1546) and John Calvin (1509–1564), the pope had become the antichrist through falling away from the faith of the earliest Church. He was the one "who opposes and exalts himself against every so-called god and object of worship, so that he takes his seat in the temple of God, proclaiming himself to be God" (2 Thes 2:4). When they identified the dragon and the beast from the abyss in the Revelation of John (12:3; 13:1) with the pope in Rome, they believed that they had in fact produced the biblical proof of their belief that the pope was the antichrist of the last days. One must, of course, add that even this extreme polemic was not completely baseless, when one remembers that some extreme papalist authors grotesquely exaggerated the pope's title of *Vicarius Christi* to make him a kind of *Deus in terris.* In the memorable religious conversation in the Kremlin about the reunion of the Russian Church with Rome on February 21, 1582, Ivan IV the Terrible (1530–1584) accused the pope of allowing himself to be venerated as God: the pope was not a shepherd but a wolf. This was due to the anti-Catholic propaganda that the agents of Queen Elizabeth I of England (r. 1558–1603) were spreading in the Russian empire. The learned papal legate Antonio Possevino (1533–1611), who also mediated the peace between Russia and Sweden in the Northern Seven Years' War, replied that just as there were bad and good grand dukes, so too there had been good and bad popes—but this did not change any of the rights and duties of their office.[8] For these words, Ivan the Terrible almost killed him with his own hands.

The pope is the Vicar of Christ as servant of the servants of Christ, in the imitation of Jesus, who came in order to serve and to lay down his life. It was no longer possible at that time for the Reformers to recognize in him the Vicar of Christ and the successor of Simon Bar-Jona, the rock of the Church's unity and of the truth of the Gospel.

8 See Pastor, *Geschichte der Päpste,* 9:698–708.

This is why the history of the Church was read as a progressive falling away from the pure biblical origin, and as the spreading of the corruption of the Church through the papacy (Flacius Illyricus, the Magdeburg Centuries). In his treatise *Against the Papacy in Rome, Instituted by the Devil* (1545), Luther asserted the erroneous view that Gregory the Great was the first pope to become the head of the universal Church.[9] He claimed that the origin and beginning of the papacy went back to Pope Boniface III (r. Feb. 19–Nov. 12, 607), who had received from Emperor Phocas sovereignty over all the bishops.[10]

All that was involved there, however, was the rejection of Constantinople's extensive claims to jurisdiction at the expense of Rome, claims that were supported by the Eastern Roman emperors. But even Emperor Justinian I, the very embodiment of caesaropapism, who wanted to reduce Rome de facto to a patriarchate in the Western Empire, had acknowledged—with complete theological correctness—Rome as the "head of all priests and head of all churches," and the Roman church as the apex of the priesthood, through which all the heresies had been overcome.[11] Similarly, Emperor Valentinian III (r. 425–455) had acknowledged the Roman primacy, founded in Peter, as a truth of the faith.[12] Even the pagan Emperor Aurelian (r. 270–275) had ordered the recalcitrant heretic Paul of Samosata to vacate his church, because the only legitimate proprietor was "the one with whom the bishops of Italy and Rome are in union."[13] Luther was thus wrong to assert that the primacy of the Roman church was conferred on it by the emperor, not by Christ. (It is, of course, another question to what extent the Byzantine emperors acknowledged this truth of the faith in ecclesial rather than in political terms.)

The assertion of the late medieval critics was therefore that the papacy, as it had developed in history, involved not the true successors of Peter but rather an intensifying despotism of usurpers who perverted the spiritual reality of the community of faith into an empire of secular power with a pseudotheological justification.

The accusation they made was that Christianity had become a worldly matter. This, of course, did not refer to the transformative impact of Chris-

9 *Wider das Papsttum zu Rom vom Teufel gestiftet,* WA 54, 195–299; see Martin Brecht, *Martin Luther* (Stuttgart: Calwer Verlag, 1987), 3:351–61.

10 WA 54, 230–231.

11 *Cod. Just.* I. tit. q.q. 7.8.

12 Konrad Kirch, *Enchiridion fontium historiae ecclesiasticae antiquae* (Barcelona: Herder, 1965), 799–800.

13 Eusebius of Caesarea, *Hist. eccl.* VII.30.

tianity on the world but rather to the alteration of its message into an inner-worldly doctrine of salvation. They held that true Christianity is a purely spiritual movement, the exact antithesis of the entanglement of the Church in politics from Constantine the Great (270–337) onwards.

This meant that the true essence of the Church is the invisible community of faith of the true believers and of the predestined. It is not an external body politic subject to the pope as its absolute prince.

Catholic Counter-Reformation apologetic historiography responded by seeking to present the path taken by the Church as a continuous upward movement, but without also realistically seeing the great crises in which a divine institution can land through the human beings who are its representatives.

For Adolf von Harnack (1851–1930), the leading historian of the liberal Protestant history of dogmas, the Gospel is a personal experience, freedom of conscience, interior disposition, and action. He regards Catholic Christianity as a religion that externalizes and reifies truth and grace into cult, dogma, the rule of faith, sacred law, and the devout and uncritical obedience of the laity to the teaching authority of the pope. He regards Catholic Christianity (and Orthodox Christianity *a fortiori*) as merely historically conditional preliminary and transitional stages en route to the purely spiritual-moral Christianity in its modern form in liberal cultural Protestantism.

The allegedly purely charismatic Church of the origins is contrasted with the institutionalized, hierarchical, sacramental, dogmatic, and legally regulated Christianity that took the form of the second-century "early Catholicism" that was essentially different from biblical Christianity. An unbridgeable chasm yawns between what Jesus wanted and envisaged, on the one hand, and what became of this—namely, the Catholic Church. The Reformers were the first to discover the purely biblical Christianity and free it from its historical encrustations and distortions. Nevertheless, the liberal Protestant church historians Adolf von Harnack and Rudolph Sohm (1841–1917) acknowledge as a historical fact the leadership of Rome for the whole of Christianity, which can be seen ever more clearly from the second to the fourth centuries. They interpret this, however, as a deviation even at this early period from the Gospel ideal. The development of the genuine, interior Christianity leads from Hellenistic metaphysics to the modern view of Christianity as trust in God the Father, in imitation of Jesus of Nazareth, as its ideal. Faith in the form of trust bids farewell to every faith that has defined contents, and this is why it does not come into conflict with philosophy or the modern human and natural sciences.[14] Harnack sees today's Catholicism

14 See Adolf von Harnack, *Das Wesen des Christentums: 16 Vorlesungen für Studierende aller Fakultäten im Wintersemester 1899/1900* (Leipzig: Hinrich, 1900).

as the anachronistic presence of the ancient and medieval Christianity in the modern age, something that must necessarily seem a foreign body. It is only a Christianity that is reduced to interiority and ethics and is liberated from belief in dogmas and in authorities that is compatible with the modern age. The modern age is the cipher here for the perfect emancipation of subjectivity and of the Protestant freedom from all mediatory authorities, leading to an immediate relationship to the God who is always transcendent, or else to the establishing of the authority of historical truth against the dogmatic Christianity that disguises the simple biblical message in the rigid material of Greek metaphysics. The influential Lutheran legal scholar Rudolf Sohm had similarly defined Catholicism as the outcome of a transition from the pure charismatic Church of love to the Church of law, a legally regulated institution that mediated salvation—thereby perverting Jesus's intention into its exact opposite. Something similar must also be said about the historically narrowed-down view taken of the development of the papacy in Gallicanism, Febronianism, and Old Catholicism: they did not succeed in reconciling the supposition of the divine institution of the papacy with the empirical analysis of the historical sources. This was also the problem of Ignaz Döllinger (1799–1890), the important nineteenth-century Catholic historian, in whom a supernaturalist and a historical-critical approach stand unmediated alongside one another. This led to a breach with the Church, because he regarded the dogma of 1870 as a contradiction of the historical facts.[15] Only a few years earlier, however, he had written:

> Like all that lives, and like the Church itself, of which it is the crown and the keystone, the papacy has undergone a historical development that is full of the most varied and surprising turns and twists. But in this history, one cannot fail to recognize the law that is the basis of the Church's life, the law of continuous development, of growth from within. The papacy had to experience all the destinies and transformations of the Church, it had to be present in every formative process. Its birth begins with two powerful, weighty, and far-reaching words of the Lord. The one to whom these words are addressed realizes them in his person and activity, and transplants the institution into the center of the Church that was just coming into being, into Rome. Here it grows in stillness, *occulto velut arbor aevo.* In the oldest period, it emerges only in some traits; but the outlines of the authority and of the ecclesial activity of the Roman bishop become ever clearer and better defined. The popes are already in the time of the Roman empire the

15 Ignaz von Döllinger, *Das Papsttum* (Darmstadt: WBG, 1969).

guardians of the entire Church, who exhort and warn in every direction, who make dispositions and judge, who bind and loose."[16]

The great theological challenges of the present day cannot be resolved by means of a "positivism of the magisterium," because one must first of all demonstrate the possibility and the reality of a self-revelation on the part of God. In the same way, one cannot employ a "positivism of church history" in dealing with the theological and historical sources, in order to leap over the questions concerning the relationship between the Word of God and its historical mediation. This is because the sources—sacred scripture, tradition, and the magisterium—are not the expression of human thoughts and actions. Because of the Incarnation, they are also bearers of information and the media of the Word of God in the spirit and the mouth of the Church that proclaims and believes.

5.
THE HISTORY OF THE PAPACY IN CONFORMITY WITH ITS DIVINE INSTITUTION

THE ORIGIN OF THE PAPACY LIES IN GOD'S WILL for the Church as the "universal sacrament of the salvation of the world in Christ."[17] And precisely this universal salvific will of God is the key to understanding the essence and the mission of this institution that has a divine origin and belongs to the sacramental law. One can adequately grasp and present the mission of the papacy in world history only in the light of the supernatural revelation. The supernatural faith cannot be justified in empirical, historical terms, but nor can it be refuted. It is, however, possible to demonstrate in the historical documents whether its understanding develops according to the principles of its own logic. Theological and historical methods contradict each other only in the thought pattern of the metaphysical dualism of rationalism and empiricism that has indeed left its mark on modern philosophy from Descartes onwards, but is not in the least insuperable.[18]

16 Ignaz von Döllinger, *Kirche und Kirchen, Papsttum und Kirchenstaat: Historisch-politische Betrachtungen* (Munich: J. G. Cotta, 1861), 31–32.

17 cf. LG 1; LG 48; GS 45.

18 For further reflection on the question of the relationship between the form and the content of a theological theme in its historical development, see Klaus Schatz, *Der päpstliche Primat: Seine Geschichte von den Ursprüngen bis zur Gegenwart* (Würzburg: Echter, 1990).

When one inquires into the essential element of the papacy, one must not begin with the developing doctrine and praxis of primacy. The recognition of the primacy, drawn from the Church's living consciousness of the faith, is anterior to the reflexive and systematic justification of the primacy.[19]

It is doubtless true that in the early centuries, the Holy See *reacted* to doctrinal challenges or heard appeals, rather than *governing* the Church centrally in a system defined by canon law. The dogmatic basis of all the legal and political activities is that Rome constitutes the first and the last criterion of the granting or the withdrawal of communion fellowship. The eucharistic ecclesiology that sees the Church as the *communio ecclesiarum*, with the Roman *ecclesia principalis* as its midpoint, is in fact the systematic approach road that enables us to discern a basis for an understanding of the Petrine ministry that is shared by both East and West.[20] And the formation of a systematic canon law, as both a structure of divine right and the regulations about the implementation of purely ecclesial law, began only from the twelfth century onwards.

But the universal pastoral ministry bestowed by Christ is not identical with a central form of Church government, although it is no simple task to turn back the wheel of history with regard to the methods of Church administration. In an age of globalization, one must make use of the possibilities of communication to benefit communion in faith and in Church life.

Hearing the word of revelation is materially and temporally antecedent to its theological explication. The real-life history of the people of God is not deduced from human theories; rather, it always forms the greater and never fully graspable horizon of the formation of theories.[21]

And one certainly must not try to approach the formative principle of the papacy via phenomena that are merely secondary (because they are mixed with political options), such as the Symmachian forgeries, the donation by Pippin as the basis of the Papal States (ca. 756–1870), the "forgeries" of the Constantinian donation and the Pseudo-Isidorian decretals, the program

19 The application of the principles of doctrinal development in the sense of the Catholic faith towards the "Papal Supremacy" in John Henry Newman, *Essay on the Development of Christian Doctrine* (London: Toovey, 1846), Part I, ch. 4, section 3, is enlightening here.

20 For further reflection here, see Paul McPartlan, *A Service of Love: Papal Primacy, the Eucharist, and Church Unity* (Washington, D.C.: The Catholic University of America Press, 2016); Patrick Granfield, *The Papacy in Transition* (New York: Doubleday & Co., 1980); Albert Brandenburg and Hans Jörg Urban, *Petrus und Papst: Evangelium, Einheit der Kirche, Papstdienst*, 2 vols. (Münster: Aschendorff, 1977–78).

21 On the process whereby the criteria of Catholic theology were elaborated, see Michel Fiedrowicz, *Theologie der Kirchenväter: Grundlagen frühchristlicher Glaubensreflexion* (Freiburg: Verlag Herder, 2007).

of the freedom of the Church in the medieval feudal society in the *Dictatus papae* of Gregory VII in the period of the Investiture Conflict, or the doctrine of the direct or indirect authority of the pope over secular government, et cetera. The vacillations of Pope Liberius (r. 352–366); the seesaw politics of Pope Vigilius (r. 537–555) in the controversy about the Three Chapters; and the case of Pope Honorius I (r. 625–638), whom the Third Council of Constantinople condemned as a heretic because of his negligence and unclarity in the fight against Monothelitism—none of these instances can be adduced as a trump card against the dogma of papal infallibility (as opponents of the First Vatican Council argued), because none of the characteristics of a doctrinal decision *ex cathedra* in the later sense of the term was present.[22]

There was certainly a historically significant dualism and struggle in the Western Middle Ages between the emperor (or national kings and regional princes and city magistrates) and the pope about the superiority of the spiritual or the secular power, which began roughly with the coronation of Charlemagne and lasted until the "Babylonian Captivity of the papacy in Avignon." But from an ecclesiological perspective, this was certainly not the zenith of the importance of the papacy in church history. The positive outcome of the struggle for the freedom of the Church from every form of subjection to the temporal power, or the subordination of the Church to the *raison d'état*, has lasted down to the present day, albeit under different presuppositions, since even in a democracy, the dignity of the human being, grounded in his or her nature, with inalienable basic rights, is antecedent to the validity of the positive laws of the state and puts limits to these laws.

The core of the conflict concerned the Church's freedom from the tight embrace of feudal lords and the sacral exaltation of secular power, with its tendency towards an absolutization in the sacral or absolutist monarchy, and later in the omnipotent or totalitarian state of the nineteenth and twentieth centuries.

The sacral government of Christian princes in the Middle Ages is, however, conceptually different from the so-called theocracy that is found in non-Christian religions. Today's terrorism in the name of Islam cannot be relativized by the fact that force was used (which at that time was legal) in the medieval states where Christianity was the dominant influence. And there is no historical period in which crimes against humanity can be justified in "religious" terms.

In the struggle between emperor and pope about the higher authority, the central idea was the sanctification of political power—it was not about

22 See Georg Kreuzer, *Die Honoriusfrage im Mittelalter und der Neuzeit* (Stuttgart: Hiersemann, 1975).

the religious justification of the arbitrary use of power, and still less about a "theocracy." That is a diametrical contradiction of the basic Christian principles, since Jesus himself formulated the essential principle of the relationship between Church and state: "Render to Caesar the things that are Caesar's, and to God the things that are God's" (Mt 22:21).

Innocent III, with the Fourth Lateran Council in 1215, was acknowledged by many rulers as the feudal lord in the chaotic societal circumstances of the Middle Ages, but this did not in the least mark the high point in the development of the doctrine of *faith* about the pope as the universal pastor of the Church. In precisely the same way, what happened to Boniface VIII at Anagni in 1303 did not launch the demise of papal authority.

And the fact that, in the aftermath of the events of 1870, the Vatican State is only a tiny remnant of the Papal States of the past is no loss in today's political constellations. On the contrary, the history books regard this as a win for the papacy.

The papal diplomacy today is unhindered by any interests of its own in the field of power politics. This allows the religious-moral authority of the Church to act in pursuit of the goals of peace, the universal validity of human rights, and social justice in the world. The ascent of the medieval papacy to a universal spiritual-moral power that was also a political power, and the loss of this political power with the emergence of the modern nation states that elevated the *raison d'état* to the highest criterion of politics, did not shed any light on the "essential character" of the papacy. Indeed, it tended rather to obscure the religious-ethical mission of the Petrine ministry—especially from an agnostic perspective on the human being and the world.

The paradigm shift is, however, not simply the result of external circumstances, as if one had been forced to make a virtue out of necessity.

When the Vatican declaration of the pope's infallibility is understood as a compensation for the loss of the Papal States, and this assertion is passed on to others as an insider tip for understanding this matter, all that this reveals is a profound ignorance.

One might add that the secular inheritors of the region that once formed the Papal States have not ruled it better, down to the present day. The pope does not need political power in order to exercise his moral authority for the good of humankind. He needs nothing other than the freedom of the Church and the recognition of the universal freedom of religion and of conscience over against the totalitarian behavior of states and of ideologies of self-redemption.

The Church's saving mission takes priority over its public and cultural tasks, thanks to the very essence of what the Church is: "The mystery of the holy Church is manifest in its very foundation" (LG 5). The meaning of the imitation of Christ becomes clear when we look at the Incarnation, through which "God sends his Son in the likeness of sinful flesh" (Rom 8:3), God's self-abasement even to the death of his Son on the Cross (Phil 2:6–11), and the redemption of humankind through the "stumbling block and folly of the crucified Christ" (1 Cor 1:23). "Just as Christ carried out the work of redemption in poverty and persecution, so the Church is called to follow the same route that it might communicate the fruits of salvation to men. [...] Thus the Church, although it needs human resources to carry out its mission, is not set up to seek earthly glory, but to proclaim, even by its own example, humility and self-sacrifice" (LG 8).

6.
THE PAPACY IN THE STRUCTURE OF THE SACRAMENTAL CHURCH

STRICTLY SPEAKING, if we were to follow the Idealist-Platonist presuppositions of historiography, Christianity would have only a history of ideas, not a real-life history. This real-life history, however, necessarily arose as a consequence of the Incarnation. On the other hand, if one were only to make a purely external list of facts, the Church would have only a real-life history; one would not be able to recognize the idea of God in history.

The Incarnation of God in his Son Jesus Christ is, however, a historical fact and not merely an idea that would have only lightly brushed the surface of our cruel world that is entangled in wickedness. Nor is it merely a matter of brute facts to which one would arbitrarily have to ascribe a significance, in order for them to acquire a meaning for me.[23]

A hermeneutic of the breach and contradiction between the Church of the time of Jesus and the apostles and the post-apostolic period in the second

23 The sacramentality of the Church is the decisive hermeneutical context for understanding all the fundamental institutions of the Catholic Church. On this, see Karl-Heinz Menke, *Sakramentalität: Wesen und Wunde des Katholizismus* (Regensburg: Pustet, 2012); Louis Bouyer, *L'Église de Dieu, Corps du Christ et Temple de l'Esprit* (Paris: Cerf, 1970); Werner Löser, ed., *Die Römisch-Katholische Kirche* (Frankfurt: Evangelisches Verlagswerk, 1986); Angelo Scola, *Chi è la Chiesa? Una chiave antropologica e sacramentale per l'ecclesiologia* (Brescia: Queriniana 2005); Leo Scheffczyk, *Katholische Glaubenswelt: Wahrheit und Gestalt* (Paderborn: Schöningh, 2008); Joseph Ratzinger, *Joseph Ratzinger: Gesammelte Schriften*, vol. 8, *Kirche—Zeichen unter den Völkern* (Freiburg: Herder, 2010). It is still worth reading the profound presentation by Möhler (1825), which overcame the theological rationalism and naturalism of the Catholic Enlightenment theology: Johann Adam Möhler, *Die Einheit in der Kirche: Oder das Prinzip des Katholizismus: Dargestellt im Geiste der Kirchenväter der drei ersten Jahrhunderte*, ed. J. R. Geisleman (1825; repr., Cologne: Hegner, 1957). Citations refer to the Hegner edition.

and third centuries not only contradicts the meaning and the realization of God's self-revelation in Jesus Christ, the *verbum incarnatum.* It also contradicts the purely historical evidence of the sources. If a substantial alteration of the message had already been undertaken in the biblical sources and in their earliest reception in the most important second-century church fathers and writers, how would it be possible to recognize the apostolic tradition apart from these same fundamental documents, and to distill out of them the pure proclamation by Jesus and the original Christianity?

7.
THE PAPACY BETWEEN DIVINE POWER AND POWERLESSNESS IN THE WORLD

WITH THE END OF ITS EARTHLY, TRANSIENT POSITION OF POWER, the Church lost little and gained much. This applies both to its religious and moral mission and to its political-cultural task in the world. But it does not mean a recognition *post eventum* of all the breaches of law and violent assaults on the part of state authorities, beginning with the pagan and Christian emperors in the Roman and Byzantine Empires, via the kings and rulers in the West, to the liberal cultural warriors of the nineteenth century and the brutal enemies of the Church in the twentieth century, who were responsible for the greatest persecution of Christians in history up to now.[24]

The kingdom of Christ is not of this world (Jn 18:36), and it is not subject to the law of the rise and fall of all the empires founded by human beings. This is why it does not suffer the fate of death, the fate that awaits all the kingdoms and states of this world and all other human institutions and enterprises. The true indestructibility of the Church is displayed through the "gates of hell" in the persecution of the Church and in the suffering of Christians, which can go as far as the temporary extinction of the faith in some countries.

As a divine institution, the Church proves indestructible in its existence and in the truth that it proclaims precisely in the midst of the rise and fall of all earthly kingdoms and ideologies. After Pope Pius VI was taken captive and died in Valence on August 29, 1799, the Jacobins' triumphalism

24 See, for example, Manuel Borutta, *Antikatholizismus: Deutschland und Italien im Zeitalter der europäischen Kulturkämpfe* (Göttingen: Vandenhoeck & Ruprecht, 2010); Jan Mikrut, ed., *La Chiesa cattolica e il Comunismo in Europa centro-orientale e in Unione Sovietica* (Verona: Gabrielli, 2016).

proclaimed the end of the Church and of the papacy, and a bright future of freedom without reason.

The later "Emperor of the French" declared his intentions on November 8, 1797 in the "Instruction of General Bonaparte to Director Gian Galeazzo Serbelloni" of the Cisalpine Republic. This was a product of opportunism, and it contains the destructive program of all the "enlightened" despots down to the present day: "This old idol will be destroyed. That is what freedom and philosophy require. [...] It is the will of the Directorate that the pope shall utterly perish, and that his religion shall be buried with him."[25]

The bloodthirsty tyrant Joseph Stalin—who was totally drunk and died as wretchedly as he lived—made a cynical allusion to the powerlessness of the Catholic Church in worldly terms at Yalta in 1945. His words have become proverbial: "How many divisions does the pope have?"

But these dictators confirm, despite themselves, that at the end the one who triumphs is not the one who can kill living persons but "the one who has the power to make the dead alive" (Jn 5:21). It is precisely here that the chasm yawns between "the rulers of this age," who "crucified the Lord of glory" (1 Cor 2:8), and the messengers of the Gospel who rely on the power and the wisdom of God (1 Cor 2:5–6.). The innumerable throng of those who were saved sing joyfully, with palm branches in their hands: "Salvation belongs to our God who sits upon the throne, and to the Lamb!" (Rv 7:10). This is the path that imitates Christ, the path taken by the Church, "the bride of the Lamb, who has made herself ready for the wedding of the Lamb" (Rv 19:7–8.; 21:2, 17).

This is the theological-historical methodology that allows us to grasp the events and developments of church history in their significance for faith. But the question of faith is: Is the papal primacy based on a divine promise, or is it merely a chance historical phenomenon that has its origin in a human claim to leadership or in the sheer lust for power of an obscurantist clerical caste, a claim generated by the sociological necessities of a worldwide organization?

Explanations are offered that are the fruit of one's ideological prejudice: the papal primacy is due to religious-political constellations, or the imperial genius of ancient Rome was transposed into the spiritual realm. What is involved here, however, is not the continuation of the Roman Empire but its replacement by the kingdom of God, the keys of which were given into the hands of Saint Peter.

25 See Heinrich Elsner, *Umfassende Geschichte des Kaisers Napoleon*, vol. 4 (Stuttgart: Lepizig Rieger, 1837).

8.
THE PAPACY AT ROME—FOUNDED IN REVELATION

According to the Catholic faith, the primacy of the Roman church is a fact founded on revelation. This fact is antecedent to its theoretical and conceptual formulation and its practical implementation in a doctrine of primacy (which was by no means exclusively developed in Rome) and in the elaboration of the details of the primatial rights (the infallible magisterium of the pope and his primacy of jurisdiction).

The real idea of the papal primacy is established in its institution by Christ, and it is expounded historically in its basic principles and aspects in the medium of the Church's consciousness of faith. It would be illogical to believe in the divine institution of the Church and to evaluate the historical development of its consciousness of faith in purely secular categories. The Holy Spirit is involved in the origin of the Church just as much as in its path through history. Indeed, the Holy Spirit is not only involved; he is above all and in all the inherent power of the Church's development and the principle of the knowledge of its faith. This means that what we find is a homogeneous doctrinal development, that is to say, the preservation of the basic principles—not a conglomerate of contradictory affirmations and claims (*complexio oppositorum*) that could be detached from each other mechanically, like the layers of an onion. The individual understanding and the Church's collective understanding of the faith, which unfolds in the course of history, can bear witness to the mystery of the revelation without leaving anything out, but can never exhaust in concepts the entire fullness and depth of this revelation, "for the act of faith has its goal not in the affirmation, but in the content. For we form affirmations only in order, by means of them, to arrive at the knowledge of the contents, both in knowledge and in faith."[26] This is why the development of doctrine and dogma is coextensive with the mission of the Church as a divine institution in this world and in the history of the human race.

And this is why, although God's self-revelation in his Word made flesh and in the Spirit who is poured out over us is unsurpassable and unique, there is necessarily a history of doctrinal development. This does not increase, decrease, or falsify the substance. Rather, it makes this substance more deeply its own: intellectually, conceptually, and spiritually. In the history of dogmas and in constitutional reflection, this also applies to the dogma of the pope's infallible teaching office and primacy of jurisdiction,

26 Thomas Aquinas, *S.th.* II–II q1 a2 ad 2.

since, as the Vicar of Christ, he is the visible representative of the invisible Head of the Church.

History does teach us. In the sequence of generations, in the endless variety of interpersonal interactions, and in the unpredictability of the effects of the decisions that human beings take, we find that history helps us to understand and to learn God's saving plan. God wants everyone to be saved and to come to the knowledge of the truth through the one mediator, the man Christ Jesus (1 Tm 2:4–5), his incarnate Word through whom everything was created and in view of whom all things have been ordained. All creatures in heaven and on earth are to receive through the apostles and the Church the knowledge of the eternal plan of salvation that God has carried out in history through Jesus Christ (cf. Eph 3:9–11). An inherent goal of church history and of doctrinal development is also linked to this: "until we all attain to the unity of the faith and of the knowledge of the Son of God, to mature manhood, to the stature of the fullness of Christ" (Eph 4:13).

Just as we attain knowledge of the existence of God as the Creator through the works of creation, so too we are meant to be led through the history of world and through salvation history, as well as through the historical unfolding of the consciousness of faith, to knowledge of God as the one who redeems and perfects the human being. The comprehensive meaning and the goal of history can be seen in the light of God's revelation. They cannot be constructed by human beings. Neither a gnostic self-redemption in the absolute Idea, in which the human being sets himself in the place of God (theosophy, anthroposophy, New Age), nor a dissolution of the person in the material stream of evolution or in the eternal return of the same, offers the magic formula "that I may know what keeps the world together in its innermost core."[27]

This means a priori that a dualism of the real-life history of the papacy, on the one hand, and of the papacy as a supratemporal idea, on the other, is impossible. The un-Catholic idea of a supratemporal-invisible Church that floats above history unmoved as a lofty Platonic ideal, untouched by all earthly vicissitudes and by the reality of failure and sin, contradicts the incarnational and kenotic form of God's grace and forgets that the Church is "always in need of being purified, always follows the way of penance and renewal" (LG 8)—not, indeed, as a divine foundation but as a community that consists of human beings.

The timeless Church, with no relation to the world, in pure interiority and unmediated immediacy to God from pure Spirit to pure spirit, is the product of a spiritualist fantasy that contradicts the relationship, mediated

27 Johann Wolfgang von Goethe, *Faust: Der Tragödie Erster Teil* (Stuttgart: J. G. Cotta, 1833), ch. 4.

by the creation, between the bodily-spiritual human being, one the one hand, and God and the sacramental reality of the Church, on the other. In exactly the same way, the opposite extreme—a secularized and politicized Church that, at most, seeks to offer its services as an ethical-charitable organization in a secularist and laical society—has nothing to do with the Church that Christ founded. Only God is immediate to God; the human being needs mediation into immediacy. The God-man Jesus Christ, in his divine person, is the unity of immediacy and mediation. In the Church's sacramental existence and work, the Church, which is his body, continues God's saving work in Christ, in the power of the Holy Spirit, until the end of the world.

It is only by means of a human, spiritual-bodily, and social-historical mediation that is appropriate to the human being that he or she enters into immediacy to God. In the human nature of Christ, which subsists in the person of the Father's Son, we find the unity between God's immediacy to his own self and the perfect mediation of human beings to God through their sharing in the Holy Spirit in the Son's relationship to the Father. Since the Church in its sacramental life is the body of Christ, we have access to God in faith, hope, and love through the Son, the Head of the Church (see Rom 5:1–11).

The description of the essence and the mission of the Church by Johann Adam Möhler, the most brilliant representative of the Tübingen School, seems to me one of the most successful syntheses of the Catholic concept of the Church: "Catholics understand the Church on earth to be the visible community of the believers, established by Christ, in which the activities that he carried out during his earthly life for the atonement and sanctification of humankind are continued under the guidance of his Spirit until the end of the world, and all peoples are brought back to God in the course of the ages."[28]

The Son came into the world "in the fullness of time" (Gal 4:4). "In him the entire fullness of the Godhead dwells bodily (*sômatikôs*)" (Col 2:9). The Church is not a society organized by human beings that preserves as faithfully as possible its founder's ideas, instructions, and programs for improving the world, or his mysticism of flight from the world, and attempts to put these into practice. It "is his body, the fullness of him who fills all in all" (Eph 1:23). The word of its proclamation, its sacred symbolic actions, and the guidance of the faithful by their pastors are the visible expression of the working of the exalted and risen Christ. He is the Lord and Head of his Church, as Teacher, High Priest, and Shepherd of the faithful.

28 Möhler, *Symbolik*, §36.

The Church is a mystery, and it is only with what Pierre Rousselot (1878–1915) called the "eyes of faith" that it can be recognized in its innermost being—which is expressed and realized in its historical form—as the sacrament of God's universal salvific will.[29] Christ marches through time in the pilgrim form of his Church. This is why the historical unfolding of the revelation in the Church's thinking about the faith and living the faith belongs essentially to the incarnational-sacramental form of Christianity. Its form, which grows in history, thus belongs to the abiding essence of the Church that has its foundation in the Incarnation.

Just as the body and soul of the human being penetrate each other and are realized in the person of the individual human being, so too the external form and the internal essence of the Church are united in Christ, who holds it together as its head. He is the divine person of the Son, who unites hypostatically his own divine nature and the human nature taken from Mary. The visible Church with its hierarchical-sacramental constitution is not in the least juxtaposed, separated and detached, alongside a supposedly pneumatological-charismatic immediacy to the Spirit, as a transient phenomenon would stand alongside its supratemporal essence.

The historical self-revelation of God in Jesus Christ is attested in sacred scripture and in the apostolic tradition. But it unfolds progressively in the Church's consciousness of faith under the guidance of the magisterium, "for as the centuries succeed one another, the Church constantly moves forward toward the fullness of divine truth until the words of God reach their complete fulfillment in her" (DV 8). Since it is only in faith that we have access to the reality of the Church as a fellowship of grace with God in a visible form, there can exist a methodological distinction between an empirical-historical approach and a theological approach, but there cannot be an absolute antithesis—unless the historical phenomena are evaluated a priori from an agnostic and rationalist standpoint. But a philosophical rationalism or a fundamental skepticism about the possibility of the historical self-revelation of God cannot be justified in empirical-historical terms, nor in a priori epistemological terms; nor is such a position evident per se with regard to the illimitable openness of the spirit for the being of the real world and for the Word of God. A critical consideration of church history also helps us to draw a distinction between historical realities that were determined by circumstances, and the authority that Jesus Christ, the founder of the Church's mission, bestowed on Peter and his successors.

29 Pierre Rousselot, "Les yeux de la foi," *Reccherches de Science Religieuse* 1 (1910): 241–259, 444–475.

It is easy, from a safe distance, to denounce the "Constantinian turning point" and the subsequent constellations of the Church-state relationship in the later Germanic dominions of the Western Roman Empire as a falling away from the pure earliest Christianity or from the Church of the martyrs of the first three centuries. But the state and public institutions were disintegrating, and the Church—and especially the pope, who was acknowledged as the ultimate authority in Western Christianity—faced the challenge of employing its authority in the spheres of governance and culture, which even included military initiatives. Examples are the Hun invasion in the fifth century, the Saracen invasion in Italy in the eighth century, and the threat to Christian Europe by the Ottoman Empire from the fifteenth to the eighteenth centuries. How could the Church have simply refused these challenges, without thereby incurring guilt with regard to the common good?

The subsidiary political activity of the Church under specific political circumstances does not invalidate the basic knowledge of the relationship between Church and state, with each enjoying its own proper authority, and preserving the autonomy of earthly realities (GS 36). And a certain political dimension belongs to this ministry, since the pope reminds Christians and all those of good will of the need to contribute constructively to building up society in accordance with the criteria of justice, of social balance, of peace, and of the preservation of basic human rights.

One of the tasks of the pope is to remind the laity of their apostolate and of their commission in the world, and to encourage them to get involved. In the face of all the totalitarian ideologies of the present day and of the recent past, the popes have consistently proved to be the true interpreters of the natural dignity and the inalienable rights of the human being. In the love and the authority of Christ, they showed themselves to be the fathers of the poor and exploited, and the protectors of those who suffer and are deprived of their rights. John Paul II wrote the striking words: "Man is the primary route that the Church must travel."[30] In its Pastoral Constitution *Gaudium et spes*, the Second Vatican Council gave a valid description of the Church in today's world. It responds to a laical interpretation by presenting the relationship between ecclesial and secular authority not as a disinterested or hostile separation but as a respectful cooperation at the service of human beings.

If, however, we are to grasp the theological essence of the papacy, the only sources on which we can draw are sacred scripture and the documents of the apostolic and ecclesiastical tradition with their doctrinal (that is, dogmatic) content, as well as the definitive form of their confession of faith in the dogmatic decisions of the conciliar and papal magisterium.

30 John Paul II, Encyclical Letter *Redemptor hominis* (March 4, 1979), 14.

The all-decisive question is whether there is a real and historical self-revelation of God, so that Jesus of Nazareth is true God and true man. And the consequence of this is that, given the presupposition of the Incarnation of God, the Church as the body of Christ does indeed consist of human beings, but it must be acknowledged in its existence and in its salvific activity as a divine foundation.

The Church belongs to the content of the revealed faith: *Credo sanctam ecclesiam catholicam*. The Church, in its necessarily visible, sacramental, and hierarchical form, is the object of the supernatural faith that alone is capable of perceiving and acknowledging its inherent role as the mediation, with the aid of grace, into the immediacy of human beings to God. It is only in the faith that is enlightened by the Holy Spirit that one can grasp what is expressed in its sacramental form, and the mission on which its path in history is based.

Theology, in its desire to grasp revelation in its factuality and in its logical coherence, cannot, however, present *more geometrico* a conclusive theory that depicts its object materially or develops it syllogistically from its principles and deduces it rationalistically, so that the inner truth of the faith would be accessible without the illumination of the Holy Spirit. Every science that goes beyond the knowledge of matter and relates to that which is living, intellectual, and personal, and ultimately even to the transcendent God, integrates into its work the experience of life, the circumstances of time, the mentalities and cultures of the various epochs, and the development of the personalities of the knowing subjects.

The Catholic's relationship to the Roman pope is not generated first and foremost by a complex theory about his primacy of teaching and jurisdiction, but by the insight, supported by supernatural faith, that in the pope, the bishop of Rome, there are present the authority and the power that Christ bestowed on Simon Peter and on his successors. This is the overwhelming testimony of the Word of God in the earliest Church in its written and oral tradition. The understanding follows the faith (*fides quaerens intellectum*) and is meant to lead to a deepening of the faith. Very few Catholics can study the papal primacy in professional theological and extensive biblical and historical investigations. But all believe in the promise that Jesus made to Peter. Every Catholic (and only the Catholic) therefore understands that Peter's successors have the task of uniting the universal Church in Christ, its head.

The tomb of Cardinal Stanislaus Hosius (1504–1579) in the church of Santa Maria in Trastevere in Rome bears the following inscription: "One who deviates from the Roman church in the doctrine of the faith is not a Catholic" (*Catholicus non est, qui a Romana ecclesia in fidei doctrina discordat*).

III

He Who Founded the Church Also Founded the Papacy

Our starting point was that it is first and foremost in persons, and especially in their relationship to Christ who is the foundation and the founder of the Church, that we see what the Church is. After looking back, from the perspective of my own life history, at the seven popes in my own lifetime, I would now like to go back to the origin of the papacy—namely, to the relationship between Jesus and the fisher from Lake Gennesaret, whom he declared to be the rock on which HE would build his Church. We do not proceed in a deconstructivist manner, by breaking down a complex theory into its individual elements. What we shall do is to go to the ever-living source of the life of the Church and of the working of its pastors, who are the successors of the apostles. The Petrine apostolate, and hence also the papacy, is based on the relationship between two persons, Jesus the Christ, the incarnate Son of the eternal Father, and Simon, whom he made Peter, the rock on which the Lord has built his Church and continues to build it until he returns in glory. The risen Lord made him for all time the universal shepherd of the sheep of his flock. We must begin by clarifying what we understand when we speak of revelation and say that it is made present in the Church.

1.
DIVINE REVELATION AND THE HUMAN KNOWLEDGE OF THIS REVELATION

Everything that is said about the Church in its origin in God, its historical beginning, its universal mission, and its apostolic authority makes sense only in relation to Jesus Christ. The mystery of the Church in God's salvific plan, which was realized in history, is accessible only when HE is known and acknowledged in faith as the self-revelation of God. Historical-critical scholarship is fully entitled to study the biblical sources and the entire history of the people of God in the old and new covenants, and its historical-theological interpretation corresponds appropriately to God's encounter with human beings in salvation history. The decisive difference, however, is whether its methodologies are employed within a naturalistic worldview or in a perspective on the reality of the being of the world, and on the essential relationship of the human being to God, that is open to transcendence.

All knowledge of the human being, a spirit with a bodily constitution, needs an empirical basis or a starting point in history (*omnis cognitio incipit a sensibus*). But the spirit is not limited to empirical knowledge, since it transcends these, in accordance with its own nature, in the direction of the metaphysical ground of its being and its knowledge. One can and must infer from the being in which the transient things and living creatures participate, and through which they exist, the existence of a being that exists through itself, in itself, and of itself (*ipsum esse per se existens*). "For what can be known about God is plain to them [i.e., human beings], because God has shown it to them. Ever since the creation of the world, his invisible nature—namely, his eternal power and deity—has been clearly perceived in the things that have been made."[1] This has a decisive consequence when we speak about God as the origin and the goal of all finite being, which exists by participation and is realized really and individually in the framework of its own nature. God is not only transcendent *above* the world; he is also immanently present and actually working *in* the world. This applies to the human being who realizes himself in his intellectual and social nature in time and in history.

Paul, the apostle for "the Greeks" (as the Jews called the Gentiles), took his stance in the center of the Areopagus (see Acts 17:22) and held a keynote speech in which he joined the philosophical question to the theological answer. A dualistic or even antagonistic contrast between Greek and biblical thinking, between natural knowledge through the reason and supernatural

1 Rom 1:19–20; Wis 13:1–9; Sir 17:8.

knowledge through faith, between nature and grace, or between metaphysics and history contradicts the essence of the human being as God's creature and the hearer of his Word, as well as the basic datum of Christology—namely, the Incarnation of the eternal Word that was with God, and that with the Father and the Holy Spirit is the one and triune God.

Paul says: "What you worship as unknown"—namely, God as the theme of philosophy, of the love of wisdom and the search for truth—"this I proclaim to you"— namely, the God of Jesus Christ:

> The God who made the world and everything in it, being Lord of heaven and earth, does not live in shrines made by man, nor is he served by human hands, as though he needed anything, since he himself gives to all men life and breath and everything. And he made from one every nation of men to live on all the face of the earth, having determined allotted periods and the boundaries of their habitation, that they should seek God, in the hope that they might feel after him and find him. Yet he is not far from each one of us, for "In him we live and move and have our being," as even some of your poets have said, "For we are indeed his offspring." Being then God's offspring, we ought not to think that the Deity is like gold, or silver, or stone, a representation by the art and imagination of man. The times of ignorance God overlooked, but now he commands all men everywhere to repent, because he has fixed a day on which he will judge the world in righteousness by a man whom he has appointed, and of this he has given assurance to all men by raising him from the dead (Acts 17:23–31).

The eternal is in time. The Word of God speaks to us *hic et nunc*—here and now. Jesus Christ, the person of the Son of God who has taken on our human nature, is the *universale concretum* and the *plenitudo temporum.* The universal manifests itself in the concrete, and all times and spaces are gathered together in Christ. Time is transient, and it is impossible to grasp space in its endlessness; but this does not mean that the human race disintegrates into nothing. God became man in the fullness of time (Gal 4:4–6), and he recapitulates time and space. In Christ, God has brought about the fullness of time, in order to unite everything in Christ: heaven and earth, times and spaces, the world and history, and at the end, humankind in God (Mk 1:5; Eph 1:10).

The promise of salvation has the character of a historical event that is in accord with the human being's seeking, in accord with the aid given by our theoretical and practical reason. Our contact with God does not take place in timeless ideas and moral principles that are merely formal, without any content; nor does it take place in internal experiences of salvation unconnected to the world and floating above real history. On the contrary, God encounters us in and through the human nature that his Son received from his mother Mary. We are beings of flesh and blood, and he gives us himself as food and drink for eternal life, with his own flesh and blood under the sacramental signs of bread and wine (Jn 6:53–58). Through baptism, we become members of his body, which is the historical Church. Through the fellowship with his human nature, that is to say, with his flesh and blood, we are nourished by his divine life, we are kept alive and are established with God in love. The *kairos* of the Greeks is united to the "fullness of time," the lengthy time of salvation history and the covenant with the chosen people Israel, which reaches its fulfillment in Jesus, who represents its totality (see Rom 9:5). The "new covenant in the blood of Christ" (Lk 22:20) did not put an end to the old covenant: rather, it signified its fulfillment through the reception of the whole of humankind through faith in Jesus the Messiah, thanks to his human nature, into the eternal relationship of the Son to the Father in the Holy Spirit. "But when the time had fully come, God sent forth his Son, born of a woman, born under the law, to redeem those who were under the law, so that we might receive adoption as sons. And because you are sons, God has sent the Spirit of his Son into our hearts, crying, 'Abba! Father!'" (Gal 4:4–6).

The historical-critical methodology in exegesis came into existence at a period that saw a dualism between empiricism and rationalism and between the experience of the senses and the pure deductions of the reason, a period that saw an unbridgeable chasm between objective facts and subjective interpretations. If human knowledge has no access to the transcendence of Being (as in the metaphysical critical philosophy and in agnosticism), all that remains is a phenomenalism. In that case, historical phenomena can be explained only as the application of subjective individual or collective ways of thinking and language patterns, of depth-psychological ciphers and metaphors, or cultural ways of looking at persons and events. And Jesus—to put it in supposedly "objective and realistic" terms—cannot have been anything other than a Jewish rabbi whose self-understanding can be completely deduced from the religious-cultural traditions of contemporary Judaism, with its Greek, Roman, and Syriac points of reference. This means that the faith professed by his disciples and by the entire Church would be nothing other than the illustration and conceptualization of his existential significance for his followers, with the aid of era-specific subjective interpretative tools, collective fictions, ciphers from the history of religion, and universal philosophical concepts. The profession of faith in Christ would be only a Jewish and Hellenistic encrypting of the importance of a historical person for a self-referential mysticism and morality, to be employed in a merely functional sense. In short, Jesus Christ would not truly be the Word that has become flesh, the God who is consubstantial with the Father and the Spirit. He would be a human being with an importance for religious feelings, who was held to be the Son of God in the days before the Enlightenment and critical scholarship, although he is not the Son of God. An enlightened consciousness ascribes to the formulae of the Christological profession of faith only a functional claim to truth (*as if* he were the Son of God, and *as if* he had redeemed us).

The tradition of the Christian faith would then no longer bear witness to God in our consciousness. It would merely present the history of our consciousness of God. This naturalistic epistemological presupposition would relativize the phenomena of the Christian faith, of its dogma and its liturgy, and of the divine law; indeed, it would suspect them of being an ideology. And this presupposition generates the antagonism between the historical pre-Easter Jesus and the dogmatic post-Easter Christ—which diametrically contradicts the New Testament tradition as "Gospel"—that is, as the synthesis of the message of salvation and the account of historical facts. A dualistic epistemology, which no longer recognizes any link between empirical knowledge and the knowledge that uncovers the essence of things, must necessarily reduce the ecclesial and biblical testimony to Jesus in the Gospels to the subjective and arbitrary interpretation of historical facts that per se are meaningless and a matter of chance. This epistemology does not uncover the real meaning of the events. It subjectively ascribes a meaning to them and employs this meaning functionally. Even the declaration in the profession of faith that persons and events are significant for me would have no basis in reality. It would be appearance and illusion, rather than reality and truth.

2. THE THEOLOGICAL-HISTORICAL CONTENT OF THE GOSPELS

IN REALITY, IT IS NOT THE INTENTION OF THE GOSPELS to be a mixture of objective historical facts and a subjective interpretation on the part of enthusiastic individual followers of Jesus, or of enthusiastic anonymous communities who believed in him. On the contrary, they are the proclamation and attestation, supported by the Holy Spirit, of the true mystery of the person of Jesus, who "for us men and for our salvation came down from heaven, and by the Holy Spirit was incarnate of the Virgin Mary, and became man."

In his birth as a descendant of David, in his proclamation of God's kingly rule, in the messianic gathering together of the people of God, in his calling of the disciples and his entrusting of authority to the apostles; with his parables of the kingdom of God, with his mighty deeds in wonders and miracles for the salvation and the health of the poor and the sick; with the new covenantal ethics in the Sermon on the Mount; with his final rejection by the Jewish authorities; and at the end, in his suffering, his death, and his Resurrection from the dead, he *realizes* within history the kingdom of God in his own person. As person, Jesus, as the Father's Son, is God's "being there" and "being with us," and this can be seen in his whole history down to the Cross and Resurrection. He takes us in the Holy Spirit into his own relationship to the Father. It is through the Spirit that the Church carries out its mission to realize fully, through all generations, God's saving will.

Paul knows that he is "called to be an apostle, set apart for the gospel of God which he promised beforehand through his prophets in the holy scriptures, the gospel concerning his Son, who was descended from David according to the flesh and designated Son of God in power according to the Spirit of holiness by his resurrection from the dead, Jesus Christ our Lord" (Rom 1:1–4; see Heb 1:1–4).

The earliest Church bears witness to the mystery of the person of Jesus, the mystery in which God reveals himself as the Father of Jesus Christ, and in which the Son makes the Father known to human beings.[2] The linguistic and conceptual formulation of the mystery of Christ took place in the light of the Resurrection from the dead, in which God's self-revelation reaches its culmination both historically and eschatologically. Recourse to the writings in the Old Testament is a recourse, not to a collection of religious metaphors and analogies but to the expression of Israel's covenantal history. The Old Testament is the profession of faith in the real history of God's loving care for his people. This faith finds expression and becomes present in the people's faith and in prayer (the Psalms).

The biblical faith in the history of the revelation to Israel up to that point is united, in the person of Jesus, to his proclamation of the kingdom of God and to the apostolic tradition to form one single revelation of God. This is his self-communication to the whole of humanity. The unity of the Old and New Testaments is not only something that can be observed on the literary level; it has its inherent reason in the unity of the self-revelation of God the Father in the Son through the Holy Spirit. The "teaching of Jesus" is made present and receives a linguistic form in the "teaching of the apostles" (Acts 4:42) and is celebrated in the liturgical life of the Church, especially in baptism and the Eucharist. In the teaching of the Church, we have before our eyes the teaching of the apostles, and hence the teaching of Christ. The

---

2 Jn 1:18; Mt 11:25–30; Lk 10:21–23.

oral proclamation and its written form in the Gospels and in the apostolic Epistles are, as it were, the living and physical media of the abiding presence of the Word of God in Jesus, the Christ. "God's Word speaks to us in the human word" (1 Thes 2:13) of the apostles and their successors. And the apostolic inheritance in its entirety, the healthy doctrine (*sana doctrina*) of Jesus Christ (1 Tm 6:3), the *depositum fidei* (1 Tm 6:20), was entrusted to the Church in order that, until the return of the Lord, everyone might learn everything that Jesus taught. Faith in Christ is taught in order that we may be able to translate this faith into a life that imitates Jesus. This is his commission to the apostles and to the entire Church: the communication of salvation in word and sacrament (see Mt 28:19–20). The full deposit of the Church's faith is not kept safe and conserved like some rare archaeological finding in a museum. A merely mechanical transmission would contradict the living Word of God, which can be communicated across the generations only in living faith and in a rational reflection on this faith that leaves nothing out.

The teaching of Jesus and the apostolic "teaching about Jesus Christ the Lord" (Acts 28:31) is the perennially gushing spring of salvation. The spring of God's Word in sacred scripture always flows into the wide and deep stream of the apostolic and ecclesial tradition; but without this stream, the life-giving water could not reach those in later generations. A sterile contrast between doctrine and pastoral care would be merely the outer surface of a Christological heresy that denies that Christ the Truth and Christ the Life are one and the same Christ. One must reject the reduction of the exegesis of the teaching of scripture and of the Church to subjective perspectives. At the same time, of course, one must pay tribute to the positive, productive contribution of human testimony and of the conceptual and intellectual work of theology.

It belongs of its very nature to God's revelation in human words that the identity of the revelation and the unity of the profession of faith can be ensured only in their changing expression in other intellectual horizons. Fidelity to the Word of God in history is not possible without supreme achievements on the part of human reason. The church fathers and the doctors of the Church in the patristic and scholastic periods, and the great theologians down to the present day are not independent scholars who work for a small circle of specialists. On the contrary, theology is a necessary "function of the Church" in the history of salvation, as Dietrich Bonhoeffer put it in his 1932 lecture on "The Essence of the Church."[3] This intellectual labor, which makes demands of all the powers of the reason and goodwill, means that the doctrinal decisions taken by ecclesial authority are subject to

3 Dietrich Bonhoeffer, *DBW*, vol. 11, *Ökumene, Universität, Pfarramt 1931–1932* (Gutersloh: Chr. Kaiser, 1994), 251.

the working of the same Holy Spirit who accompanied the apostles in their oral proclamation and in the writing down of the early Church's testimony to Christ. "No one can say 'Jesus is Lord' except by the Holy Spirit" (1 Cor 12:3). The Word of God in scripture and the tradition of the Church remains true to itself in its substance only in passing through the spiritual process whereby the Church's consciousness of the faith develops:

> In this developmental process of the divine Word during the apostolic period, we may esteem the divine guidance of the disciples of Christ very highly indeed and expand it greatly; but without the human being, without the specific human activity, this process would surely not have happened. Freedom and grace penetrate one another in the Christian work, and one and the same undivided act is simultaneously divine and human—and precisely that is what we find here too. When the Church confronts aberrations by declaring and safeguarding the original doctrine of the faith in the way we have just set out, the apostolic expression necessarily crosses over into another expression which is exactly the most suited form to disclose the specific error at that time and also to reject it. [...] The genesis of the Nicene formula is the best example of this. This form is human and belongs to the dimension of time; it is *per se* transient, and it could surely be exchanged for a hundred other formulae. [...] Just as we are finally allowed to see the truths of salvation in greater clarity already in the apostolic writings, so too the doctrine of scripture encounters us in a continuously increasing comprehension in the doctrine of the Church. And just as it is meaningless to identify anything more than a formal distinction between the teaching of Jesus and that of the apostles, so too it is meaningless when another antithesis is discerned between the later and the original tradition. The charge that this formal antithesis exists is based on the failure to grasp clearly that Christ was the God-man, and that he wanted to continue to work in a divine-human manner. [...] Catholics have gained much in the conflict with the Protestants; but it would be absurd for the Catholic to deny this, and for the Protestants to shower themselves with ignorant praise on this account. [...] It is doubtless true that we stand on a higher level of Christian knowledge than the pre-Reformation period; the difference between the formulation and justification of all the relevant dogmas, and the formulation and justification of the earlier dogmas, is obvious, without any great effort or a lengthy investigation, to anyone who compares recent theological works with the pre-Tridentine presentations. The phenomenon that the deeper awareness of the Christian truth, which is eternally one and immutable, is linked to strife and struggle [...] explains the necessity of a visible, living authority that in every conflict recognizes

> with certainty the truth and distinguishes it from error; otherwise, we would have nothing but uncertain and disputed manners, and finally we would be left with nothing at all. Accordingly, where sacred scripture is acknowledged as the sole source and norm of the institution of salvation, without the tradition and the authority of the Church, there is a great tendency to ignore completely—indeed, to misconstrue completely—all the more acute developments and further formulations of the Christian dogma. Following the principle that I have mentioned, they are incapable of seeing any rational goal in the history of the believing intelligence in the Christian Church, and therefore show themselves impatient with everything that has taken place in this direction in the Church.[4]

Jesus did not simply found one community among many in the course of the history of religion, one that differs from others through a mystical-ethical program. He is not one in a long line of founders of religions and teachers of morality, and that is why he did not provide "his" religion with an organizational structure. In this sense, we can also say that his Church is not a religious community, a moral institution, or a social aid organization. The purpose of its existence is to be the universal sign and instrument of the most intimate union with God and of the unity of the human race (LG 1). It is the sacrament of the kingdom of God. Although its foundation makes it a part of history, it transcends the transience of all that is temporal, because it anticipates the goal of history. In the word that God speaks to the human being today, the imperishable meaning of his existence is proclaimed to him. The Church leads human beings to eternal life in the name and in the authority of Christ, who is its Head. It is in this way that one attains the meaning and the goal of created existence—namely, the knowledge of God in the eternal communion of love with him. Jesus was "sent by the Father." He is the Messiah whom the people of God awaited, the one anointed by the Holy Spirit. God, the "Lord of heaven and of earth" (Lk 10:21), chose Israel out of many peoples and made it his own covenantal people. Jesus comes from this people "according to the flesh" (Rom 9:5) and brings it the message that the kingdom of God is close at hand. The universal dominion of salvation, which comes from God, has dawned in him. The kingdom of God can be discerned in the signs, miracles, and mighty deeds of the Son of God. The kingdom of Christ manifests itself as the realization of God's universal saving will and the making of the eschatological covenant with the new people of God. The kingdom of God, which came in the person and the fate of Jesus

4 Möhler, *Symbolik*, §40. See also Möhler, *Athanasius der Grosse und die Kirche seiner Zeit, besonders im Kampfe mit dem Arianismus* (Frankfurt: Minerva, 1972).

Christ, was realized historically in a genuine manner in his death on the Cross and his Resurrection, in the Ascension, and in the eschatological outpouring of the Spirit of the Father and the Son. This kingdom remains real and active until its victorious perfecting at the return of the Son of man at the end of time, thanks to the teaching, the life, and the liturgy of his Church. Through his gospel of the forgiveness of sins and the establishing of the new and eternal covenant, Jesus has brought together once more the people who had been violently scattered, thereby universalizing the mission of the covenantal people. In his own person, he founded the Church of Jews and Gentiles (Eph 2:14). The Church is the fellowship in Christ with the triune God, and the participation in, and the continuation of, the mission entrusted to the Son by the Father (LG 4). The Church is "built upon the foundation of the apostles and prophets, Christ Jesus himself being the cornerstone, in whom the whole structure is joined together and grows into a holy temple in the Lord; in whom you also are built into it for a dwelling place of God in the Spirit" (Eph 2:19–22). As members of the body of Christ, Christians are "fellow citizens with the saints and members of the household of God."

The Church has its origin in the mission entrusted to Christ by the Father, and it continues this mission, which was realized through the gathering together of those who were lost as a result of sin. The Church of Christ is thus, as God's eschatological covenant people, *communio* and *missio,* communion and mission, gathering around Christ and receiving a commission from him. The Church is the people of the new covenant thanks to Christ—it is therefore not an earthly organization with lofty ideals but the body of Christ. And Christ is the Head of his body. The Church is filled completely by the Spirit of the Father and of the Son, and is thus also the temple and house of God and his holy priesthood, the vineyard of the Lord. It is commissioned by Christ and continues his kingly, prophetic, and priestly working in the world, in the power of his Spirit. The Church has a mediatory-priestly mission to accomplish in view of humanity as a whole.

3.
JESUS MAKES SIMON AN APOSTLE WITH THE SURNAME PETER

WHEN WE CONSIDER THE APOSTOLATE OF SIMON PETER, which is also relevant to faith, we can do so only under the presupposition that Jesus is the Son of God, who came into the world for our salvation, and that he remains among us in the human word of the profession of faith and of the proclamation of the Church of the apostles and of the apostolic Church.[5]

Peter is a historical person who is very closely linked to the historical Jesus and to the earliest Church. Jesus himself defined his authority and mission and put him at the head of the apostles and of the entire Church by giving him the surname *Peter.* And it is this rock on which he places his Church once and for all, and continually builds it up. Besides this, much of what links the story of his life to Jesus has an exemplary significance, both for the successors to his ministry, the shepherds of the church of Rome—the place where he glorified God through his death—and indeed for every disciple of Christ. The Simon Peter of the Bible is, as an individual, the founder of the *cathedra Petri* in Rome and an abiding paradigm of the papacy in terms both of the inalienable authority and of the possibility of personal failure. This is why we cannot restrict ourselves here to the classical biblical passages about the primacy, since that would show us only his authority; we need also to see the specific character of his exercise of his office as well as its human risks.

The picture of Peter in the four Gospels and the Acts of the Apostles is based on the historical relationship of Jesus to Peter, and explains theologically, in the light of revelation, his abiding mission and authority for the Church of Christ until the return of the Lord. The various historical and theological accentuations and modes of presentation do not destroy the unity of the testimony to revelation. In their diversity, they display the many aspects and facets that cannot be tied down to one simple concept or approach, and that invite us to look at this theme again and again. The differences in individual points do not in the least prevent us from defining the essence of this unique ministry. Rather, they indicate the many aspects that are involved when we look at the Petrine ministry in its unity and its totality. This applies first and foremost to the inexhaustible fullness of the mystery of Christ, "which not all the books in the world could contain" (see Jn 21:25). The same must also be said by analogy about the understanding of

5 On this, see the overall presentation by Joachim Gnilka, *Petrus und Rom: Das Petrusbild in den ersten zwei Jahrhunderten* (Freiburg: Herder, 2002).

the Church or about Mary's mission in the history of salvation, and about the understanding of the Petrine ministry in its Christological foundations and in its ecclesiological elaboration under the conditions of the various epochs of church history.

4.
THE CALLING AND APPOINTMENT OF THE APOSTLES

In virtue of his divine authority, Jesus called disciples to follow him. He was not a rabbi and teacher of the law whom one could choose for oneself as one thought best.

Within the community of disciples whom he called to follow him, he appointed twelve disciples whom he also called "apostles," and who are known to us as the stable group of the twelve apostles. They were to share in his divine authority and power (*exousia*) and in his mission, and to carry it out where he himself could not come. Since Jesus as a human being could work only at one particular time and in one limited space, the fulfillment of his universal salvific mission means that he needed to call—and that he still needs to call—people at all times and at all places to carry it out until the end of time. The mystery of the apostolic authority and mission has its basis in the logic of the Incarnation and is an essential form of the representation of Christ. The apostles had to carry on their mission and to hand it on to their successors beyond the time of Jesus's earthly activity, beginning with his Resurrection from the dead, until the end of the world. In the circle of the twelve apostles before and after the Resurrection, in the gathering of the disciples for the kingdom of God, and in the founding of the community of disciples as the Church of Christ through the eschatological sending of the Spirit, Simon, whom Jesus had made Peter, has a special task and position. In the oldest Gospel, named after Peter's pupil and collaborator Mark (1 Pt 5:13), which was written in Rome, Simon is appointed to be a future fisher of men, together with the first disciples (Mk 1:17; Lk 5:10). When Jesus established the institution of the twelve apostles, Simon, to whom he had given the surname Peter, was put at the head of this college (Mk 3:13–19). It is he who declares to Jesus the confession of the disciples: "You are the Messiah" (Mk 8:29).

After the women who come to Jesus's grave to anoint him hear the Easter message from the lips of the angel, they are told: "Go, tell his disciples and Peter that he is going before you to Galilee; there you will see him, as he told you" (Mk 16:7). Peter and the twelve disciples are the guarantors of the identity between the earthly and the Easter Jesus. When we seek a precise definition of the concept of apostle, it is not a question of the wider or narrower group of persons that this encompasses. The content of the definition is more important. The mission and authorization by the pre-Easter Jesus is taken up anew by the risen Lord. But now the twelve disciples become apostles of the risen Lord. And the core of their message and their mission, the Easter kerygma, is the making present of the crucified Son of God, who was raised from the dead. Since the apostles have held out with Jesus in all his trials, Jesus bequeaths to them the kingdom of God, just as his Father had bequeathed it to him. The eternal fellowship with the victorious Christ is their reward, and they are given a share in the final judgment by the future judge of the living and the dead: "I appoint for you that you may eat and drink at my table in my kingdom, and sit on thrones judging the twelve tribes of Israel" (Lk 22:30).

One must draw a distinction between the aspects of the spiritual following by all the disciples and the ministerial succession of the bishops in the spiritual authority and mission of the apostles; this applies both to pre-Easter discipleship and to the post-Easter Church. On the one hand, all who believe and are baptized have a spiritual fellowship in following Christ—this is what we call the participation of all the members of his ecclesial body in his priestly, kingly, and prophetic work (the common priesthood of all believers). On the other hand, there is the calling, the sending, and the authorizing of individual disciples to serve as apostles with their successors in the office of bishops (in union with their priests and deacons).

The sacramental-hierarchical constitution of the Church does not come from the later, sociologically necessary institutionalization of an originally free, charismatic, community constitution. Nor is it, in keeping with theory of the degeneration from the pure earliest Christianity, to be condemned as the falsification of this original constitution. It is based on the foundation of the Church by Jesus himself. In any case, since the Church is in its essence the body of Christ and his temple, it cannot be shaped and reshaped by human beings in accordance with models of political organization. Jesus chose twelve disciples out of the crowd of disciples whom he had called to follow him: "He appointed twelve to be with him, and to be sent out to preach and have authority to cast out demons (Mk 3:13–15).

The apostolic ministry essentially consists in fellowship with Christ and in the participation in his messianic mission, in order that they may proclaim the Gospel on his authority (not on their own) and carry out his saving work of forgiving sins until he returns at the end of the world.

After Easter, this means that the apostles and their successors have the task of preaching with *spiritual* authority—with the consecratory authority of the Holy Spirit—and of administering the sacraments and guiding the Church of God, thereby bringing about grace in Christians *instrumen-*

taliter through the rites established by Christ. They are the representatives of Christ. In them and through them, the risen Christ who is exalted to the Father speaks in the power of the Holy Spirit. And he acts through his messengers as through instruments, communicating his grace to those to whom their preaching is addressed: "He who hears you hears me, and he who rejects you rejects me, and he who rejects me rejects him who sent me" (Lk 10:16; Mt 11:40). These are the words that Jesus spoke to the group of seventy-two disciples, who represent the total number of the peoples of the world. This group is the expansion of the group of twelve apostles, and also demonstrates the continuation and the universalization of the apostolic mission and authority after the Lord's Resurrection.

This is how Saint Cyprian of Carthage explains the authority of the bishops, who "are appointed as representatives and successors of the apostles" and who work "as representatives of Christ and priests of God."[6] In Luke's two-volume work and the New Testament writings that reflect the various phases of the Church's growth and the transition to the post-apostolic age, it is the bishop-presbyters who, initially together with the apostles and then after them, carry on the authority and the mission of the apostles. It is only from the second century onwards that the concepts of bishop and presbyter become increasingly exact designations of two degrees within the one apostolic ministry. The apostles Barnabas and Paul "appointed presbyters for them in every church, with prayer and fasting."[7] For the flock that is entrusted to them, "the Holy Spirit has made" them "guardians, to feed the church of the Lord" (Acts 20:28). The decisive points are the participation in the mission that Jesus received from the Father and the salvific activity of the apostles and of their successors, not in the power of their own spirit and word, but in the power of the Spirit of the Father and of the Son: "'As the Father has sent me, even so I send you.' And when he had said this, he breathed on them and said to them, 'Receive the Holy Spirit. If you forgive the sins of anyone, they are forgiven; if you retain the sins of any, they are retained'" (Jn 20:21–23).

The twelve disciples whom he had appointed to be his apostles (Mt 10:1–2) were initially to go "only to the lost sheep of the house of Israel" (Mt 10:6). But the risen Lord commanded the twelve disciples to go a mountain in Galilee, where he appeared to them and revealed himself to them. He overcame all their doubts and gave them the certainty of the victory of the kingdom of God. Then he said to them that now they were to go to all the peoples and to impart salvation to them in his authority: "All authority in heaven and on earth has been given to me. Go therefore and make disciples

6 Cyprian of Carthage, *Ep.* 66.4–5.

7 Acts 14:23; 2 Tm 1:6; 1 Tm 4:14.

of all nations, baptizing them in the name of the Father and of the Son and of the Holy Spirit, teaching them to observe all that I have commanded you; and behold, I am with you always, to the close of the age" (Mt 28:16–20).

With their testimony, the group of the twelve apostles guarantees the identity between the historical, pre-Easter Jesus and the Easter Lord. The essence of the Christian faith consists in the confession, sustained by the Holy Spirit, that Jesus is the Christ, the Messiah, the Son of the living God. God has made himself known as Truth in the relationship between the Father and the Son, and has communicated himself as the life of human beings: "The word is near you, [...] (the word of faith which we preach); because, if you confess with your lips that Jesus is Lord and believe in your heart that God raised him from the dead, you will be saved" (Rom 10:8–9).

The apostles, with Peter at their head, belong constitutively to the earliest kerygma and to its continuous tradition. The Gospel exists in and through the tradition of the Church because the Lord lives in his Church and works through it. Christ is the subject of revelation, and he equally remains the subject of its handing on in the Church's consciousness of faith and in the decisions taken by the magisterium of the pope and the bishops. In the original confession of faith in Christ, which shows us the essence of the Church as the community that hands on the revealed faith, Paul says: "For I delivered to you as of first importance what I also received, that Christ died for our sins in accordance with the scriptures, that he was buried, that he was raised on the third day in accordance with the scriptures, and that he appeared to Cephas, then to the twelve" (1 Cor 15:3–5).

5.
PETER IN THE COLLEGE OF THE APOSTLES

After Jesus, Simon Peter is the person most frequently mentioned in the New Testament. The name of the fisher from Lake Gennesaret was Simon (Simeon in Hebrew). When he was called, the son of John (Jn 1:42) or Bar-Jona (Mt 16:17) from Bethsaida, who was married in Capernaum where he exercised his profession, received from Jesus the surname Peter, the stone or rock (*kîphâ* in Aramaic, usually translated into Greek by Paul as *Kêphas*).

According to the testimony of the synoptic Gospels, Peter is the first disciple to be called, together with his brother Andrew;[8] in the Gospel of John, it is first Andrew who is called to follow Jesus together with another disciple, and who then leads his brother Simon to Jesus the Messiah (Jn 1:42). Out of the many disciples whom Jesus has called to follow him, he

8 Mk 1:16; Mt 4:18; Lk 5:10–11.

then chooses the twelve disciples who are then known as apostles because of their participation in his mission. They represent both the totality of the twelve tribes of Israel and the people of God in the last days.

Simon is mentioned first in all the lists of the "twelve disciples" or "apostles," as their "head." He is a member of this circle and speaks on behalf of all; he represents the unity and the totality of this group and body, and thus also represents the entire people of God of the old and new covenants. The "first" (Mt 10:2) of the "names of the twelve apostles" is always "Simon, called Peter."[9] Peter declares the confession of Jesus as Messiah before Easter.[10] And it is Peter who speaks on the day of Pentecost, in order to bear witness to the crucified Jesus as the Messiah accredited by God, and to proclaim him (Acts 2:36). At the beginning of the Church's history, it is he who is the first to have people baptized, thereby allowing the Church to take its sacramental form. And he integrates the Gentiles into the world mission, so that from now on, the Church consists of Jews and Gentiles (Acts 10:44–48; Eph 2:14–22). In the earliest Christian tradition, the concept of "apostle" in a narrower and a wider sense acquires an ever clearer theological profile. The calling of the twelve disciples—with Peter as their spokesman and representative—establishes the historical and theological basis of the visible Church of Christ. When the world is made new, Jesus says, "when the Son of Man shall sit on his glorious throne, you who have followed me will also sit on twelve thrones, judging the twelve tribes of Israel" (Mt 19:28). The Church is "the bride, married to the Lamb," the messianic Jerusalem, the city of God. "The wall of the city had twelve foundations, and on them the twelve names of the twelve apostles of the Lamb" (Rv 21:14; see Eph 2:20). Thanks to the Easter appearances of Christ and the sending of the Holy Spirit at Pentecost, the Church has its roots in the pre-Easter community of disciples; and an essential element of this community is the apostolic authority and the mission of the group of the Twelve.

6.
PETER AS HEAD OF THE COLLEGE OF THE APOSTLES

SIMON PETER RECEIVED THE SAME MISSION as the other apostles: to proclaim the kingdom of God with divine authority and to mediate with power Christ's salvation. The apostles, and their successors in the ministry of bishops and priests, do not create grace in the manner of Christ, who is the Redeemer and the Head of the Church; what they do is to make the grace of

9 See Mk 3:16–19; Lk 6:13–16; Acts 1:13.

10 Mk 8:29; Mt 16:16; Lk 9:20.

Christ present in accordance with the institution of the signs of salvation—namely, baptism, confirmation, the Eucharist, penance and absolution, and the anointing of the sick. Marriage and ordination also belong to the sacramental form of the Church.

There is, however, something specific that characterizes and distinguishes the apostolate of Peter. He is not elected by the others, nor is he appointed by Christ as the spokesman of the apostles and of the entire Church. The Lord made Simon the rock on which the Church stands securely, the rock that guarantees its existence. In Peter, the *protos* or *primus* of the apostles, the Church possesses the principle of its unity with the head of the body, the principle that is embodied in the apostolate and in the Church itself. It is only as the Vicar of Christ, who acts in the person of Christ as head and shepherd of the universal Church, that Peter and, in him, his successor on his cathedra in Rome can be the visible head of the pilgrim Church. This means that, with regard to the Church's unity with Christ its Head, Peter is the representative of Christ and his Vicar for the universal Church. The unity of the Church with Christ and the *communio* of the local churches and of their bishops with the bishop of Rome are manifested visibly and tangibly.

The apostles and Peter are not functionaries of a religious group but messengers in whom the one who sends them makes himself present. Peter and his successors, the bishops of Rome, have not made a claim to leadership of their own volition, inspired by a crazy wish to walk in the footsteps of the Caesars of ancient Rome. They are called by the Lord himself and appointed to manifest and to embody the unity of the disciples and of the entire Church. The Second Vatican Council affirms on this point that:

> Jesus Christ, the eternal Shepherd, established His holy Church, having sent forth the apostles as He Himself had been sent by the Father (Jn 20:21); and He willed that their successors, namely the bishops, should be shepherds in His Church even to the consummation of the world. And in order that the episcopate itself might be one and undivided, He placed Blessed Peter over the other apostles, and instituted in him a permanent and visible source and foundation of unity and communion (LG 18).

The individual apostles do not have a limited share in the total apostolate. Rather, they exercise it in a whole and undivided manner in their person, but in such a way that the unity of the universal Church and the corporate body of the apostles are manifested and realized in the person of Peter. Peter, the *prôtos*, is the first of the apostles. He does not have an office of a different nature than the other apostles, nor does he stand at the head of the apostles only in a numerical sense as the first to be mentioned, or thanks to a recognition on the part of the other apostles (a primacy of honor). His position is due to his special mission to be the rock that keeps the entire building of the Church of Christ in union with Jesus the Messiah. Through him, Christ preserves the house and people of God from falling apart. He preserves his body from the detachment of its members. He may do so, and he can do so, only in virtue of a special mandate by Christ, who is the true foundation stone and cornerstone of the Church as the community of salvation.

This is already expressed when the name Cephas—Peter—is bestowed on Simon the fisher: "'You shall be called Cephas' (which means Peter, the rock)."[11] He was to become a "fisher of men" in fellowship with the other apostles, to be the one who gathers everyone in his net and "draws" human beings "to the shore" for Jesus (Jn 21:11; Lk 5:6) and wins them for the kingdom of God.

7. THE PETRINE APOSTOLATE IN THE TESTIMONY OF THE GOSPEL OF MATTHEW

What we call the "primacy" (or "principate") of Peter and his successors, the bishops of the Roman church, unfolds its deepest and most genuine meaning only in the intimate and indissoluble connection between Jesus's Messiahship and Peter's confession of Christ.

It is also true that the stories of the rich catch of fish or of Peter's ship in the storm and the rescue of Peter (see Mt 14:22–33) have a symbolic and paradigmatic meaning for the Church in the ups and downs of history. Here and always, Jesus strengthens Peter in faith, asks for the constancy of Peter's love for him, and gives him encouragement. And it is only with the power of God that the Church can hold firm against external threats and internal dangers. Every pope, therefore, will affirm the "weaknesses, hardships, persecutions, and calamities that I bear"—as his fellow apostle Paul says—"for the sake of Christ; for when I am weak, then I am strong" (2 Cor 12:10).

When the Gospel of Matthew was finished and put into circulation around 80 of the Christian era, the Church had already lived for half a century in the "teaching of the apostles" and in the faith in Jesus, the Christ, "who redeemed his people from its sins" (see Mt 1:21), a faith that had been handed on in all its vitality. The pre-Easter story of Jesus and his disciples is related in the light of the Resurrection and is understood and expounded as

11 Jn 1:42; see Mk 3:16; Mt 16:18.

the continuing revelation of the mystery of his person. He is the Son of God, who was sent into this world as the Messiah. All the hopes in salvation from God that were already linked to this title "Messiah" in the Old Testament, in their priestly or prophetic or kingly accentuations, cluster together in the messianic mystery of Jesus.

The reciprocal understanding and interpretation of the gathering of the pre-Easter community of disciples and the abiding *communio* with the risen Lord are also the hermeneutical keys to the understanding of the Church as the sacrament of the *basileia tou theou,* the kingly rule of God. This means that the texts of the Gospel do not offer an arbitrary collection of impressions left on people's memory. They are not interest-based constructions, nor are they projections from the present back onto the past; still less are they the expression of "the unintentional creation of a poetic saga" by people who were captives of their own mythical and prescientific worldview.[12] Just as it is only through the Holy Spirit—that is, through the revelation of God in Jesus Christ—that Jesus can be recognized and confessed as Lord (1 Cor 12:3), so too it is only in the same Spirit of God that the apostolic tradition in the earliest Church can have been written down—in other words, thanks to the inspiration of the sacred writers.

The tradition about Jesus was "written so that you may believe that Jesus is the Messiah, the Son of God, and that believing you may have life in his name" (Jn 20:31), since the Gospel accounts "of the things which have been accomplished among us" hold fast to what was "delivered to us by those who from the beginning were eyewitnesses and ministers of the word," so that everyone who believes in Christ "may know the truth concerning the things of which you have been informed" (Lk 1:1–4).

The passage about Peter's messianic confession and the promise of the primacy must likewise be understood in the structure of the (horizontal) link between the pre-Easter and the post-Easter apostolic tradition and of the (vertical) relationship between the divine assistance and the human act of putting the revelation into writing.

The appointment of the twelve apostles with Simon Peter as their *prôtos* serves the mission, first to "the lost sheep of the house of Israel" (Mt 10:8) and then to all the Gentile nations (Mt 28:19). Jesus calls the twelve apostles and sends them out: "He gave them authority over unclean spirits, to cast them out, and to heal every disease and every infirmity. [...] And preach as you go, saying, 'The kingdom of heaven is at hand.' Heal the sick, raise the

12 David Friedrich Strauss, *Das Leben Jesu: Kritisch Bearbeitet* (Tübingen: C. F. Osiander, 1835), 75.

dead, cleanse lepers, cast out demons. You received without pay, give without pay" (Mt 10:1, 7).

Among the apostles, Peter is the first missionary, the one who leads the total mission of the Church. Peter and the apostles are the representatives of Christ on earth. At the end of the mission discourse (Mt 10:1–42), Jesus says to Peter and the apostles, and to all who will follow them in the Petrine ministry and the episcopal office: "He who receives you receives me, and he who receives me receives him who sent me" (Mt 10:40). The Father's sending of Jesus into this world is continued by Jesus in the apostles whom he sends into the whole world, in order to lead everyone through the Gospel into the kingdom of God. We must see the entrusting of the keys to Peter (Mt 16:18) and of the power to bind and loose to Peter and the other apostles (Mt 18:18) in the framework of this universal sending of Christ and of his Church by the Father.

Jesus comes with the twelve disciples into the region of Caesarea Philippi, where they have crossed the boundary of the Jewish territory and entered the Gentile world. And it is here that the event that is decisive for the future Church of Christ takes place. Later, thanks to the event of Pentecost, the Church from both Jews and Gentiles came into existence through the initiative of Simon, the Peter. In faith, it is spiritually united in the same Spirit, and bound together corporately through baptism into the body of Christ. The very choice of this place for the messianic confession and the promise to Peter shows how Jesus's salvific mission and the mission of the Church cross over the borders of Galilee and Judea, aiming at all of humankind, who are to be led in the Church and through the Church to Jesus, the Redeemer of the entire world. The link between the promise of primacy and the sending of the apostles into the entire world at the close of Matthew's Gospel is obvious. Matthew 16:13–20 displays so many Aramaic formulations and typical images of the Hebrew Bible, which echo through the Greek language of the Gospel text, that it is thought likely that this text has its genesis in the earliest Church in Jerusalem.

We find confirmation in the Letters of Paul, and his adoption of the wording of the pre-Pauline Jerusalem tradition (1 Cor 15:3–5), that Peter is the guarantor of the identity between the earthly and the risen Lord, and between the unity of the pre-Easter group of disciples and the Easter Church, the unity that is indeed based on this identity. The evangelist, who put into writing the Jerusalem tradition with the special Petrine material around the year 80 in Syria, certainly did not want merely to preserve early Christian reminiscences. He wanted to present normative and constitutive principles of the origin and of the historical development of the Church. For Matthew,

Peter's mission and authority belong to the abiding essence of the Church founded by Christ.

Jesus asks his disciples who people think the Son of man is. The disciples had already recognized and confessed who Jesus truly is in relation to God. When their boat, the barque of the Church, the little barque of Peter, was tossed around by the waves in the storm, they saw Jesus walking on the lake and coming towards them. Trusting in Jesus, Peter stepped out of the boat and walked towards Jesus. But instead of entrusting himself completely to the Lord, who alone was able to rescue him from drowning, his "little faith" put him at risk of sinking. When they were with Jesus in the boat and the storm had abated, they adored him and confessed: "Truly you are the Son of God" (Mt 14:33).

This confession of faith in Christ after the storm on the lake is related to the specific situation; but Jesus's question about who the disciples think he is transposes it into the confession of the disciples for all times to come—the confession that lays the foundation of the Church. The people who hold that the Son of man is John the Baptist, Elijah, Jeremiah, or another of the prophets were not chance passers-by in an opinion poll. They were members of the people of God, who believed in the promise of an eschatological Savior whom God would send to his oppressed people. The disciples differ from the rest of the people not because they hold a different view but because the God of Israel, the Lord of heaven and of earth, has revealed to them the insight that *this Jesus of Nazareth* is the promised Messiah. This revealed insight, and this alone, is the foundation of the confession that is supported by the Holy Spirit, and hence also the foundation of the community of disciples as the Church of the Messiah.

Peter replies *personally* and *alone* to the question put to the apostolic college. He does not speak as their designated spokesman but as their representative appointed by Christ, as his *vicarius*. Since Peter's confession is the fruit of the revelation by the Father, who discloses to him his Son and the consubstantiality between the Father and the Son, Peter speaks first of all in the authority that God has over the Church (*ex auctoritate Dei*), and he expounds to the disciples the faith that has been revealed, in order that they may accept it. It is only in the second place that he replies to the revelation with the Church's confession, thereby also speaking in the person of the Church (*ex persona ecclesiae*). His confession of the Messiah binds the Church to Jesus, the Son of God, and through him to God the Father.

It is not only the *content* of the confession that is the foundation on which the Church is built, because the *person* of the one who makes the confession addresses it to Christ. And this is why the apostolic tradition can never congeal (so to speak) in a book; the living spirit can never become a dead letter. What we find in the sacred scripture of the New Testament is only the *content* of the apostolic teaching. The *act* of confessing and the *person* of the one who confesses are linked to the authorized successors of the apostles. In this way, the apostolic scripture and the apostolic succession of the bishops through sacramental ordination belong inseparably together. The Spirit doubtless enlightens the hearers of the Gospel and the readers of the sacred scriptures (*testimonium internum spiritus sancti*), but it is also the same Spirit who preserves in the truth of God the testimony and the confession of the teachers of the Gospel and the shepherds of the Church who are appointed by Christ (*assistentia spiritus sancti*—for the ecclesial magisterium).

The teaching of the apostles continues in the teaching of the Church, just as the mission of the apostles continues in the mission and authority of the pope and the bishops. There is thus a dynamic connection between the proclamation and salvation, between the message and the authorized messengers of the Gospel, which Paul expresses as follows: "'Everyone who calls upon the name of the Lord will be saved.' But how are they to call upon him in whom they have not believed? And how are they to believe in him of whom they have never heard? And how are they to hear without a preacher? And how can men preach unless they are sent?" (Rom 10:13–15). Simon Peter utters the confession for the entire Church: "You are the Messiah, the Son of the living God" (Mt 16:16).

The obvious contrast to the confession of Christ made by the apostolic college, with Peter at its head, and by the entire Church is the anti-Christological confession (Mt 26:62–66) that is uttered by the Sanhedrin of the Jews, with the high priest at its head. The high priest Caiaphas adjures Jesus to say whether he is the Messiah. He rejects as blasphemy Jesus's self-confession that he is "the Messiah, the Son of the living God," and "the Son of man." Peter's confession of Christ, the Son of the living God, unites the Church in faith and distinguishes it from other communities of faith. Peter is an important criterion of Christian identity.

When the Church confesses Jesus as Messiah and Son of the living God, it does not commit blasphemy. On the contrary, its confession of Jesus's divine sonship glorifies God, his Father, in the highest possible way. This is why God clothes the disciples of his Son with his own glory: he deifies them by making them in Christ sons and daughters of God, and by giving them eternal life (Jn 17:3).

Matthew differs from the confession of the Messiah in Mark and Luke by adding to the title Messiah the words *Son of the living God*; and in Christ, we too "are called sons of the living God" (Rom 9:26). The Messiah is the one anointed by the Holy Spirit. In Christological terms, this is related to the human nature of Jesus, through which he accomplishes the work of salvation in the world in his human life. Jesus is not only the Messiah in keeping with the various expectations among the Jews: he is the Messiah in accordance with the divine promise. The figures of a new and eschatological prophet, of a kingly and a priestly Messiah, and of the Suffering Servant of the Lord flow together and are realized concretely in Jesus of Nazareth, who is in truth "the Son of the Father." The addition "Son of the living God" points to the divine nature. The unity of the divine and human natures of Christ has its foundation in the unity of the person of the Logos, the second person in the Trinity.

The confession that Jesus is the Messiah and the Son of the living God far transcends the sphere of a mere knowledge of who and what Jesus is. The Christian confession always mediates salvation too. This is how Paul speaks of "the word of faith that the apostles preach": "Because, if you confess with your lips that Jesus is Lord and believe in your heart that God raised him from the dead, you will be saved. For one believes with his heart and so is justified, and he confesses with his lips and so is saved" (Rom 10:9–11). Orthodoxy means more than the correct formula of the confession. It proves its truth in the confession made in words and in confession of a life lived for Christ. Peter's messianic confession implicitly contains the reference to the mystery of the triune God as the ultimate ground of truth and of salvation. Jesus is the Son of the Father, of the living God (Mt 11:25–27; 16:16), and as Messiah, he is the Anointed One of the Holy Spirit (Mt 1:16). In the line of thought in Matthew's Gospel, this is made explicit in baptism "in the name of the Father and of the Son and of the Holy Spirit" (Mt 28:19).

8.
PETER'S INFALLIBILITY IN THE CONFESSION OF JESUS'S DIVINE SONSHIP

For Peter, the representative of the people of God of the new and eternal covenant in the blood of Christ, of the Church formed of Jews and Gentiles, the confession of Jesus, the Son of man, as Messiah and Son of the living God is not a blasphemy but a glorification of God, "for flesh and blood has not revealed this to you, but my Father who is in heaven" (Mt 16:17). Jesus calls Peter "blessed," not in the sense that the knowledge of the person and work of Jesus Christ would give him a state of natural and transient happiness, but because the human search for truth finds its fulfillment in the revelation that brings grace and the knowledge of God. "This is eternal life, to know you the only true God, and Jesus Christ whom you have sent" (Jn 17:3). The blessedness with which we are filled in the knowledge of Christ is the knowledge of God in truth and in love.

The heavenly Father permits Peter, and the Church that is recapitulated integrally in his person, to recognize in the Holy Spirit both Jesus's mission in salvation history and its own origin in the *communio* of the Father and the Son. This is why the Church's confession of Jesus is no mere intellectual ascription of a predicate, something depending on the limited power of judgment of the fallible human understanding. The judgment about the identity between Jesus and the Christ is undergirded by the infallibility of the divine Reason, which never errs and never leads into error. The Father reveals the Son's unity with him in his divine being, and at the same time in his historical mission, as the Word that has become flesh. Between the Father and the Son there is a unity in revelation, a unity in knowledge, and on the deepest level a unity of being; this already exists before the creation and the revelation in history, and it constitutes the being of God as the Trinitarian *communio* of Father, Son, and Holy Spirit. We are baptized in his name and taken up into the eternal fellowship of life with him (Mt 28:19).

Shortly before the scene in Caesarea Philippi (Mk 8:27; see Lk 9:18–21), where the heavenly Father reveals to Peter the messiahship and divine sonship of Jesus, Jesus reveals the Father and himself as the Father's Son. "I thank you, Father, Lord of heaven and earth. [...] All things have been delivered to me by my Father; and no one knows the Son except the Father, and no one knows the Father except the Son and anyone to whom the Son chooses to reveal him" (Mt 11:25–27).

And now, in Peter, the Father has revealed to the entire Church the sonship of Jesus, both within the Godhead and as Messiah. The entire confession of the Church's faith with its individual articles is radically summed up in the knowledge of the Father in the Son through the Holy Spirit (Lk 10:21–22). All the declarations of the magisterium in the course of two thousand years about the mysteries of the Trinity, the Redeemer as God and man, about grace and the sacraments are nothing other than the unfolding and the safeguarding of the confession that Jesus is the Messiah, the Son of the living God.

All the doctrines of the Church's faith are contained and concentrated in the faith in Christ's divine sonship, "for there is no other name under heaven given among men by which we must be saved" (Acts 4:12; see 1 Tm 2:4–7). In the confession of the Christian faith, we are not declaring our private opinions about God; on the contrary, it is God who makes himself known to us in faith as our salvation. And this is why the Church is not a conventicle of mystics in flight from the world, nor a religious group that finds its bliss here on earth. The Church is "the city of the living God, the heavenly Jerusalem" (Heb 12:22), "the household and the temple of God." It is only this that allows us to understand why "the Church of the living God" is "the pillar and bulwark of the truth" (1 Tm 3:15). The truth of God is "the mystery of the faith" (1 Tm 3:16) that recognizes the revelation of God in the flesh of the Logos, in his Cross, in his Resurrection and Ascension, in the sending of the Spirit, and in his return as the judge and savior of all human beings.

It was only in virtue of the divine revelation that Peter could reply to Jesus's question—not through the natural powers of "flesh and blood" and human reasoning but through the supernatural illumination of our intellect by the Holy Spirit.

9.
THE INSTITUTION OF THE ENDURING PETRINE MINISTRY

The Son of the living God now turns to Simon, the son of Jona, and says to him with his divine authority: "And I tell you, you are Peter."

In sovereign authority, he makes the disciple "Peter," the rock that bears his Church. This is not the ascription of a significant name and a decorative title; he gives him the name "Peter" and bestows on him the authority that, after Peter's death, must be exercised through his successors for the good of the Church.

One cannot separate the Peter of faith from the faith of Peter. And this is why the church of Saint Peter in Rome also offers the guarantee of the unity of faith of the universal Church in the confession of Christ, because this confession has always been preserved faithfully and completely in the Roman church.

Whereas Jesus, the Son of the living God, *is* with the Father the one God, Simon is *made* Peter. By gathering together the believers in his Church as the house and people of God and making them his body, Jesus establishes in it a ministry of service that exists and must be exercised for as long as the Church fulfills its missionary task, "to the close of the age" (Mt 28:20).

The Petrine ministry, and hence the papacy in Rome, is thus instituted by Christ, the Son of the living God—not by the devil, as Luther's polemical pamphlet of 1545 asserted. And the Petrine ministry is operative in the Holy Spirit, despite all the human weakness of those who hold it. It is not a claim to power by those who bear this office that integrates Peter and the pope into the building of the Church of the living God as a foundation: this is the work of the founder of the Church himself. The laying of the foundation takes place one single time, but it fulfills its function perennially, and this is why Peter exercises in his successors the tasks of bearing everything as the foundation, holding it together in unity, and making use of the keys of the kingdom of heaven to forgive sins and to retain them, to take disciplinary measures for the protection of the Church. This foundation of the visible unity of the Church is, of course, based on the foundation in which Peter confessed his faith, when he said to Jesus: "You are the Messiah, the Son of the living God."

There are three metaphors that explain what Peter's ministry means for the Church:

And I tell you, you are Peter,
and on this rock I will build my Church,
and the gates of Hades shall not prevail against it.

And I will give you the keys of the kingdom of heaven,

and whatever you bind on earth shall be bound in heaven,
and whatever you loose on earth shall be loosed in heaven (Mt. 16:18–19).

The expression "Church" as a technical term for the post-Easter community of Christ (and possibly for the pre-Easter community) did not yet at that point refer to the community of Jesus's disciples but the later self-designation of the new covenant people, and the messianic community rightly saw therein the expression of Jesus's will for it as the Church of Christ.

Jesus, the Messiah and Son of God, builds on a rock *his* Church, which, thanks to the gift of his body and to the blood of the covenant, belongs to the eschatological reality of the kingdom of God.[13] The names of those on whom the Lord builds up the unity in faith and the community of the Church change, from Simon Bar-Jona to Jorge Bergoglio, but the authority and the mission of Peter remain. The foundation of the "papacy" lies, not in the fact that the official title of "pope" became established for the universal pastoral task of the bishop of Rome in the first centuries of church history, but in the fact that Jesus makes and appoints each Roman bishop to be "Peter," the rock on whom he builds his Church: this is the essential core of the "papacy." As long as the house stands, the rock on which it was built fulfills its function. One cannot restrict to the temporal beginning of the Church the task of Peter as the rock on whom the Lord built his Church. The Church was built for the first time on Simon, but it is built once and for all time on Peter. Without Peter, who is present and exercises his office in the popes, the pilgrim Church would fall apart, and the house of the Church would totter. Surely it is unthinkable that the prudent man who built his house on a rock (*qui*

13 See Mt 26:26–30; Mt 28:18–20; Eph 5:25.

aedificavit domum suam supra petram, Mt 7:24) is anyone other than Jesus himself? The people and the house of God will never collapse, despite all the storms that shake it—*fundata enim erat super petram* (Mt 7:25).

The individual human being Simon has the general task of being the rock on which Jesus once and for all erects the house and temple of God, the rock on which he continuously builds up the Church. As the risen Lord, Jesus fulfills what he promised at Caesarea Philippi for the time after Easter. But he does not do this in the manner of an architect who has erected a mighty building that will be admired after his death as a monument to his genius. The Colosseum in Rome stands before our eyes as a grandiose architectural monument to a past that will never return. Saint Peter's in Rome is a building made of stone, and as such, it can be destroyed.

But after his martyrdom on the soil of Rome, Peter forever remains in his successors, the bishops of the church of Saint Peter, the witness and the confessor of Jesus Christ, the Son of God. The *ecclesia Petri* is indestructible, and the *fides Petri* remains infallible, because the pope never falsifies the confession of Jesus the Christ, and never turns the believers away from the path of salvation. This is because Jesus prays for the weak human being on the *cathedra Petri*, that his faith may not waver—*ut non deficiat fides tua* (Lk 22:32). "All power in heaven and on earth is given" to the Son of the living God, whom Peter confessed, and who built his Church on Peter. Through the preaching of the Gospel and baptism, the disciples make people in every generation his disciples, in a process that will never come to an end in history. He confirms them in the certainty that "I am with you always, to the close of the age" (Mt 28:19–20).

Jesus built his Church historically, once and for all, on Peter and the other apostles, and that is why the Church is not a timeless community of ideas and values but a historical-societal and salvation-historical reality. But even after the death of the apostles and the earliest Christian missionaries, the Lord himself builds up his Church as a temple made of living stones, as his body to which he gives nourishment and growth. He does this through the pope and the bishops, who, as the successors of the apostles, teach, govern, and sanctify his Church in his name.

Did Jesus have in mind successors, when he appointed Simon as Peter and the rest of the apostles, or did he not? This is an all too human question that does not get deeper than the surface. The Son of God, who laid down his life for all human beings on the Cross, who instituted the eschatological covenant of God with his people in his blood, and who sent out his disciples to the ends of the earth surely was not restricted in his intellectual horizon and his salvific will only to the past and the present of his life on earth in the first three decades of our Christian era. The Church of the living God and the temple of the Holy Spirit always remains the same, although more and more living stones are inserted into it through baptism, for the simple reason that people die and others become through baptism members of the body of Christ in the next generations. If the command to baptize is valid forever, and the unique sacrifice of the Cross must be celebrated again and again in the Eucharist in memory of him until the end of time, then the promise that the Lord will build the visible unity of his Church on Peter, the rock, also holds good without interruption. After the deaths of Simon Bar-Jona and all his successors (266 up to the present day), it is Christ himself who appoints an individual person to carry out the task and the mission *of* Peter and *as* Peter. The gates of hell will never overwhelm the Church because Jesus built it on Peter and continuously builds it on him.

One thing is certain—namely, that he also had in mind the future of humanity and of the Church as the sacramental mediator of salvation. This is why he also gave the apostles a share in his own mission, in order that they should give their successors after their deaths a share in the mission and the messianic authority he had received from the Father. Since God willed the new covenant in the blood of his Son, he also willed the sacramental mediation of the saving work of Christ until the end of the world. This means that the pope and the bishops are rightly called the successors of the apostles because, far from merely presenting the apostles' views about Jesus and propagating religious-moral values, they proclaim the word of God in the name of Christ and in the power of his Spirit and make this word effectively present in sacred signs.

Accordingly, the Church was not built only once upon the mortal man Simon Bar-Jona, so that Jesus would have left it to its own devices after Simon's death. Such an idea would call into question the divine sonship of Jesus. Simon was the first to be "Peter," the rock on which Christ continuously founds his Church and builds it. The promise of indestructibility is made to the rock on which the Lord builds the Church. This means that the Petrine mission and the confession of Christ are indestructible—while Simon Bar-Jona and those who hold this office must die, and they can indeed waver and fail in carrying out their office. Despite human weakness, the Petrine ministry remains the rock on which Jesus infallibly builds up the confession and the life of the Church. It is only because all authority in heaven and on earth is given to the Son of God, and because he has overcome sin, death, and the devil (the author of evil) and the antichrist in the Resurrection from the dead, that the "gates of hell" cannot conquer, destroy, and annihilate the Church, his body of which he himself is the Head.

It would be absurd to look for the "rock in the turbulent waves" in the character traits and the psychological qualities of Simon and some of his successors, such as Clement, Damasus, Innocent III, Benedict XVI, or Francis. It is Christ's promise to Peter that supports the mortal and wavering men in this Petrine ministry. And this is the only reason why the pope is the perpetual principle and foundation of the Church in the unity of faith and of communion with Christ (see LG 18).

The "gates of heaven" are mightier than the "gates of hell, of Hades." Peter rules and judges with authority here on earth, in accordance with the directives of the Lord of the Church—and this corresponds to the invisible working of God's grace, because it is God himself who brings about his grace in the signs of salvation instituted by Christ, which the Church administers. This does not mean that God would be dependent on the Church. He can bring about grace even without the sacraments of the Church in those who seek him and love him and who, through no fault of their own, do not find the path to the Church's confession of faith. But in accordance with Christ's commission, the Church's working has the promise of God's certain working: it is God who employs the Church as the instrument of his universal saving will.

The Church's external existence is threatened by worldly rulers who place themselves at the service of hell and of the devil, who was a liar and a murderer from the very outset (see Jn 8:44–45). But thanks to Christ's promise, the Church cannot be destroyed. It is threatened from within by heresies, schisms, and a secularized mentality, but these dangers do not lead it astray from the true confession of faith in Jesus, the universal bringer of salvation and the Son of God. This is the infallibility of the Church in questions of the doctrine of faith and morals, which belongs in a specific way to the pope and to the bishops in communion with him.

The keys of the kingdom of heaven serve to open the gates to God's grace and his life. Peter must close the gates to one who wishes to enter into the Church without faith, and out of false motives (as we already see in Simon Magus, the protoheretic, in Acts 8:20). He does so not in order to anticipate the divine judgment but in order to protect the sinners and the sacrilegious from the judgment of God by preaching the need for repentance. The key that opens up access to the kingdom of heaven is a metaphor for the apostolic testimony to Christ that awakens faith, and for the sacraments that mediate grace—but it also symbolizes the exhortation to lead a life in the spirit and the imitation of Christ. There is another key too, which closes the kingdom of God for all those who resist the knowledge of Christ as Messiah, who oppose the truth of God in heresy, or who exclude themselves from the kingdom of God through grave sins, unless they repent (see 1 Cor 6:8–11).

With the key that binds, the ecclesial authority can exclude, and remove from the union with the living community of the Church, a person who has incurred grave guilt with regard to the truth of the faith and the unity in love. This is the meaning of the canonical or sacramental excommunication that can be imposed as a sanction by the Church's pastors. The disciplinary authority of the Church mostly makes use of penalties that are intended to bring the sinner or heretic to insight and repentance. The key that binds is subordinate to the key that looses, and serves it.

The metaphor of opening and closing the gates of heaven corresponds to the metaphor of the keys (see Is 22:22; Rv 3:7). The logion about the power to bind and loose, which probably was originally an independent saying, is added here in reference to Peter's authority over the keys. When it is also applied to the other apostles (Mt 18:18), this refers to the Church's authority to forgive sins or—in instances where penance and repentance are lacking—to retain them (Jn 20:23). This, however, does not mean a relativizing of the Petrine authority. Apart from the fact that Peter alone is the rock on whom Jesus built and builds his universal or catholic Church, and that the keys of the kingdom of heaven for the entire Church belong to him alone, he alone also receives the power to bind and loose for the entire Church, while it is given to the other apostles as a group, and they can exercise this authority for the good of the Church only in unity and fellowship with Peter. Matthew 18:18 confirms (rather than relativizing) the fact that Peter's primacy is to be exercised within the fellowship of the apostles, not in opposition to them. The authority to bind and to loose is given to all the apostles together, and to Peter in a primatial manner. The link between the two passages, Matthew 16:18 and Matthew 18:18, shows that there exists between the apostles and Peter a unity that must also be the model for the unity between the pope and the bishops. There is no biblical basis for the idea that Jesus first bestowed the authority on the entire Church, and that the Church bestowed it at a secondary stage on its office-bearers. On the contrary, Peter and the apostles received the authority directly from Jesus, and they exercise it for the Church and in their fellowship, so that here, too, there is no antithesis between the community and the office-bearers.

It is, at any rate, clear that the authority to teach and to exercise discipline in relation to the Church was entrusted to Peter and the apostles, to the pope and the college of bishops, by Jesus Christ, the founder of the Church, its Lord and its Head.

The logion about "Peter, the rock on which Jesus will build his Church," needs an explanation. Is the rock on which Christ builds the Church Peter or Christ himself? One could ask why Jesus builds the Church on Peter if he himself is the rock and the fundament of the Church. Or does he build the Church only on the faith of Peter? But in that case, what is faith without the one who confesses it, and what is the preacher without the one who has sent him and authorized him? Or does this "rock" function apply only to Simon, so that when he dies, the Petrine function—the use of the keys and of the power to bind and to loose that Jesus bestowed on the apostles for all time—dies with him? How does Peter exercise this authority after his death? There is in fact a certain tension here vis-à-vis the other affirmations about Christ himself as the fundament and foundation stone or cornerstone of the Church (but also about Peter and the other apostles as rocks and foundation stones of the Church).[14] Christ himself is the rock (1 Cor 10:1), and scripture states that "no other foundation can anyone lay than that which is laid, which is Jesus Christ" (1 Cor 3:11; see Is 28:16).

At first sight, there may appear to be a tension on the symbolical level here, but things are clearly distinct on the level of substantial affirmations. With regard to the relationship between Christ's mediatorship and the ecclesial-sacramental mediation through the priests or through the bishops and the pope as Vicar of Christ in his office as teacher, priest, and pastor, Thomas Aquinas draws the following distinction, which is important for the ecumenical dialogue: "The priests of the new covenant can be called mediators between God and humankind because they are servants of the true Mediator, in whose stead they offer to human beings the sacraments of the Church that bring salvation. This means that they exercise the ministry of mediator not *principaliter et perfective,* but only *ministerialiter et dispositive.*"[15]

It is clear that the images are true in relation to Christ not in the same perspective but in a differing perspective. Christ himself builds his Church, and he builds on the content and on the act of the confession by Simon, the first bearer of the Petrine function, that is to say, of being the perennial rock, the principle of the visible unity and fellowship of the Church that has become, in the pope, a person. Accordingly, Saint Augustine can say that "Petrus" comes from "petra," and that this "petra" is Christ as the true fundament of the Church—just as "Christ" does not come from the term "Christian," but rather "Christian" from "Christ." The visible Church—or, to use a better term that avoids the dialectical dualism between "visible" and "invisible," the pilgrim Church—is represented by the apostle Peter in his person:

> because of the primacy of his apostolate, in metaphorical universality. The Church, then, which is founded on Christ, has received from him, in Peter, the keys of the kingdom of heaven, that is, the authority to bind and loose sins. For what the Church in the genuine sense is in Christ, that is Peter symbolically in the "petra"; in this symbolic sense, the "petra" is

14 Mt 21:42, Eph 2:20, 1 Pt 2:4–8; Eph 2:20, Rv 21:14.

15 Thomas Aquinas, *S.th.* III q26 a1 ad1–2.

to be understood to mean Christ, and Peter is to be understood to mean the Church.[16]

For Christ instituted the Church through his saving work, which he transmitted to Peter and the other apostles, who were to proclaim it and mediate it.

Who then is the fundament of the Church, Christ or Peter? Thomas Aquinas gives the following answer:

> Christ is [the fundament] in himself, Peter because he has the confession of Christ and because he is his Vicar. [...] This means that Christ is in himself the fundament of the Church. The apostles are not the fundament in themselves, but through Christ's entrusting this to them, and through the authority that they were given by Christ. [...] And this applies especially to the house of Peter, which was founded upon the rock in in order that it might not collapse—like the prudent man who built his house on rock rather than on sand (Mt 8:24–27). The Church can indeed be assailed, but it cannot be conquered.[17]

The logion about the primacy in Matthew 16:18–19 found a varying and, indeed, controversial exposition in patristic exegesis, and later also in the debate about the existence and the precise definition of the precedence of the Roman church. It is difficult or impossible to find a biblical or systematic-theological justification for doubting that Christ intended his Church to be a visible community of faith and of confession, which has in Peter the principle of its unity with the God who has revealed himself in Christ as Truth and Life.[18]

16 Augustine, *Tract. in ev. Ioh.* 124.5; *serm.* 295.

17 Thomas Aquinas, *Ev. Matt.* ad c 16, 17.

18 See Joseph Ludwig, *Die Primatsworte Mt 16,18.19 in der altkirchlichen Exegese* (Münster: Aschendorff, 1952); Franz Obrist, *Echtheitsfragen und Deutung der Primatsstelle Mt 16,18f. in der deutschen protestantischen Theologie der letzten dreißig Jahre* (Münster: Aschendorff, 1961); Richard Baumann, *Was Christus dem Petrus verheißt: Eine Entdeckung im Urtext von Matthäus 16* (Stein am Rhein: Christiana Verlag, 1988).

10.
THE PETRINE MINISTRY IN THE MORTAL CRISIS OF FAITH IN THE MESSIAH

THE DRAMATIC TURNING POINT IN JESUS'S PUBLIC ACTIVITY comes with the decision of the Sanhedrin to kill him. This would eliminate any basis for belief in his messiahship, "for it is written, 'Cursed be everyone who hangs on a tree'" (Gal 3:13; Dt 21:23). But the messiahship and the divine sonship triumph on the Cross and are confirmed after Jesus's Resurrection from the dead by God his Father. Peter confesses later on, together with the apostles: "The God of our fathers raised Jesus whom you killed by hanging him on a tree" (Acts 5:30). Paul proclaims "the gospel of God [...] concerning his Son, who was descended from David according to the flesh and designated Son of God in power according to the Spirit of holiness by his resurrection from the dead, Jesus Christ our Lord" (Rom 1:1–4). The Church professes that Jesus is Messiah; indeed, the Church in its life and work is the bodily presence of the eschatological bringer of salvation. As a fellowship equipped with hierarchical organs, it is his body, his visible presence in the world.

During his life on earth, Jesus was present among his disciples in his natural body. After his Resurrection, he is visible and tangible in the world in his body—that is, in the social form of the community of disciples. The Church is the tangible risen Christ, and this is why it is called "the body of Christ." In addition to his presence in his ecclesial body, he is also present in the sacramental body and blood of the Eucharist. The Church shares the fate of the Messiah and understands its mission in the light of what it means to imitate the Christ who suffered, was mocked, and was killed.

The path that Jesus took came to its decisive turning point through the hostile rejection, by both the religious authorities of the people of God (the Sanhedrin) and the political authorities of the Gentile peoples (the governor appointed by the Roman emperor), of his messiahship and his message that the kingdom of God had drawn near. The great task of the Messiah is accomplished in the fate of the Suffering Servant of the Lord (Is 52:13–53:12). The disciples on the road to Emmaus admit that their faith in Jesus as Messiah has collapsed because he was crucified by the chief priests and the leaders of the people of God. They had hoped in vain "that he was the one to redeem Israel" (Lk 24:21). It was only the risen Lord who could let his Church understand God's plan of salvation: it is in the folly and weakness of the Cross that he reveals his divine power and glory (see 1 Cor 2:8), and it is only in the light of Jesus's rising from the dead that one can recognize and believe that the Messiah had to go through suffering to enter into his glory (Lk 24:26).

Our reason must first be drawn by the Holy Spirit into the higher wisdom and power of God. "None of the rulers of this age understood this; for if they had, they would not have crucified the Lord of glory" (1 Cor 2:8). It was not the Messiah of our expectations and demands but the Messiah of God's promises who "was wounded for our transgressions, bruised for our iniquities; upon him was the chastisement that made us whole, and with his stripes we are healed" (Is 53:5).

This drama of dying and rising in Christ occurs on the path of every believer. In virtue of his or her baptism, the Christian reaches Christ through death; but one must die every day the death of the old Adam and come to new life with Jesus. One must put off the deeds of the old human being and live as a new human being (Rom 6:1–11). There is no following of Christ without participation in his *via dolorosa*: "If anyone would come after me, let him deny himself and take up his cross and follow me" (Mt 16:24). It would be too superficial to declare the disciples' consternation when Jesus predicts his suffering, and announces that he will meet a violent death, as merely a lack of knowledge on their part before Easter. The connection between the Passion and the glorification of the Messiah encompasses the total existence of the disciple of Jesus.

The evangelists show us the learning process of the disciples up to the point when they recognize that it was only through suffering that the Messiah could enter into his glory. Their initial belief that Jesus was the Messiah broke down in the face of the utterly shameful death of Jesus on the Cross (*mors turpissima crucis*). It needed to be set back on its feet (so to speak) and established on a new foundation through the Messiah who rose victoriously from the grave.

The crisis of the faith in the Messiah can be seen in an exemplary and paradigmatic manner in Simon, whom Jesus had chosen to be the rock on which he wished to build his Church. If Peter in his mission and in his person embodies the Church in its organic totality, and the "we" of the disciples is synthesized in his "I," so that he acts *in auctoritate Christi et in persona ecclesiae,* this means that we also see in him what the imitation of Christ means. This is the daily path of the Church from the Cross to the Resurrection, from powerlessness to the glory of God.

In the Gospels, Peter's messianic confession is linked to Jesus's prediction of his suffering. He rebukes Peter very sharply: "Get behind me, Satan! For you are not on the side of God, but of men" (see Mk 8:33) and "You are a stumbling block to me" (Mt 16:23).

The primary concern of Matthew's Gospel is not in the least a look back on Jesus's pre-Easter relationship to Peter that would paint everything in rosy hues. Peter's confession of the Messiah and Jesus's rebuke of him frame the promise of the primacy. It would certainly be exegetically naïve to speak here of a withdrawal of the promise, by playing off one biblical quotation against another; we must not lose sight of the context and the total affirmation of scripture. The bestowal of the keys was a promise for the future, after the Resurrection, when the Church would emerge in the sending of the Spirit at Pentecost. But it is clear that the pope, as the successor to Peter's office, must remain aware of the danger of understanding the messiahship according to worldly criteria and of "being a stumbling block" for Jesus in the faith of human beings, if "he is not on the side of God, but of men" (Mt 16:23).

It has often been thought that one could give greater help to the Church through skilled diplomatic dealings with those who are powerful in politics and the economy and with the opinion makers in the mass media, thereby adapting to their standards, than through fidelity to the teaching of Christ and a humble and misunderstood life according to the directives of the Lord. This is the temptation inherent in every power, and especially in spiritual authority—and it is not absent from the Church and from its highest office, the papacy. This is why it was a mistake when the 1965 reform of the Curia gave the Secretariat of State precedence over the congregations of the Curia, especially over the Congregation for the Doctrine of the Faith. The considerable disadvantage for the Church is above all the fact that decisions in questions of the doctrine of faith and morals are subordinated to diplomatic perspectives. The magisterium of the pope is instituted by Christ and must therefore have an unrestricted precedence in all the measures that are taken and the declarations that are made. The question of truth must never be sacrificed to the diplomacy and the politics of the Holy See. And this is the reason for the existence of the principle *ecclesia semper reformanda.* The criterion for the fulfillment of the Church's mission is not the cowardly or cunning adaptation to external circumstances, the denial of the cross, or the populistic desire to please people. All the "servants of Christ and stewards of the mysteries of God" (1 Cor 4:1), and especially Peter and the popes, must take to heart Paul's urgent admonition of his successor Timothy: "Preach the word, be urgent in season and out of season. [...] For the time is coming when people will not endure sound teaching, but having itching ears they will accumulate for themselves teachers to suit their own likings, and will turn away from listening to the truth and wander into myths. As for you, always be steady, endure suffering, do the work of an evangelist, fulfil your ministry" (2 Tm 4:2–5). The first of the apostles is the one mostly closely bound to the Passion of the Messiah, so that the primacy not only makes its appearance in the light of its glorious promise, but also shows the terrifying shadow side that is linked to it in the person of Simon Peter and that lurks within the primacy, at least as a risk.

During the Last Supper, in connection with the institution of the new covenant in his blood and of the eucharistic sacrifice and meal, Jesus predicts Peter's denial. And Peter overestimates human strength, which, without the grace of conversion, can do nothing: "Though they all fall away because of you, I will never fall away. [...] Even if I must die with you, I will not deny you" (Mt 26:33, 35). But despite all his protestations, he denies Jesus three times, even with a curse and an oath: "I do not know the man" (Mt 26:74). Was not this the man who had been enlightened by the revelation of the heavenly Father, the man who had declared: "You are the Messiah, the Son of the living God" (Mt 16:16)? And after the scandal in the synagogue at Capernaum, was it not he who stabilized the group of disciples and the pre-Easter Church, which had been profoundly disturbed?

At that time, many of the disciples had taken offense at Jesus and had left him, protesting loudly. Jesus then asked the twelve apostles, the hierarchically organized leadership of the group of disciples, the core community of the Church, "Will you also go away?" Simon Peter gave the answer that deeply touches every Christian heart: "Lord, to whom shall we go? You have the words of eternal life; and we have believed, and have come to know, that you are the Holy One of God" (Jn 6:68–69).

In Luke's version of the Passion narrative, the task of the primacy is linked to Peter's repentance after his denial of the Lord in his suffering and Cross (in the first sentence "you" is plural; in the second sentence it is singular): "Simon, Simon, behold, Satan demanded to have you, that he might sift you like wheat. But I have prayed for you that your faith may not fail; and when you have turned again, strengthen your brethren" (Lk 22:31–32).

Jesus had now fulfilled the apostles' request to their Lord: "Strengthen our faith" (Lk 17:5). This refers not to the subjective faith that demands an absolute certainty of salvation, but to the faith of Peter's confession when he confessed that Jesus was the "Messiah of God" (Lk 9:20) in the name of all the disciples and of the entire Church. This is because the disciples' faith that Jesus was the Messiah had collapsed and totally disintegrated because of what they saw as his failure on the Cross. There was no remnant of faith in them that could have raised Jesus to life in their imagination; their faith was really dead and could really rise again only through the raising of Jesus from the dead. In this way, God establishes through the Resurrection of his Son from the dead the faith of Peter and of the Church in Jesus, the Son of God. Peter must not deviate from his faith—*ut fides tua non deficiat.* He must not desert (*eklipsein*) the confession of the faith through cowardice and fear. Jesus always prays to the Father for Peter and for the pope that the faith of the Church, which is built on him as on a rock, may not waver. But how does Peter strengthen his brothers and sisters in the Easter community?

11.
THE INITIAL GATHERING OF THE CHURCH BY PETER AT PENTECOST

The evangelist himself explains this in his two-volume work. In the Pentecost event, the Holy Spirit had brought together in the one Church of Christ people from all the languages. In this way, all the peoples were united in the Church, and the Church is one in all the peoples. The Church, which is sent into all the world and is thereby "catholic," exists in the peoples as the bond that progressively unites them in Christ. Peter demonstrates with his sermon that he stands at the head of the visible pilgrim Church, and now confesses Jesus as the crucified and risen Messiah: "'Let all the house of Israel therefore know assuredly that God has made him both Lord and Messiah, this Jesus whom you crucified.' [...] And he testified with many other words and exhorted them, saying, 'Save yourselves from this crooked generation.' So those who received his word were baptized" (Acts 2:36, 40–41).

Thanks to the sending of the Holy Spirit, Peter thus not only established the Church as a visible gathering by means of his sermon. He also gave its sacramental reality a concrete form in baptism. Those who came through the Holy Spirit and the sermon to faith in the crucified Lord Jesus asked Peter and the apostles what they ought now to do. Peter gives the answer that is valid now and for all generations to come: "Repent, and be baptized every one of you in the name of Jesus Christ for the forgiveness of your sins; and you shall receive the gift of the Holy Spirit" (Acts 2:38).

This is the visible community of faith that Peter calls together, thanks to the working of the Holy Spirit, as the Church of Christ—through the Word of God and the sacraments of baptism and the bestowal of the Spirit. It continuously comes into being and is renewed in its youth through bearing witness to the Gospel of the crucified Messiah whom God has authenticated. Those who believe in Jesus are added to their community through receiving the Word and baptism in the name of Jesus, who is the Father's Son and the one anointed by the Holy Spirit. The Church's identity consists in the confession of Jesus the Messiah, in baptism in the name of the one in whom alone is salvation (Acts 4:12), and in holding fast "to the apostles' teaching and fellowship, to the breaking of the bread and to the prayers" (Acts 2:42).

The Church of Christ is also the Church of the apostles, and it is apostolic because its identity lies in the apostles' confession of faith. It follows their teachings and finds its orientation in Peter and the apostles as the witnesses to Christ, "the author of life, whom you killed, but whom God raised from the dead. To this we are witnesses" (Acts 3:15).

Peter strengthens his brothers and sisters in this faith in Jesus, with all that this faith implies, when "the apostles and elders gather together" (Acts 15:6) to examine the doctrinal question of the admission of the Gentiles to Christ, and to reach a dogmatic decision. Dogmatics, as the formation of a theological judgment, does not mean inferring conclusions from a priori concepts. It means defining the revealed truth that the living consciousness of the Church's faith determines, through the authority of Peter and the apostles or of the pope and the bishops.

The "presbyters" or "elders" (*presbuteroi*) are the "bishops" whom God has appointed as pastors (Acts 20:28; 14:23), such that the connection between the apostolic and the episcopal ministries is already recognizable in the Acts of the Apostles, and the bishops emerge as the apostles' successors. ("Presbyter" is not yet the technical designation of the second grade in the threefold ministry after the bishop, but a general term for the highest office-bearers who succeed the apostles and accomplish their mission of preaching and mediating salvation with the authority and power of the apostles. It is only at a later date that they appear in two grades of ministry and form the college of presbyters, the *presbyterium,* with the bishop at its head.)

Peter now speaks in this assembly with the supreme teaching authority of the Church. It is, so to speak, the first dogmatic decision *ex cathedra Petri*:

> Brethren, you know that in the early days God made choice among you, that by my mouth the Gentiles should hear the word [logos] of the gospel and believe. And God who knows the heart bore witness to them, giving them the Holy Spirit just as he did to us. [...] But we believe that we shall be saved through the grace of the Lord Jesus, just as they will (Acts 15:8–11).

This definitive and authoritative doctrinal decision by the apostles and presbyters, confirmed by God and inspired by the Holy Spirit—and thus "dogmatic"—declares the revealed truth and shares in their authority, which was bestowed by God: "It has seemed good to the Holy Spirit and to us" (Acts 15:28).

12. THE PETRINE PRIMACY IN THE GOSPEL OF JOHN (AD 95–100)

THE ASTONISHING THING IS NOT THAT THE PETRINE PRIMACY is handed down at such a late date in the Gospel of John, so long after its institution by the historical Jesus, but that it is attested with such surprising truth and clarity in the earliest Church after the death of the apostles and proves to be a fundamental element of the apostolic tradition that is so indissolubly anchored in the biblical Word of God. It is the risen Lord who bestows the primacy over the entire Church when he makes Peter the universal pastor. He had already given Simon, the son of John, the name Cephas (that is, Peter, the rock) when he called him to enter the group of his disciples (Jn 1:42). Simon Peter's confession of Jesus as Messiah (Jn 6:69) and his denial of Jesus (Jn 18:17, 25) are followed by the revelation of the risen Lord at the Sea of Tiberias (Jn 21:1–23). Simon Peter had taken the initiative and gone fishing with six other disciples. After they had toiled in vain throughout the entire night, they once again threw out their net on the instructions of Jesus, who was waiting for them on the shore, and they caught an immense number of large fish. It was Simon Peter who drew this net ashore, and although it was filled with so many fish, "it was not torn." This is doubtless a metaphor for the Church with the innumerable crowd of believers, and for its worldwide mission to fulfill God's universal salvific will. Peter ensures that, despite its vast size, despite the many generations in the course of history and the billions of persons who belong to it, the Church does not fall apart. He sees to it that "the net is not torn" (Jn 21:11). After the meal, Jesus three times addresses Simon Peter: "Simon, son of John" (Jn 21:15–17), just as he had done when he called him and gave him the name Cephas-Peter (Jn 1:42).

Jesus recalls the threefold denial and forgives him by asking three times whether Peter loves him: "Do you love me more than these?" The Church and its ministers live on the basis of the forgiveness of their "little faith," of their numerous denials of Christ through fear of other people, and of all the sins through which they have obscured the reflection of the splendor of Christ on the face of the Church. This is (so to speak) the scrutiny that must precede every appointment to the episcopal and priestly ministry and that belongs to the daily examination of conscience of every Christian who exercises the ordained ministry (see 1 Tm 5:22). In his spiritual life, the pope, every bishop, every priest and deacon, and every Christian must continually face this question by the Lord—both with joy (because of his promise) and with sadness (because of one's sins).

Jesus's question about my love for him should move me very deeply, so that I cry out: May no one ever dry out in the routines of his ministry, so that he carries out his duties without love! The consequence of Jesus's forgiving love is "the boldness of Peter" (Acts 4:13), and the apostles pray in a time of persecution: "And now, Lord, look upon their threats and grant to your servants to speak your word with all boldness." The text continues: "And when they had prayed, the place in which they were gathered together was shaken; and they were all filled with the Holy Spirit and spoke the word of

God with boldness" (Acts 4:29, 31). It is only when we entrust ourselves completely, without any reservation, to Jesus, the Lord and Head of his Church, that we can say with Peter: "Lord, you know everything; you know that I love you" (Jn 21:17). Only love overcomes our fear and our sins, which are always a denial of Christ (1 Pt 4:8), for when Christians fall away from the faith, "they crucify the Son of God on their own account and hold him up to contempt" (Heb 6:6).

The pastoral love of the pope and the bishops for the "lambs and sheep" of God's flock will be more than a human friendship based on reciprocity only if they make a response to the love of Jesus, who laid down his life for his sheep. What matters is neither the breadth of the phylacteries and the length of the fringes nor having the seats of honor at a state reception and being greeted obsequiously by people (Matt 23:6-7). The apostles are not "rabbis" in the proper sense of that word—that is, teachers and fathers. They are teachers when they impart to their brothers and sisters in faith what Jesus has charged them to teach, and always provided that they themselves first acknowledge Jesus as their teacher and God as the Father of all (Mt 28:20). This is the "abiding" in the love of God that makes us a community of love in Jesus Christ:

> As the Father has loved me, so have I loved you; abide in my love. If you keep my commandments, you will abide in my love, just as I have kept my Father's commandments and abide in his love. These things I have spoken to you, that my joy may be in you, and that your joy may be full. This is my commandment, that you love one another as I have loved you. Greater love has no man than this, that a man lay down his life for his friends" (Jn 15:9-13).

One who does not love Jesus, or one who loves only his own self, is not suited to the ordained ministry. One who does not feel driven onward by the love of Christ would be in the wrong place.

Caritas Christi urget nos—"the love of Christ drives us onward" (2 Cor 5:14). In this context, loving means not a sentimental attachment but supreme sensitivity to the responsibility that Jesus entrusted to Simon Peter and to his successors. The love with which Peter loves the Lord has its origin within the Godhead in the fellowship of love of the Father and the Son, which hands over the Son for the salvation of the world (Jn 3:15-16) and moves the Good Shepherd to offer his life as a sacrifice on the altar of the Cross (Jn 10:14). Loving means knowing "the Son of God" and confessing him as "the true God and eternal life" (1 Jn 5:20).

Jesus's question to Peter, "Do you love me more than these?" thus signifies the challenge to Peter as the universal pastor to surpass the other apostles in the knowledge of Jesus and in the confession of Jesus, and thereby to go ahead of the Church. His greater love for Jesus is the distinctive mark of the disciples, which the pope must continually bear ahead of the Church of Christ. He must love Christ more than the others because the universal pastor must do more than the others for the entire flock. One who has the primacy in the pastoral ministry must daily stand the test of an ever-greater pastoral love.

The pope bears the supreme responsibility for the Church's confession of Christ. The entire magisterium of the Church, and especially the pope, has the aid of God (*assistentia divina Spiritus sancti*) when the bishops, with Peter and united in him, teach the faithful everything that he has enjoined upon them (Mt 28:19–20), because "If a man loves me, he will keep my word [...]. The Counselor, the Holy Spirit, whom the Father will send in my name, he will teach you all things and bring to your remembrance all that I have said to you" (Jn 14:23, 26). In the Gospel of Luke, Peter receives the charge during the Last Supper to strengthen the disciples after his repentance, on the basis of Jesus's abiding intercession for him. He is to strengthen them in faith in the crucified and risen Lord, the Son of God (Lk 22:32).

It is at this point that we find in the Gospel of John the account of the washing of the feet. This gives a vivid picture of Jesus's service as a slave, which goes to the point of his atoning death on the Cross: "For God so loved the world that he gave his only-begotten Son, so that whoever believes in him should not perish but have eternal life" (Jn 3:16). This is thus a narrative that makes an immensely high Christological and soteriological claim. It must not be reduced to a mere pedagogy about the Christian virtue of humility and readiness to serve. On the contrary, it is the salvific laying down of Christ's life on the Cross that is the presupposition of our Christian thinking and acting. Simon Peter, the official representative of the disciples and of the entire flock that is to be entrusted to him, indignantly rejects the intention of his master and Lord to wash his feet. But it is only in this way that Peter with the other disciples has a share in the baptism of the bloody atoning death on the Cross, and in fellowship with Jesus (Jn 13:8). This means that the disciples not only perform their ministry in the same humble attitude as Jesus; in their preaching and in their care of Jesus's sheep, they also really communicate the salvation that has come into the world through the death of Jesus.

He glorifies the Father through his death on the Cross, and Peter too will one day glorify God through his martyrdom (Jn 21:19). The disciples are slaves and apostles of the Lord (Jn 13:16). "If you know these things, blessed are you if you do them" (Jn 13:17). Jesus predicts his betrayal by Judas, one of his disciples, in order that when this takes place, he may reveal himself to the disciples as the Son of God: "I am he" (Jn 13:19).

From the room of the Last Supper, looking ahead to the glorification of the Lord on the Cross, Jesus speaks with divine power the words that send and empower the apostles: "Truly, truly, I say to you, he who receives anyone whom I send receives me; and he who receives me receives him who sent me" (Jn 13:20).

At Caesarea Philippi, Jesus had said: "You are Peter, and on this rock I will build *my* Church" (Matt 16:18). So now, at Lake Gennesaret, he commands Peter three times: "Feed *my* lambs!" (Jn 21:15). "Tend *my* sheep!" (Jn 21:16). "Feed *my* sheep!" (Jn 21:17).

God himself is the shepherd, the bishop of Israel. And the shepherd promised for the messianic age is Jesus (Ezek 34:11–24). God speaks against the bad shepherds: "*I, I myself* will search for *my* sheep, and will seek them out" (Ezek 34:11; italics added). "And I will set up over them one shepherd, my servant David, and he shall feed them; he shall feed them and be their shepherd. And I, the LORD, will be their God, and my servant David shall be prince among them" (Ezek 34:23–24). Jesus is thus the archetype and the criterion of every shepherd who pastures the sheep of Christ in his name and in his love, through the Word and the sacred signs of grace (see Acts 20:28). When Jesus calls the new people of God, which he has gained for himself through his own blood, his "flock," and calls his disciples his "sheep," he reveals himself as the Word that was with God and that is God, as the consubstantial Son of the Father: "You are my sheep, the sheep of my pasture, and I am your God" (Ezek 34:31). When he charges someone to pasture his sheep, he makes him his visible representative and the visible head of His Church. This Church is in its innermost essence one, holy, catholic, and apostolic because it continues the universal salvific mission of the Son, through which the Father realizes in history his universal saving will.

The apostle Peter would later give the presbyters, who shared with him the same responsibility for the Church, the serious admonition: "Tend the flock of God that is your charge" (1 Pt 5:2).

The church of Saint Peter writes from Rome to Corinth that "in the flock of Christ," the faithful are to "submit to the presbyters."[19] It is, therefore, not their flock. It remains the property of God. As human shepherds, they are only representatives of Christ, who is the true shepherd of his sheep. Bu they are to care for the priestly and kingly people of God in his spirit of love. They do so in the name of Christ and following his example, for he is "the supreme shepherd" of the sheep, "the shepherd and bishop of your souls."[20]

19 *1 Clement* 57.1.

20 Ignatius of Antioch, *Ep. ad Rom.* 9.1; 1 Pt 2:25.

In relation to the leaders of the Church, "who spoke to you the word of God" (Heb 13:7), scripture says: "Obey your leaders and submit to them; for they are keeping watch over your souls, as men who will have to give account. Let them do this joyfully, and not sadly, for that would be of no advantage to you" (Heb 13:7).[21]

The pastoral office of the pope and the bishops is not juxtaposed to the pastoral office of Christ, equal in rank to it. Rather, it is subordinate to Christ's office, or secondary to it, so that Christ who is the true pastor of his Church exercises through them his pastoral office in the Church. If the apostles, bishops, and priests are also called "vicars" of Christ, this is not presumptuous, as if they wanted to exalt themselves above other believers or to place themselves between the others and Christ. The contrary is true: "All this is from God, who through Christ reconciled us to himself and gave us the ministry of reconciliation. [...] *So we are ambassadors for Christ,* God making his appeal through us" (2 Cor 5:18–20; italics added).

However, Peter is not the only one who exercises the pastoral ministry in the Church. In his person, he is, so to speak, the embodiment of the principle of the unity of all the pastors. The doctrine of the Catholic faith says that the pope has the pastoral office for the universal Church, which lives in the fellowship of the local churches, but all the bishops are united in the care for the entire Church under his leadership. This is why Thomas Aquinas interprets the bestowal of the pastoral office on Peter as the bestowal of the pastoral office on the fellowship of the apostles and the entire body of bishops, which has its origin and its unity in the *cathedra Petri* in Rome: "It was fitting that this pastoral office was bestowed on Peter without mentioning the others. According to Chrysostom, he was the outstanding one among the apostles, the voice of the disciples, and the head of the college (*vertex collegii*)."[22]

Accordingly, when the bishop of Rome is addressed as "Holy Father" and he is called the Vicar of Christ as the successor of the apostle Peter, this makes clear in a substantially appropriate manner the character of this mission and of the commission to tend the lambs and the sheep of the entire people of God in the fatherly love of God and in the name of Christ, who is the good shepherd of the whole Church. To address the pope in this way is to profess one's faith in the authority that Jesus has bestowed on him; at the same time, it always reminds the pope that the honor belongs not to him but to the one who sent him. One who is called to the ministry of a teacher of the Gospel and shepherd of the Church must continually look to Jesus and

21 Heb 13:7; *1 Clement* 1.3.

22 Thomas Aquinas, *Ev. Jo.* 21 lect III/III.

follow the one who has revealed himself as the Son of the Father: "I am the good shepherd. The good shepherd lays down his life for the sheep" (Jn 10:11).

It was Pope Gregory the Great who grasped most deeply the spirit of the papacy. As the universal shepherd of the community of the Messiah, the successor of Peter is the servant of the servants of God: "Whoever would be great among you must be your servant, and whoever would be first among you must be your slave" (Mt 20:26). The Roman primacy receives its spirit and its form, not from the victory sign of a conquering general, not from the triumphal procession of the heroes of the public, nor from the ranking among the celebrities of this world, but exclusively from the shepherd's love of Christ.

"Our Lord Jesus, the great shepherd of the sheep" (Heb 13:20), "the good shepherd who lays down his life for the sheep" (Jn 10:11), was appointed by the Father to be "the Lamb of God, who takes away the sin of the world."[23] No one can become a shepherd unless he himself is first and foremost a lamb like Jesus, who in his own person is both the shepherd of his sheep and the Lamb of God, *pastor ovium* and *agnus Dei*. The rule of God, which Jesus proclaims and which he has realized once and for all, is exercised by the Lamb who was slain on the wood of the Cross. Peter can tend the Church in the name and in the authority of the Good Shepherd, provided that he tends the pilgrim Church in love for Christ. In this way, "the Lamb in the midst of the throne will be their shepherd" (Rv 7:17).

13. PETER'S APOSTOLIC TEACHING

LUKE'S TWO-VOLUME WORK, the Gospel and the Acts of the Apostles, redacted in the 80s of the first Christian century, shows us the transition from the pre-Easter community of disciples to the Easter Church and its unity in faith in the same Jesus, the Christ, the Son of God, the founder of the eschatological community of salvation.

Simon Peter had been put at the head of the group of the twelve apostles. This does not mean that the apostolate is monopolized in him, but that it is integrated into his person, so that in his office, the principle of the unity of the faith and of the community of faith becomes visible and is made concrete through him. In the earliest apostolic kerygma of Jesus's atoning death and his glorious Resurrection, Peter had already been mentioned, first in his person alone, and then also as the representative of the college of the twelve,

23 Jn 1:29, 36; Is 53:7; see 1 Pt 1:19; 1 Cor 5:7.

the guarantor and witness of the identity between the historical-earthly Jesus of Nazareth and the exalted Christ, the Head of the Church (see 1 Cor 15:3–5; Lk 24:34).

In the Easter apparitions, Jesus reveals himself to the apostles: "Then he opened their minds to understand the scriptures, and said to them, 'Thus it is written, that the Christ should suffer and on the third day rise from the dead, and that repentance and forgiveness of sins should be preached in his name to all nations, beginning from Jerusalem. You are witnesses of these things'" (Lk 24:45–48) "in the power of the Holy Spirit" (Acts 1:8). The apostles are thus not merely historical witnesses to purely inner-worldly events. They are Spirit-filled witnesses to events revealed by God: to the Incarnation of God, to the death of Jesus on the Cross, which has brought about the universal reconciliation of humankind with God, and to the eternal life that is promised to all who believe. Accordingly, their oral preaching and its written record in the New Testament is not a piece of historical information like the information Caesar gives us about his war in Gaul. Their testimony to Jesus generates in us, through the Holy Spirit, the supernatural faith through which we are eternally saved. Whether or not I know everything about the military adventures of a Roman general, who in his own way was a genius, means nothing whatsoever for my eternal salvation and for the meaning of my existence. But the knowledge of the name of Christ and faith in the Messiah and the Son of the living God determines my eternal bliss, the absolute success or failure of my entire being and life.

After Jesus returns to his Father in heaven and sits at the right hand of the Father, entering upon the divine rule in virtue of his saving death and his Resurrection from the dead, the age of the Church with its testimony to Christ begins. This age lasts until the accomplishment of God's universal saving will at the end of time. The Church is not a Christian religious society founded by human beings. God is the founder and Lord of the Church. Its basis and its content are Christ's grace and his Gospel (Acts 20:21). The Father has acquired "the Church of God" (Acts 20:28) as his own possession in the Holy Spirit through "the blood of his own Son." God gathers together and protects his flock, which is led under Christ, the true Shepherd, by the bishops who are its human shepherds. It is the eschatological and messianic people of God, formed from both Jews and Gentiles, who "repent to God and have faith in our Lord Jesus Christ" (Acts 20:21), who "are baptized in the name of Jesus Christ for the forgiveness of their sins and receive the gift of the Holy Spirit" (Acts 2:38). Through the preaching of the Gospel of Christ, the work of sanctification in the sacraments, and the exercise of the pastoral office—that is to say, through their *munus praedicandi, sanctificandi et regendi* (LG 20)—the apostles make Jesus, the Messiah and Lord, visible and audible in his Church on earth.[24] They are the mouth of Christ through which he speaks to us, the eyes with which he looks at us lovingly, the "hands of the apostles" through which "many signs and wonders were done among the people" (Acts 5:12), and the "feet of those who preach good news" (Rom 10:15); they point the flock of Christ and the people of God in the right direction and lead them.

In the first pages of the Acts of the Apostles, Luke is, of course, not giving a narrative of the chronological beginnings of the Church. What he shows is how Jesus, from his place with the Father in heaven through the Holy Spirit, founds the Church by means of Peter and the twelve apostles once and for all as a fellowship of life with God. It is through God himself that the transition takes place from the pre-Easter community of disciples to the Church of Easter and Pentecost.

The calling, empowerment, and sending of the disciples take on a new form. The apostles were Jesus's companions: now, the Holy Spirit appoints them to be witnesses and preachers of the entire mystery of Christ, as "servants of Christ and stewards of the mysteries of God" (1 Cor 4:1).

The college of the twelve apostles (Lk 6:12–16) is the link to the Church that comes into being after Easter (Acts 1:12–14). The first place is held by Simon, "whom he named Peter" (Lk 6:13) and who is therefore known both inside and outside the Church as "Simon who is called Peter" (Acts 10:5, 18). Peter holds Luke's two-volume work together. In the Gospel, it is Simon to whom the Lord appeared, and therefore he is the guarantor of the reality of the Resurrection (Lk 24:34). And Peter gathers with the eleven to wait for the descent of the Holy Spirit, in accordance with the promises of the risen Jesus (Acts 1:13). The "apostles' teaching" (Acts 2:42) is preserved collegially by all the apostles, and by Peter as the principle of their unity, because he is at the head of the college. He is without doubt the first among the "eyewitnesses and ministers of the word" (Lk 1:2), and he calls himself "a witness of the sufferings of Christ as well as a partaker in the glory that is to be revealed" (1 Pt 5:1).

The first primatial and likewise collegial act takes place when Peter stands up among the brethren (*in medio fratrum*) and speaks to the community of disciples, in order to reestablish the number of twelve apostles who represent the full number of the people of God, after Judas Iscariot has gone his way—"For he was numbered among us, and was allotted his share (*klêros*) in this ministry" (Acts 1:17). One of the men who can join the apostles as a witness to the identity between the earthly Jesus and the risen Lord (Acts 1:21–22) is to receive a share in Judas's *episkopê* (Acts 1:20; see 20:28: the

24 Mt 28:16–20; Mk 16:15–20; Jn 20:21–23.

pastoral ministry of the bishop).The apostles respond to Peter's initiative by putting forward two candidates. "And they prayed and said, 'Lord, you know the hearts of all men, show which one of these two you have chosen to take the place in this ministry and apostleship'" (Acts 1:24–25). It is God who chooses and calls the apostles and equips them with spiritual authority. This is why, at a later date, bishops and priests are introduced into their ministry through the prayer and the laying on of hands of the successors of the apostles (Acts 14:23). Matthias was "enrolled with the eleven apostles" (Acts 1:26) as the twelfth.

At the beginning, it is the presbyters who "together with the apostles form a college" (see Acts 11:20; 15:6), just as at an earlier date the calling and sending of the seventy-two disciples was an extension of the apostolic ministry (Lk 10:1–20). After they left Jerusalem, they were to carry out the teaching and pastoral ministry of the apostles in the city and in the communities that came into being in other places.[25]

The sending of the Holy Spirit is decisive for the historical genesis of the Church. The Holy Spirit comes down on the "Jews, devout men from every nation under heaven" (Acts 2:5). From Jerusalem, the center of the people of God, where the universal Redeemer had died, the mission of the Church goes out into all the world, to the ends of the earth (Acts 1:8). It is precisely in this utterly decisive hour of the history of salvation and of the Church that Peter stands up "*together with* the eleven" (Acts 2:14; italics added). Through his voice and his words, all who hear his sermon learn that in the last days, in the *eschaton* (Acts 2:17), God has brought about in Jesus the salvation that was promised.

Peter's confession of Jesus on behalf of the community of disciples (Lk 9:20) becomes the foundation and the center of the Church's confession of faith: "Let all the house of Israel therefore know assuredly that God has made him both Lord and Christ, this Jesus whom you crucified" (Acts 2:36). The following sermons of Peter, who always acts together with the apostles as witnesses to the Resurrection and exaltation of Jesus and to the sending of the Spirit, are sermons that lay the foundations of the Church. They contain all the articles of the faith that were included in the Apostolic Creed of the Roman church and of other churches, down to the great Nicene Creed (325) and the Creed of Constantinople (381).

The confession and the teaching of the apostles are not in the least applications of interpretations and theories to a human being with a subjectively intense relationship to God. The "teaching of the apostles and of the Church"

25 Acts 14:23; 15:4, 6, 22.

mediates a participation in the salvation that is real and effective in Jesus, "the author of life" (Acts 3:15).

The Church is born from above through the working of God, with the cooperation of the apostles, who proclaim the events of salvation and preach the Gospel. People come to faith in Jesus, the crucified and risen Messiah. Through baptism in the name of Jesus, they are integrated into the Church, the house of God, and receive the Holy Spirit. Living in and with the Church means holding fast "to the apostles' teaching and fellowship (*communio, koinônia*), to the breaking of the bread and to the prayers" (Acts 2:41–42).

"Filled with the Holy Spirit" (Acts 4:8), Peter confesses before the entire people of Israel and their leaders the unique and universal mediation of salvation by Christ: "Jesus Christ of Nazareth [...] is the stone which was rejected by you builders, but which has become the cornerstone. And there is salvation in no one else, for there is no other name under heaven given among men by which we must be saved" (Acts 4:10–12).

Heresies about the person and work of Jesus Christ endanger the truth of the faith and the salvation of souls and destroy the Church and Christianity as a whole. This is why Rome, the place where Peter suffered martyrdom, had to become the guardian of orthodoxy, the rock of Peter on which all the heresies must be shattered.

14.
PETER FOUNDS THE CHURCH OF JEWS AND GENTILES

A SECOND SETTING OF THE COURSE AHEAD, which is almost equal in importance to the foundational act of the one, holy, catholic, and apostolic Church in the event of Pentecost, and is indeed merely its logical consequence, is the opening up of the Church to the world mission. The apostles and presbyters assemble in Jerusalem, the place of Jesus's Passion and Resurrection. At this *syn-hodos* (Acts 15:6), the mother of all the general councils of the Church:

> Peter rose and said to them, "Brethren, you know that in the early days God made choice among you, that by my mouth the Gentiles should hear the word of the gospel and believe. And God who knows the heart bore witness to them, giving them the Holy Spirit just as he did to us. [...] We believe that we shall be saved through the grace of the Lord Jesus, just as they will" (Acts 15:7–11).

At the baptism of the Gentile centurion Cornelius, Peter had already realized, through God's working, that the Gentiles were called to enter into the eschatological community of salvation. Cornelius said to "Simon who is called Peter": "Now we are all here present in the sight of God, to hear all that you have been commanded by the Lord" (Acts 10:33).

Once again, it is characteristic—and decisively important for the understanding of the Petrine primacy—that Peter does not appeal to his own personal reflections and the conclusions he has drawn. He presents the Gospel of the calling of Jews *and* Gentiles into the Church of Christ as something that must be believed, because in his person the Church has recognized God's universal saving will, and from now on proclaims it *definitively and irreversibly.*

He understands the truth that "in every nation anyone who fears him and does what is right is acceptable to him" (Acts 10:34–35). The *Word* is sent to the Israelites. Through Jesus Christ, peace has been established between God and human beings (see Eph 2:11–22): Jesus Christ "is Lord of all" (Acts 10:36). Through the Holy Spirit, the confession of the person and the saving work of Christ brings about in the Gentiles faith in Jesus, "the one ordained by God to be judge of the living and the dead" (Acts 10:42). This is linked to faith in the forgiveness of sins in his name. Peter now directs that those who have come to faith in Jesus the Messiah and have received the Holy Spirit are to receive baptism. In this way, they are incorporated visibly into the Church as the community of grace and of confession (see Acts 10:48).

From Pentecost onward, the Church spread from Jerusalem to the ends of the earth. The martyr Saint Ignatius, bishop of Antioch at the beginning of the second century, was the first to declare that its universality or catholicity, which encompasses in its fellowship all those who believe in Christ, is the consequence of Christ's universal mediation of salvation.[26] Its unity in faith and in salvation reflects the uniqueness of Christ. There is only one visible Church, because "there is one mediator between God and men, the man Christ Jesus" (1 Tm 2:5). The universal Redeemer is no Platonic idea that is realized in varying degrees in its individual bearers, so that Jesus would differ only in degree from the prophets and religious geniuses and gurus. No, Peter confesses that in this one name alone the salvation of all is decreed (Acts 4:12).

26 Ignatius of Antioch, *Ep. ad Smyrn.* 8.2.

IV

The Catholic Church in the Apostolic Tradition

1. THE METAMORPHOSIS OF THE CHURCH OF THE APOSTLES INTO THE APOSTOLIC CHURCH

THE WORD THAT WAS WITH GOD and that is God became flesh and dwelt among us (Jn 1:1, 3, 14). The *universale* thereby became concrete in Jesus. Thereafter, the Church developed in the realization of its universality and its local concreteness. The Church followed an inherent logic as it took the form of a *communio ecclesiarum*, each of which is led by its own individual bishop. The ensemble of bishops is the *corpus episcoporum* or the college of bishops, with the *pope* as its highest member. All the bishops are united by one and the same confession of faith, and by one and the same sacramental fellowship; and all the local churches, each with a bishop as head of the clergy and of all the believers, represent locally the universal Church of which they are members.

The transformation of the Church from the foundational period of the apostles to the form of the local churches led by the bishops means that the primacy of Peter now becomes the Petrine primacy of the local church of Rome, with its bishop at its head. It is not the case that the primacy of Peter passes over in general terms to the Roman church, which would then give its bishop the mandate to exercise this primacy—for in that case, the head would be merely a function of the body. The pope receives his authority directly and personally and immediately from Christ, not from a collective: neither from one local church nor from the universal Church.

There is a reciprocal relationship between the bishop and the Church, which is expressed in the celebrated formula of Cyprian of Carthage: “The bishop is in the Church, and the Church in the bishop.”[1] Ignatius of Antioch wrote at the beginning of the second century: “Where the bishop appears, there the community ought to be, just as where Jesus Christ is, there the Catholic Church is. Without the bishop, one may neither baptize nor hold the *agape*. But what he approves of, that is also pleasing to God.”[2]

The apostolic and episcopal constitution of the Church is necessarily linked to its sacramental being and working:

> The visibility of the Church, and the continuity that is linked to this, thus require an ecclesiastical ordination that begins from Christ as its starting point and continues in an unbroken succession. This means that, just as the apostles were sent by the Savior, they too appointed bishops, who in turn gave themselves successors, and so on down to our own days. This episcopal sequence, which has its origin in the Savior and has been continued without interruption, is a primary external mark (so to speak) that shows which is the true Church instituted by him. The episcopate, which is the continuation of the apostolate, is therefore venerated as a divine institution. And the same applies, for precisely this reason, to the pope, who is the point of unity and the head of the episcopate.[3]

2. THE TRANSLATION OF THE PRIMACY AND THE TEACHING OF PETER TO ROME

THERE IS, HOWEVER, NO PRIMACY OF A BISHOP isolated from the local church of Rome, in the sense that he could locate his see at any place he desired. Simon, the fisher from Lake Gennesaret, brought the primacy with him to Rome and integrated it into the fundament of the Roman church. There can be no reasonable historical doubt about Peter’s residence in Rome and his work there in his role as the first among the apostles. To the eyes of faith, the divine guidance of the Church can be seen in the fact that, after the

1 Cyprian of Carthage, *Ep.* 66.8.

2 Ignatius of Antioch, *Ep. ad Smyrn.* 8.2.

3 Johann Adam Möhler, *Symbolik*, §43.

risen Lord had sent out the apostles from Jerusalem to the ends of the earth, the martyrdom of the apostle whom he had appointed to be the rock that bears up his universal Catholic Church providentially united his primacy forever with the local church of Rome. The Incarnation of God means that contingent events make manifest the concrete location of the universal history of salvation.[4] No general principles can explain why God chose precisely Abraham, why Israel was to become the covenant people, or why the Son of God was brought into the world by Mary precisely in Bethlehem. But faith accepts God's salvific working in exactly the manner that he ordains (Gal 4:4). And so, I can readily accept that divine providence directed Saint Peter's steps to Rome and that the see of his successor is in Rome, rather than in my own home diocese of Mainz. At any rate, Mainz was blessed with an Englishman as bishop: Saint Boniface, whom we revere as the "apostle of the Germans." He was famous for the very close connection of his activity to the pope in Rome, a union that made his mission to the Germans (who were rather wild at that date) fruitful and long-lasting. It is an irony of history that people in *that* region are proud of their anti-Roman sentiments today.

Since God's providence has ordained it so, the Roman church is the *ecclesia apostolica principalis,* in which the universality of the Church can be grasped concretely in one local church. And one individual man in the episcopal see of Rome embodies, in all his limited individuality, the abiding principle and fundament of the Church's unity in faith and of the fellowship of life in grace. All the bishops are successors of the apostles in a general sense, but only the bishop of Rome is in a personal sense the successor of one specific apostle. The bishop of Rome takes his place on the chair of Peter the teacher, the *thronos Petrou,* from which he governs the entire Catholic Church, for it is only to him that the Lord has said: "Tend *my* sheep!" The apostolic fundament of the church of Rome and the universal teaching authority of its bishop in succession to Peter are the rock on which the Lord builds his Church.

There was, of course, a Christian community in Rome before the arrival of the two princes of the apostles (see Rom 1:1; Acts 28:15). But it was through their preaching of the Gospel of Christ that Peter and Paul gave the Roman church the apostolic fundament.[5] In this way, the Petrine primacy in Rome became the providential foundation of the papal primacy, and this is why the Roman episcopal see is called a fortiori the Apostolic and Holy See. The primacy of Peter, from its first bearer, Simon Bar-Jona, down to today's

4 See Christian Gnilka, Stefan Heid, and Rainer Rieser, eds., *La morte e il sepolcro di Pietro* (Vatican City: Libreria editrice Vaticana, 2014).

5 Irenaeus of Lyons, *Adv. haer.* III.1.1.

pope, Jorge Bergoglio, is certainly of divine right. This is a truth that must be accepted with divine and Catholic faith as a binding criterion of belonging to the Catholic and apostolic Church of Christ.[6]

The link between the *cathedra Petri* and the church of Rome likewise proves to be indissoluble because the apostolic preaching and the fullness of Peter's apostolic authority form a part of the fundament. There is not an episcopal office for the local church of Rome *and* a separate papal ministry for the universal Church, nor is there a personal union between two different ministries. The bishop of Rome in his person is the pastor of the believers of the diocese of Rome *and* the universal pastor of the Catholic Church. And the universal pastor is always the bishop of Rome.

This truth of the faith is not overturned by the fact that some popes resided outside of Rome, either because they were forced to do so or through distressing circumstances. The exile of the papacy in Avignon was doubtless a grave abuse, and the damage to the Church was enormous. The intrigues of French cardinals and the French king had made the papacy a political football, an instrument of the French *raison d'état.* The urgent appeals to Gregory XI and Urban VI by Saint Catherine of Siena (1347–1380), a doctor of the Church, have a prophetic power that remains impressive even today. They are also the expression of the universal consciousness of the Church that the successor of Peter is only the bishop of Rome, and that he belongs to Rome. She boldly castigates the poor conduct in office and the lifestyle of priests and even of popes, but she has a radically different understanding of Church reform than Martin Luther, who published a treatise in 1545 claiming that "the papacy in Rome was founded by the devil." In her Letter 207, Catherine writes: "Even if the pope were a devil incarnate, rather than a kind father, we must nevertheless still obey him—not because of his person, but for the sake of God, since Christ wants us to obey his Vicar."

The Roman Curia, which (like the Roman synods in earlier times) assists the pope in the exercise of his primacy today in the form of the College of Cardinals (who represent the Roman church), is also linked to the pope in a local sense. It cannot have decentralized branches (so to speak) in other local churches. The Roman Curia supports the pope in his ministry *for* the local churches—but not *in* the local churches, since that would endanger their own rights: "In exercising supreme, full, and immediate power in the universal Church, the Roman pontiff makes use of the departments of the

6 Pierre Batiffol gives a detailed presentation of the understanding of the Church and of the primacy in Irenaeus of Lyons, Clement of Alexandria, Tertullian, Origen, and Cyprian of Carthage, with a synoptic comparison of the two versions of Cyprian's *De unitate ecclesiae* that concern the primacy. *L'Eglise naissante et le catholicisme* (Paris: Lecoffre, 1909). Translated by Henri L. Brianceau as *Primitive Catholicism* (New York: Longmans, Green, 1911; Forgotten Books, 2015).

Roman Curia which, therefore, perform their duties in his name and with his authority for the good of the churches and in the service of the sacred pastors" (CD 9).

If "the Church of the living God" is "the pillar and bulwark of the truth" (1 Tm 3:15), this applies all the more strongly to the church of Saint Peter in Rome. The church of Rome exists only together with its bishop, who is appointed by God to exercise the primacy as the supreme pastoral care for all the churches of the *communio ecclesiarum* in the authority of Peter and in accordance with the teaching of the apostles.

The Roman church assists him in his task for the universal Church through the clergy of the Roman church—namely, the heads of the principal Roman churches: the cardinal bishops of the Roman ecclesiastical province and the cardinal priests and cardinal deacons of the Roman church. It was in Rome that Simon, "the Peter," finished his mission and the course of his life on earth. It was in Rome that he had "glorified God" through his martyrdom, as Jesus had promised (Jn 21:19; see 13:36). But the task of the universal mission had also led the apostle Paul to Rome, where he "preached the kingdom of God and taught about the Lord Jesus Christ quite openly and unhindered" (Acts 28:31). Through their apostolic witness to "Jesus, the Messiah of the Jews and the Gentiles" and their martyrdom under Emperor Nero between 64 and 67 of the Christian era, they made the community of Christians in Rome an apostolic foundation. The first of the apostles (*princeps apostolorum*) made his church the first church (*ecclesia principalis*) in the fellowship of the local churches in which, and of which, the one Catholic Church subsists (LG 23).

The church of Rome takes up into its apostolic tradition the Petrine primacy and the Pauline zeal for the world mission. These transform the pagan Rome, which their contemporaries called "Babylon" (see 1 Pt 5:13), the adversary of the people of God, into the Christian Rome of the martyred princes of the apostles, Peter and Paul.[7]

Saint Ambrose formulated this admirably in the late fourth century in a sermon honoring the princes of the apostles:

> These are the men by whom the light of the Gospel was brought to you, O Rome. You had been a teacher, but now you became a pupil of the truth. [...] Through the Holy See of the blessed Peter, you became a race consecrated to God, [...] the head of the whole world. Through the divine religion, you were to spread your rule wider than your worldly power had been in the past.[8]

7 1 Clement 5.4–7.

8 Ambrose, *Sermones*, 82.1.

There is, incidentally, a grain of truth in the assertion that the Catholic Church is only the continuation of the Roman Empire with spiritual means. The kingdom of God, which is founded visibly on the rock of Peter, is in fact a spiritual rule that brings all the peoples together peaceably in one spirit as the family of God. In the past, the Roman emperor bore in his hand the insignia of worldly power; now, the Roman pope bears in his hands the keys of the kingdom of God. Thanks to the sending of the Spirit of truth and of love at Pentecost, the Church is one in the multitude of peoples, and she unites the many peoples in the one people of God. The Holy Roman Church guarantees this as the succession to Peter.

Even before the apostles arrived in Rome, Paul wrote to "all God's beloved in Rome, who are called to be saints, [...] because your faith is proclaimed in *all* the world" (Rom 1:7–8). And the great martyr Bishop Ignatius of Antioch (d. 108) addressed his letter at the beginning of the second century:

> To the Church that has obtained mercy in the greatness of the Most High Father and of Jesus Christ, his only Son, beloved and enlightened by the will of him who has willed all that exists, in accordance with the love of Jesus Christ our God—the Church that presides in all the country of the land of the Romans [the local church], worthy of God, worthy of glory, worthy of blessing, worthy of praise, worthy of success, worthy in holiness, and presiding in love [over the universal Church], an observer of the law of Christ, bearing the name of the Father—which I greet in the name of Jesus Christ, the Father's Son: to those who are united in flesh and spirit in every one of his commandments, filled with the grace of God without wavering and purified from every foreign stain, abundant greetings blamelessly in Jesus Christ our God.[9]

When he speaks twice about "presiding in love," he points both to the local church of Rome and to the universal Church, which is a fellowship in "the love of the Father and of the Son" (see 1 Jn 1:3). The Roman church, where Saint Peter presides on the principal cathedra, has thus the primacy in the fellowship of the local churches, of which, and in which, the one and entire Catholic Church subsists (LG 23).

There is a probable allusion to the First Letter of Clement, the exhortation sent by the Roman church to the church in Corinth circa 96 of our era, when Ignatius writes "You taught others."[10] He goes on: "I am not issuing commands to you, like Peter and Paul."[11]

9 Ignatius of Antioch, *Ep. ad Rom.* preamble [translation from Greek: B.McN.; the words in square brackets are clarifications by Cardinal Müller].

10 Ignatius of Antioch, *Ep. ad Rom.* 3.1.

11 Ignatius of Antioch, *Ep. ad Rom.* 4.3.

A few decades later, Irenaeus of Lyons, who is the best witness to the Eastern and the Western traditions (since he came from the East, lived for some years in Rome and died as a martyr in Gaul), writes: "The tradition that comes from the apostles and the faith that is preached for human beings has always been preserved [...] in the especially great and ancient Church in Rome, which is known to all the world, which was founded and established by the two most glorious apostles, Peter and Paul, as this has come down to us in the succession of the bishops."[12]

The paths of their apostolic journeys reunited the two apostles in Rome, where these "ministers of the word" jointly bore witness to Christ with their blood. Their paths had first crossed in Jerusalem: three years after his conversion, Paul went there to meet those who had already been apostles before him, and especially "to visit Cephas" (Gal 1:18). The kerygma of the earliest Church in Jerusalem, which spoke of Jesus's saving death, his burial, and his Resurrection on the third day, contains a fundamental element that sustains the Church as a community of witnesses: "and he appeared to Cephas, then to the Twelve" (1 Cor 15:3).

Paul also takes over from the earliest Church in Jerusalem the tradition of the institution of the new covenant and of the Eucharist at the Last Supper (1 Cor 11:23–26). The Eucharist establishes the unity of the Church as the body of Christ, a unity that is nourished by the sacramental body of Christ: "The bread which we break, is it not a participation in the body of Christ? Because there is one bread, we who are many are one body" (1 Cor 10:16–17). The unity of the Church in the Eucharist and the building up of the Church through the Eucharist are insights of faith that have their roots directly in revelation. This is why the eucharistic ecclesiology is not an intellectual theological construction but is the basis of every ecumenical striving to attain the unity of all Christians in the one Church and the one Eucharist.

Some years later, Paul came once again to Jerusalem to the synod of the apostles and presbyters, who had to clarify the question whether or not the Gentiles who had come to faith in Jesus must first be circumcised (Gal 2:1–10; Acts 15:1–35). Paul is confirmed in "the truth of the Gospel" that he had preached "among the Gentiles" (Gal 2:2, 5) and he had presented it to "those of repute, lest somehow I should be running or had run in vain" (Gal 2:2). James, Cephas, and John, the "pillars" who enjoyed great respect, gave him "and Barnabas the right hand of fellowship (*koinônia*)" (Gal 2:9).

In this passage, Paul switches between the names "Peter" and "Cephas" which go back to Jesus himself.[13] Peter had begun his work of evangelization

12 Irenaeus of Lyons, *Adv. haer.* III.3.2.

13 See 1 Cor 3:22; 9:5; cf. 1 Clement 47.3.

among the Jews in Palestine, while Paul had assumed the mission among the Jews of the Diaspora.

Then, however, Peter came to Antioch, where tactical perspectives and a desire not to give offense led him to abandon table fellowship with the Gentiles. Paul "opposed him to his face, because he stood condemned." Peter's hypocrisy and that of others "were not straightforward about the truth of the Gospel." Paul said, "to Cephas before them all, 'If you, though a Jew, live like a Gentile and not like a Jew, how can you compel the Gentiles to live like Jews?'" (Gal 2:11–14). Peter has departed from the truth of the Gospel not on the level of the confession of faith but because of his hypocrisy, which has dangerous consequences.

The orthodoxy that the pope must preserve also includes the concern lest salvation might be imperiled through erroneous consequences that might be drawn from any ambiguity on his part. There is also a heresy of praxis. This certainly applies to the sale of indulgences by Tetzel, who had the backing of his ecclesiastical superiors—and this became the occasion for the schism in the sixteenth century.

Peter's conduct was per se neutral with regard to salvation, as we see from the fact that Paul himself behaved similarly, albeit in a different context.[14] But precisely in this situation, in the face of the pressure from the associates of James, Peter ought to have stood firm and overcome his own fear, lest he gave the wrong impression and thereby sowed doubts about whether we are indeed "justified, not by works of the law, but through faith in Jesus Christ" (Gal 2:16).

Although those who adduced the incident in Antioch as an argument against the papal primacy and the infallibility in definitions *ex cathedra* were wrong, this story nevertheless contains a providential warning. Taking account of power relationships, the fear of looking bad in other people's eyes, the ineradicable craving to please human beings rather than God—all these are dangers that always lie in wait for those who hold the highest spiritual offices, and that can bring them down. Thomas Aquinas, appealing to Augustine, did not hesitate to speak of a sin in this case, although it is only a venial sin since, after the Resurrection, the apostles were preserved from mortal sin; and this shows that the fraternal correction of one apostle by another, or the criticism of one who holds a higher position, is sometimes not only a right but actually a duty.[15]

One cannot exclude a priori the possibility that popes in their personal morality can commit venial or even mortal sins. It is also clear that in their

14 Rom 14:21; 1 Cor 8:13; 9:20.

15 Thomas Aquinas, *Com. ad Gal.* 3.11: cap. II. lect. III.

task of faithfully and reliably expounding the faith and confronting heresies *a limine* firmly and securely they can fail to do what the Church requires. In such a dramatic hour for the Church, the cardinals of the Holy Roman Church would have the grave responsibility of confronting the pope, as Paul did, with the entire truth and fullness of the Gospel—for the Roman church is also founded on Paul. Saint Cyprian of Carthage offers an interpretation of the confrontation between Peter and Paul that should be taken to heart for what it says about the spirituality of the papacy and the episcopal ministry:

> In the case of regulations, one must not appeal to their provenance: the reason must conquer. For Peter too, whom the Lord chose as the first [apostle] and on whom he built his Church, did not raise any loud claims, nor did he display any proud presumption when Paul once again brought up the question of circumcision with him. He did not say that he held the primacy, and that newcomers and late arrivals must obey him; nor did he in any way take a negative view of Paul as a former persecutor of the Church. Instead, he took his reasonable advice to heart and joyfully agreed with the correct view that Paul put forward.[16]

The service of the truth of the Gospel has a theoretical, but also a practical aspect; the latter cannot be separated from the former. The two letters that the apostolic tradition in Rome handed on under the name and the authority of the apostle Peter show the "reconciliation" of the two princes of the apostles. Silvanus, who accompanied Paul on missionary journeys and, like Timothy, appears as the joint author of some of his letters—inspired writings that are the Word of God[17]—was very familiar with the theology of Paul, and Peter doubtless charged him to play a central role in the composition of the First Letter (see 1 Pt 5:12), where we can see that essential elements of the Pauline presentation of the Gospel are taken up and developed.

In "the second letter that I have written to you, beloved" (2 Pt 3:1), Simon Peter recalls "the commandment of your Lord and Savior through your apostles" (2 Pt 3:2). Peter speaks against the heretics who falsify the apostolic tradition and against the apostates who "turn back from the holy commandment delivered to them by their apostles" (2 Pt 2:21; 3:2). "There will be *false teachers* among you, who will secretly bring in destructive *heresies*" (2 Pt 2:1, italics added). He invokes his apostolic testimony when he tells the believers: "I will see to it that after my departure you may be able at any time to recall these things" (1 Pt 1:15). Peter thus has in mind the time after his death, and he makes provision for the Church by committing the believers

16 Cyprian of Carthage, *Ep.* 71.3.

17 1 Thes 1:1; 2 Thes 1:1; 2 Cor 1:19.

to the apostolic tradition. Remaining faithful to the apostolic tradition and to the Church's orthodoxy is "the way of truth" (2 Pt 2:2). Peter confirms the inspiration of the sacred scriptures and the Church's authority to give their authentic interpretation: "No prophecy of scripture is a matter of one's own interpretation, because no prophecy ever came by the impulse of man, but men moved by the Holy Spirit spoke from God" (2 Pt 1:20–21).

He also reserves the right to protect "our beloved brother Paul" (2 Pt 3:15) against the incorrect interpretation of his Letters, which he "wrote to you" about salvation "according to the wisdom given him. There are some things in them hard to understand, which the ignorant and unstable twist to their own destruction, as they do the other scriptures" (2 Pt 3:16).

We see here that Peter expounds the "holy scriptures" in a binding manner.[18] And Paul's exhortation to his successors applies even more to the successors of Peter: "Follow the pattern of the sound words which you have heard from me, in the faith and love which are in Christ Jesus; guard the truth that has been entrusted to you by the Holy Spirit who dwells within us" (2 Tm 1:13–14).

With his sermon at Pentecost and his other confessions of the faith, Simon Peter defined the apostolic teaching and brought it with him to Rome. This means that no one other than Peter himself raised the Roman church to the position of the first and highest guardian of the Catholic doctrine of faith. At the same time, the Pauline preaching of the Gospel likewise entered into the fundament of the Roman church. The primacy of the Roman church and of its bishop is based on the apostolic teaching and authority of Saint Peter. As the successor of Peter, the head of the college of apostles, the pope is the head of the college of bishops, but he integrates into the exercise of his universal ministry the unique world mission of Paul, the apostle of the Gentiles.

We can sum up the New Testament teaching about the primacy of Peter in the various phases of its development, down to the age of the apostolic fathers, by saying that, for the period between 90 and 150, the faithful of the Catholic Church:

> Look back to the apostolic generation and venerate their leaders, above all the twelve apostles with Peter and Paul at their head, as the abiding authority in the Church of Jesus Christ. The apostles are present and at work in the post-apostolic Church through their writings, their witness to Christ, their function as models, and their continuing work in the communities that they either founded or formed. The latter applies in a particular fashion, after the fall of Jerusalem and the slow disappearance of the Palestinian

18 1 Clement 53.1.

Jewish Christians, to the great community of Rome. The Church of Rome knows that it is called, more than the other communities, to care for the unity of the Church of Christ and the life of the individual communities far and wide. It does so through fraternal admonition and aid, appealing thereby to the apostolic order of the Church and to the example of the two leading apostles, Peter and Paul, who worked in Rome and died there for Christ.[19]

The succession of the apostolic authority of the bishops of Rome begins with Peter. And this is why the bishop of Rome is:

1. the legitimate successor of Peter as the rock on whom the Lord builds his Church;
2. the universal pastor who strengthens his episcopal brothers in the faith in Jesus, the Messiah and Son of God;
3. the personal principle of the unity of the episcopate and of all the Churches.

In the bishops of Rome, Peter continuously cares for the lambs and sheep of the one worldwide flock of God, which Jesus has entrusted to him.

3. THE RULE OF THE FAITH AND EPISTEMOLOGICAL PRINCIPLES OF CATHOLIC THEOLOGY

IRENAEUS OF LYONS, LIKE OTHER AUTHORS BEFORE HIM and after him, elaborated the fundamental hermeneutics of the Catholic faith in a reaction to the heretical and pagan gnosis, and to the disintegration of the Catholic faith that was caused by its idealistic speculations that dehistoricized revelation. The faith is based on the historical revelation that the apostles received and faithfully handed on, in its spirit and its content, to the post-apostolic Church. This "oral" (that is to say, lived) tradition is present in the sacred scriptures of the old and new covenant, in the life of the Church in preaching, confession, liturgy, and the sacramental means of grace, and in a life according to the commandments of God. And all of this is handed on not in the manner of a "thing" (as in a "book religion" or in a traditionalistic sense, as a mechanical transmission) but from person to person. These persons are the authorized witnesses and preachers—namely, the bishops who are the

19 Otto Knoch, "Petrus im Neuen Testament," in *Il primato del Vescovo di Roma nel primo Millennio: Ricerche e testimonianze: Atti del simposio storico-teologico*, ed. Michele Maccarone (Vatican City: Libreria editrice Vaticana, 1991), 1–52, 259.

successors to the apostles in their ministry. The principle of scripture, tradition, and succession is not in the least a criteriology applied to Christianity *ab extra* in order to ward off the gnostic danger. Real problems cannot be solved with fictitious means. A placebo cannot cure a real illness! It is only when an illness is life-threatening that the body's own immune system comes into play, and in this case, the organism—the Church—was able to survive and emerge from the deadly threat stronger than before.

The constitutive elements of the Catholic doctrine were present long before Irenaeus. If God is the author of revelation, this means that not only its content but also its logical structure derives from him, although this is grasped by the Church, the hearer of the Word, only in its reflection on the content and on what this content means. How many people there are who speak their mother tongue correctly and are able to communicate with each other in this language about the problems of daily living, as well as about essential questions of life—but there are far fewer who can analyze its grammar, rhetoric, and dialectic with certainty. And it is often the case that people have a reflexive mastery of a foreign language that is superior to their mastery of their own mother tongue. The grammar of the revelation of the Logos was already inherent in it before it was made explicit, by men like Irenaeus of Lyons (ca. 135–200) in the *Adversus haereses* (ca. 180) or Origen (185–254) in the *De principiis* (ca. 212), in the debates with the heretical gnosis and its alleged access to secret apostolic traditions. The *Traditio apostolica* of Hippolytus of Rome (ca. 220), which unites the best traditions of Alexandria and Rome, is also extremely important. The decisive point is that while one can separate logically and conceptually the content of the revelation from the forms of its tradition and the principles that govern its knowledge, one cannot separate these in real life.

The formation of the biblical canon had long been underway, and we find already at the close of the apostolic age the exhortation to protect the apostolic *depositum fidei* against the machinations of the heretics. The vital point is to hold fast to the canon of the truth, the *regula fidei,* that we have received in the baptismal confession of faith: "Although the Church is spread over the whole inhabited world to the ends of the earth, the entire Church throughout the world possesses one and the same faith" in the Father, the Son, and the Holy Spirit, and in their saving work for us.[20] The Church carefully preserves this message, which it received from the apostles:

> For although the languages everywhere in the world differ, the content of the tradition is identical everywhere. The Churches in Germany believe

20 Irenaeus of Lyons, *Adv. haer.* I.10.3.

> and hand on nothing other than the Churches in Spain and in Gaul, just like those in the East and in Egypt, in Libya, and in the midpoint of the world. [...] And even the most gifted preacher among the heads of the Churches does not preach differently than the others, for no one is "above the teacher" (Mt 10:24); and the preacher with weak gifts does not do any harm to the tradition. It is one and the same faith; one who can say a great deal does not thereby add to it, and one who can say little does not diminish it.[21]

Irenaeus of Lyons knew Polycarp of Smyrna (69–155), who had personally known the apostles and their successors; he was Polycarp's most celebrated pupil.

This is why Irenaeus did not put forward one intellectual construct against another. All that he did, when he elaborated the principle of scripture, tradition, and succession, was to bring to light and to put into words the principle of unity in the transmission of the faith, a principle bestowed by Christ on his Church. He summarized this principle in the Petrine principle: *ad hanc enim ecclesiam* [*Romanam*] *propter potentiorem principalitatem necesse est omnem convenire ecclesiam, hoc est eos qui sunt undique fideles, in qua semper ab his qui sunt undique conservata est ea quae est ab apostolis traditio.*[22]

This is a full statement of the essence of the Roman primacy. In order to remain in the true faith of the apostles, which mediates salvation, it is necessary to be in agreement (*con-venire necesse est*) with the Roman church. This does not in the least contradict the apostolicity of the other Petrine churches or of the other churches that were founded by apostles. On the contrary, it brings this apostolicity into the light:

> Many testimonies, from a very early date, confirm that, on the analogy of Peter's precedence in the college of the apostles, the see of the Roman bishop had a special position. When Irenaeus used the sequence of the Roman bishops to explicate the principle of succession, he stated emphatically: "For because of its especial foundational authority, every other Church, that is to say, the faithful in every place, must agree with this Church. The tradition that stems from the apostles has been preserved at all times for all those who are in all places." What Irenaeus says goes beyond the perspective of Tertullian (*praescr.* 36.2), who writes that Rome was the essential point of orientation only for the Churches of the West.

21 Irenaeus of Lyons, *Adv. haer.* I.10.2.

22 Irenaeus of Lyons, *Adv. haer.* III.3.2.

> Irenaeus ascribes to the Roman Church a special position on the level of the universal Church in questions that concern faith and teaching. This is why the Roman Church was the decisive criterion of the true form of the tradition.[23]

There is no competition between the other churches and the Petrine apostolicity of Rome, since each of these is present in the other. The Roman church is one local church in the *communio ecclesiarum*, and precisely as the see of Peter, it is the principle of the unity of the plurality of the local churches; at the same time, it is the representation of the totality of the Church. The Church is thus organized by the principles of unity, plurality, and totality. This makes it possible for the pope, as the bishop of one Church, to represent the Church that is universal and one, without abolishing the plurality of the individual local churches. He confirms this plurality in such a way that the plurality does not damage the unity, while the unity does not allow the plurality to get lost. The Petrine primacy does not replace and absorb the apostolate of other witnesses and messengers of Christ. Nor does it replace or absorb the episcopate that is based on divine institution. Rather, it integrates the episcopate into the Church and into the mission of all the bishops, "in order that the episcopate might be one and undivided" (LG 18).

Lest anyone might think that the apostolic foundation and succession of the Roman church is merely a theoretical construct without any basis in history, Irenaeus, who had lived for some years in Rome (ca. 177), lists the sequence of its bishops, who came after Peter and Paul (*loco episcopatum ab apostolis habentes*):

> This is the ordering and this is the succession in which the tradition of the Church, which comes from the apostles, and the preaching of the truth have come down to us. And this is the firm proof (*plenissima ostensio*) that there is one and the same life-giving faith (*unam et eandem vivificatricem fidem*) that has been preserved in the Church from the time of the apostles down to the present day and has been handed on in truth.[24]

The *potentior principalitas* of the Roman church reflects the insight that Peter and Paul are the *principes apostolorum*, the heads and princes of the apostles. Thanks to the power of the keys, which Jesus bestowed on Peter, the Church has received from Peter's see inerrancy in the faith.[25]

23 Michael Fiedrowicz, *Theologie der Kirchenväter: Grundlage frühchristlicher Glaubensreflexion* (Freiburg: Herder, 2007), 7–8; Irenaeus of Lyons, *Adv. haer.* III.3.2.

24 Irenaeus of Lyons, *Adv. haer.* III.3.3.

25 Theodore the Studite, *Epistolarum Libri, ad Naucratius*, II.63.

It is surely not by chance that, thanks to the foundation of the Roman church in the universal authority and mission of the apostle Peter, the oldest baptismal confession of faith, the Apostles' Creed, has its origin precisely in Rome. In the oldest of the four canonical Gospels, after the death of the two founding apostles of the Roman church, "Mark, the pupil and interpreter of Peter, has likewise left for us in written form what Peter had preached."[26] It is also in Rome that we find the oldest list of the canonical New Testament writings, the Muratorian Canon. The Petrine-primatial succession is theologically and historically demonstrated by the oldest list of bishops.

Like Hegesippus, who during his journey to Rome between 154 and 166 "met many bishops and discovered everywhere, as in Rome too, one and the same apostolic teaching,"[27] Irenaeus too records at this point the succession of the Roman bishops from Peter onwards.

After the first indications of the apostolic succession of the pupils of the apostles and of the bishop-presbyters whom they had appointed,[28] the letter of the church of Rome to a Pauline foundation, the church of Corinth, clearly states the reality of the authority and mission inherent in the apostolic succession of the bishop-presbyters, which has its origin in the apostles:

> The apostles received the good news for us from the Lord Jesus Christ; Jesus, the Christ, was sent by God. Christ therefore comes from God, and the apostles come from Christ. [...] They appointed men, after testing them in the Spirit, as bishops and deacons for the future believers....[29]
>
> Our apostles too knew through our Lord Jesus Christ that there would be conflict about the office of bishop [see 1 Tm 3:1]. For this reason, since they had received exact information beforehand, they appointed the above-mentioned [bishops and deacons] and then gave instructions that, when these men died, other men who had been tested should take on their ministry.[30]

In the case of Rome, it is certain that the bishop-presbyters were appointed by the apostles, whose successors they were. And this makes it clear that the chief pastor of Rome is Peter's successor. The *cathedra Petri* in Rome gives orientation in orthodoxy (a word that literally means the correct glorification of God) and proves again and again to be the unconquerable rock on which all the heresies are shattered to pieces. And the facts that

26 Irenaeus of Lyons, *Adv. haer.* III.1.1.

27 Eusebius of Caesarea, *Hist. eccl.* IV.22.1–3.

28 Acts 14:23; 20:28; 1 Tm 4:14; 2 Tm 2:2; Ti 1:5–6.

29 1 Clement 42.1–5.

30 1 Clement 44.1–3.

most of the heretics attempted to justify themselves in Rome, and that the orthodox fathers sought and found protection and support there, demonstrate the supreme authority of the Roman church with regard to the truth of the Catholic and apostolic faith and to the sacramental unity of the faith.

Irenaeus of Lyons, the great warrior against the gnostic dehistoricization of the mysteries of the Christian faith and the most important theologian of the second century, always argues concretely and precisely. He shows how the Roman church exercises its primacy as a service of the truth of the faith and of the unity of the Church. He mentions Clement of Rome as the third who exercised the episcopal ministry in Rome, after the apostles had first "laid hands" on Linus "for the government of the Church."[31] Linus had heard the preaching of the apostles in Rome.

The letter that the church of Rome sent ca. 96 to the church of Corinth calls to order the agitators in Corinth, who had mounted an opposition to the presbyters whom the apostles had appointed. Its tone is respectful, but at the same time authoritative, because it is "written in the Holy Spirit."[32] It demands not an external obedience but a religious obedience to the structure of the Church, which was given by God.[33] The church of Rome is concerned about the unity of the brothers and sisters in faith and love and writes this letter, these *potentissimas litteras,* to the church in Achaia "in order to give it *reconciliation in peace,* in order to *renew its faith*, and to *proclaim the tradition* that it had lately *received from the apostles.*"[34] The content of the confession of faith, directed against the gnostic destruction of the unity and uniqueness of God, affirms that there is only one God, the Creator of all the world, whom the apostolic churches confess in the Holy Spirit as the Father of our Lord Jesus Christ.

It is precisely this that is the service rendered by the Roman church to the entire Catholic fellowship of faith and of life. The outcome of the entire tradition from the age of the church fathers down to seventh and eighth centuries has been summed up as follows:

> It is indisputable that one of the constant elements of the early Christian understanding of the faith is that the apostolic see of Rome, thanks to its special foundational authority, is a privileged place where the tradition is both attested and confirmed. Despite many conflicts and varying degrees of willingness to accept this in the churches of the East and the West, the

31 Irenaeus of Lyons, *Adv. haer.* III.3.2.

32 1 Clement 63.2.

33 1 Clement 57.1–2.

34 Irenaeus of Lyons, *Adv. haer.* III.3.3. Italics added.

conviction that the Roman Cathedra had a specific responsibility for the authentic transmission of the faith was manifested repeatedly at times of crisis in church history, either when the successors of Peter took the initiative in the form of interventions or when those outside Rome consulted the faith of its Church or appealed to the authority of its bishops.[35]

4. THE ROMAN PRIMACY IN THE LIFE OF THE CHURCH

After the fellowship of the local churches in the universal Church took an ever-clearer form at the close of the apostolic age and was recognized very clearly in the second century as the divine constitution of the Catholic Church, the final essential orientation to the Roman-Petrine church emerged. It is only from the mid-third century that one can speak of an incipient theology of the primacy, but the faith in the Roman primacy is not based on its reflexive and thematic understanding; rather, it is thanks to its divine institution that it unfolds and becomes explicit.

Historically speaking, this emerges in the ultimately decisive role that Rome plays in the rejection of all the heresies and schisms in the early centuries: of the Jewish Christianity that had become heretical, of Gnosticism and Manichaeism, and of Montanism. Without Rome, the universal Church would never have been able to elaborate the mysteries of Christianity—the mysteries of the Trinity, of the one God in three persons, of the unity of the divine and human natures of Christ in the person of the Logos—as happened in the great councils of the patristic age. The heresies directed against the Trinity (tritheism, Monarchianism, modalism, and Patripassianism) met a decisive resistance in Rome, as did the denial of the divine or the human nature of Christ, or the obscuring of the hypostatic union (Arianism, Nestorianism, Monophysitism, Monothelitism) and the denial of the divinity of the Holy Spirit (the Pneumatomachians). In the questions of the possibility of penance for grave sins (Novatianism), the validity of the administration of sacraments outside the full communion with the Church (the conflict about baptism by heretics, and Donatism), and the absolute necessity and gratuitousness of grace (Pelagianism and Semi-Pelagianism), while the popes did not decide these matters on their own, they had the ultimately decisive voice, thereby preserving the Catholic Church on the path of the revealed truth.

35 Fiedrowicz, *Theologie der Kirchenväter*, 80.

"The church of the living God" remains "the pillar and bulwark of the truth" of God in the flesh of Jesus (1 Tm 3:15–16) never without, and still less against, the *cathedra Petri* in Rome, but only together with the apostolic faith of the Roman church in Christ, the Son of the living God (Mt 16:16).

5.
THE EMERGING THEOLOGY OF THE PRIMACY

THE FACT THAT ROME WAS THE CENTER of political power in the Roman world-empire plays absolutely no role in the testimonies to the exercise of the primacy of the Roman church in the centuries of the persecution of Christians, down to the beginning of the fourth century. Since Rome was the center of the pagan deification of the emperor and of the absolute state cult, Rome also became the focal point of the persecution of Christians until the reign of Constantine. The Rome of the martyrs is the Rome of Saint Peter, who placed his primacy in the very fundament of the Roman church, thereby founding once and for all its task and its mission for the worldwide Church. The concern for unity in faith becomes apparent in the admonitory First Letter of Clement, in the controversy about the date of Easter, in the conflict about baptism by heretics, or in the letter sent by the Roman bishop Dionysius to the other Dionysius, the bishop of Alexandria, about the latter's heterodox or unclear statements about the divine Trinity.

The Petrine-Roman primacy had an *ecclesial* basis, but the claim of the bishop of Constantinople to leadership in the Church, after the transfer of the imperial capital, was in fact a pretext for a *political* relativization of the primacy and for restricting it to the western half of the empire.[36] Down to the present day, these thought patterns and traumas influence the question of the full communion between the Catholic Church and the Orthodox Churches that are found everywhere in the world. It is as if the old Roman Empire or its division into a western and an eastern part or (later on) the contrast between the West and Byzantium deserve more than a reverent nod in the direction of past history. It is as if all this would possess even today some kind of theological significance.

Saint Cyprian, the martyr-bishop of Carthage (d. 258), deserves a special mention when we discuss the primacy of the Roman church. Despite

36 On this, see the major study by Anton Michl, "Der Kampf um das politische oder petrinische Prinzip der Kirchenführing," in *Das Konzil von Chalkedon: Geschichte und Gegenwart,* ed. Alois Grillmeier and Heinrich Bacht, 5th ed. (Würzburg: Echter-Verlag, 1979), 2:491–562; Hugo Rahner, *Kirche und Staat im frühen Christentum: Dokumente aus acht Jahrhunderten und ihre Deutung* (Munich: Kösel-Verlag, 1961); Franz Dvornik, *Byzance et la Primauté Romaine* (Paris: Cerf, 1964).

his opposition to Pope Stephen I (r. 254–257) in the controversy about the validity of the baptism administered by heretics, Saint Augustine defended him against the Donatists, who appealed to him as *catholicus episcopus*.[37] In a letter to Pope Cornelius (r. 251–253), we find the impressive formulation that the Roman church is *Petri cathedra atque ecclesia principalis, unde unitas sacerdotalis exorta est*.[38] Cyprian writes against those who accused him in Rome:

> And after all this, they even dared to appoint one from the ranks of the heretics as a successor bishop and to board a ship and bring letters from apostates and godless men to the see of Peter and to the principal Church, from which the unity of the bishops takes its origin, without reflecting that it is the Romans whose fidelity to the faith the apostle praises and glorifies, and to whom heresy finds no access.[39]

The interpretation of his treatise *De unitate ecclesiae* with its two versions of chapter 4 was long a matter of dispute, because it was employed anachronistically as evidence for or against the jurisdictional primacy of the pope in the sense in which this was defined by the First Vatican Council. One must bear in mind that Cyprian is concerned not about the papal primacy in a more proactive or reactive sense but about the unity of the episcopate as the principle of the unity of the Church. The Church is not only morally one, but also ontologically *one* Church; indeed, as one person, the Church is *one* (Gal 3:28), as we see from the fact that the episcopal ministry in the many individual bishops who are the heads of their churches is only one single and undivided ministry. "It is only one, in which every individual has his share—provided that the totality is preserved."[40] The primacy is given to Peter: *primatus Petro datur*.[41] This is the meaning of the words of promise and commission that Jesus speaks to Peter (Mt 16:18; Jn 21:16). Jesus's sending by the Father passes to all the apostles (Jn 20:21–31.). Nevertheless, the will of Christ is that the unity should proceed from one man, although the other apostles too are what Peter is, and, like him, "they are equipped with the same share in glory and in power. But the beginning proceeds from the unity, in order that it may be seen that the Church of Christ is one."[42]

37 Augustine, *De baptismo* 3.3, 5.

38 Cyprian of Carthage, *Ep.* 59.14; see 55.8.

39 Cyprian of Carthage, *Ep.* 59.14.

40 Cyprian of Carthage, *Eccl. unit.* 5.

41 Cyprian of Carthage, *Eccl. unit.* 4; cf. *Ep.* 71.3.

42 Cyprian of Carthage, *Eccl. unit.* 4.

The defect in Cyprian's argumentation is his derivation of the apostolate of the other apostles from the primacy of Peter; in reality, this apostolate has its origin in the unity of Jesus with the Father and in their share in the one authority and mission of Jesus. Peter is not in his own person the origin of the apostolic succession and the authority of the many bishops and of the Church, whose heads they are in the individual churches; rather, he is the visible principle of their unity and of their origin in Christ. This means that the unity of the bishops and of the churches does not possess its unique principle in Simon Peter in a merely chronological sense. On the contrary, its principle and fundament remains perpetually in the bishops of Rome as the successors of Simon Bar-Jona in the Petrine ministry.

Cyprian is completely correct in what he says about the unity of the episcopate and of the Church, but his theological argumentation is not fully developed and free of tensions. In the classical biblical texts about the primacy, he overlooks the fact that what is involved is not directly the unity of the episcopate but the bestowal of the universal pastoral office on one person, whose successor in office exercises this ministry of teaching and government for the universal Church—naturally, in unity with those bishops who are in ecclesial communion with him. It is not only the unity of the Church that is founded on Peter, the rock, but also its continued existence, its very being. This is why Cyprian's question is addressed to everyone who abandoned the unity in faith and the sacramental fellowship with the bishop of Rome: "One who abandons the see of Peter, on which the Church is founded—is he still convinced that he is in the Church?"[43] The bishop on the *cathedra Petri* is important for the intercommunion of all the bishops, and hence he is both sign and foundation of the unity of the Catholic Church: being in communion with the legitimate bishop of Rome in Peter's place, the *episcopus sanctissimae catholicae ecclesiae*, means being in communion with the Catholic Church.[44] The question whether one can claim Cyprian as a supporter or as an opponent of the dogma of the doctrinal and jurisdictional primacy of the Roman pope fails to do justice to his actual concern, which is to ensure the unity of the Church through the unity of the episcopate.

The fact that he had a substantive controversy with Pope Stephen about the validity of the baptism administered by heretics, and that he did not accept the Roman decision about the objective efficacy of the sacraments, cannot be seen as a contradiction of the primacy, for this was a matter of *how* the papal doctrinal and jurisdictional primacy was to be exercised. This

43 *Qui cathedram Petri, super quam fundaata est ecclesia, deserit, in ecclesia se esse confidit?* Cyprian of Carthage, *Eccl. unit.* 4.

44 Cyprian of Carthage, *Ep.* 55.8; 49.2; 55.1.

question, which always involves a tension, had to be clarified on the fundamental level. The papal primacy does not seek to call into question or diminish the doctrinal authority and jurisdiction of the bishops in their own dioceses; nor, indeed, can it do so, since this jurisdiction is given by God. Doctrinal questions cannot be resolved in a positivist manner with a reference to the formal obedience vis-à-vis the successor of Peter. The pope does indeed have the final decision, but this is always connected rationally to the content of the tradition of the faith. The ultimate competence of the pope in questions of the doctrine of faith and morals, and the unity of the Church as a legal community, are not in the least matters of "issuing decrees." They are the humble service of the ultimate insight of the Church into the truth that God has given it.

The doctrinal primacy of the pope is not a material principle of the Church's teaching—that can be predicated only of the revelation that comes to us in the scripture and in the tradition of the apostles and of the Church. The papal and conciliar magisterium is only the formal principle of definition. It is never the principle of the origin of the truth of the confession and of the unity of the Church. This means that is perfectly possible for tensions to exist between the bishops and theologians, with vehement controversies at councils and sharp intellectual debates between the various theological schools, until finally the magisterium decides which teaching agrees, or does not agree, with sacred scripture and tradition.[45]

This applies equally to the historical evaluation, and even more to the theological evaluation, of the controversy about the date of Easter, or of the later prohibition by the Synod of Carthage (418) of appeals to Rome. What was called into question was not the act of appeal as such but the attempt by troublemakers to evade every decision through procedural questions.[46] This must be eliminated today as well, since the right of every believer to appeal to the pope is not meant to circumvent the bishop's authority or to employ pressure in the social media in such a way that the bishop caves in for the sake of a peaceful life and is driven from the episcopal see on which he sits by divine (not by papal) right. "The bishop's primary obligation is not to ensure peace and quiet." In Rome too, one must be careful not to let oneself be instrumentalized in local conflicts.

45 See Georg Schwaiger, *Päpstlicher Primat und die Autorität der Allgemeinen Konzilien im Spiegel der Geschichte* (Munich: Schöningh, 1977).

46 On this, see the valuable study by Werner Marschall, *Karthago und Rom: Die Stellung der nordafrikanischen Kirche zum Apostolischen Stuhl* (Stuttgart: Hiersemann, 1971); Otto Wermelinger, *Rom und Pelagius: Die theologische Position der Römischen Bischöfe im pelagianischen Streit in den Jahren 411–432* (Stuttgart: Hiersemann, 1975).

There can be no doubt that the bishops and all the faithful have the right, for good ecclesiological reasons, to appeal to the pastor whom Christ has appointed for the universal Church. But this must be regulated concretely in such a way that the immediate, direct teaching authority and spiritual jurisdiction that Christ has bestowed on the bishop is not called into question either by the one who makes the appeal or by the authority to which the appeal is made. This is because the bishop does not derive his authority from the pope, nor from the believers of his diocese. He receives it immediately and personally from Christ in the Holy Spirit through episcopal consecration. An essential element in the exercise of this authority is, however, his collegial union with all the bishops and in reference to the pope, the person who is the principle of the unity of the Church and of the episcopate in Christ, the Head of the Church.

Saint Cyprian's intention is expressed clearly when he refers to the confession Peter addresses to Jesus: "Lord, to whom shall we go? You have the words of eternal life; and we have believed, and have come to know, that you are the Holy One of God" (Jn 6:68–69), that is to say, "the Son of the living God" (Mt 16:18). And the greatest African father of the Church before Augustine explains:

> Here, it is Peter who speaks, the one on whom the Church had been built, and he teaches and shows in the name of the Church that the Church, even if a defiant and arrogant crowd of disobedient persons separates from it, nevertheless does not depart from Christ, and that only the people united to the bishop, and the flock that adheres to its shepherd, form the Church. You must therefore know that the bishop is in the Church and the Church is in the bishop, and if anyone is not with the bishop, he is likewise not in the Church. Those who creep up, without having peace with the priests of God, and imagine in secret that they have fellowship with a few other persons, flatter themselves in vain, since the one Catholic Church is not split and divided. On the contrary, it is intimately united and is held firmly together through the bond of the bishops who are very closely united to each other.[47]

47 Cyprian of Carthage, *Ep.* 66.8.

6.
ON THE DEVELOPMENT OF DOGMA

WE MUST BEAR IN MIND that we cannot read the testimonies from the patristic age about the significance of Peter and of his successor as bishop of Rome from the perspective of a systematic ecclesiology that was elaborated at a later period. It is only from the de facto perception of the primacy as a concern for the fidelity of the entire Church to the apostolic tradition, and for the unity in the confession of the faith, that there gradually emerges a theological reflection on the foundations, the extent, and the specific competences of the pope with regard to the doctrine of the faith and the constitution of the Church by divine right, as well as on the concrete order and discipline of the purely ecclesial law. The real development of the papacy and its perception in theological reflection can be grasped better in the category of a coherent intellectual development than in that of a merely organic-biological development. In any case, one cannot employ the categories of a clattering mechanical functioning and a dusty study of archives (as in the rationalism of the Enlightenment ecclesiology) if one wishes to formulate intellectual processes and the inner unfolding of an insight in a way that is even roughly adequate.

When one's reason has accepted a historical fact, or an undeniable truth of logic and the knowledge of being, a learning process can take place. This will be more or less differentiated according to the varying power of judgment of a person's mind, and it can lead to a deeper intellectual and conceptual understanding of what was recognized in an initial perception.

Let me give another example. It is only as they pass through the ups and downs of their shared path through life that a man and a woman who have said to each other the "I do" of their love and held fast to it unswervingly come to know what married love is—as it stands the test, overcomes crises, and finally reaches the maturity of the union that God has in fact given them from the outset in his grace, when he established in the sacrament a genuine fundament for the love that they would live.

The Church's consciousness of faith is realized as it passes through time, thanks to the intellectual work of many gifted thinkers, when a deeper logic and a spiritual perception of the depths of the revealed faith shine out in the spiritual lives of the saints. The history of dogma does not run automatically (so to speak), according to formal rules and patterns that are laid down in advance, because history cannot be separated from the contingency of events, the individuality of the persons involved, and the circumstances and coincidences over which we human beings have no control. What course would history have taken, if the Roman Empire had not been divided and then had disappeared in each of its halves? No matter what would have happened in this particular case, the contingent course of history has no influence on the revealed truth. But it does have a not insignificant influence on the intellectual, cultural, and political conditions under which this truth is grasped and is put into practice in the Church's life. Undesirable developments and dead ends are also possible in the history of the Church and of dogma; these are left aside by the broad stream of the apostolic tradition. Nevertheless, the reflexive and conceptual understanding of the revealed truth must exist, an understanding that is definitively given in the Church's consciousness of the faith. Once a dogma has been presented by the Church as a proposition of the faith revealed by God, as a truth that must be believed, one can no longer deconstruct it backwards: one can only preserve it and study it more deeply forwards, in a constructive and living manner. This is because church history has only one direction—towards the Christ who is to come—while faithfully preserving the faith that is revealed.

In the patristic age as a whole, it is the central mysteries of Christianity that are the focus of debate. The material and formal principles such as scripture, tradition, and the magisterium are brought into play and elaborated theologically only to the extent that they serve to ward off heresy and strengthen orthodoxy in the faith in the Trinity, the faith in Christ, the confession of the objective efficacy of the sacraments, and the absolute necessity of grace. This means that the historical and theological justification of the episcopal office and of the Petrine primacy was studied in a concrete and pragmatic sense. It was not a systematic academic theme of exegetical studies and dogmatic dissertations.

Until the mid-fourth century, the path of the Church was marked by the continued bloody persecution of Christians, which broke out with varying degrees of virulence. There is no doubt that the Roman church, as the foundation of the apostles Peter and Paul, was the ultimately binding criterion—both for the heretics who appealed to it and for the orthodox who found orientation in its authoritative witness to the faith—of the catholicity and apostolicity of the Church that Christ build upon the rock of Simon Peter.

The French scholar Louis Duchesne (1843-1922), who cannot be suspected of a naïve papalism, studied early church history with a historical-critical methodology. He describes the consensus with regard to the papacy at the close of the third century as follows:

> The Churches of the entire world, from Arabia and Cappadocia to the borders of the West, experienced in everything—in faith and in discipline, in governance, in the liturgical customs, and in the works of love of neighbor—the continuous influence of the Roman Church. As Irenaeus writes, it was known everywhere, present everywhere, and respected everywhere,

> and its leadership was followed everywhere. It does not enter anyone's mind to place oneself on the same level: it is only later that patriarchates and other local primacies are formed. In the course of the third century, the first outlines of this development can scarcely be discerned. Above these organizations, and above the totality of the individual Churches, the Roman Church rises up in its sovereign majesty, represented by its bishops whose long line of succession goes back to the two heads of the apostolic college. This Church feels itself to be the center and midpoint that forms unity. This is how it describes itself, and this is how it is regarded everywhere in the world.[48]

We must certainly avoid painting the early period of the Church in romantic hues. But scarcely anyone can fail to be captivated by the splendor of holiness that radiates from the martyr Church and by the mystical depth of the unity between head and body in Christ. The lived faith sheds light on dogma and on law. Questions about power and rank are not in the foreground. The sacramental constitution of the Church is not deduced from abstract concepts and the academic exegesis of passages in the Bible and the church fathers. Rather, it develops from the vigorous power that the will of Jesus and the Spirit of God have bestowed on the called and chosen people of God.

In his impressive first work *The Unity of the Church or the Principle of Catholicism: Presented in the Spirit of the Church Fathers of the First Three Centuries*, Johann Adam Möhler traces the organic development of the visible constitution of the Church out of the spirit of the Church's unity. Möhler wrote in the spirit of Romanticism against the flattened, rationalistic, and juridically narrowed-down image that the Catholic Enlightenment had of the Church as an external institution for the instruction of the people. The Church's constitution is not imposed or enforced *ab extra* on its spiritual being, so that its being would be distorted by purely worldly forms of organization.

The emerging episcopal constitution of the individual churches with a bishop and his presbyterium, and the insight into the inherent unity of the episcopate as a whole, developed from the essence of the Church as unity and as fellowship with Christ, its Head, in the Holy Spirit. The bishop is:

> the personified reflection of this unity. But just as we would regard the bishops as a merely human product, if their institution was not apostolic—or rather, if it did not derive from Christ himself, in whose commission and

48 Louis Duchesne, *Églises séparées* (Paris: Albert Fontemoing, 1905), 155.

> in whose Spirit the apostles acted—that is also how we would be inclined to regard the midpoint of the whole Church [that is, the pope], even if it were in fact possible to find something of this kind in history, as a human work, if its basic characteristics were not also mapped out in the story of Jesus and the apostles. [...]
>
> When the phenomena appeared in which the unity of the Church and of the episcopate is displayed most completely in life, and in which this unity was elaborated in theory, the Roman Church and its bishop appear at the same time as the personified midpoint of the episcopate.[49]

In other words, *the pope of Rome is the unity of the universal Church in person.*

7.
THE CHURCH AFTER THE CONSTANTINIAN TURNING POINT

THE END OF THE STATE PERSECUTION OF THE CHRISTIANS and the transition to the imperial Church in the fourth century are a deep caesura in ancient church history. The so-called caesaropapism, the system of a state church, begins with Emperor Constantine the Great. When Eastern Rome reconquered Italy in the sixth century, this system imposed a heavy burden on the Church's freedom, and especially on the pope of Rome, for the space of two hundred years. The Christianization of society and of culture was indeed a great opportunity, but a high price had to be paid in terms of dependence on the state and of instrumentalization for the imperial politics of the Roman and Byzantine emperors. The worldwide ecclesial fellowship in faith, in the sacramental *koinônia,* and in the episcopal constitution of the local churches also experienced an administrative concentration modeled on the civil structures of the Roman Empire. This precarious situation for the Church found a continuation in the duality and rivalry of the power of the Christian state and the Church in the renewed Roman-German empire and the national kingdoms that lasted well beyond the Middle Ages.

Emperor Constantine had already made use of the Church as a binding agent for the imperial unity in 325 when he convoked the first imperial council in Nicaea, which has always been recognized by the Church as the universally binding highest authority of the shared magisterium of the bishops. It is not too much to say that he instrumentalized the Church here. This continued in the shifting claims to power by secular and spiritual authorities

49 Johann Adam Möhler, *Die Einheit in der Kirche*, §65, 70.

in the Byzantine period and in the Germanic kingdoms, for example at the Synod of Frankfurt (794) in the Frankish realm.

Ambrose of Milan (339–397) had already given the definitive formulation of the standpoint from which the Catholic Church has never deviated, and which it can never abandon: the emperor is not above the Church. As a believing Christian, he belongs to it, and in questions of the faith, he is subject to the bishops, and especially to the pope, to whom he must show religious obedience. The doctrine of the two powers was the papal response to the crushing yoke of the state church under the emperor, who went so far in Byzantium as to claim the authority to make ultimately binding doctrinal decisions. Gelasius I (r. 492–496) wrote to Emperor Anastasius: "There are above all two by whom this world is ruled, the sanctified *authority* of the bishops and the royal *power*."[50] Pope Symmachus (r. 498–514) added to this the clear subjection on the part of the imperial power, which has to do only with earthly matters, under the episcopal authority, which has to do with divine matters.[51]

This indicates how one should judge theologically the question whether the emperor or the pope can convoke an ecumenical council, or even preside at it—not only in an organizational sense but in terms of ecclesiology. Historically speaking, it was the emperors who convoked the ancient ecumenical councils, which however encompassed only the bishops within their realms, not the universal Church throughout the world. But the basis of a church assembly is never the power of the state or of the sacralized ruler, but rather the authority that Christ, the head of the Church, gave to the apostolic college with Simon Peter at its head and to the episcopate with the Roman pope as its point of unity.

Every universal council of bishops and all the provincial councils and local synods have a universal binding character in the dogmatic sense only when they are explicitly or implicitly recognized by the successor of Peter as an expression of the revealed faith that was entrusted to the entire Church. One must draw a distinction between the dogmatically binding character and the binding character in the civil law of the empire because the later antithesis between the pope and the council in late-medieval conciliarism is inherently contradictory. As a bishop, the pope is a member of the episcopal college. And the episcopal college does not exist without the successor of Peter, appointed by Christ as the visible head and principle of unity of this college. Without the pope, every council would be a torso—it would lack its

50 DH 347.

51 DH 362.

head. It would be impossible to prevent the atomization of the Church into national churches and sects. Even a later world council of confessions and national churches, which is set up by human law, could not establish and bring about the unity of the Church in Christ, because it does not owe its existence to a divine initiative. It would be at the mercy of the futile will of human beings to achieve unity.

8.
THE DEVELOPMENT OF THE DOCTRINE OF PRIMACY

No one disputed the doctrinal primacy of the apostolic Roman church, which had been founded by the princes of the apostles, until well into the period of the alienation of the Eastern Churches under the leadership of Constantinople, which increased until the de facto separation (let us avoid the technical term "schism" here) came in 1054.

This must be distinguished from the jurisdictional primacy, which is initially expressed in the recognition of Rome as the highest appellate court. At the Synod of Sardica in 343, which was recognized in theory but ignored in practice in the East because of the Arian turbulences, Rome was recognized as the appellate court for the entire Church in all important questions of doctrine and discipline: "The priests of the Lord are to give an account to the head, to the see of the apostle Peter."[52] It is in the nature of things that there cannot be any authority higher than the highest and ultimate authority in the Church on earth, nor any other authority to which one could appeal. This is declared by Pope Gelasius I in the letter *Famuli vestrae pietatis* to Emperor Anastasius I in 494.[53] This is what is meant by the principle in canon law *prima sedes a nemine iudicatur*; this principle has a dogmatic foundation. The pope writes to the emperor that the Peter-Pope is the one "to whom Christ has given precedence before all others and whom the venerable Church has always confessed and revered and reverently acknowledged as primate. Human presumption can attack what has been determined by divine decision, but it cannot be overthrown by the power of any one individual."[54]

The conflict between Rome and Constantinople grew, nourished by the damaging question whether Constantinople was the highest authority for the Eastern Churches and independent of Old Rome (Photius, Michael Cerularius), or Rome, as the *Apostolica sedes Sancti Petri*, was not by divine law higher than the jurisdiction that Constantinople exercised de facto in the

52 DH 133–135; 136.
53 DH 347.
54 DH 347.

Byzantine realm by imperial law. Did Rome act on behalf of the entire Catholic Church throughout the world? Originally, territorial synodal associations had formed under the leadership of a primate (Rome, Alexandria, Antioch, Carthage, Caesarea, Arles, etc.). The claim by the bishop of the royal capital to an ecumenical patriarchate in the realms of the Byzantine emperor was not in accordance with the synodal praxis of the early Church. The primacy of Rome was perceived early on as the ultimate orientation of the unity of the various synodal associations. The pope never took "solitary" decisions. He always understood a final doctrinal decision as the culminating point of a synodal process, as we see in the many important Roman synods. There is, however, a formal distinction between the final papal decision and the overall decision of a synod, although the latter is integrated into the former.

The reshaping of the synodal associations into regions of patriarchal jurisdiction meant that the doctrinal primacy of the Roman church was also called into question, because the doctrine of the primacy was incorrectly understood and was interpreted to mean that Rome was entangled in error, or even in formal heresy. Down to the present day, however, the existence of the Petrine primacy in Rome is acknowledged in all the Orthodox Churches as a fact of church history.

The coming into existence of the great primacies and the theory of the five patriarchates belong to a later period, which sought to justify theologically the de facto development. It has, however, no dogmatic basis in the sacramental reality of the Church if one prescinds from the three Petrine sees (Jerusalem, Antioch, and Rome). There is no need to take issue with the venerable tradition that is expressed here, *provided that* the idea of the pentarchy or of Moscow as the Third Rome does not obscure the essential difference between the Petrine primacy of Rome and the idea of the pentarchy, which has its origins in the imperial church politics of the Byzantine Empire. When the Eastern Roman Empire collapsed, the idea of the patriarchate gave way to the theory of the autocephaly of national churches under a "patriarch," a kind of super-archbishop over the other bishops of the country.[55] In the various Eastern rites of the local churches in the Catholic Church today, the real synodal associations, which are older than the theory of the pentarchy, have their acknowledged place.

There can be no denying the innumerable "appeals" to Rome in matters of faith and jurisdiction in the epoch of undivided Christianity by Origen, Athanasius the Great, John Chrysostom, Flavian of Constantinople, and Maximus the Confessor. There were also heretics who wanted to justify themselves there (Marcion, the Novatians Felix and Felicissimus, Nestorius,

55 See the precise description of this development by Hans-Georg Beck, *Kirche und theologische Literatur im Byzantinischen Reich* (Munich: Beck, 1959), 32–35.

Pelagius, Eutyches, and the Monothelites). It belongs to Rome, thanks to the Petrine authority, to provide the ultimately decisive orientation, because the apostles Peter and Paul are still present there not as dead historical documents but as living examples and witnesses to Christ.

This is seen in the role played by Pope Damasus in the struggle against Apollinarianism, by Celestine I against Nestorianism at the Council of Ephesus (431), and by Leo I vis-à-vis the Synod of Ephesus (449), which he annulled, and in the confession of the Fourth Ecumenical Council, at Chalcedon, against Monophysitism, which he approved.[56] And this is expressed perhaps even more clearly in the position taken by Pope Agatho (r. 678–681) vis-à-vis the Third Council of Constantinople and by Adrian I (r. 772–795) vis-à-vis the Second Council of Nicaea (787).

The correlation between the Petrine apostolate of the pope and the apostolate of the bishops—or, to put it in brief terms, between pope and council—is not a matter of the majority opinion that ultimately prevails; nor is the pope a president who has the deciding voice in a tie vote, and still less one who imposes his own individual view on everyone else. One arrives at moral unity through the unanimity of the testimony of everyone about the Catholic faith that the Church has received from the inheritance of the apostles. At the apostolic council, the entire testimony of the apostles and bishop-presbyters is brought together and finally defined in the responsibility for the unity of the faith that Christ bestowed on Simon Peter, and this is what happens at an ecumenical council. The pope, with the synod of the Roman church, authoritatively makes the contribution of his apostolic authority, and this is compared with the testimony of other bishops to the faith. At the end, the pope approves the overall decision of the council and proposes it to the entire Church with the highest authority of the magisterium, as something that must be believed. In this way, the equilibrium between the plurality and the unity is maintained, and the totality of the Church's testimony to the truth is realized. History shows that this can always be linked to tensions, and even to a parting of the ways. If conciliar assemblies do not run harmoniously like a piece of clockwork, if the beams of the house can creak and undignified scenes take place, this is not because of a failure on the part of the Holy Spirit. These confrontations, which are sometimes highly un-fraternal, are a consequence of the risk that God entered into through the Incarnation, when he entrusted the revealed truth to frail human beings with all their per-

56 Stefan Otto Horn, "Das Verhältnis von Primat und Episkopat im ersten Jahrtausend: Eine geschichtlich-theologische Studie," in *Il primato del successore di Pietro: Atti del Simposio Teologisco* (Vatican City: Libreria editrice Vaticana, 1998), 194–213; *Petrou Kathedra: Der Bischof von Rom und die Synoden von Ephesus (449) und Chalcedon* (Paderborn: Bonifatius-Druckerei, 1982).

sonality defects and intellectual shortcomings. But one must also remember that the intellectual struggles have led to deeper clarifications of matters of faith— "For there must be factions among you, in order that those who are genuine among you may be recognized" (1 Cor 11:19).

The controversy about the higher rank of Constantinople, which was justified by political reasons, must be seen as the decisive rejection of the attempt to relativize the Roman primacy by linking it to the rank of the old imperial capital of Rome, as if Rome owed its primacy not to Christ but to a conciliar decision or even to the emperor. Canon 6 of the Council of Nicaea had stipulated that the ancient prerogatives of the bishops of Rome, Alexandria, and Antioch, the bishops of the Petrine-apostolic churches and of other leading metropolitan sees, must be preserved. The Council of Constantinople in 381, which was later to enjoy universal recognition as the Second Ecumenical Council thanks to its acknowledgment by Rome, spoke of a primacy in honor of New Rome immediately after the precedence of Old Rome, while the celebrated canon 28 of the Council of Chalcedon with 158 signatures (although in the absence of the papal legates) decided to raise the rank of Constantinople and to put it on the same level as Rome, Alexandria, and Antioch, whose bishops have been called "patriarchs" from the sixth century onward. This was prima facie a matter of changing the areas of jurisdiction, but the *political* justification of the altered ranking meant that the primacy of Rome, which has an *ecclesial* justification, was obscured.

Pope Leo I initially opposed the decision, in order to safeguard the prerogatives of the other bishops and to satisfy the requirements of the ancient canons. The decisive point here is, however, the emphasis on the completely different character of the precedence of the Holy Apostolic See of Rome, as a presupposition for the acceptance of the decisions of the council, which belong entirely to the sphere of church law. The Roman primacy cannot be shared with New Rome or with other ecclesial and political metropolitan cities, because only one man can be the fundament of unity and the head of the visible Church. Only one man was appointed by Christ himself in Saint Peter—namely, the bishop on the *cathedra Petri* in Rome. And he is the integrating point of unity of the consultations and decisions of the ecumenical councils and of the entire episcopate. When they arrived in Ephesus, the legates read Pope Celestine's letter to this assembly, which expressed its agreement with Celestine, "the guardian of the faith." Philip, the papal legate, thanked Cyril, the patriarch of Alexandria, and the other council fathers for their agreement in belief in the unity of the divinity and the humanity in the person of the Logos "together with our sacred and blessed Pope, for the blessed apostle Peter is the head of the entire faith, just as he is the head of the apostles." And he sums up the whole of the doctrine of the Roman primacy and of the unity of the pope with the bishops as follows: "We thank the sacred and venerable synod that, after the reading of the letter from our sacred Pope, you as sacred members with sacred voices have proclaimed your adherence to the sacred head with your sacred acclamations. For you are not unaware that the head of the entire faith and of all the apostles is blessed Peter."

On the following day, July 11, 431, he added:

> No one doubts, and indeed no one has ever at any time doubted, that the most sacred and most blessed Peter, the first and the head of the apostles, the pillar of faith and the foundation stone of the Catholic Church, received from our Lord Jesus Christ, the Redeemer of the human race, the keys of the kingdom and the power to bind and to loose. And it is he who down to the present day and for all time to come lives and judges in his successors. His successor and vicar in due order, our most blessed Pope, Bishop Celestine, has sent us to this synod to take his place in his personal absence. The most Christian Emperors have commanded this synod to gather, always mindful of the Catholic faith and protecting it, and preserving the doctrine of the apostles, which they have received from their fathers and ancestors.[57]

Bishop Capreolus of Carthage, the successor of Saint Augustine, judged that Nestorius "has been condemned by the authority of the Apostolic See and the unanimous sentence of judgement of the bishops." And with regard to the later debates about the superiority of the council or of the pope, Cyril of Alexandria states clearly how the council works together, in its composition as the assembly of all the bishops with the pope: the fathers decide together with the pope, and the pope confirms the decision that all have taken.[58] In his sixth letter to the bishops of the East, Pope Pelagius II (r. 579–590) emphasizes that no synod had ever succeeded in claiming a binding character for the entire Church without the authority of the Apostolic See. He writes in the letter *Dilectionis vestrae* (585/586) to the schismatic bishops of Istria that anyone who does not preserve the unity with the successor of Peter separates himself from the Church and loses the truth of the faith.[59]

The council fathers recognize in Leo I's synodal letter the pope as the voice of Peter and as the head who guides the members of the body of the conciliar assembly, and hence of the entire Church.[60] It is thus clear that a

57 Erich Caspar, *Geschichte des Papsttums*, vol. 1 (Tubingen: J. C. B. Mohr, 1930; Münster: Stenderhoff, 1985), 409–411. Citation refers to the Stenderhoff edition. DH 3056; ACO I.I.3.8.

58 Pierre-Thomas Camelot, *Ephesus und Chalcedon* (Mainz: Matthias-Grünewald 1963), 62–63.

59 DH 486.

60 DH 307.

council can decide definitively about matters of faith and morals only with the approval of the Roman pontiff as the successor of Peter in the authority of Christ, whom he represents visibly in the Church. Pope Gelasius I declares: *Prima Sedes unamquamque synodum sua auctoritate confirmat et continuata moderatione custodit.*[61] The affirmations of many popes, such as Siricius, who introduced the decretal style of the official Roman documents, in 385, Innocent I in 417, Zosimus in 418, Boniface I in 422, or Gelasius I in 494, show that the primacy in doctrinal questions was taught by the Roman bishops as a doctrine of the faith, and that it was accepted by the other churches.[62]

The *Decretum Gelasianum* contains documents that go back to the time of Pope Damasus I. The Roman Synod of 382 formulates the unease about the political justification of the ascent of Constantinople (and the relativizing of the Roman primacy) by pointing to the origin of the ascent in the position and the power of the imperial capital.

This declaration is of decisive importance for understanding the dogmatic significance of the primacy over all the churches in the world. Damasus I underlines the Petrine-apostolic qualification and authority of the Roman church. In addition to the sacred scriptures, the authority of the councils, and the earlier papal decisions in doctrinal matters, it is necessary to underline one other factor, on which the Catholic Church is built up through the grace of God:

> Although the one bridal chamber of Christ belongs to the entire Catholic Church that is spread throughout the world, the holy Roman Church does not take precedence over the other Churches because of decisions by any council. It has received the primacy on the basis of the words of the Lord and Redeemer in the Gospel, for he said: "You are Peter, and on this rock I will build my Church." In addition, there is the fellowship with the most blessed Paul.[63]

Unity with the Apostolic See and with the Roman church is decisive for the unity of the Catholic Church in the faith. This emerged very clearly in the settling of the Acacian Schism (484–519), the first schism between "East" and "West." Christ built his Church on the rock when he said to the reigning bishop of Rome, at his installation in office, *Tu es Petrus.* This means that one belongs to the one, holy, catholic, and apostolic Church in the full and true sense of the term only if one submits to the highest doctrinal authority

61 Gelasius I, *Ep.* 26: "The first see confirms every single synod with its own authority and guards it with continued guidance."

62 DH 181–82; DH 217–18; DH 221; DH 233–35; DH 347.

63 DH 350.

of that Church. Acacius liked to appeal to canon 28 of the Council of Chalcedon, with the privileges it formulated for his diocese, but he distanced himself from the Christological confession of that council. This is a good example of how one can appeal to a council in a secondary question about the extent of one's own jurisdiction, while relativizing its central statement of the faith in the mystery of Christ. On the basis of the Henotikon (482), an edict of the Eastern Roman Emperor Zeno (r. 474–491), Acacius attempted a compromise with the pre-Chalcedonian Churches and the Monophysite opponents of the council, proposing a formula that contradicted the true Catholic faith in the unity of the divine and human natures of Christ in the person of the divine Logos. This led to the separation of Constantinople from the Apostolic See. This was a foretaste of the growing alienation, and ultimately of the loss of the full fellowship of the Eastern Churches under Constantinople with the Roman and Catholic Church—first in the dispute with Patriarch Photius (ca. 810/20–898) and then definitively under Patriarch Michael Cerularius (ca. 1005–1059). In retrospect, however, the year 1054 is more of a symbolic date than a date in real history; one cannot speak of a definitive loss of ecclesial communion before the thirteenth century, since despite all the conflicts, there remained an overarching consciousness of belonging in faith to the one, catholic, apostolic and hence orthodox Church.

The schism was overcome and the Roman doctrinal primacy was universally acknowledged as a truth of the faith through the signing of the *Libellus fidei* (519) that Pope Hormisdas (r. 514–523) had sent to Emperor Justin I (r. 518–527) and Patriarch John II in Constantinople. Number 1 of the *Formula Hormisdae*, which they were requested to sign, and which was later proposed anew by Emperor Justinian I (r. 527–565), by Patriarch Menas, and by the Fourth Council of Constantinople (869–70), runs as follows:

> Salvation begins with paying heed to the rule of the right faith and not in any way deviating from the decisions of the fathers. And since once cannot ignore the saying of our Lord Jesus Christ, who declared: "You are Peter, and on this rock I will build my Church," that which was said is proved to be true by its genuine effects, since the Catholic religion has always been preserved unstained [*immaculata*] at the Apostolic See.[64]

Number 4 then states:

> This is why we accept and approve of all the letters of the blessed Pope Leo that he wrote about the Christian religion. As we have said above, we follow in all things the Apostolic See and proclaim all its decisions; and

64 DH 363.

> therefore I hope that I may deserve to be in the one fellowship with you that the Apostolic See proclaims, the fellowship in which is the intact and true and perfect stability of the Christian religion. I also promise that in future, the names of those who are separated from fellowship with the Catholic Church, that is, those who are not in agreement with the Apostolic See, will not be read aloud during the sacred mysteries [the liturgy].[65]

Number 5 of the *Formula Hormisdae* then affirms: "I have signed this confession of faith with my own hand and have given it to you, Hormisdas, the holy and venerable Pope of the city of Rome."[66] The letter *Inter ea quae* of Pope Hormisdas to the bishops of Spain in 517 uses almost identical language.

9. THE DOGMATIC CONTRIBUTION OF THE UNDIVIDED CHRISTIANITY TO THE DOCTRINE OF PRIMACY

The development of the doctrine of the faith in the early Church with regard to the Church and the Roman primacy can be summed up as the universal recognition of the doctrinal primacy of the Roman bishop as the successor of Peter. Like Peter, the Roman pope is the rock and fundament of the unity of the Church in the truth of the faith, and of the fellowship of all the churches in the Catholic and apostolic faith. Metropolitan Sergius of Cyprus wrote to Pope Theodore I (r. 642–649): "Christ our God has appointed your Apostolic See, O sacred head, to be the immovable foundation and pillar of the faith. For as the divine word truly says, you are Peter and on you, as the foundation stone, the pillars of the Church are made firm."[67]

The subsequent dissolution of the ecclesial communion of the Churches of the East and those churches that remained united to the pope (a separation that never became complete) was sparked by the question of the understanding and the praxis of the Roman primacy of jurisdiction. The unclarity in the understanding of what precisely "jurisdiction" means also played a role here. It is only once the basic concept has been clarified that one can go on to ask what it ultimately is, on the level of the universal Church, that holds together the jurisdiction of the individual bishop over the local church

65 DH 365.

66 DH 365.

67 Sergius of Cyprus, *Ep. ad Theodorem,* ACO (ser. 2) 1, 60–65, quoted in Josef Hergenröther, *Anti-Janus: Eine historisch-theologische Kritik der Schrift "Der Papst und das Konzil" von Janus* (Freiburg: Herder, 1870), 41.

and the jurisdiction of the councils over the universal Church, as well as the jurisdictions of the synodal associations, ecclesiastical provinces, and patriarchates that have come into existence in the course of history. Catholic theology has never understood the primacy of jurisdiction as replacing the jurisdiction by divine right of the bishops of the local churches, but rather as holding them together: this is a service rendered by the pope in the authority that the Lord of the Church gave to Peter, in order to preserve the fellowship of all the churches in the universal Church. A theological evaluation of the historical sources from various epochs and historical constellations must pay more attention to the precise substance than to the fluctuating terminology. When, for example, Ambrose of Milan ascribes to Rome a primacy in the confession and the faith, but not a primacy of honor and in organization,[68] he is rightly professing the truth of the Catholic faith that the papal jurisdiction never absorbs the episcopal jurisdiction or the share in jurisdictional responsibility that the episcopate as a whole exercises for the universal Church. It was the task of a later development to formulate the precise meaning of the papal primacy of jurisdiction over the universal Church in the service of the unity in faith.

Ambrose wrote to Emperor Gratian in support of Pope Damasus: "Do not permit the head of the entire Roman world, the Roman Church, and the most holy apostolic faith to be confused; for it is from there that the rights of the venerable ecclesial fellowship pass over to all the Churches."[69] Saint Ambrose attests the Catholic faith in the unity of the universal Church with the pope as the rock of unity in Peter: "It is Peter to whom Christ has said: 'You are Peter and upon this rock I will build my Church.' Where therefore Peter is, there is the Church; where the Church is, there is not death, but eternal life."[70] *Ubi Petrus—ibi Ecclesia. Ubi Ecclesia—ibi vita non mors.*

To be in fellowship with the Catholic bishops means to be in fellowship with the Roman church.[71] Naturally, the authority of the Roman church is based in the apostolic confession of faith, which it preserves; its authority is not based on the need to establish among human beings a unity of a secular, sociological kind.[72] The Ambrosiaster calls the Roman pope the *rector domus Dei,* the leader of the house of the living God.[73] Archbishop Eugenius of Carthage, the primate of the North African church which was hard pressed under the Vandal rule, speaks of the assurance of the common Catholic

68 See Ambrose, *De incarnatione dominicae sacramento,* 4.32.

69 Ambrose, *Epistulae,* 11.4.

70 Ambrose, *Expositio Super Psalmos XII,* 40.30.

71 Ambrose, *De excessu fratris sui Satyri libri duo,* I.47.

faith of the bishops when they look to "the Roman Church, the head of all the Churches."[74]

Jerome (347–420), who sees the pope as the most important guardian of the truth of the faith and as the guarantor against the invasion of heresy, describes the relationship of the pope to the bishops as analogous to the relationship of Simon Peter to the apostles: "The Church is founded on Peter; in another passage, the same is done for the apostles [Mt 18:18]. All receive the keys of the kingdom of heaven, and the Church is firmly founded on all of them. But among the twelve, one single man is chosen, in order that a head may be established and every occasion of division may be excluded."[75]

It is probably Leo the Great who offers the most concentrated overview of the essential elements of the Petrine primacy. His decisive contribution to Chalcedon's confession of Christ against Nestorianism and Monophysitism displays the inherent connection between Peter's confession of Christ and the appointment of Peter to be the guarantor of the Church's fundament in Christ.

The Catholic Church is the unity of all the individual churches under their bishops in the fellowship of the doctrine of the faith, in the sacred mysteries, in the sacraments, and in the hierarchy. Every local church is led by one single bishop with the college of presbyters and the deacons who assist him. The total episcopate represents the universal Church. This *Catholica* has its unity in the Roman church. Although some may insist on their autonomy, especially the churches in the sphere of Byzantine influence, the fact remains that the unity and fellowship of all the churches in the one and only Catholic Church can exist only in fellowship with the Roman pope, and never without him—still less, against him. This is the consensus of all the church fathers and ecclesiastical authors, of the councils and synods. And this was expressed in the consciousness of the primacy and in the primatial action of the important popes of the fourth and fifth centuries.

It is, of course, not yet possible to speak of a theology of the primacy in the sense of a thoroughly reflected theory formation.

Above all, it is not a question of establishing a thesis by presenting academic evidence from scripture and tradition. Theology in the systematic and academic sense has existed since the twelfth century, when an academic theology came into being. The real reason for the primacy lies in the promise of the primacy to Simon Peter and in the continued transmission of his authority and mission to those who sit on his *cathedra* in the Roman church.

72 Ambrose, *De Trinitate*, 7.

73 Ambrosiaster, *Commentaria in Epistolas Pauili*, 314.

74 Victor of Vita, *Historia Persecutionis Africae Provinciae*, II.43.

75 Jerome, *Adv. Iovin.* I.26.

For reality is not the representation of an academic theory. The theory is merely the speculative grasping of the reality—in this case, the reality of the institution of the Church that has, through Christ, its being and its life as the ecclesial body of Christ. The Church mediates sacramentally the internal fellowship of grace with Christ, but at the same time it is a visible fellowship and is thus a social body that must necessarily be seen as a worldwide, hierarchically structured fellowship in faith and the sacraments:

> No failure was possible for a mystery that the one and triune Godhead himself had undertaken to carry out. And yet, in the whole world only Peter was chosen to be the head of all the peoples that would be called, head of all the apostles and of all the fathers of the Church. Therefore, although there are many priests and many shepherds among the people of God, Peter is in the true sense of the word the leader of all those over whom Christ too is the primary ruler.[76]

The Petrine function of being the rock and fundament of the Church is not derived from the idea of the Church as a spiritual, social body, since that would entail that, just as its secular pendent, the Roman Empire, had one single head—namely, the emperor—so too, the Church would have to have one single head—namely, the pope. One cannot take a theologoumenon and infer from it the existence of an essential element in the Church's constitution (in this case, the pope as the fundament of its unity in faith). Nor did the popes deduce the primacy from the exegesis of passages in scripture. Rather, they saw it as authorized by the real transmission of the Petrine-apostolic authority to the Roman church and to its episcopal head. At a secondary stage, they then understood, in the light of the biblically attested words of the institution by Jesus, the task they had to undertake in his name for the universal Church.

The papacy in Rome is instituted by Christ. It is not the product of a human will to dominate other people; still less is it the work of the devil, as Luther asserted in the most polemical of his treatises (1545). Naturally, the devil can also sow weeds among the wheat. But the wheat comes from the good sower and the weeds from the evil foe (see Mt 13:24–30). This is the reply to the objection that the first pope to appeal to the Matthean passage about the primacy was Stephen I in the mid-third century. Peter's primacy is not theoretically *constructed* on the basis of the exegesis of the Gospel of Matthew; it is *attested* in Matthew as an ecclesial institution of divine right. The Petrine authority came to Rome with Peter; its origin is not in an exegesis

76 Leo I, *Serm.* 4.2.

of the books of the Bible that aimed to justify a worldly claim to rule over the Church. The theological reflection on the Roman primacy is based on the fact that it is revealed in the words of Jesus. This is why Leo I can write: "Through Peter, the blessed prince of the apostles, the sacred Roman Church has the principate over all the Churches of the entire world."[77]

When we read the five sermons that Leo the Great gave on the anniversary of his episcopal ordination, and thereby of his elevation to the chair of Peter, we see with particular clarity the foundation of faith on which the papacy stands, and the spiritual fellowship with Christ that alone permits a pontificate to be a blessing for the Church. The papacy owes its existence to the Redeemer's will for his Church. It is not the accumulation of worldly aspirations to rule, such as we find in the realm of an emperor or prince.

Peter speaks every day through the mouth of the entire Church: "You are the Christ, the Son of the living God." And that is why Jesus says to each one who sits on Peter's chair with responsibility for the salvation of all the sheep of Christ's flock: "You are Peter, the rock," the fundament, the doorkeeper of the kingdom of heaven, the one who uses the keys of the kingdom of heaven, the brother who strengthens the brethren in faith:

> We enjoy the perpetual favor of the almighty and eternal high priest who is like us and is equal with the Father, who lowered the divinity to the humanity and elevated the humanity to the divinity. Although he entrusted to the many shepherds the care of his sheep, this did not mean that he himself ceased to watch over his beloved flock. He who perennially gives us his especial assistance also bestowed on us in blessed Peter a helpful support that, of course, will never be lacking to his work. The solidity of this fundament on which the vast building of Church is constructed remains unshakable, no matter how heavy the burden of the temple that rests on it may be. What Peter believed about Christ remains for all times. In the same way, what Christ instituted in Peter remains forever.[78]

This is why every priest ought to celebrate the anniversary of his ordination, in order to be reminded of the dignity that he has received and to be able to bear the burden that lies on his shoulders: "Therefore, my beloved, one celebrates today's feast in true submissiveness when one sees and honors in my lowly person that one [namely, Peter] who unites in himself forever the cares of all the shepherds who have the charge of the sheep that are

77 Leo I, *Ep.* 65.2.

78 Leo I, *Serm.* 3.2.

entrusted to him, and who loses none of his dignity even when a successor is unworthy."[79]

Despite all his emphasis on the unique position of the pope in the universal Church, Leo I does not shift the constitution of the Church in the direction of a papal (political) monarchy. We find in his words nothing of the caricature of the papacy as a kind of spiritual absolutism at the cost of the authority and mission of the bishops. Instead of speaking of a "monarchical" escalation of the Church's governance, one ought to see here the idea of a universal episcopate. One should avoid speaking about a monarchical episcopate or papacy, because it suggests that one could impose upon the spiritual essence of the Church an arbitrary political ordering, in keeping with the circumstances and needs of the time. But the Church is not a monarchy, an aristocracy, or a democracy in the political sense; nor is it the opposite of any of these. The Church is a societal body that has a sacramental constitution: "Now you are the body of Christ, and individually members of it. And God has appointed in the church first apostles, second prophets, third teachers [...]. Are all apostles? Are all prophets?" (1 Cor 12:27–31). A body does not have changing political constitutional models; it has an organic form. The ecclesiastical offices are not concentrations of power. They represent Christ as shepherd, teacher, and priest.

The pope does not belong to a different category than the bishops. In the midst of his brothers, he represents the unity of the episcopate and of the entire Catholic Church under Christ, who is its only shepherd in the true sense of the term. The bishops share in the pastoral care of the entire Church, but they do not possess fully the Petrine authority over the entire Church. Unlike the pope, they do not have the *plenitudo potestatis*.[80] The pope was never a *primus inter pares* in relation to his fellow bishops, nor can he become a monarch who is flanked by subordinate administrators, in the sense that the episcopal authority to sanctify the Church would be bestowed on them by the pope, not by Christ. The episcopal office remains of divine right. The pope was made the "head of the entire Church"[81] in order to guide the Church through Peter and thereby, like Peter, to fulfill Jesus's charge to "strengthen the brethren in the faith in Jesus, the Messiah" (Lk 22:32).

Leo the Great is thus a witness to the Catholic doctrine of the collegiality of the exercise of the episcopal ministry. But Peter, the rock on whom the Lord built his Church, is the principle and the fundament of the unity of the college, especially when it bears the supreme responsibility for the entire

79 Leo I, *Serm.* 3.2.

80 Leo I, *Ep.* 14.1.

81 Leo I, *Serm.* 4.4.

Church in an ecumenical council. The power of the keys was delivered to Peter alone. He does not exercise it in dependence on anyone else, even when he exercises the power to bind and loose together with the other apostles.[82]

Thanks to the exclusive bestowal on Peter of the power of the keys, the Church is one in its origin and is one single mother. The primacy of Peter passed to the Roman church, which is therefore the *locus Petri* and *cathedra Petri*.[83] This allows Saint Augustine to observe: *Ideo unus pro omnibus, quia unitas est in omnibus*.[84] Jerome put it as follows: "Among the twelve, one single man is chosen, in order that a head may be established and every occasion of division may be excluded."[85] The Roman primacy is a functional cause and a visible criterion of the unity of the bishops and of the entire Church: "For the heretics do not have the keys that Peter alone received."[86] "For the salvation of the Church rests on the dignity of the highest priest; accordingly, if he is not given a wholly eminent authority that exceeds everyone else, we will experience in the Church the same number of divisions as there are priests."[87] This is why the Roman bishop is called *Vicarius Petri* and *Vicarius Christi*.[88] And the pope is called "Peter, who has spoken through Leo" or Peter, who has spoken through Pope Agatho.[89]

This is why Pope Gelasius makes fun of the archbishop of Constantinople, who wanted to equate his own position with that of the successor of Peter in Rome by referring to the imperial rank of his diocese.[90] The same Gelasius I writes: "Although the Church that is spread throughout the whole world is the one and only bridal chamber of the Lord, the Roman Church is placed above the other Churches not through synodal decisions, but because it has received the primacy through the words of our Lord and Savior in the Gospel."[91] For "that which the holy apostle Peter received from the Lord, he has handed over to his successors."[92] Later, Pope Nicholas I writes in 867 in his eighth letter to Emperor Michael: "The privileges of this Holy See, which were planted by God and have taken firm root, cannot be lost. They can be

82 See Optatus of Milevis, *C. Parmen.* 7.3; Leo I, *Ep.* 10; Chrysostom, *Homiliae in Matthaeum*, 54.2; Augustine, *Sermo* 295

83 Cyprian of Carthage, *Ep.* 75.17; 70.3; 66.8; 59.5.

84 Augustine, *Tract. in ev. Ioh.* 118.4.

85 Jerome, *Adv. Iovin.* I.26.

86 Optatus of Milevis, *C. Parmen.* 1.19.

87 Jerome, *Altercatio Luciferani et Orthodoxi Epistulae*, 9.

88 Gelasius I, *Ep.* 30.

89 Council of Chalcedon, *Acta*, 2; Second Council of Constantinople, *Acta*, 18.

90 Gelasius I, *Ep.* 26.10.

assailed, but they cannot be taken away. They can be stolen, but they are not extirpated."[93]

In a sermon on the Feast of Saint Peter, Leo the Great speaks of the handing over of the power of the keys to Peter alone, and of the power to bind and loose that is given to Peter (Mt 16:18), and in which the other apostles have their share:

> The other apostles too were, of course, given the right to make use of this power. But it is not without reason that that in which all were to have a share is entrusted to one man. It was precisely because the person of Peter is superior to all the leaders of the Church that the authority is given to him separately. This prerogative of Peter applies also to his successors, as often as they are filled with his sense of justice and pronounce a judgment.[94]

At the end of the patristic age stands the outstanding figure of Gregory the Great (r. 590–604). In the midst of political collapse and cultural degeneration, the papacy experienced in Gregory a high point of its world-historical mission. He was the great promoter of the mission to the Anglo-Saxons. The Arians in the West Gothic kingdom converted to the Catholic faith, as did the Lombards, thanks to the Catholic Queen Theodelinda (r. 589–626). The Catholic baptism of the Franks was an event of world-historical significance. He played an important role in liturgical reform and church music, and his extensive charitable activity during terrible natural catastrophes had an exemplary character. His *Pastoral Rule* set standards for all who are engaged in pastoral work. He exercised his office with an exemplary humility that is itself a lesson about the meaning of the papacy. He opposed the claims made by Patriarch John IV (the Faster) of Constantinople (r. 582–595), who was the first to insist on the extremely ambitious and arrogant title of "ecumenical bishop," thereby doing harm to the brotherly relations among the bishops and to the unity of the members of the one body.[95] He resisted the all-too-human temptation to go one step further than John and call himself "universal pope." Instead, he summed up the true spirit of the papacy by calling himself *servus servorum Dei* ("servant of the servants of God").[96] He is the first in serving, just as Christ came to serve, not to be served (Mk 10:45). The *princeps apostolorum* is the *primus servus ecclesiae*. The truth of

91 Gelasius I, *Ep.* 42.

92 Xystus I, *Ad Ioannem Antiochiae*.

93 Nicholas I, *Epistulae*, 8.

94 Leo I, *Serm.* 83.2.

95 Gregory I, *Ep.* 5.19.

the faith, that Christ entrusted to Peter the care for the entire Church and the principate (primacy), accords with this principle.[97] The Roman bishop is thus the head of the faith—that is, of the fellowship of believers.[98] And this is why the Roman see also has the duty to communicate to the universal Church its decisions in questions of faith and canon law.[99] The spirituality of the papacy is seen not in the demonstrations of power of worldly potentates but in the faithful testimony to the King on the throne of the Cross. This is the self-understanding of the one who ascends the *cathedra Petri* as the father of Christians and shepherd of all the faithful.

Pope Gregory I, one of the four great western doctors of the Church, was a man of profound humility, the great model for a pope who wants to be a pastor in a missionary Church.

Leo the Great and Gregory the Great represent in the early centuries of the Church the ideal embodiment of the primacy of the holy Roman church in the care for all the churches.

With Leo I, the theology of the Roman primacy reached a high point. His definition of the relationship between primacy and synodality is ideal, as one can observe when looking back on the collaboration of the pope with the Council of Chalcedon.

With his immense missionary energy and his humility as servant of the servants of God, Pope Gregory I personifies what one could call the spiritual internalization of the papacy. The papacy is a service of the Catholic truth against heresy, and a service of the Catholic unity of the Church against every tendency to division that reduces the credibility of the Church.

10.
TENSIONS BETWEEN EAST AND WEST IN THE CATHOLIC CHURCH

The transition from the early period of the Church to the Christian Middle Ages is accompanied by the increasing alienation between the Western and Eastern Catholic Churches. Such a distinction makes sense, historically speaking, only from the perspective of the old Roman Empire, since the Catholic Church is universal in all peoples and is not in the least

96 Gregory I, *Ep.* 1. 1.

97 Gregory I, *Ep.* 5.20.

98 Gregory I, *Ep.* 13.47.

99 Gregory I, *Ep.* 3.57.

tied anachronistically to the old empire that was divided by Emperor Theodosius in 395 into a western and an eastern half. And when we speak of the schism that occurred between those Catholic churches that accept the primacy of the pope in the totality of its dogmatic elaboration and those Catholic churches that dispute this totality, it is false to speak of a schism that was virtually inevitable, since there existed a doctrine of the primacy and a praxis of the Apostolic See of the Church of Saint Peter, and this doctrine and praxis were accepted as belonging to the substance of the faith of the Church of Christ. This provided a sufficient basis for a profound reconciliation and for a healing of the historical wounds.

This is the meaning of the affirmation by Cardinal Joseph Ratzinger, at that time Prefect of the Congregation for the Doctrine of the Faith, that the churches of the Eastern Orthodox patriarchates need not accept more of the doctrine of the primacy (but also not less) than was common to all the Catholic churches in the first millennium. This affirmation rejects the historically and theologically unjustifiable opinion that the primacy of Rome was never known and acknowledged in the East. There was no point in time in the first millennium when the Catholic Church lacked the primacy of the church of Saint Peter in Rome and his primacy in the teaching and the eucharistic fellowship of the Church.

What we can learn from the Church of the patristic age is the insight that there are different forms of its exercise, while preserving the substance. This does not mean a historicizing step backwards into an alleged golden age in the first centuries. In the history of dogma, the Roman primacy, both in its theological understanding and in the drama of its part in the history of the Church and of the world, shares in the unfolding of the entire doctrine of the faith in the ecclesial consciousness.

The principal reason for the alienation and the final separation of the Catholic church in the Byzantine sphere of influence from those churches that were in full unity with the Apostolic See was ultimately not ecclesiological but lay in the religious politics of the Roman and Byzantine empires. Later rulers in both East and West imitated this caesaropapism, albeit on a smaller, national scale, inflicting great damage on the credibility of the Church and on its universal mission.

After the destruction of the Gothic kingdom in Italy and the Vandal kingdom in North Africa in the sixth century, the reestablishing of the Roman-Byzantine rule for almost three centuries also promoted the ecclesial fellowship between Rome and the Catholic churches in the realms of the East Roman emperor; but the two halves of the empire never grew together again, either spiritually or intellectually. The Gothic wars in Italy kindled long-lasting resentments against the Byzantines, who replied with aversion vis-à-vis the Latins. It is highly regrettable that such human limitations and weaknesses could not be overcome through the faith and the love in the one Church of Christ, and that they block the realization of the full communion in faith, in the sacraments, and in the apostolic governance of the Church down to the present day. The Church in the East was profoundly shaken by the Monophysite and Monothelite turbulences and by the unfortunate attempts by the emperors and some of the patriarchs of Constantinople to overcome these confusions with political force. Whole regions were alienated from the imperial church. Some (like Egypt) became Monophysite, others Nestorian. The phenomenon of the pre-Chalcedonian churches came into existence. The iconoclast strife deeply disturbed the Byzantine Empire and the Church in the East and deepened the alienation from the emerging Western Christianity (Synod of Frankfurt, 794; the *Libri Carolini*).

The Arabic storm brought the Islamization of other historical regions of Christendom. The ascent of the Ottoman Turks later sealed the fate of the last remnants of the East Roman Empire with the conquest of Constantinople in 1453. This confirmed the alienation; and above all, it put an end to the lively exchanges and thus to the common growth of the one Catholic Church in East and West.

It was only through the alliance of the papacy with the emergent Frankish kingdom that Western Christendom slowly came into being under the spiritual leadership of the pope and began to flourish.

There is a tension between the comprehensive claims to jurisdiction by the imperial patriarch in Constantinople, which were justified by an appeal to the political position of New Rome, and the spiritual leadership of the entire Church by the Apostolic See of Saint Peter in Rome.

The East-West "schism" has basically political, not theological, reasons. The attempts to supply a theological justification in the reciprocal accusations of the "errors of the Latins" (Photius) and the "haughtiness of the Greeks" against the rites of the Latins (the Fourth Lateran Council) are obviously not the causes but reasons put forward at a later date (the use of leavened or unleavened bread, the doctrine of purgatory, different customs with regard to fasting, the *Filioque*, the formative element of the consecration in the words of institution or the epiclesis, priestly celibacy, and so on).

In the patristic age, the theology of the Roman primacy was accepted in the Eastern Catholic churches. This acceptance later weakened as it became overlaid with the idea of the unity of the imperial church under the supreme leadership of the pope. The Christianized kingdoms of the West under the emperor of the Holy Roman Empire were identified with the Church under the spiritual leadership of the pope. Christendom, the *corpus christianum*, was almost equated with the Church of Christ. This led to the conflict about whether the pope or the emperor was the supreme head of the Christian empire—that is to say, of Western Christendom—and this was linked to a reinterpretation or expansion of the papal jurisdictional primacy as a universal papal monarchy from roughly the time of Gregory VII onwards. This could not be accepted by the churches with an Eastern tradition; nor could Rome in fact demand it of them. And this in turn went hand in hand with a praxis of the central government of the universal Church where canon law and church politics predominated. However, these are not the content of the dogma of the Roman primacy, nor are they the only binding model of its exercise.

There is a strong tension between the centralization and juridification of the Church on the model of the imperial governance of the empire, on the one hand, and the ecclesiology of the *communio ecclesiarum* in which the Roman church has the primacy in the task of preserving the unity in faith and in the *koinônia*, on the other hand. The jurisdictional primacy, which is implied in the doctrinal primacy, does *not* mean that the pope exercises the ordinary and immediate episcopal jurisdiction, nor that he replaces all the jurisdictions by metropolitans and patriarchs. It means the authority given by Christ to the pope in Saint Peter to preserve the unity of the universal Church in the faith and to prevent the churches from ending in schism. A faulty development in the East meant that the priest-emperor (on the model of the priest-king Melchizedek) was even permitted to intervene in dogma. Likewise, the theory that the Roman primacy was first transferred to Constantinople as New Rome and then, after the union of the churches at Florence (which was suspected of heresy) and the end of Constantinople as a Christian city, was transferred further to Moscow as the third Rome, is conceived in political terms and lacks any dogmatic basis. This sixteenth-century theologoumenon was elaborated by the starets Philotheus in letters to Ivan IV the Terrible and to other correspondents. It provided the tsars, as heirs to the Byzantine emperors, with a state theory of "holy Russia," and was still employed, paradoxically enough, by the atheistic Soviet Union. The original intention of this theory was not so much to justify the Russian Orthodox state-church system as to identify in apocalyptic terms Orthodox Christianity in Russia as the holy remnant ("… there will be no fourth Rome"); it lacks any basis in ecclesiology.

The Petrine primacy is bound to the church of Saint Peter because, as Irenaeus of Lyons said at an early date, it has in Peter and Paul the apostolic fundament *principaliter.* This is the source of its primacy and principate. This also includes the infallibility of the Roman church and of its bishop when he proclaims the Catholic truth *ex cathedra* and as the visible head of the entire Church (not when he is expressing his own private opinion). The case of Pope Honorius is no argument against this. Even if individual popes have made unclear statements and performed questionable acts, this does not shake the Petrine and Pauline fundament of the church of Rome, nor does it make the primacy transferrable. It was only Simon whom Jesus made the rock on which the Lord builds his Church, and it is only to the bishop of Rome, as the successor of Peter, that Jesus says, when he elevates him to the *thronos Petrou*: *Tu es Petrus et super hanc petram aedificabo ecclesiam meam.*

11. RAPPROCHEMENTS BETWEEN EAST AND WEST IN THE QUESTION OF THE PRIMACY

THE UNITY THAT JESUS WILLED can grow only if we strip away the superimpositions of religious politics on the real idea of the *communio ecclesiarum* under the leadership of Saint Peter and go back to the essential elements of the Roman primacy—that is, the Catholic truth and the unity of all the bishops and faithful in the one, holy, catholic, and apostolic Church.

In the context of the schismatic confusions surrounding the Constantinopolitan Patriarchs Ignatius and Photius, Pope Nicholas I (r. 858–867) emphasizes both the freedom of the Church vis-à-vis the meddling of the emperor in dogmatic questions and the fundament of the Roman primacy in the will of Christ. In the letter *Proposueramus quidem* to Emperor Michael (865), the pope writes that:

> The prerogatives of the Roman Church, confirmed through the mouth of Christ in blessed Peter, were mandated in the Church itself, were observed from ancient times, were praised by the sacred general Councils, and continuously venerated by the entire Church. They cannot in any way be diminished, cannot in any way be restricted, cannot in any way be altered; for the foundation laid by God cannot be removed by any human activity, and what God has set up stands strong and firm [...]. The prerogatives that Christ bestowed on this holy Church were not bestowed by the Councils. All the Councils did was to acclaim them at once and to venerate them [...]; these prerogatives compel Us to have "care for all the Churches" of God.[100]

The basis of the primacy of the church of Saint Peter in Rome thus lies in the will of Christ and in the appointment of the Roman bishop as universal shepherd. But the goal of all the Roman shepherds and of all their activity is

100 DH 640.

not a quasi-imperial domination of secular matters but the concern for the eternal salvation of human beings. They also have the task in this world of proclaiming and defending the dignity of the human being as God's image and likeness.

Even at the zenith of the papal (not the imperial) universal monarchy, in the hour of triumph of the Gregorian movement, Pope Innocent III (r. 1198–1216) justified the primacy in letters to Catholicos Gregory of the Armenians and to King Leon, as well as in the letter *Apostolicae Sedis primatus* to the Patriarch of Constantinople (1199), in purely Christological terms, by appealing to Jesus's words of promise and institution. The primacy of the Apostolic See is instituted by the God-Man Christ, not by any human being. This is confirmed by the Gospels and the writings of the apostles, which are the origin of the regulations of canon law, so that the *ius mere ecclesiasticum* is based on the *ius divinum*. It is thus the unanimous testimony of the entire apostolic and ecclesiastical tradition:

> That the most holy Church that is consecrated in the blessed prince of the apostles, Peter, is superior to the other Churches as teacher and mother. He deserved to hear the words: "You are Peter [...] I will give you the keys of the kingdom of heaven." [...] For although the first and outstanding fundament of the Church is Jesus Christ, the only-begotten Son of God, [...] the second and secondary fundament of the Church is Peter. He is not the first in the temporal order, but in his authority he has the preeminent position among the others.[101]

"Cephas" and "Peter" are translated literally as "rock," and this must be understood to mean "head," since the head represents the unity of the body—that is, of the entire Church in its many members that are the local churches:

> So that, as the head has the precedence among the other members of the bodies, since the fullness of the senses lives in the head, so too Peter is preeminent among the apostles, and his successors are preeminent among all those who preside over the Churches, because of their precedence in dignity. At the same time, the others are called to share in [Peter's] care [for all the Churches] in such a way that they lose nothing of the fullness of their authority.[102]

101 DH 774.

102 DH 774.

It was only to Peter that the Lord three times gave the charge to pasture his flock, and thus the entire Church of Christ; but this is done in such a way that in the universal Church, which exists in and out of the local churches, the bishops are true shepherds in their dioceses in the name and in the authority of Christ. They exercise their authority of ordination and jurisdiction not in the name and the authority of the pope but in fellowship with the one who is the principle of the visible unity of the Church in faith and in the fellowship of all the churches.

The Fourth Lateran Council explicitly confirms the ancient prerogatives of the patriarchates and their established ranking. After Rome comes Constantinople, as Canon 28 of the Council of Chalcedon wished, and then Alexandria, Antioch, and Jerusalem. But the Roman church has not only the patriarchal dignity but also "as the mother and teacher of all the faithful, by the decree of the Lord, the precedence (*principatum*) of ordinary authority over all the others."[103]

The attempts to reestablish full communion with the churches of the Eastern patriarchates were made difficult by diverging developments in ecclesiology and by adverse political circumstances. The very existence of Byzantium was threatened by the expansion of Islam from Arabia and by the emerging Ottoman Empire, but despite some sincere endeavors, it never found a support in the West that would have staved off disaster. The great error was to make military aid dependent on an acceptance of the exercise of the primacy, which was overlaid even in its core by a narrowly juridical ecclesiology. In the East, this could be viewed as blackmail. It seemed that in their threatening situation they were being forced to make a submission in terms of power politics; it did not look like a reconciliation of the differing traditions aiming at the synodal collaboration of all the bishops with the apostolic-Petrine authority of the Roman Church.

Nevertheless, the important documents of the attempts to renew the *communio* of all the Catholic churches under the recognition of the Roman primacy were formulated theologically, rather than politically. The confession of faith of Emperor Michael Palaeologus at the Second Council of Lyons (1274), which was also reiterated by Patriarch John XI Beccus of Constantinople and the members of his synod in 1277 and was presented by the popes to the Greeks who entered into church union, is very moderate and concentrates on theological questions (much more so than the *Dictatus papae* of Gregory VII). The affirmations about the primacy come at the close, after the shared confession of the central mysteries of the Christian faith, because it is not a matter of substantial principles here but of the formal principle

103 DH 811.

of unity. The basis of the Catholic Church is the Trinitarian-Christological dogma that was formulated in the universally accepted councils of the early centuries; "Catholic" and "Orthodox" faith are synonymous. This is why even today, one cannot regard the Catholic Church with the pope and the other patriarchates of the East, which do not acknowledge the primacy in one particular sense, as separate confessional churches. The difference that makes full communion not yet possible consists solely in the principle of the unity of the total episcopate of the one, catholic, orthodox, apostolic Church.

The affirmation that the unity of the total episcopate lies not in the decision of the pope but in the complete consensus of all the bishops fails to convince because this is a false antithesis. Both the moral unanimity and the definitive conclusion of the decision in a question of the faith through the approval of the successor of Saint Peter are constitutive elements of the Catholic magisterium. The Roman primacy is mentioned *after* the clarification of controversial questions that concern the theological explication rather than the substance of the shared faith (the *Filioque*, the doctrine of purgatory, the permission to enter a second marriage after the death of one's first partner).

The Roman church has received the primacy or principate over the entire Catholic Church with the plenitude of authority "from the Lord himself in blessed Peter, the *princeps et vertex apostolorum,* whose successor is the bishop of Rome."[104]

What is this power that is spiritual, not secular? And why was it bestowed? Its purpose is to defend the truth of the faith and to take a definitive decision in questions of the faith. It is also possible to appeal to the Apostolic See in legal questions. In this sense, all those who preside over the churches are subject to the Roman church, but in such a way that they share in its care for the universal Church. The bishop is thus not a teacher and shepherd in the name of Christ for his local church alone. Through the unity of the episcopate, which has its summit in the successor of Peter, all the bishops share, especially in particular and ecumenical synods, in the magisterial and jurisdictional responsibility for the universal Church.

The Latin-Greek union at the Council of Florence (1439, doubtless an ecumenical council) has an outstanding place among the many attempts to achieve union with the Greeks, the Armenians, and the Jacobites (Copts and Ethiopians). The East was represented by the Byzantine emperor and the Eastern patriarchs, either in person or through legates. Ultimately, the propaganda by Mark Eugenikos of Ephesus (1391–1444) and Gennadius II (George) Scholarios (1405–1473), whom Sultan Mehmed the Conqueror

104 DH 861.

(1432–1481) appointed patriarch after the fall of Constantinople on May 29, 1453, and the deeply rooted aversion of the people and many of the monks to the "heretic Latins" meant that the union did not last long. Nevertheless, the declaration about the Roman primacy is a dogmatically binding definition of the Catholic faith and is relevant to salvation.

The modest—or better, the exact—theological title of the pope is interesting. The definition of the faith, in agreement with the bishops, states:

> Eugene, bishop, servant of the servants of God, for perpetual remembrance, with the agreement of the emperor, of the Patriarchs, and of the other representatives of the Eastern Church: We define that the Holy Apostolic See and the Roman bishop have the primacy over the entire earth, and that this Roman bishop is the successor of Saint Peter, the prince of the apostles, the true Vicar of Christ, head of the entire Church, and father and teacher of all Christians; that in Saint Peter, the *potestas plena* to pasture, to rule, and to administer the entire Church has been entrusted to him by our Lord Jesus Christ, as the acts of the ecumenical Councils and the sacred canons state.

The last sentence can only be explicative, not restrictive, since the councils cannot set limits to the authority that Christ gave to Peter. But when the old ranking of the patriarchs is confirmed anew, together with all the rights and privileges that have belonged to them from ancient times, this points to what will later be called episcopal collegiality. The Roman bishop belongs to the fellowship of bishops, so that he represents and realizes the principle of the unity of the episcopate. There is no fellowship of the bishops without the pope, and no pope without the fellowship of the bishops.

The Greek and Latin Bull *Laetentur caeli,* which was solemnly promulgated on July 6, 1439, was signed by all the Latin and Greek conciliar fathers, apart from Mark Eugenikos of Ephesus and Isaias Stauropolos. Sadly, this union did not last long. From today's perspective, however, the doctrinal decision can be seen as a milestone on the path to the reestablishing of the full unity of the Church. The Orthodox resistance refers to the medieval theological-political theory of the universal papal monarchy, which found its most prominent representatives in Gregory VII and Boniface VIII. This, however, is not a component of the Catholic doctrine of faith about the primacy of the pope, and this is why our contemporary discussion must concentrate exactly on the question of the faith.

A careful analysis of the dogmatic decisions shows that in binding documents of the magisterium it is only the true essence of the primacy that is defined. This is compatible with the *communio* ecclesiology of the ancient Church and with the collegiality of the bishops, and it can be reintegrated into it, as happened at the First Vatican Council, and even more strongly at Vatican II. Primacy and synodality are communicable fundamental principles, and they are certainly capable of being integrated into a unified ecclesiology. Basically, this is a disagreement within Catholicism about the precise description of the Roman primacy in relation to the totality of the episcopate.[105] The hierarchical constitution of the Church, with belief in the apostolic succession of the bishops and the sacramental mediation of salvation through the Church on the foundation of the Trinitarian-Christological dogma, is the shared framework for the faith in the one, holy, catholic, and apostolic Church. In comparison to this divergence on one single point, the Catholic-Protestant conflict is a more fundamental conflict about the understanding of salvation and of the Church, a conflict that took on an especially drastic intensity with regard to the papacy.

105 On this, see the groundbreaking work by Karl Rahner and Joseph Ratzinger, *Episkopat und Primat* (Freiburg: Herder, 1961).

V

The Dogma of the Doctrinal and Jurisdictional Primacy of the Roman Pope

1.
CHURCH AND PRIMACY IN THE SUPERNATURAL ORDER

IN THE PRESENT CHAPTER, our concern is with the dogma of the papal doctrinal and jurisdictional primacy in its belief content—not with the time leading up to the First Vatican Council (1870) and its aftermath, with the political side effects and its lasting effects on the Church (the *Kulturkampf* in Germany, the Old Catholic secession from the Church, the alleged incompatibility between the Catholic Church and the modern age), or with the serious theological reception of the two Vatican councils. What is the revealed content of faith with regard to the papacy? What must every Catholic accept, with both internal and external assent, for the sake of eternal salvation?

We can understand the essence and the mission of the Church only in the light of the supernatural revelation that is God's self-communication in truth and love. The intellectual atmosphere in the nineteenth century was characterized by a rationalistic limitation on faith, or alternatively by a fideistic and supranatural justification of faith—in other words, by an apparent antithesis between reason and faith. There was no way of getting from the Kantian critical philosophy, from Hegel's Idealism, or from materialistic monism to a real revelation of God in salvation history by means of the Incarnation.

The First Vatican Council emphasizes the ability of the reason to arrive at the certain knowledge of God as Creator of the world by means of a rational analysis of the world and of the metaphysical principles of its existence. The supernatural and historical revelation of God, which cannot be deduced from any principles, has its ground in his free decision and his infinite goodness "to give the human being an orientation to a supernatural goal, namely, to share in the divine goods that completely transcend the epistemological capacity of the human mind."[1]

It is, accordingly, a dogma of the Church and a revealed truth that must be firmly held with divine and Catholic faith that, beyond the knowledge of God with the natural light of the human reason as the origin and goal of all things, "it has pleased God in another, supernatural manner to reveal to the human race both his own self and the eternal decisions of his will."[2]

The concept of revelation at Vatican I should not in the least be dismissed as information-theoretical, in a supposed antithesis to the communication-theoretical understanding at Vatican II. In reality, *Dei Verbum* (from the latter council) takes the concept of revelation in *Dei Filius* (from the former council) to a deeper level in the light of the personalism and the dialogical philosophy that draw their categories from the biblical revelation itself: "Therefore, following in the footsteps of the Council of Trent and of the First Vatican Council, this present council wishes to set forth authentic doctrine on divine revelation and how it is handed on, so that by hearing the message of salvation the whole world may believe, by believing it may hope, and by hoping it may love" (DV 1).

The triune God has communicated to us the fellowship of the Father, the Son, and the Holy Spirit in such a way that we say "Abba, Father" to God in the Holy Spirit; we are called the children of God, and that is truly what we are. This is why Christ called the apostles and made those who believe their message his Church. He is not a founder of a religion who addresses the natural religious-ethical disposition of human beings and gives it one specific cultural form. He is the Father's Word who has become flesh and who acquires the community of salvation as his body, in order to make it alive through his word and his Spirit.

The Church does not recall Jesus as its founding figure from a remote historical period. Jesus was not a founder of a religion. With the Father and the Holy Spirit, as the consubstantial Son of God, he is the unique Creator and the only ground of being and vital principle of his Church. It is HIS body, and HE is its Head. He has acquired it as his bride through his self-giving

1 DH 3005. [Translations from the Latin text of Vatican I by B.McN.]

2 DH 3004.

love (Eph 5:23–25). And the Church is not a human religious fellowship; in Christ, the Son of God made man, it is the universal sacrament of the salvation of the world. In its liturgy and its proclamation, it celebrates the living Christ who is alive in the Church and brings about the salvation of human beings in the medium of his Church. The Church is "Christ existing as a community" (to borrow the felicitous formulation by the Protestant theologian Dietrich Bonhoeffer in his 1927 doctoral dissertation).[3] For this reason, the Church does not give itself a constitution in keeping with the changeable criteria of this world. It does not adapt forms of political organization, because it is not a secular society, still less a state. It is not a monarchy (in keeping with the principle of unity), nor an oligarchy (in keeping with the principle of plurality), nor a democracy (in keeping with the principle of universality). More appropriate natural analogies are the family founded by God, or the people that is a bond uniting the various generations over time. In the special case of Israel, this is a family called by God, who *made* it his people. As a body, the Church is the vitalizing link between Christ as the head and the individual Christians as members of this living entity. We find the best orientation in the biblical images of the Church: the sheepfold and flock of Christ, God's planting and field, the vineyard of the Lord, God's house, temple, and building. The Church is our mother, the bride of Christ (see LG 6).

Its hierarchical-sacramental constitution is coexistent with its foundation, its essence, and its origin in the *communio Trinitatis*. The apostolic office of the bishops, with its Petrine summit in the bishop of Rome, is not an alien, time-conditioned organizational principle that is tacked on to a *civitas platonica* or a *societas perfecta*. The sacramental constitution has its origin in the Incarnation and gives the Church its divine-human character.

2.
THE ECCLESIOLOGICAL INTRODUCTION TO THE CONSTITUTION *PASTOR AETERNUS*

THE PREAMBLE AND INTRODUCTION to the Dogmatic Constitution *Pastor aeternus* are of decisive importance for the understanding of this text, for is only this section that shows us the inherent principle that unites the four chapters about the institution, the continued existence, the significance, and

3 Dietrich Bonhoeffer, *DBW*, vol. 1, *Sanctorum Communio: Eine dogmatische Untersuchung zur Soziologie der Kirche* (Munich: Chr. Kaiser, 1986).

the essence of the papal primacy and the infallible teaching office of the Roman bishop.

"'The eternal shepherd and bishop of our souls' (1 Pt 2:25) resolved, in order to make permanent the saving work of redemption, to build the holy Church in which, as in the house of the living God, all the believers would be united through the bond of the one faith and of love."[4] In order to continue his mission and to build up the Church in the future, Christ appointed "shepherds and teachers" as successors of the apostles for those who would believe because of their word, until the present world comes to its end. And now comes the fundamental insight into the meaning and essence of the primacy of the Roman church and of its bishop as the personal successor of Peter:

> But in order that the episcopate itself might be one and undivided, and the entire throng of the faithful might be preserved in the unity of the faith and of the fellowship through priests who were closely united to one another, he placed blessed Peter at the head of the other apostles and established in him a permanent principle of this twofold unity and a visible fundament. The eternal temple was to be erected on the strength of this fundament. And the sublimity of the Church, reaching up to heaven, was to rise up in the strength of his faith.[5]

The exposition of the doctrine of the Catholic faith about the Roman primacy and the rejection of the damaging errors about the papacy and the Church are made with the consent of the council, that is to say, of the entire episcopate that is headed by the pope, "for the protection, the maintaining, and the flourishing of the Catholic flock."[6]

The doctrine of faith about the primacy in jurisdiction and teaching was not wrested from the council by the pope and the ultramontanists, nor was it a concession to him by those opposed to it, in order to give him a personal pleasure. On the contrary, this doctrine is clearly laid down in revelation and is shown to be a supporting element in the full and unabridged presentation of the mysteries of salvation. The bishops in union with the pope bear witness to this revealed truth and present it as a truth to be believed.

This truth is not an additional condition, extrinsic to the faith that brings salvation, but an intrinsic element of the deposit of faith within the *nexus mysteriorum,* the inherent structure of the saving truths. One must, of course, add, in the ecumenical spirit of Vatican II, that in the context of

4 DH 3050.

5 DH 3051; see LG 18.

6 DH 3052.

the hierarchy of truths it is not a dogma about the fundament and the center of the divine and Catholic faith (UR 11). A Catholic does not believe in the pope or the bishop, just as he or she does not believe in Mary or the saints, who are venerated. But we believe that the Lord has given his Church the teaching office that serves the Word of God and proclaims it with authority without standing above the Word, and still less without being a source of new revelation. A positivism with regard to the magisterium that holds that whatever the pope says is true, even in a casual remark in an interview, is heretical. In reality, the opposite is the case: because a doctrine of the faith is true, the pope expresses it. The substantial authority of the revealed truth is antecedent to its binding exposition and guides this exposition. The inherent conditions of admission to the sacraments cannot be changed by the pope—not even with the supreme use of his authority. This means that the pope could not give sacramental absolution to a Catholic in a state of mortal sin, unless that person repented and resolved to avoid sin from then onwards; nor could he admit that person to receive Holy Communion without sinning against the truth of the Gospel and the salvation of the believer concerned, who would be led into error by what the pope did.

The magisterium is not inspired in the same way as the biblical authors. The inspiration of sacred scripture is an inherent element of revelation, whereas the magisterium only serves its historical communication and actualization with the aid of the Holy Spirit. The magisterium of the pope enjoys the aid of the Holy Spirit only in order that no error may sneak into the Church's confession of faith and put our salvation at risk. This is why the principle *Roma locuta—causa finita*[7] is not to be interpreted to mean that there must be one person who speaks the final word that puts a stop to the discussion. Nor does the pope enjoy a secret knowledge that is unavailable to others. The essence of the Catholic faith is not determined arbitrarily but is the outcome of sacred scripture, the confession of faith, the catechisms, and the previous doctrinal decisions of the Church. The questions of the faith that have already been decided cannot be reversed under the pretext of further development, for:

> This teaching office is not above the word of God, but serves it, teaching only what has been handed on, listening to it devoutly, guarding it scrupulously and explaining it faithfully in accord with a divine commission and with the help of the Holy Spirit, it draws from this one deposit of faith everything which it presents for belief as divinely revealed. It is clear, therefore, that sacred tradition, Sacred Scripture and the teaching author-

7 Augustine, *Serm.* 131.10.

> ity of the Church, in accord with God's most wise design, are so linked and joined together that one cannot stand without the others, and that all together and each in its own way under the action of the one Holy Spirit contribute effectively to the salvation of souls (DV 10).

Opponents of the council have suspected the teaching of Vatican I to be ideological. They have said that, for all the great theological rhetoric, the real aim was to make good the loss of power, with regard not only to the Papal States, where the pope was no longer ruler, but also with regard to human minds, which had emancipated themselves through their autonomous consciences and the Enlightenment from the Church's anthropology and worldview, which science had rendered obsolete. The autonomous thinking of the modern age was contrasted to obedience vis-à-vis the magisterium. The idea in circles hostile to the Church that priests seek power is nothing short of pathological and absurd, when they think that priests have a special feeling of power over people's souls as a compensatory satisfaction for the renunciation of sex in celibacy, when the priests assure people even in delicate situations of the promises and the consolations of the grace of God.

The wording and the intention of the Constitution *Pastor aeternus* have little or nothing to do with this myth of liberalism and the narrative of nineteenth-century anti-Catholicism. The themes of the constitution are the presentation of the reality and the truth of the divine revelation and its mediation through the Church.

3.
THE DOCTRINE AND CANONS OF *PASTOR AETERNUS*

It is a historical and dogmatic certainty that Jesus made his apostle Simon, the son of John, "Peter," the rock on whom he wished to build his Church. This makes Jesus himself the author of the Church's constitution. He did not leave it up to the Church to provide itself with a constitution and to call its servants in each instance: it is not the totality of the believers who hand over their own authority to one single man. The bishops are appointed for the Church, but not by the Church. Peter and the apostles received personally and immediately from Christ the divine authority for their service of the Church. The apostolic ministry is a sharing in his sending by the Father. This is why their authority is handed on to their successors through episcopal ordination. The successor of Peter in the office of the Roman bishop is thereby directly set by Christ himself at the head of the college of bishops. The *first canon* of the dogma closes the first chapter about the institution of the apostolic primacy in blessed Peter by drawing the following conclusion: "Whoever therefore says that the blessed apostle Peter is not the prince of all the apostles and the visible head of the entire Church militant, appointed by Christ the Lord; or that he received directly from the same Christ our Lord only the primacy of honor, but not the true and genuine primacy of jurisdiction: let him be anathema."[8]

The doctrine of the continued existence of the primacy of blessed Peter in the Roman bishops then follows in the second chapter.

The Church was not founded as an association holding one particular worldview that keeps alive the ideas of its founder, or as a philosophical school that struggles to identify the true inheritance of its pioneer thinker. It was founded as a fellowship of the divine life in Christ. The only reason for the existence of the Church is to mediate eternal salvation. And this is why the institution of the Petrine office must continue to exist for as long as the Church fulfills its mission. This means that every man who follows Simon Bar-Jona on this episcopal *cathedra Petri*, "according to the institution by Christ, has himself the primacy of Peter over the entire Church."[9] The members—that is to say, the local churches (the dioceses and the synodal associations that have come into existence in the course of history)—can live and work together as a unity in the structure of the body of the entire Church only provided that they remain united and grow together in the head—that is, in the Roman church with its bishop.

The *second canon* concludes the second chapter as follows: "Whoever therefore says that it is not through the institution by Christ the Lord himself, or of divine right, that blessed Peter continuously has successors in the primacy over the entire Church; or that the Roman bishop is not the successor of blessed Peter in precisely this primacy: let him be anathema."[10]

The third chapter presents the significance and the essence of the primacy of the Roman bishop, which originates in the directive given by the Lord. This means the rejection of every purely worldly reason for its genesis and its validity. In its existence and in its essential structures, which do not serve earthly goals but are orientated to eternal salvation, the Church is the fruit of God's will to reveal himself and to bring about salvation. In the same way, the Petrine ministry is anchored in God's will for his Church, as can be seen from the testimonies of sacred scripture and all the central doctrinal documents of the Church. The doctrinal definition of the Council of Florence is explicitly renewed and presented to those who believe in Christ as

8 DH 3055.

9 DH 3507.

10 DH 3058.

something that they must believe. No one can deviate from this Catholic truth without detriment to the faith and to salvation.[11]

The Roman church has the primacy of ordinary authority in regard to all the churches with their pastors and faithful. This jurisdictional primacy is, of its very nature, an episcopal and ordinary authority. Its sole origin is therefore in the one episcopal ministry that is exercised by all the bishops together, in submission and true obedience to the bishop of Rome. Besides this, it goes without saying that the obedience to the pope is not unconditional and absolute, since the authority he has is bestowed on him by God for the service of the Church. The pope is not father, teacher, and shepherd in virtue of his own authority: it is Christ who exercises his salvific power through the shepherds of the Church in the Holy Spirit. This is the answer to those who somewhat self-righteously apply to the apostles whom Christ appointed, and to their successors, the words of Jesus against the self-authorization of the Pharisees and scribes (see Mt 23:8–12). The religious and canonical obedience to the pope or the bishop has its intrinsic reason and its external boundary in obedience to God in the word of his revelation and in his will, which is manifested in the natural moral law. When the Spanish King Philip II (1527–1598) put the pointed question to Ugo Boncompagni (papal legate and later Pope Gregory XIII, r. 1572–1585) whether there were any conditions under which he would not obey the pope, he replied: "Should the pope command me to do something that is against my conscience or is detrimental to the Holy See, I will not obey."[12] Since it involves the unity of the Church under Christ, who is the supreme, the real, and the true shepherd of the Church, this service of unity and fellowship naturally refers to the doctrine of faith and of morals, and, deriving from this and at the service of this unity, also to the discipline and the governance of the universal Church.

This has two further consequences. First, the contact between the pope and the bishops must be free from every influence from the political power, from economic interests, or from manipulations in the media. Under no circumstances can the consent by the various states to the doctrinal and governmental decisions of the pope for the Church be regarded as necessary. The governance of the Church must not be oriented to the hoped-for or feared reactions of public opinion, nor must it sacrifice its positions or its persons on the altar of this modern idolatry.

Secondly, the divine right of the apostolic primacy of the Roman bishop over the entire Church means that the pope is the supreme judge in all matters of the doctrine of faith and of morals, and in all matters of disci-

11 DH 3060.

12 Pastor, *Geschichte der Päpste*, vol. 9:16.

pline and church order, and that an appeal to a higher authority is therefore impossible—precisely because the pope is the highest judicial authority in the visible Church. A legal infinite regress is not possible. Accordingly, the successor of Peter has the final judgment in the Church. This must be distinguished from the judgment of God, who alone can see into the heart, about the ultimate fate of a human being.

The conciliarist theories of the superiority of a council to the pope refute themselves through their self-contradiction. There is no council at all without the Roman bishop, who qua bishop is the most important member of the council, and qua successor of Peter is the head of the entire episcopate which is gathered together at the council. He is thus the principle and fundament of the unity of the universal Church. The totality of the members of a body *without* its head certainly does not stand over against the head of body and the principle of its life—namely, the pope—as an ensemble that is capable of acting on its own. Head and body are essentially bound together and thus form an indissoluble unity of life and of action.

In view of the fact that the primacy of the pope lies in his ministry as bishop of Rome, the clash between papalism and episcopalism, which is so significant in church history and in dogmatics, proves to be the result of a false ecclesiological approach. The pope is not above the council—nor is the council above the pope, because there cannot be any Church and any council without the successor of Peter in Rome who was appointed by Christ himself, and because the episcopate that was appointed by God himself remains one and undivided *cum et sub Petro.*

The decisive question cannot be whether the decree *Haec sancta* of the Council of Constance (April 6, 1415) and the affirmations of the Council of Basel in its second session, chapter 3 (1431), with and without the approval of the pope, possess validity and the rank of a dogma, quite apart from the unclarified concept of "council" on which they are based.[13]

In the case of conciliarism, it is impossible a priori to speak of a dogma—that is, a doctrine revealed by God that each Catholic must believe with divine and Catholic faith for the sake of his or her salvation. And the hopes that one can convict Catholic doctrine of a self-contradiction or that one can lead every Catholic into a hopeless dilemma by offering the choice between deciding for *Haec sancta* or for *Pastor aeternus* are futile, since a council is an assembly of bishops, not a representation of Christendom with all its nations and its institutions that belong to church law. Its importance lies rather in the fact that in an extreme case, when it is impossible to determine

13 Walter Brandmüller, *Das Konzil von Konstanz (1414–1418),* 2 vols. (Paderborn: Schöningh, 1991–1998).

who is the legitimate pope, the entire episcopate has a responsibility to put an end to the emergency of a schism in the Roman church. In this sense, the entire Church has a higher right vis-à-vis dubious claimants and illegitimate occupants of the *cathedra Petri*.

The legitimate pope is in and above the college of bishops, not because he is separated from it, but because he is organically linked to it like the head to the body and because he is the highest representative of a corporate body over which he presides. But one must not forget the principle that the episcopate does not elect the pope as a kind of episcopal president, since that would destroy the essential unity of the Church in Christ and form a contradiction of the principle: *unus et totus Christus et corpus—caput et membra.* In the creed, the sacramental Church is recognized with divine and Catholic faith as *una ecclesia,* because it has one faith (*una fides*). "There is one body and one Spirit, just as you were called to the one hope that belongs to your call, one Lord, one faith, one baptism, one God and Father of us all, who is above all and through all and in all" (Eph 4:4–6).

The Roman church, in the form of the College of Cardinals, has the task of electing a bishop of the Roman church and thereby ensuring that the universal Church too receives in the pope the shepherd whom Jesus has appointed to pasture his lambs and his sheep. The entire Catholic concept of the Church would be unhinged if one were to take as a dogma—that is to say, as a doctrine coming from God that is to be believed for the sake of one's salvation—the formula (born of an emergency situation) that the council is superior to the pope (who is by nature its head). Such a doctrine is contrary to scripture and contradicts the entire Catholic tradition; it would also generate an unbridgeable contradiction between the principle of the plurality of the bishops and the principle of unity that is embodied in the bishop of Rome with the Roman church and in this way realizes the total unity of the universal Church in and out of the local churches. This affirmation that the pope is subordinate to the entire Church is thus merely for pragmatic use in an emergency situation when no indubitably legitimate pope can be identified: it is only with regard to the doubts about the legitimacy of a papal pretender that one can speak of a superiority of the Roman church, or even of the universal Church. Where there is a fully justified doubt about the legitimacy of a papal election, the College of Cardinals has the right to conduct an examination, which may then lead to a new election. It is true that the College of Cardinals in this form has belonged to church law only since the decree about the papal election issued by Pope Nicholas II in 1059, but since it represents the Roman church and the Roman ecclesiastical province in its most important clergy (cardinal bishops, priests, and deacons), it certainly also has a fundament in divine right. This is because the primacy is given personally to the Roman bishop, who, however, as a bishop cannot be separated from his local church. Accordingly, the oldest sources (Irenaeus of Lyons, etc.) also speak of a primacy of the Roman church, and of its bishop as the successor of Peter.

It goes without saying that the pope, with the entire Church, stands under the Word of God and remains obligated to obey it in every respect. Whether, and in what form, a pope has accepted or relativized the decrees from Constance and Basel on this subject does not say much about the dogmatic rank of these decisions, in the strict sense of that term, because not even a pope can reshape or define anew the revealed faith in the primacy of the pope.

The teaching of Vatican I about the essence of the Roman primacy is not constructed upon a diminishing of the office of his fellow bishops, since the bishops are not instituted by the pope; they are instituted directly by the Holy Spirit through their episcopal ordination to be the bishops of the flock that is assigned to them. This means that they pasture and guide their flocks, their dioceses, in their supreme, ordinary, and immediate authority and in their own jurisdiction. As successors of the apostles, they are their true vicars. A strict distinction must be drawn here from the perspective of the Vatican. The apostolic nuncios, most of whom are ordained as bishops, and other bishops who serve in the Curia are functionally dependent in their ministries on the pope, but one cannot in the least affirm that there is the same relationship between the pope and the diocesan bishops. The Secretariat of State is responsible for the nomination of the nuncios of the papal diplomacy, but the appointment of the local bishops is the task, not of the Secretariat of State, but of three congregations of the Roman church (in the narrower sense, of the Curia). Unlike the pope, the bishops are not the successors of one individual apostle; it is as members of the college of bishops that they are the successors of the apostles. Accordingly, they do not have as individuals the authority over the universal Church that the apostles had. They possess this authority only in union with the entire college of bishops in fellowship with the pope as the head of this college.

Naturally, the pope is Peter's successor in his authority over the entire Church, and this means that as the head of the college of bishops, he can also make doctrinal decisions alone and in his own person for the entire Church. But the jurisdiction of the diocesan bishops, and a fortiori their authority to ordain, do not have their source in the jurisdiction of the pope over the entire Church but are exercised in the authority of Christ that is given to all the bishops together for the entire Church, and to each one individually for his own local church. This is not relativized when the ordinary, immediate, and personal authority of the bishop in the district entrusted to him (see

Acts 20:28) must be exercised in relation to the pope's service of the unity and the fellowship of the entire Catholic Church.[14]

When Saint John Henry Newman (1801–1890) gave the preference to the conscience rather than to the pope in his celebrated toast, what he meant was that, as persons, we are immediately related in our conscience to God, mediated through the Church's teaching of his commandments, and that the papal authority is not above the moral law but proclaims it prophetically and in a way that criticizes the contemporary age.

An exact ecclesiology must affirm that the pope is the bishop only of Rome, not of any other diocese. But he teaches and acts as the universal shepherd for the universal Church and is thus inherently present in every local church not as its own bishop but as the episcopal principle of the unity of the entire Church since the local church is a part and a representation of the entire Catholic Church. As the perpetual principle and fundament of the unity in faith and of the fellowship of the episcopate and of the universal Church, the pope is therefore also present in every local church as the guarantee of its unity with the universal Church. He is thus the principle of the unity of every diocese with the entire Church and can also issue orders for every pastor and believer in the local churches.[15]

This passage about the divine right of the episcopate and the consequent impossibility of hollowing it out in theory and in practice is the bridge to the teaching of Vatican II about the hierarchical constitution of the Church, and especially about the episcopal office, in chapter III of *Lumen gentium*. The key to the new interpretation lies in the more comprehensive ecclesiology of Vatican II. It is not enough to reflect only on the relationship between the Roman bishop and the other bishops. One must at the same time bear in mind the relationship of the bishops to each other and to their head, the bishop of Rome, together with the relationship between the local churches and the universal Church of which they are a part, since the universal Church subsists in and out of the local churches whose heads are the bishops.

More is involved here, of course, than the theological clarification of the relationship between the Roman church and the other local churches in the totality of the Catholic Church. It is also a question of the spirit of the exercise of the primacy by the pope himself and by the congregations of the Roman Curia that share, in his name and his authority, in the governance of the entire Church. In this context, Vatican I quotes the letter from Pope Gregory the Great, one of the most energetic and humble successors on the *cathedra Petri*, to his brother bishop, Eulogius of Alexandria: "My honor

14 DH 3601.

15 See DH 3113–3116.

is the honor of the entire Church. My honor is the unbroken energy of my brothers. I am truly honored when no individual is deprived of the honor that is his due."[16]

The *third canon,* following the doctrinal chapter of *Pastor aeternus,* reads as follows:

> Whoever therefore says that the Roman bishop possesses only the office of supervision or guidance, but not the full and supreme jurisdictional authority over the entire Church, not only in matters concerning faith and morals, but also in those that concern the discipline and governance of the Church which is spread over all the earth; or that he possesses only the larger part, but not the entire fullness of this supreme authority; or that this authority of his is not ordinary and immediate, both over all the Churches and the individual churches as well as over all the pastors and faithful and the individual pastors and faithful: let him be anathema.[17]

There now follows the celebrated fourth chapter about the infallible teaching office of the Roman bishop. The apostolic primacy of the pope also includes the supreme authority of the magisterium with regard to the revealed truth of the Church's confession of Christ, the Son of the living God. All the truths of the Christian faith are contained in this confession. It was only in virtue of a revelation by God, the Father of Christ, that Peter was able to declare the confession of Christ that is the foundation supporting the Church's fellowship of faith; and it is in the gift and in the power of Holy Spirit that the magisterium of the bishops and of the pope likewise works to preserve and develop this confession.

While the apostles were the bearers of revelation, and the sacred authors of the biblical books enjoyed the gift of the inspiration of the Holy Spirit, the highest magisterium of the bishops with the pope as the head of their college is guided safely in the presentation of the faith to the Church. Their task is to present and to expound the *depositum fidei,* and this involves an *assistentia spiritus sancti.* The testimony of the entire Church at many councils and in the authoritative documents of the doctors of the Church proclaims that the successors of Peter in Rome:

> have laid down what must be maintained, what they recognized with the help of God as in agreement with the sacred scriptures and the apostolic traditions.

16 DH 3061.

17 DH 3064.

> For the Holy Spirit was not promised to the successors of Peter in order that they might bring a new teaching to light through his revelation, but in order that, with his assistance, they might sacredly preserve and faithfully expound the revelation handed on through the apostles, or the deposit of faith."[18]

All the orthodox teachers of the faith have been firmly convinced that the *cathedra Petri* has remained free of every error and always will remain free of error, not because of the brilliant intellectual gifts and the moral strengths of its occupants, but because of the divine promise to Peter: "I have prayed for you that your faith may not fail; and when you have turned again, strengthen your brethren."[19]

"This charism of truth and of unfailing faith" was bestowed on Peter and his successors, not in order that they might shine with a miraculous omniscience in every branch of knowledge, but because the true faith is the presupposition of salvation. An error in the faith would mean not only that the Church and the Christians would succumb to a mistake in the construction of a theory, but that they would lose their orientation to the light that leads to the fellowship of life with God. This is why the Church preserves orthodoxy and fights against heresy and schism, in order that the Church may be maintained in unity with Christ and in the truth of God. Peter is the fundament of this unity in truth, in order that the gates of hell—internal and external disintegration—may not triumph over the work of God. The gift of the infallibility of the bishops in union with the pope and the entire Church, as well as the infallibility of the person of the pope on his own as the head of the Church, is implied in the pastoral obligation of the successor of Peter and has its basis in a special prerogative that Christ has given him. This is why the pope declares with the entire council that it is a dogma revealed by God that:

> When the Roman bishop speaks ex cathedra, that is, when in the exercise of his office as shepherd and teacher of all Christians in virtue of his supreme apostolic authority he decides that a doctrine of faith and morals is to be held fast by the entire Church, then he possesses, thanks to the divine assistance promised to him in blessed Peter, that infallibility with which the divine Redeemer willed his Church to be equipped in the definition of the doctrine of faith and morals; accordingly, such definitions of the Roman bishop are unalterable of themselves [ex sese], not because of the assent of the Church. Whoever—which may God forbid!—should undertake to contradict our definition: let him be anathema.[20]

18 DH 3069–70.

19 DH 3070.

20 DH 3074–75.

4.
THE ECCLESIOLOGICAL SIGNIFICANCE OF THE PRIMACY IN TEACHING AND JURISDICTION

THIS IS NOT THE PLACE TO GO into the controversial reception of this conciliar decision inside and outside the Catholic Church; I wish only to point out that the Roman primacy is justified purely in terms of the theology of revelation and of ecclesiology. Every commingling with political and sociological motifs inherited from the Middle Ages is carefully eliminated. Nor can one say that papalism has triumphed over episcopalism (conciliarism, Gallicanism, Febronianism, Josephenism, etc.). Anyone who expounds the dogma of the primacy of the Roman pope in terms of power politics, rather than in terms of the theology of revelation, has fundamentally misunderstood the Church by seeing it in the logic of the struggle for power and influence.

In a philosophical-epistemological perspective, the platitude that every human being is fallible in theory and in praxis can reduce the dogma of the infallibility of the episcopal and papal magisterium *in docendo fidem divinam et catholicam* to absurdity only if one denies the supernatural character of revelation and its realization in the Incarnation and its being made present in the sacraments. It is indeed true that the human understanding is not immune to error in the perception and evaluation of intellectual and material phenomena—and this applies equally to the understanding of the relativists, who take their own position to be absolutely obvious. But already in the recognition of the metaphysical principles of being and in the recognition of the transcendent ground of these principles in the knowledge of the existence and working of the personal God and Creator of the world, the human understanding can arrive at the unshakable certainty that it knows genuinely and truly. This is all the more possible when the Church not only receives the revelation from God but also receives through the same God the gift of his Spirit in order to preserve and expound this revelation faithfully.

Peter speaks as the head of the Church: "We have believed, and have come to know, that you are the Holy One of God" (Jn 6:69; Mk 1:24). It is only in the Holy Spirit that we are able to confess: "Jesus is the Lord" (1 Cor 12:3; Rom 10:9). The external revelation in the incarnate Word, which is transmitted to us in the Church's confession, becomes our own internally when our understanding is elevated to a share in God's self-knowledge in the WORD and the SPIRIT: "God has revealed everything to us through the Spirit. For the Spirit searches everything, even the depths of God. [...] We have received the Spirit which is from God, that we might understand the gifts bestowed on us by God" (1 Cor 2:10–13).

If the pope is the perpetual principle and the fundament of the unity of the Church in the truth of revelation, then, in accordance with the words of Jesus's promise to Peter, his successor must be the rock on which Jesus will build his Church, which cannot be shaken by the power of unbelief and of erroneous belief.

Faith in the infallibility of the pope as the visible head of the episcopate and of the entire Church is not a grotesque burden added on to everything else that one would have to believe. It is the certain overcoming of skepticism (a fruit of original sin) vis-à-vis God's definitive word of salvation, through "the grace and the truth" that came into this world in a definitive manner through Jesus Christ (Jn 1:17).

"The Spirit of truth," whom the world does not see and know but whom the Father will send down on the Church in the name of the Son, will assist the apostles as shepherds and teachers. The Paraclete will "*teach them everything*" and "*remind them of everything*" that Jesus, the incarnate Word has *said* to them (Jn 14:26).

The Catholic concept of the Church as the sacrament of the salvation of the world in Jesus Christ, its Lord and Head, stands and falls with the faith in the infallibility of the councils and the pope.

Long before the First Vatican Council, Johann Adam Möhler had declared, in response to the Catholic theology of the Enlightenment that found expression in Febronianism, with its rationalistically narrowed-down concept of faith, its ecclesiology that was flattened down moralistically, its reduction of revelation to the confirmation of natural truths for the uneducated, and its narrowed-down understanding of history in an archival and positivistic sense: "The dogmatic decisions of the episcopate are unerring, since it represents the universal Church, and a doctrine of faith that the episcopate understood falsely would surrender everything to error. If then the institution that Christ set up in order to maintain and to declare his truth is not subject to any error in this function, the same applies to that organ through which the Church makes its declaration."[21] One cannot (like the Febronians) arbitrarily tie down the distinction between what is essential in the papal primacy and what is time-conditioned to one particular point in history—for example, in the supposedly ideal state of the Church anterior to the Pseudo-Isidorian decretals—in order then to enter into "ecumenical negotiations." One cannot restrict the primatial rights in order to "accommodate" the Protestants or the Orthodox. It is only in the context of a shared basic understanding of the essence, the form, and the mission of the Church that one can survey the content of the faith, both historically and theologi-

21 Möhler, *Symbolik*, §43.

cally, with regard to the episcopate and the primacy; and only then is it possible to speak about its concrete form that is required for the Church today.

5.
PAPAL INFALLIBILITY AND INTELLECTUAL AND ETHICAL RELATIVISM

THE ANTI-CHRISTIAN IDEOLOGIES of the twentieth century showed in an oppressive manner how relevant and necessary the Roman primacy is for the preservation of the truth of revelation. On Palm Sunday 1937, Pope Pius XI (r. 1922–1939) declared in his encyclical *Mit brennender Sorge* against National Socialism, in face of the brutal threat to human beings and the total extinguishing of the saving faith in God, in Christ, and in his presence in the Church:

> Faith in the Church cannot stand pure and true without the support of faith in the primacy of the bishop of Rome. The same moment when Peter, in the presence of all the Apostles and disciples, confesses his faith in Christ, the Son of the living God, the answer he received in reward for his faith and his confession was the word that built the Church, the only Church of Christ, on the rock of Peter (Mt 16:18). Thus was sealed the connection between the faith in Christ, the Church, and the primacy. True and lawful authority is invariably a bond of unity, a source of strength, a guarantee against division and ruin, a pledge for the future: and this is verified in the deepest and sublimest sense, when that authority, as in the case of the Church, and the Church alone, is sealed by the promise and the guidance of the Holy Ghost and his irresistible support. Should men, who are not even united by faith in Christ, come and offer you the seduction of a national German Church, be convinced that it is nothing but a denial of the one Church of Christ and the evident betrayal of that universal mission, for which a world Church alone is qualified and competent. The live history of other national churches with their paralysis, their domestication and subjection to worldly powers, is sufficient evidence of the sterility to which is condemned every branch that is severed from the trunk of the living Church.[22]

These are truly prophetic words that are obviously significant today too, in the confrontation with totalitarian claims to rule originating in the media,

22 Pius XI, *Mit brennender* Sorge, 22; see Heinz-Albert Raem, *Pius IX. und der Nationalsozialismus: Die Enzyklika "Mit brennender Sorge" vom 14. März 1937* (Paderborn: Schöningh, 1979).

or that have a pseudoreligious and laicist-state provenance. The agnosticism of an earlier period and the relativism vis-à-vis the natural and the revealed truth that dominates today have not in the least led to freedom of conscience and tolerance. On the contrary, they are never safe from their dialectic reversal into ideological and political totalitarian claims. It is not despite the Enlightenment, but precisely in the age of the aggressive de-Christianization or "secularization," that Europe and the whole world are experiencing a greater physical and moral persecution of Christians than at any time in history. Our contemporaries who are "enlightened" in a rather vulgar sense ought not to ask how it is still possible in the twenty-first century to believe that the human being is the image of God, and to believe in the infinite mercy of God, the resurrection of the body, eternal life, and the unique mediation of salvation by Christ. They ought rather to be profoundly shaken by the fact that the truth and the life of God are withheld from them, and they are fobbed off with "Esau's lentil broth"—that is to say, with materialism and a nihilism that is empty of thought.

Faith is the truth of the reason. But the reason of the truth is faith. And the truth of truth is God in whom I believe.

Jesus gives Pilate this reply: "I am a king. For this I was born, and for this I have come into the world, to bear witness to the truth. Everyone who is of the truth hears my voice" (Jn 18:37).

It is not the renunciation of the truth but the shared love of the truth that binds people even of different faiths to a peaceful coexistence, since the opposite of the truth is not freedom but the error and falsehood that deprive people of solidarity. Satan comes "with all wicked deception for those who are to perish, because they refused to love the truth and so be saved. Therefore, God sends upon them a strong delusion, to make them believe what is false" (2 Thes 2:10–11). This is a striking description of propaganda, from the Jacobins to Fascism and Stalinism and every form of spying on one's fellow citizens and supplying them with false information in totalitarian systems.

At every period, we are faced with the alternatives of listening to God, so that we thereby become free, or of listening to human beings, so that we thereby become their slaves. It is the task and the mission of the pope and the bishops in unity with him, like Peter long ago as the visible head of the Church together with the apostles, to confront the chief priests of the zeitgeist and the rulers of this earth as witnesses to the truth and as advocates of freedom.

At every period, Peter confesses through the pope: "We must obey God rather than men. The God of our fathers raised Jesus whom you killed by hanging him on a tree. God exalted him at his right hand as Leader and Savior, to give repentance to Israel and forgiveness of sins. And we are witnesses to these things, and so is the Holy Spirit whom God has given to those who obey him" (Acts 5:29–32).

This is precisely what is affirmed by the dogma of the primacy and the infallibility of the Roman bishop as successor of the apostles and the visible principle and fundament of the unity of the Church in the truth of the definitive self-revelation of God in Christ and in the Holy Spirit.

VI

The Integration of the Papacy into the Church and the College of Bishops

1.
THE DOGMA THAT THE EPISCOPATE IS OF DIVINE RIGHT

THE THEORY OF A BREACH IN CONTINUITY between the First and Second Vatican Councils is not only historically audacious and ignorant but also, in dogmatic terms, a heretical contradiction of the faith in the unity of revelation and in the uniqueness of the Church of Christ. The history of the Church, which was instituted once and for all by Christ as the sacrament of the salvation of the world, is not a sequence of foundations of new churches or of ecclesiological constructs that were generated as theories in human minds and then saw the light of day thanks to tactical and political maneuvers. Behind this theory lie an ecclesiological nominalism and an agnostic refusal to accept the transcendence of God.

The Second Vatican Council not only stands in the theoretical-conceptual continuity of doctrine; it also attests the real identity of the one Church instituted by Christ as a socially constituted fellowship of faith and of confession, because the Church brings us concretely into the fellowship of salvation with God. It is founded by Christ as the instrument through which God accomplishes in history his universal saving will. *Lumen gentium* must be read and understood as a whole in the larger framework of the Dogmatic

Constitution on Divine Revelation, *Dei Verbum,* and of its implementation in the Pastoral Constitution on the Church in the Modern World, *Gaudium et spes.*

In the chapter about the hierarchical constitution of the Church, the Second Vatican Council explicitly declares itself to be the continuation of the path taken by the First Vatican Council. Before doing so, the council fathers unfold in the first two chapters of the Dogmatic Constitution on the Church, *Lumen gentium,* the mystery of the Church in God's plan of salvation and the existence and essence of the Church as the people of God, the body of Christ, and the temple of the Holy Spirit. In relation to the teaching of Vatican I "about the institution, the perpetuity, the meaning and reason for the sacred primacy of the Roman Pontiff and of his infallible magisterium" (LG 18), the doctrine about the bishops as successors of the apostles in unity with the pope, the Vicar of Christ and visible head of the Church, does not in the least signify a relativizing of the primacy but rather its integration into the totality of the Church and of the episcopate.

When Vatican II "again proposes" the doctrine about the primacy "to be firmly believed by all the faithful" (LG 18), the council fathers unambiguously reject every theory and hypothesis about a breach in the tradition of the Catholic faith. A populistic oversimplification declares the difference between the two councils to lie in the change of the image of the Church: from a pyramid to a circle. All at once, the pope ceases to be the summit of a building constructed "from above," because now the laity constitute "from below" the "basis" of the Church, which supports the superstructure (that is to say, the hierarchy). This would mean that the office-bearers carry out their ministry as bearers of a representative mandate. Since the Church is the people of God, and this definition is now understood politically rather than theologically, this necessarily entails a democratization of the Church—in other words, a rule by the people, who are the source of all power. An old hierarchical image of the Church would stand in contrast to an up-to-date, democratized Church.

This forgets that the hierarchical office is not a structure of domination. This term refers to the apostolic foundation of ecclesial ministry. In reality, all power in the Church has its source in Christ, to whom this power in heaven and on earth has been given by the Father (Mt 28:19). In the Bible, however, power (*munus et potestas*) signifies the authority in the name of Christ to lead and sanctify the faithful and to proclaim the Gospel to them. It is only by analogy that this spiritual power (*exousia*) has anything in common with the legitimate power of the state, because the Church's concern is eternal salvation, whereas the state's concern is the common good here on earth. The ecclesial authority is the exact opposite of the power that breaks the law in rogue states. These ideas of a "democratization of the Church" are nothing new. They were already spread by the Jansenist Synod of Pistoia and were condemned by Pope Pius VI in the constitution *Auctorem fidei* (August 28, 1794) as false fundamental understandings of the constitution of the Church, which is of divine right.[1]

It is alleged, in support of this excessively simple explanation, that the first two chapters of *Lumen gentium* speak of the Church in the general, and it is only in the third chapter that we read about the hierarchical constitution of the Church; and this looks rather like an afterthought. Two concepts of the Church, one new and one traditional, are juxtaposed with no connection. The progressive forces who believe that the spirit of the council (and thus the true intention of the council, intended by God) is on their side now have the task of vanquishing the conservative interpretations and marginalizing the obscurantists who still maintain them. And if the latter are unwilling to submit to the dictates of those who are the stewards of the spirit of the council, they must as a final resort be driven out of the Church. The end justifies the means here, and it is a matter of fact that after every council there are some who have failed to catch the train of time and are left behind on the platform. Indeed, it is only realistic to assume that there will be losses.

All this, however, is the logic of political struggles for power, not the logic of the Church as the family of God. Since that time, an ideological power struggle has played out in some countries when bishops are appointed, a struggle that is antithetical to the spiritual meaning of this ministry and to the question who is best suited to serve as teacher of the Gospel and shepherd of the Church. The decisive factors are not so much the theological and pastoral competence and the personal spiritual and moral integrity of the one who becomes bishop, but rather loyalty to the party line of the progressive-liberal ideology.

All these maneuvers, which have driven the Church in some countries to the edge of the abyss of insignificance, have nothing whatever to do with the spirit and the teaching of Vatican II. At the same time, these maneuvers do not justify the resistance to the further development of doctrine and to the reforms in the liturgy and the *diakonia* of "the Church in the modern world." Extremes not only meet; they also threaten the Church's orientation to the "sound doctrine." Paul writes to his fellow apostle Timothy:

> Teach and urge these duties. If anyone teaches otherwise and does not agree with the sound words of our Lord Jesus Christ and the teaching which accords with godliness, he is puffed up with conceit, he knows noth-

1 DH 2601–2605.

> ing; he has a morbid craving for controversy and for disputes about words, which produce envy, dissension, slander, base suspicions, and wrangling among men who are depraved in mind and bereft of the truth (1 Tm 6:2–5).

The Church as a visible societal entity and as the mystical body of Christ, the Church as the fellowship of all the baptized and its hierarchical constitution, that is to say, the equipping of some Christians with spiritual authority to build up the body and to serve its baptized members, those who believe in Christ (Eph 4:11–12)—this Church does not disintegrate into two parts but forms a complex reality that is united in Christ himself (LG 8). The participation of all the baptized, and precisely of the laypersons who do not belong to religious congregations nor act (like the ordained priests) in the person of Christ as the head of the body, has its foundation in Christ (LG 8).

The apostolate of the laity has a sacramental basis which is established in baptism and confirmation and is nourished by taking part in the Eucharist and in the entire life of the Church in *martyria, leitourgia,* and *diakonia.* In an ecclesiological sense, the "lay person," the baptized person, is a sacral term that means the exact opposite of what is meant in the Romance languages by "laicism" or "just being a layman."

Just as Christ is one and undivided, so too the differing participation in his priestly, kingly, and prophetic office will not bring about the collateral damage of a separation between laypersons and priests and thereby the disintegration of the Church. On the contrary, it will be the basis of the unity of the people of God in the same mission and in the differentness of the charisms and ministries (LG 10).

"For those ministers who are endowed with sacred power serve their brethren, so that all who are of the People of God, and therefore enjoy a true Christian dignity, working towards a common goal freely and in an orderly way, may arrive at salvation" (LG 18). The Church paralyzes itself when various groups and states of life, from "mature" laypersons to "authoritarian" office-bearers, fight for shares in "power" instead of employing their charismatic and hierarchical gifts to build up the people of God under its head, Jesus Christ (LG 9–14).

This is why, in the line of thought of *Lumen gentium,* the third chapter about the bishops with their presbyters and deacons, and the fourth chapter about the laity, are not addenda to the general ecclesiology but are to be understood as its concretization.

With regard to our present subject, we must note that the primacy of the pope is not a principle in opposition to the episcopate, but rather the principle of the unity of all the bishops and of the entire Church. The bishops are indeed taken up by the pope into the hierarchical fellowship of the *corpus episcoporum,* but they are made bishops and successors of the apostles not by him but by the Holy Spirit in their ordination (LG 21). One element of Christ's will that the Church should last to the end of time is the will that the apostolic ministry, too, shall continue in the ministry of the bishops and in their offices of proclaiming the Word, sanctifying the believers, and guiding their flock.

2.
THE UNITY OF THE EPISCOPATE WITH AND IN THE POPE

"AND IN ORDER THAT THE EPISCOPATE ITSELF might be one and undivided," the eternal Shepherd of his Church, Jesus Christ, "placed Blessed Peter over the other apostles, and instituted in him a permanent and visible source and foundation of unity of faith and communion" (LG 18).

The doctrine of the collegial unity of the entire episcopate with the bishop of Rome as the principle of its unity is not an innovation by Vatican II. This is not only a demonstrable fact at every epoch of church history; it is entailed in the institution of the office of apostle and bishop and thus belongs to the *depositum fidei.* The "collegial character and aspect of the Episcopal office" (LG 22) means that it can be exercised legitimately only in fellowship with the entire episcopate. This liturgy already shows this: a bishop is ordained by several bishops acting together, and when he is consecrated by God at the moment of his ordination, he is simultaneously inducted thereby into the episcopate, whose principle of unity is always the pope. The induction into the college of bishops is identical to his ordination as bishop. This must be distinguished from his welcome into the *practical* collegiality among bishops, since whereas God's action is the basis of episcopal collegiality, its realization among human beings, like all human behavior, can also break down. This is why the doctrine of the collegiality of the bishops with and under the pope is a dogma revealed by God. To dispute this is a grave error in the divine and Catholic faith. Although the Second Vatican Council refrains from promulgating a canon with the *anathema sit,* one cannot reject the dogma of the collegial nature of the episcopal office, which has a wide foundation in scripture and tradition, because the episcopate is one and undivided. Nor can one reject the responsibility of every individual bishop for the entire Church, which finds its highest expression in an ecumenical council, because this is what the dogma expresses.

Johann Adam Möhler, a theologian whose orthodoxy cannot in any way be doubted, presented very clearly the Church's teaching about the primacy and episcopate half a century before Vatican I and 130 years before Vatican

II. He shows that the teaching of the two councils about the primacy of the pope and the collegiality of the episcopate is nothing other than the elevation of the Church's universal awareness of the faith to the epistemological rank of a dogma:

> The episcopate (the continuation of the apostolate) is hereafter revered as a divine institution; and the same is true, precisely for this reason, of the focal point of unity and the head of the episcopate, namely, the pope. If the episcopate is to be a self-contained unity bound together both internally and externally, in order to unite all the believers to the true life in common that is the very urgent requirement of the Catholic Church, the episcopate itself must have a midpoint thanks to whose existence all are held together and firmly joined to one another. [...] If the universal Church did not have a head appointed by Christ, and if this head did not have an influence on each one of its parts, an influence revealed in acknowledged rights and obligations, the Church would be left to its own devices and would take a path that was mutually contradictory and was conditioned merely by local circumstances. And that would be the path of the dissolution of the entire Church. [...] Without a visible head, nothing would be left of the Catholic Church's self-understanding as a visible institution that represents Christ; indeed, such an understanding would never have come into being in the first place. A visible Church necessarily entails a visible head. [...] Besides this, it is well known that, partly because of the changes of the times and of abuses in the Church, and partly automatically as a result of the internal course of development of the concepts in contradictory senses, two systems have come to dominate the relationship between the pope and the bishops, namely, the episcopal and the papal system. The latter, while not denying the divine institution of the bishops, emphasized especially the power of the center; the former, without denying the divine institution of the primacy, sought to direct the use of power primarily in accordance with the periphery. Since each acknowledged the existence of the other as divine, they formed antitheses that brought great benefits to the Church's life. In the contrast they formed to each other, the autonomous, free development of the parts was preserved, and the union of the parts to an indivisible and living totality was held fast.[2]

It would be difficult to find a better commentary that anticipated the definition of the relationship between primacy and episcopate in accordance with the dogmatic teaching of Vatican II.[3]

2 Mohler, *Symbolik*, §43.

3 Umberto Betti, *La dottrina sull'episcopato del Concilio Vaticano II: Il capitolo III della Costituzione dommatica* Lumen gentium (Rome: Pontificium athenaeum Antonianum, 1984).

The bishop of Rome is a member of the one college of bishops. As its head, he is the Vicar of Christ and shepherd of the entire flock of God. This is why he possesses the full, supreme, and universal authority over the entire Church, which he can exercise freely at all times. He always remains bound to the divine constitution of the Church. He cannot share his primatial rights with others, nor can he define them differently. And he cannot either reduce or increase the divine right of the bishops. But human canon law does not place limits on the divine right of the primatial authority. Instead, it serves the realization of this authority to the good of the entire Church (LG 22).

This is the meaning of the words in the *Nota praevia explicativa*, number 4 of the Constitution on the Church, *Lumen gentium*: "As Supreme Pastor of the Church, the Supreme Pontiff can always exercise his power at will (*ad placitum*), as his very office demands" (LG 4). His action here cannot be accused of arbitrariness. His initiative must serve the *bonum ecclesiae*, which cannot be achieved in every individual case through the positive *ius mere ecclesiasticum*.

It must nevertheless be admitted that this opens a breach through which a potential arbitrariness can enter into the exercise of his office. The plenitude of the apostolic authority, over which only God stands, demands that the one who holds it must very strictly examine his conscience before the Lord of the Church and practice supreme self-discipline; he must also be ready to listen to the fraternal counsel of his fellow bishops. He must be willing to accept constructive criticism from the cardinals and his closest collaborators in the Curia, just as once Peter accepted the criticism by Paul; the authority and teaching of these two has entered into the apostolic fundament of the Roman Church. When he is ordained a bishop and then called to assume the Petrine ministry, the highest spiritual authority is conferred on him for the good of the Church, but his human nature and character are not changed. This is not a chance for him to impose his own special theological ideas on the Church, to settle old scores, to succumb to megalomania in the new guise of populism in the media, or to force his way into the role of a media favorite. The supreme authority can be exercised only in the spirit of the uttermost dedication to Christ and of the selfless love of a shepherd for the true good of the Church.

The objective total power and the subjective powerlessness, in the footsteps of the Good Shepherd who laid down his life for the sheep—this is the true Petrine spirituality. Jesus says in Saint Peter to every pope: Now you must stretch out your hands. You can no longer do what you want. You belong completely to me, and I will bind the girdle around your traveling garment "and carry you where you do not wish to go" (Jn 21:18). It is only through death or through the anticipation of death in the daily spiritual dying of the old Adam in us that we shall "glorify God" (Jn 21:19).

This is the morning and evening prayer of the pope: *Non nobis, Domine, sed nomini tuo da gloriam* (Ps 115:1).

The contradiction between a superiority of the council over the pope, or vice versa, is dissolved in the context of the doctrine of collegiality. What remains is the fruitful tension between the principle of unity and the plurality of the episcopal college. It is only in the tension between unity and plurality that the *bonum commune* of the totality is realized: "This college, insofar as it is composed of many, expresses the variety and universality of the People of God, but insofar as it is assembled under one head, it expresses the unity of the flock of Christ" (LG 22). There is a mutual indwelling of the universal Church and the local churches, which belong together according to the principles of unity, plurality, and totality. The Church is a whole. The pope represents its unity and totality in the plurality, while the bishops represent the plurality of the local churches and, since they are united with the bishop of Rome as the head of the Church, they also represent the universal totality—that is, the catholicity of the Church. As the head of the Church, the pope can act alone and represent the Church without thereby excluding the plurality of the local churches and their bishops, because he represents the totality of the Church in its unity.

However, an individual bishop, too, represents the Catholic Church when, as a member of the college of bishops in union with the pope, he authentically proclaims the doctrine of the Church or carries out the sacred ordinations whereby the ordinands are taken into the college of bishops or into the presbyterium of the diocese (or of a religious congregation). The bishop is the head of the presbyterium and guarantees the apostolic authority of the teaching, pastoral, and priestly ministry of the presbyters (LG 28). The council did not find either a weak or a strong compromise between the extremes of a centrifugal episcopalism and a centralistic papalism. Its inherent ecclesiological synthesis allowed it to overcome and exclude the extremes, thereby depriving them of their power to harm the life of the one Church in the plurality of the local churches and the plurality of the expressions of their life:

> Just as in the Gospel, the Lord so disposing, St. Peter and the other apostles constitute one apostolic college, so in a similar way the Roman Pontiff, the successor of Peter, and the bishops, the successors of the apostles, are joined together. [...] But the college or body of bishops (*corpus episcoporum*) has no authority unless it is understood together with the Roman Pontiff, the successor of Peter as its head. The pope's power of primacy over

> all, both pastors and faithful, remains whole and intact. [...] The order of bishops, which succeeds to the college of apostles and gives this apostolic body continued existence, is also the subject of supreme and full power over the universal Church, provided we understand this body together with its head the Roman Pontiff and never without this head. This power can be exercised only with the consent of the Roman Pontiff (LG 22).

In the light of the dogmatic teaching about the primacy of the pope and the collegiality of the bishops, the anachronistic and historicizing debate about whether it was the emperor or the pope who convoked the early councils proves to be a pseudoproblem. The Christian emperors convoked the bishops de facto—but not *de iure divino*—to a council in the region under their rule, but they could not give the bishops any spiritual authority. And even when they did claim competence to take decisions in dogmatic matters, as happened later on in the imperial Byzantine Church, this was a usurpation of competence that was diametrically contradictory of the divine constitution of the Church, and that must be rejected as a heretical opinion and praxis. The magisterium of the episcopate for the entire Church was bestowed on Peter and the apostles, and on their successors in the papacy and the episcopate, by Christ, the invisible and true head and "bishop" of the Church (1 Pt 2:25). The question whether the Roman bishop confirmed or did not confirm, through a formal legal act, synods of the eastern half of the empire, of the entire empire, or of individual provinces says nothing about the binding character or the reversibility of these assemblies for the Catholic and universal Church. Even when the office of the ruler is understood in a sacral manner, the participation by the emperor can be understood only in terms of a political theology—it belongs under no circumstances to the revealed truth, to the *depositum fidei.* For Jesus did not send the apostles only as far as the *Limes* and Hadrian's Wall, nor only as far as the Great Wall of China. He sent them into the whole world, to the furthest bounds of the earth. And the apostolic authority of the pope and the bishops lasts until the end of the ages and encompasses human beings on all the continents and in every political system:

> This collegial union is apparent also in the mutual relations of the individual bishops with particular churches and with the universal Church. The Roman Pontiff, as the successor of Peter, is the perpetual and visible principle and foundation of unity of both the bishops and the faithful. The individual bishops, however, are the visible principle and foundation of unity in their particular churches, fashioned after the model of the universal Church, in and from which churches comes into being the one and only

> Catholic Church. For this reason the individual bishops represent each his own church, but all of them together and with the pope represent the entire Church in the bond of peace, love and unity (LG 23).

The immediate relationship between every bishop and the pope within the college as a whole does not exclude but instead favors the partial fellowships of the bishops of a larger region or nation, or under the primacy of honor and jurisdiction held by the ancient synodal associations that were described by the councils, as well as the later patriarchates (Constantinople, Alexandria, Antioch, Jerusalem, etc.). Here, the episcopal conferences in the Latin Church also possess their own law, and they have a great significance for the proclamation of the faith and for pastoral work (CD 36–38). Independently of the historically conditioned genesis of the political-imperial theology of the pentarchy, Vatican II expresses its esteem for the ecclesiological significance of the synodal and patriarchal constitution of the Catholic Churches of the Eastern tradition. It encourages their restoration or the foundation of new patriarchates:

> The patriarchate, as an institution, has existed in the Church from the earliest times and was recognized by the first ecumenical councils. [...] Though some of the patriarchates of the Eastern Churches are of earlier and some of later date, nonetheless all are equal in respect of patriarchal dignity, without however prejudice to the legitimately established precedence of honor. By the most ancient tradition of the Church the patriarchs of the Eastern Churches are to be accorded special honor, seeing that each is set over his patriarchate as father and head. [...] The patriarchs with their synods are the highest authority for all business of the patriarchate [...] without prejudice to the inalienable right of the Roman Pontiff to intervene in individual cases (OE 7–9).

This also applies to major archbishops who "rule the whole of some individual church or rite" (OE 10).

At Vatican I, *Pastor aeternus* made concrete the primacy of the pope in the infallibility of the proclamation of doctrine, and Vatican II declares the infallibility of the bishops together with the pope. The bishops proclaim as teachers of the faith not only the knowledge they have acquired in personal study or what they have been told to say in order that "those higher up" may hear how the "people in the church pews" think. They are authentic teachers and interpreters of the faith because they are "witnesses to the divine and Catholic truth" (LG 25) that they receive from the apostles and expound with the authority of Christ and the power of the Holy Spirit. It is not the individual bishop on his own but all the bishops together, in union with the pope, who "proclaim Christ's doctrine infallibly whenever [...], authentically teaching matters of faith and morals, they are in agreement on one position as definitively to be held" (LG 25).

These words are followed by an authentic declaration of the doctrine of infallibility from Vatican I, linked to the classical doctrine of the infallibility of councils in matters of faith and morals:

> And this infallibility, with which the Divine Redeemer willed His Church to be endowed in defining doctrine of faith and morals, extends as far as the deposit of Revelation extends, which must be religiously guarded and faithfully expounded. And this is the infallibility which the Roman Pontiff, the head of the college of bishops, enjoys in virtue of his office, when, as the supreme shepherd and teacher of all the faithful, who confirms his brethren in their faith (cf. Luke 22:32), by a definitive act he proclaims a doctrine of faith or morals. And therefore his definitions, of themselves, and not from the consent of the Church, are justly styled irreformable, since they are pronounced with the assistance of the Holy Spirit promised to him in blessed Peter, and therefore they need no approval of others, nor do they allow an appeal to any other judgment. For then the Roman Pontiff is not pronouncing judgment as a private person, but as the supreme teacher of the universal Church, in whom the charism of the infallibility of the Church itself is individually present, he is expounding or defending a doctrine of Catholic faith. The infallibility promised to the Church resides also in the body of Bishops, when that body exercises the supreme magisterium with the successor of Peter. To these definitions the assent of the Church can never be wanting, on account of the activity of that same Holy Spirit, by which the whole flock of Christ is preserved and progresses in unity of faith (LG 25).

Christ has also endowed the whole Church with the charism of infallibility, not *in docendo* but *in credendo*. This means that it would be a complete misunderstanding of the ancient doctrine (taken up anew by Vatican II) that the totality of the faithful who have received the Holy Spirit cannot err if one were to see it as an argument for the inclusion of plebiscitary elements in the Church's constitution. Nor did the council open a door to a falsely so-called democratization of the Church (which ought more correctly to be called its "politicization"). There is no antithesis between the pope and the other bishops, as if they were a closed circle; and one cannot speak of a separation between the episcopate and the rest of the Church. The Church is not a people that gives itself a constitution and elects its government. In 1786, Pope Pius VI summed up and rejected the view of the old Febronians and Jansenists that "Christ wished the Church to be governed like a republic. This form of government does indeed need a president, because unity is a good thing. But this president must not dare to intervene in the affairs of others who also rule [...]. The pope is the head who draws his power and strength from the Church."[4]

On the contrary, the power and strength of the visible head of the Church and of all the members of the Church come only from the invisible Head, from Jesus Christ. He is the head of the Church "which is his body, the fullness of him who fills all in all" (Eph 1:23). The Church was made the people of God through his calling in grace, and Christ at the same time chose as his representatives the bishops with the pope, who were to share in his mission and his authority. The entire people of God, with all its believers and the shepherds instituted by God, enjoys inerrancy in the revealed faith, because it has a share in the prophetic office of Christ: "The entire body of the faithful, anointed as they are by the Holy One (cf. 1 Jn 2:20, 27), cannot err in matters of belief. They manifest this special property by means of the whole people's supernatural discernment in matters of faith when 'from the Bishops down to the last of the lay faithful' they show universal agreement in matters of faith and morals" (LG 12).[5]

This text does not speak of dissent from the revealed faith that is defined by the Church. Surveys taken among the faithful can help enrich a debate, but they have nothing to do with the infallibility of the totality of the faithful in the strict sense, since this is built up not on human opinions and mainstreaming in the media but on the revelation that is present in scripture and tradition and that is expounded in a binding manner by the magisterium:

> That discernment in matters of faith is aroused and sustained by the Spirit of truth. It is exercised under the guidance of the sacred teaching authority, in faithful and respectful obedience to which the people of God accepts that which is not just the word of men but truly the word of God (cf. 1 Thes 2:13). Through it, the people of God adheres unwaveringly to the faith given once and for all to the saints (cf. Jude 3), penetrates it more deeply with right thinking, and applies it more fully in life (LG 12).

In the modernistic schema of development, revelation and Church dogma are only historically conditioned transitional stages, at the end of which stands the self-deification of the human being. The history of religion shows the human being who he or she is. The revelation in Christ, and

4 DH 2595–96.

5 The text quotes Augustine, *De praedestinatione sanctorum*, 14.27.

history up to the present date, are only a prelude to an understanding of God, the world, and the Church in which the human being is himself both subject and object of revelation. This is the true background to the thesis that "existential reality" is the real source of revelation. This reduces scripture and tradition to preliminary historical stages that are abolished by the higher standpoint of the absolute spirit that comes into its own in the human being. The *depositum fidei* (1 Tm 6:20), the totality of the truth of revelation that must be preserved faithfully by the entire Church and especially by the magisterium of the pope and the bishops, is replaced in the age of global communication by the majority opinion that is orchestrated in the media, and it is here that the alleged *sensus fidei* of the people of God is to find its expression. In reality, however, no new revelation takes place in the "sense of faith" of the people of God. Rather, God's revelation of salvation in Jesus Christ, which took place "once for all" (Heb 10:10), is preserved in its completeness in this sense of faith and is applied to people today and tomorrow. It is not a matter of adapting the revelation to the world but of gaining the world for God.

3.
REFORM AND MISSION OF THE CHURCH: THE NEW IMPULSE FROM *EVANGELII GAUDIUM*

WE CAN SPEAK OF THE CHURCH only because of the question about God and the knowledge of his human presence in Jesus Christ for the world. In view of the global and daily tragedies of civil wars and terrorism, with poverty and exploitation, with the wretched situation of refugees, with people dying of overdoses and an increasing number of suicides, with 20 percent of young people addicted to pornography, with the crisis of meaning and the intellectual and moral disorientation of millions of people, the Church of God has the epochal task of giving people a new hope. But the Church is not the light. She can only bear witness to the light that enlightens every human being: to Jesus, the Son of God and Redeemer of all. It is the knowledge of God that decides whether a person becomes conscious of his divine calling and has a future in this world and beyond it.

A Church that merely revolves around its own structural problems would be frighteningly anachronistic and remote from reality. In its being and its mission, it is nothing other than the Church of the triune God who is the origin and the goal of every human being and of the entire cosmos. Any new adjustment of the autonomy and collaboration of the local churches, of the collegiality of the bishops and the primacy of the pope, must never neglect the epochal challenge of the question about God.

In his Apostolic Exhortation *Evangelii gaudium*, Pope Francis speaks of a healthy "decentralization." The life of the Church cannot be concentrated on the pope and his Curia in such a way that the parishes, religious communities, and dioceses would be merely the arena of secondary and derived matters. Rome is not the *centrum unitatis* of the Church, as the Febronians and Gallicans thought. Christ is the center of the Church in a concrete manner in the Eucharist, even when it is celebrated on a wobbly altar in a remote jungle village. On the level of the sacramentality of the Church, the pope is the visible and perpetual principle and fundament of the unity of the Church in faith and of the fellowship of the bishops and of all the local churches.

The pope and the bishops point away from themselves to Christ, who alone gives human beings hope. The pope cannot and need not assess centrally from Rome the various conditions of the Church's life in the individual nations and cultures and personally solve every local problem. An exaggerated centralization of the administration would not help the Church but would rather paralyze its missionary dynamism.[6] This is why a reformed exercise of the primacy is one element in the new evangelization that was the theme of the synod of bishops in October 2012. This concerns the institutions of the universal governance of the Church, especially the dicasteries of the Roman Curia that serve the pope in the exercise of the supreme, full, and immediate authority over the whole Church. These departments "therefore perform their duties in his name and with his authority for the good of the churches and in the service of the sacred pastors" (CD 9). The new evangelization entails that the bishops, the synods, and the episcopal conferences, too, must accept a greater responsibility, which includes "a certain competence with regard to the magisterium," since this competence is given to them through their ordination and their canonical mission, not only through a special papal authorization. "Bishops, teaching in communion with the Roman Pontiff, are to be respected by all as witnesses to divine and Catholic truth" (LG 25).

The papal magisterium does not replace the magisterium of the bishops and their collaboration on the national or continental level.[7] Rather, it presupposes this magisterium and promotes it in its responsibility for the entire Church.[8]

6 Francis, *Evangelii gaudium*, 32.

7 See, for example, the documents of CELAM: Puebla, Medellin, Santo Domingo, Aparecida.

8 Francis, *Evangelii gaudium*, 16.

The pope refers explicitly to the Motu proprio *Apostolos suos* (1998), in which Pope John Paul II described in greater detail, on the basis of the Second Vatican Council, the tasks of the episcopal conferences. Despite what superficial interpretations have claimed, this document did not give a signal for a change of direction or for a "revolution in the Vatican." Power struggles and clashes over competences would make it impossible for the Church to fulfill its missionary task, and according to the ecclesiological synthesis of Vatican II an antagonistic or dialectical interpretation of the relationship between the universal Church and the local churches is inadmissible. The historical extremes of papalism-curialism on the one hand, and episcopalism-conciliarism-Gallicanism on the other hand, as well as Febronianism and Old Catholicism, only go to show what one must *not do.* These examples make it clear that the absolutization of one constitutional element at the cost of the other contradicts the confession of faith in the *una ecclesia catholica.* The collegial and fraternal unity of the bishops of the universal Church *cum et sub Petro* has its foundation in the sacramentality of the Church and is therefore of divine right. A power struggle between centralistic and particularistic forces would mean the desacramentalization of the Church. And what would be left? A secularized and politicized Church, which would differ from an NGO only by degree. This would be a complete contrast to the Apostolic Exhortation *Evangelii gaudium.*

In its literary genre, this text is not dogmatic but paraenetic. Its dogmatic basis presupposes the doctrine about the Church in *Lumen gentium,* which was taught with the highest binding character by the magisterium.[9] The pope seeks to overcome lethargy and resignation in face of extreme secularization and to put an end to the paralyzing debates within the Church between traditionalist and modernist ideologies. Despite all the storms and headwinds, the barque of Peter must once against hoist the sail of joy about Jesus, who is in our midst. And the disciples ought to take up the oars for a missionary Church, vigorously and without fear.

If the Church presents to outsiders a picture of internal division and hostility, one cannot expect that anyone will perceive the Church as a credible witness to the love of God and will learn to love the Church as his or her mother.

In the Dogmatic Constitution on the Church, *Lumen gentium,* the Second Vatican Council does not start from a sociological-immanentist definition of the Church, as if it were constituted by the intention to form a community on the part of those who shared some religious-ethical conviction.

9 Francis, *Evangelii gaudium*, 17.

No: it is in the proceeding of the Son from the Father within the Godhead that the Church has its innermost origin. In the Son, from all eternity, every human being is already destined "before the foundation of the world" to share in the divine life. God "destined us in love to be his sons through Jesus Christ" (Eph 1:5). The fellowship of human beings with God, which becomes a historical reality when they are created, is already prefigured in Christ from the very beginning of human history. It is prepared in the covenant people in salvation history. Finally, it is constituted in the Christ event and the outpouring of the Spirit and becomes manifest as the Church of the new and definitive covenant (LG 2).[10]

Since the Church is instituted by God, it cannot become a purely human organization. This means that the question about its foundation "as a legal association" (so to speak) by the "historical" Jesus is objectively erroneous. It is also anachronistic with regard to the theological hermeneutic of the historical revelation. The Church, as a fellowship of life with Jesus, is grounded in his divine nature and in his relationship to the Father as his Son. It is revealed historically in his activity as a human being, since it is in his person that the kingdom of God has come. This includes the gathering of the disciples to whom he gives a share in his authority and his mission. As the eschatological mediator of the rule of God, Jesus established through his proclamation, through his saving deeds, and through his Cross and Resurrection the eschatological covenant people as a *communio* of human beings with God. He also gave to the fellowship of those who believe in him a share in his own mission.

It is thus the two elements of *communio* and *missio* that constitute the community of Jesus's disciples as the sign and instrument of the unity of human beings with God and with each other. The Church is thus essentially one single reality that serves and mediates this union. The Church is not the sum total of individuals in their autonomous, unmediated relationship to God. The Church is already organically united to Christ, as the body to the head. As the head, Christ is the principle of the unity of all the members of the body. Only in this way can all rejoice and share in suffering when another person rejoices and suffers. The plurality of the members of the body of Christ is *unus* (Gal 3:28) in relation to Christ—*totus Christus, caput et corpus*—who is the one and only mediator of the entire creation and the eschatological man, the new Adam. All are taken into his relationship as Son to the Father in the Holy Spirit (see Gal 4:4–6).

10 On the relationship between the Old and New Testaments, see the document of the Pontifical Biblical Commission, *The Jewish People and their Sacred Scriptures in the Christian Bible* (Vatican City: Libreria editrice Vaticana, 2001).

This is why the word "Church" (*ekklêsia/ecclesia*), which already appears in the Septuagint as the Greek translation for the assembly of the people of God, is always used in the singular in relation to God the Father, Christ the Son, and the Holy Spirit: the one and only people of God, the one and only body of Christ that is the Church, and the one and only temple of the Holy Spirit. This Church, in the service of Christ's unique and unifying and universal (catholic) mediation of salvation, is necessary universal (that is, catholic) in its being and its mission, because it proclaims salvation to all human beings. The Gospel of Christ frees them from the dispersal of Babel and calls them from the many peoples and languages into the pentecostal unity of the one people of God. One and the same Church is present in the many peoples and languages and forms them into the one humankind in Christ who is the Head of the Church and of the whole creation.

4.
THE ONE CHURCH IN ITS UNIVERSAL MISSION AND ITS LOCAL CONCRETIZATION

THE CHURCH'S SACRAMENTALITY IS GROUNDED in the Incarnation. On the analogy of the divine-human unity of Christ, the one, holy, catholic, and apostolic Church exists as a spiritual-invisible fellowship of life with God and as a visible society with a hierarchical constitution. The unity is manifested in the shared apostolic teaching, the sacramental life, and the hierarchical constitution. This means that it cannot merely be the making visible of a supratemporal idea, a *civitas platonica* that unites the peoples. As a Church for the human being who is made up of soul and body and who lives in history and in society, it is made concrete in accordance with the cultural conditions of human life in the coordinates of space and time. The Church of the Word of God who has entered into space and time realizes itself at one and the same time both universally and locally. The one and universal Church, which is guided by the pope and by the bishops in fellowship with him, exists in and out of the local churches. This is what is meant by the formula *in quibus et ex quibus una et unica Ecclesia catholica existit* (LG 23). The mission of Christ concerns all human beings in all places and at all times. However, he himself lived in one of the many places on earth and at one tiny temporal segment of human history. His mission was realized uniquely in history in the man Jesus of Nazareth, who lived and worked at one particular time in one particular place in the world. We already find before Easter the tension between universal mission and local presence when Jesus chooses the apostles and sends them to all the places where it was not possible for him to come in person. After Easter, he sends the apostles to all the places in the world where he already is, and he promises them—all of them together and each one individually—his presence, so that, through the mediation of the many apostles in every place in the world, the one Christ may be present, mediating salvation and uniting humankind. In this sense, the concept of "Church" can also be employed in the plural of the local churches: the one and only Church of God is present as the universal Church in the churches of God in Corinth, Rome, Manila, Cape Town, et cetera. And the believers locally encounter nothing other than the one Church of Christ, in which the Holy Spirit unites all the baptized with each other and integrates them into the unity of the body of Christ, so that all are one in Christ and constitute the one *familia Dei* as sons and daughters of God in Christ.

There is thus no spiritual authority that is initially in a state of suspension and is then distributed and passed to and fro between the pope and the bishops, between the universal Church and the local churches, in keeping with considerations of political and strategic expediency. On the contrary: Christ called all the apostles, and he himself placed the apostle Peter at their head as the fundament and principle of the unity of the one apostolic authority and mission for the entire Church. Episcopal ordination also manifests the collegial nature of the episcopal ministry, in which the individual bishop is related to the college as a whole and to the pope as its head, without whom the college cannot exercise any universal authority in the teaching and pastoral ministry:

> This collegial union is apparent also in the mutual relations of the individual bishops with particular churches and with the universal Church. The Roman Pontiff, as the successor of Peter, is the perpetual and visible principle and foundation of unity both of the bishops and of the faithful. The individual bishops, however, are the visible principle and foundation of unity in their particular churches, fashioned after the model of the universal Church, in and from which churches comes into being the one and only Catholic Church. For this reason the individual bishops represent each his own church, but all of them together and with the Pope represent the entire Church in the bond of peace, love and unity (LG 23).

The relationship between universality and particularity can be defined only in a consistently Christological and ecclesiological perspective. There is no analogy to it in the governmental and nongovernmental forms of organization in human societies and businesses. The unity of the Church is realized in the concreteness of the local church. This is the reason why a community of persons can never be a local church in the true sense of the term; it is also the reason why each local church is, of its nature, nothing other than the universal Church in that particular place. This mutual indwelling is the Catholic *communio* of the Church, which is constituted as the *communio ecclesiarum.*

5.
THE RECIPROCAL INTEGRATION OF PRIMACY AND EPISCOPACY

CHAPTER III OF *LUMEN GENTIUM* DESCRIBES THE UNITY of universality and particularity. It presupposes the apostolic constitution of the local church, which means that, like the Church of Christ as a whole, the local church too does not bring itself into existence through the intention of individual Christians to form an association. It is Christ himself who through his apostles and their successors in the *munus praedicandi, sanctificandi, et gubernandi* founds the universal Church in and out of the local churches as the *communio ecclesiarum.* One can speak of a local church only when it visibly realizes in the bishop, who is the successor of the apostles, the unity with the other local churches and the unity with the origin of the Church in Christ and the apostles. This is manifested in the unity of the apostolic confession of faith and the sacramental-liturgical act of making present the salvation we receive in Christ. The doctrines of the bishops as successors of the apostles, of their collegial unity with each other, and of their unity with the successor of Peter as the visible head of the entire Church and of the college of bishops are thus constitutive of what Catholics understand the concept "Church" to mean.

This is the necessary presupposition if we are to evaluate correctly the following description of universality and particularity as the realization of the unity and the oneness of the Church of Christ:

> Just as in the Gospel, the Lord so disposing, St. Peter and the other apostles constitute one apostolic college, so in a similar way the Roman Pontiff, the successor of Peter, and the bishops, the successors of the apostles, are joined together. [...] But the college or body of bishops has no authority unless it is understood together with the Roman Pontiff, the successor of Peter as its head. The pope's power of primacy over all, both pastors and faithful, remains whole and intact [...]. This college, insofar as it is composed of many, expresses the variety and universality of the People of God, but insofar as it is assembled under one head, it expresses the unity of the flock of Christ. In it, the bishops, faithfully recognizing the primacy and pre-eminence of their head, exercise their own authority for the good of their own faithful, and indeed of the whole Church, the Holy Spirit sup-

> porting its organic structure and harmony with moderation. The supreme power in the universal Church, which this college enjoys, is exercised in a solemn way in an ecumenical council. [...] This same collegiate power can be exercised together with the pope by the bishops living in all parts of the world, provided that the head of the college calls them to collegiate action, or at least approves of or freely accepts the united action of the scattered bishops, so that it is thereby made a collegial act (LG 22).

The individual local churches make up the one Catholic Church of God in the *communio* of the episcopal churches. Each local church has a share in the entire Church through its unity with it and with its apostolic origin, through the unity of the confession of faith, through the Church's sacred scripture, through its liturgical-sacramental forms of mediating salvation, and through the apostolic authority that is embodied and guaranteed by the bishop in the succession that goes back to the apostles. This does not prevent it from flourishing richly. Indeed, it promotes this richness, which can be seen through inculturation into the various peoples and epochs of history. The local church of Rome is one among many local churches, but with a special character—namely, the fact that its apostolic foundation through the martyrdom *verbi et sanguinis* of the apostles Peter and Paul gives it, among the apostolic local churches, a primacy in the total witness and the unity of life of the *catholica communio.* Because of this *potentior principalitas,* every other local church must be in concord with it.[11] With regard to the substance of the faith, the two Vatican Councils added nothing to this in their teaching about catholicity and particularity, about the collegiality of the bishops, and about the orientation to the *cathedra Petri* in doctrine and in discipline.

6.
THE POPE AND THE BISHOPS AT THE SERVICE OF THE ONE CHURCH

IT IS, HOWEVER, IMPORTANT TO UNDERSTAND the episcopal ministry itself as a sacramental reality in the sacramental Church. The bishop must not be confused with a moderator of purely human associations.

The episcopate is an office instituted perpetually by God for the Church (LG 18). The "guardians appointed by the Holy Spirit" (Acts 20:28) preside over the Church in the place of God (LG 19). In sacramental ordination, the Spirit brings it about "that bishops in an eminent and visible way sustain the

11 See Irenaeus of Lyons, *Adv. haer.* II.3.2.

roles of Christ himself as Teacher, Shepherd and High Priest, and that they act in His person" (LG 21). They are "vicars and ambassadors of Christ" in the exercise of their ministry (LG 27).

The collegial dimension of the episcopal ministry, which concerns the universal Church, is manifested by the fact that when the successor is sacramentally installed in this ministry, this is done through ordination by "neighboring bishops of other Churches." The episcopal ordination is a sign that integrates the bishop into the college of bishops and entrusts to him a responsibility for the one worldwide Catholic Church, which exists in the *communio ecclesiarum*.

In his local church, the bishop is "the visible principle and foundation of unity" (LG 23). This involves the *communio* of all the faithful and the college of the office-bearers: presbyters, deacons, and those who have other ecclesial ministries. The episcopal office on its own does not absorb into itself the plurality of missions and ministries. It prevents the individual ministries from falling apart and promotes the plurality of ministries in the individual members; it also guarantees the unity of the Church's mission in *martyria, diakonia*, and *leitourgia*.

Since the college of bishops serves the unity of the Church, it must bear in itself the principle of its unity. This can only be the bishop of a local church, not the president of a federation made up of regional and continental associations of churches. Nor can this be a purely material principle (majority decisions, the delegation of rights to an elected governing body, and so on). Since the inner essence of the episcopal ministry is a personal testimony, the principle of the unity of the episcopate itself is embodied in a person. According to the Catholic understanding, the personal principle of unity exists in the Roman bishop, both in its origin and in the present-day exercise of this ministry. As bishop, he is the successor of Peter, who himself, as the first apostle and the first witness to the Resurrection, embodied in his person the unity of the college of apostles. The characterization of the Petrine ministry as an episcopal mission is decisively important for a theology of the primacy, as is the recognition that this office belongs not to human law but to divine law, since it can be exercised only in the authority of Christ, thanks to a charism that is given personally in the Holy Spirit to the one who holds it.

In *Evangelii gaudium*, the pope envisages an improved praxis that corresponds to today's global and digitalized civilization. Although the primacy and the episcopacy belong to the essence of the Church, the forms of their realization in history are necessarily diverse. The pope's summons to a renewed perception of the collegiality of the bishops is the very opposite of a relativization of the ministry that Christ has entrusted to him to serve the unity of all the bishops and the faithful in the revealed faith, the shared life nourished by sacramental grace, and the mission to mediate the unity of the human race in God (LG 1). Since the episcopal ministry is collegial by its nature, his ordination and his canonical mission entrust the bishop also with a share in care and responsibility for the good of the universal Church: "The individual bishops, insofar as their own discharge of their duty permits, are obliged to enter into a community of work among themselves and with the successor of Peter, upon whom was imposed in a special way the great duty of spreading the Christian name" (LG 23).

In its acknowledgement of the fruitful apostolate that had been carried out by the episcopal conferences that existed up to that date, and in the desire that these bodies should be set up everywhere, the Second Vatican Council offered the following brief definition: "An episcopal conference is, as it were, a council in which the bishops of a given nation or territory jointly exercise their pastoral office to promote the greater good which the Church offers mankind, especially through the forms and methods of the apostolate fittingly adapted to the circumstances of the age" (CD 38.1). The theological and practical realization of the services rendered to the universal Church, and to the local churches that are gathered together in these conferences, is further developed and concretized in the Motu Proprio *Apostolos suos*. This also includes a competence with regard to the magisterium, which belongs to the whole body of the bishops who are the members of a conference;[12] the conference is at the service of the unity in faith and of the concrete application in one specific cultural sphere. The reference to the successor of Peter, who is the visible principle of the unity of the Church and of the totality of the bishops of the Catholic Church, is constitutive of every ecumenical council, every particular synod, and every episcopal conference, and belongs to the divine law that must be the basis of every code of canon law. An episcopal conference can never issue separate binding dogmatic definitions, and still less can it relativize defined dogmas and constitutive sacramental structures (for example, by making its own office of teaching and pastoral care dependent on bodies that belong to purely ecclesial law). Separatist tendencies and arrogant behavior inflict damage on the Church. The revelation is entrusted to the one and universal Church to be preserved faithfully, and this Church is governed by the pope and by the bishops in unity with him (LG 8; DV 10). The Catholic Church is a *communio ecclesiarum*, not a federation of national churches or a world union of ecclesiastical fellowships with similar confessions of faith that respect the Roman bishop, thanks to human tradition, as their honorary president. Nation, language, and culture are not constitutive principles of the Church that attests and realizes in Christ the

12 John Paul II, Motu Proprio *Apostolos suos* (May 21, 1998), 21; CIC can. 753.

unity of the peoples, although they are, in a regulative sense, indispensable instruments through which the entire wealth and fullness of Christ unfolds in the redeemed.

It is the aim of *Evangelii gaudium* to bring the Church together internally, in order that the people of God may not stand in its own way in its missionary service of a humanity that needs salvation and help. Pope Francis sketches in his apostolic exhortation "some guidelines which can encourage and guide the whole Church in a new phase of evangelization, one marked by enthusiasm and vitality."[13]

7.
THE MINISTRY AND THE REFORM OF THE ROMAN CURIA

HISTORICAL EXPERIENCE TEACHES that whenever the Church freed itself from the models of the worldly exercise of power, and the poison of secular thinking departed from its spirit and body, the way was open for a deep spiritual renewal in Jesus Christ, its Head and the model of its life. What matters for the Church is the Gospel, the truth, and salvation. In its teaching, life, and constitution, it finds its criterion not in the *dominium* of the kings but in the *ministerium* of the apostles: *non quia dominamur fidei vestrae, sed cooperatores sumus gaudii vestri* (2 Cor 1:24).

One can study this principle historically in every attempt at a reform *in capite et membris,* for example in the great Gregorian reform movement in the eleventh century, when the *libertas ecclesiae* was at stake, or in the Tridentine reform, or in the great new awakening of the Church at the time of the Second Vatican Council, into which the biblical, patristic, liturgical, and ecclesiological renewal movements of the nineteenth and twentieth centuries flowed. The secular power of the pope and of the prince-bishops or courtier-bishops was all too often superimposed upon the spiritual mission of the Church and did it more damage than good in not a few historical situations. Even when material possessions and secular power were intended to ensure the independence of the Church vis-à-vis the secular rulers, the unnatural liaison between political power and spiritual ministry had a corrupting influence, favoring ideas of power and prestige over a conduct of ecclesial office that was in keeping with Gospel. The state-church system of the modern period and the royal patronage in the Spanish and Portuguese empires, where the Church was totally subordinate to the *raison d'état,* were

13 Francis, *Evangelii gaudium,* 17.

even more destructive. Patterns of the courtier-bishop still have an effect when the status symbols of the CEOs of international firms and accommodation to the ideological mainstream prove that a bishop "fits our modern age well and cuts a good figure in the media." Popularity among the people, avoidance of giving offense, and keeping quiet are not criteria for a bishop. He should be guided by love for Jesus, the Good Shepherd, who laid down his life. Paul writes to Timothy, who exemplifies the biblical ideal of the bishop:

> But as for you, man of God, aim at righteousness, godliness, faith, love, steadfastness, gentleness. Fight the good fight of the faith; take hold of the eternal life to which you were called when you made the good confession in the presence of many witnesses. In the presence of God who gives life to all things, and of Christ Jesus who in his testimony before Pontius Pilate made the good confession, I charge you to keep the commandment unstained and free from reproach until the appearing of our Lord Jesus Christ (1 Tm 6:11–14).

It is not societal consensus, the functioning of Christianity as a civil religion, or the contacts with top politicians that make the Church significant, but the word of salvation for the poor on the peripheries of life.

There were often important popes on the *cathedra Petri* who were shepherds of the universal Church and initiated, supported, and promoted church reform in accordance with their ministry. The impressive motto of Pope Pius X has not been forgotten: *Omnia in Christo instaurare,* "To renew all things in Christ." God has founded the Church through and in Jesus Christ, the Word made flesh, as his house and people, as a fellowship of the saints and "sacrament" of the salvation of the world (LG 1; GS 45), so that "all may be saved and come to the knowledge of the truth" (1 Tm 2:4).

The Church cannot wish to understand itself or to justify itself before the potentates and the leaders of opinion of the "age of this world" (Rom 12:2; 1 Cor 2:12), in accord with the worldly categories of power and prestige and the human criteria of wealth, splendor, and outward show. Before one has recourse to financial and economic advisers, one must reflect on the essence and the mission of the Church of God, because the Church will not be renewed by prescinding from its spiritual and sacramental being. Although "the Church of the living God," which is "the pillar and bulwark of the truth" (1 Tm 3:15; Heb 12:22) needs human means to accomplish its mission, it "is not set up to seek earthly glory, but to proclaim, even by its own example, humility and self-sacrifice" (LG 8).

In face of the failure of the human beings in the Church—whether out of human weakness or in the frivolous instrumentalization of the means of salvation and of spiritual authority for one's own advantage, which entails the secularization of the Church—there has existed and still exists the temptation to spiritualize the Church and transpose it into the realm of the ideal and of dreams, far away from the abyss of temptation and crime, of sin, death, and the devil, as if it were not through the valley of the cross and of suffering that we are led to the glory of the resurrection. But because the Church, in a certain analogy to the Incarnation of the WORD, is an inherent unity of a spiritual fellowship and a visible gathering together and serves the Spirit of God in this way as a sign and instrument of salvation in order to continue the work of Christ among the human race until the world is perfected in Christ, we must affirm that the Church is *both* holy and sanctifying, thanks to God, and *also*—as far as we human beings on the pilgrim path of faith are concerned—"[is] always in need of being purified" and "always follows the way of penance and renewal" (LG 8).

It was in this sense that Pope Benedict XVI spoke of the necessity of a certain desecularization as the countermove to the Church's secularization. Pope Francis takes this idea up with the theme of the "poor Church for the poor" as opposed to the secular and ultimately nihilistic thinking and conduct of many of the Church's representatives. The price of the self-secularization that the Church must pay for its conformity to the secularist society without God is too high.

In his discourse to the Curia and to the entire Church before Christmas 2014, the pope emphasized the priority of the spiritual goal of the Church vis-à-vis the earthly means, which must never become an end in themselves. This was a spiritual admonition and an aid to the examination of conscience; it does not qualify as a confirmation of all the obscure legends and conspiracy fantasies about what goes on "behind the walls of the Vatican." The renewal finds its compass, not in the possessions of the Church, the size of its institutions, and the number of those employed in the dioceses and religious congregations (in schools and hospitals), but in the spirit of love in which the Church serves people in its preaching, in the sacraments, and in *caritas*.

The reform of the Curia, which was the object of the debates prior to the conclave in 2013, is meant as a model for the spiritual renewal of the entire Church. The Curia (and on analogy to it, all the ecclesial institutions) is not to be seen like a secular civil service that administers a spiritual fellowship that is actually alien to the bureaucrats, a fellowship oriented to the salvation of human beings. On the contrary, the Curia must understand itself on the basis of the spiritual essence of the Church and must give an example for the governance of the Church on various levels.

Accordingly, our first question must be about the ecclesiological *locus* of the Curia in the church of Rome. What does the Roman Curia mean for the pope in his ministry as teacher and shepherd of all Christians? The goal of a curial reform will not be reached if one expects the master plan to be supplied by experts in politics, finance, and economics. If the Church is not a worldly organization, its very nature means that it cannot be renewed with purely inner-worldly means, but only with spiritual means. The means and the end must both be spiritual. The Curia is not a profane administrative structure that escapes the tendency to form a caste of functionaries and a nomenklatura of power only thanks to a private spirituality of those who work there. Of its inherent nature, the Curia is a spiritual institution that has its roots in the sacramentality of the church of Rome, which was honored through the martyrdom of Peter and Paul with a special mission for the entire Church.

A distinction must be drawn between the Roman Curia and the civil institutions of the Vatican State, whose organization is subject to the normal laws of secular administration.

The internal organizational principle of the Roman Curia is generated by the spiritual nature and mission of the Church, because "in exercising supreme, full, and immediate power in the universal Church, the Roman Pontiff makes use of the departments of the Roman Curia which, therefore, perform their duties in his name and with his authority for the good of the churches and in the service of the sacred pastors" (CD 9). On the basis of this theological description, the Second Vatican Council called for an up-to-date reorganization of the Curia. The structural ordering and operation of the Curia find their criteria in the being and the mission of the bishop of Rome as the successor of Peter, the *first* of the apostles—a being and a mission that must be grasped with theological means. In Saint Peter, the bishop of Rome is appointed by Christ for his Church as the "permanent and visible source and foundation of unity of faith and of the unity of both the bishops and the faithful" (see LG 18; 23). Just as it is only in the light of the revealed faith that we can draw the distinction between the Church in its supernatural reality and a religious fellowship founded solely by human beings, so too it is only in faith that we understand that the pope and the bishops have a sacramental authority that mediates salvation and that unites us to God. This distinguishes them from the leaders that every religious fellowship gives itself out of a sociological and organizational necessity.

Because of the universal will to save that has become concrete in Jesus, the Church is realized both universally, by gathering the whole of humanity into a unity, and at the same time locally and concretely, where people dwell, live, and die, so that "the one and only Catholic Church comes into being in and from the local Churches" (see LG 23).

In the local church, the bishop appointed by the Holy Spirit (Acts 20:28) is the vicar of Christ, and the principle and fundament of unity—he is not in the least a delegate and vicar of the pope. In this context, we must understand the doctrine of the primacy of the pope and the collegiality of the bishops as an expression of their shared care for the entire Church as the *communio ecclesiarum*. This makes it difficult to define the relationships between the pope and the bishops, and between the universal Church and the local church, in the terms of secular organizational forms. The pope is not a superbishop (in the sense of the historical curialism of the canon lawyers) from whom the spiritual authority of the bishop is derived; nor have the bishops appointed someone to represent their unity (as the Gallicans and Febronians imagined). The universal Church is not the result of adding together the local churches; nor are the local churches branches of the universal Church. The Church is the one body of Christ as the *corpus* or *communio ecclesiarum*. There is an inherent interlacing of the universal Church and the local church, which is governed and represented by the entire episcopate together with the bishop of Rome as the successor of Peter. The universal shepherd and teacher, in whom the unity and indivisibility of the episcopate and of the entire Catholic Church are synthesized and represented, himself works as bishop of the local church of Rome and thus as the bearer of the primacy of that church. Through his martyrdom, the apostle Peter united the primacy of his successor forever with the Roman church. Just as "the bishop is in the Church and the Church in the bishop,"[14] so too the Roman bishop is never bishop and shepherd of the universal Church without his bond to the church of Rome, which is his diocese. The Roman bishop has in his person the primacy over the universal Church—but never without the church of Rome. He is its own shepherd, and just as the head cannot be separated from the body, so too the union between the bishop of Rome and the Roman church is indissoluble. This is why the tradition often speaks of the primacy of the Roman church. The pope always exercises the primacy in connection with the Roman church. As its head, he is at the same time the visible head of the entire Church. Because of the special authority due to its foundation by Peter and Paul (*propter potentiorem principalitatem*), every other church must agree with it in the apostolic faith.[15] The predicates of the "one, holy, catholic, and apostolic" Church are thus realized a fortiori in the Roman church, which from ancient times has also been called the "Holy Roman church," not because of the subjective moral holiness of its head and members, but because of the holiness of its commission to present visibly and

14 Cyprian of Carthage, *Ep.* 66.8.

15 Irenaeus of Lyons, *Adv. haer.* III.3.2.

realize concretely the unity of all the churches in Christ. Its specific mission is to preserve the apostolic doctrine and tradition, the *depositum fidei,* the *sana doctrina apostolorum,* intact and unabridged.

The primacy has nothing to do with domination of other churches. Of its inherent nature, it consists of "presiding in love." It is the first cathedra in the Church, both in the Roman local church and in the Catholic worldwide Church,[16] and at the same time it serves the unity and fellowship of all the churches and the faithful in God the Father, the Son, and the Holy Spirit. The Roman bishop exercises his service of the unity in faith and the fellowship personally and immediately, because he is in his person the successor of Peter, and because Peter is in him always the fundament on which the Lord builds his Church. But he never does this without the support that the Roman church owes him, since he is its bishop and the church of Rome remains his local church. If one were to dissolve the sacramental bond between the universal shepherd and the church of Rome, one would make the pope the manager of a Catholic world federation, thereby transmuting the divine institution of the primacy into a form of organization that was merely necessary or desirable from a sociological perspective. In the course of history, the College of Cardinals has developed from the bishops of the suburbicarian dioceses and the most important presbyters and deacons of the church of Rome. In a diocese, the body of priests is related to the bishop through its representation by the priests' council, and one could likewise say that the College of Cardinals of the Holy Roman church is the presbyteral council for the pope "in his service of the unity of the faith and the fellowship of the universal Church" (see LG 18).

The relatively recent decree that the cardinals of the Curia must also be bishops corresponds to their integration into the collegiality of the bishops. This is of no little importance, for example in the meetings when the bishops make their *ad limina* visits.

Through all the changes in history, the basic idea has been maintained that the Roman church, in the form of the College of Cardinals, helps the pope to carry out his universal ministry as shepherd and his task of teaching. Some of the cardinals created by the pope head the Roman congregations; these are a part of the entire consistory of cardinals and are assigned to one particular departmental responsibility. The Roman Curia consists basically of the congregations of cardinals, to which, in the aftermath of Vatican II, bishops also belong; in addition, there are some pontifical councils. The Curia is not an intermediate authority between the pope and each individual bishop and/or the ensemble of the bishops. The curial cardinals and bishops

16 Ignatius of Antioch, *Ep. ad Rom.*, preamble.

assist the pope in his service of the Catholic unity of the Church in relation to the Catholic plurality of the local episcopal churches and supply him with the "fitting means" (LG 25) for the exercise of his ministry as shepherd and teacher. In the context of the task assigned to them, and also of their competence to take decisions, the cardinal prefects guarantee the collaboration of the assembly of cardinals, of the college of consultors, and of the collaborators in the various offices and in the relevant commissions, and they assume responsibility vis-à-vis the pope for the results of their consultation and their work. The pope is not in any way restricted by the activity of the Curia; he is only supported in the primacy that has been entrusted to him for the worldwide Church as bishop of Rome and that he exercises in the Holy Spirit.

The Synod of Bishops does not belong to the Roman Curia, because the bishops who assemble there take part collegially, not as representatives of the pope. However, its General Secretariat is an organ of the Holy See; it is not a representation of the bishops vis-à-vis the pope. Unlike an ecumenical council, it is not a "sacred synod" qua the assembly of all the churches and of the episcopate. But it is an expression of the collegiality of the episcopal ministry in fellowship with the pope and under his leadership (CD 5). The Roman Curia, on the other hand, is the aid that the Holy Roman church gives the pope in the exercise of his primacy over all the churches with their bishops. In formal terms, the difference between the Curia and the Synod of Bishops is that the Curia supports the pope in his service of the unity of the Church, while the assembly of the bishops with and under the pope expresses and actualizes the catholicity of the Church, for all the bishops share in the *sollicitudo omnium ecclesiarum* (LG 23). In concrete terms, the two missions overlap, because the heads of the Roman dicasteries are ex officio synodal fathers and many participants at the synod are cardinals and bishops who are members of the congregations and councils.

This means that the Synod of Bishops, the episcopal conferences, and other forms of collaboration among the bishops with and under the pope belong to a different theological category than the Roman Curia. Only one who thinks in the categories of politics and the media would see the harmonic relationship between primacy and episcopacy as an unworthy quarrel about competences. A quarrel of this kind is utterly foreign to the nature of the collaboration of the pope, the Roman Curia, a council, synods of bishops, and episcopal conferences. The Holy Spirit, to whom we cannot be indifferent, creates harmony between the two poles of unity and plurality, both between the universal Church and the local churches and in the local churches themselves. The spirit of the world sows conflict and distrust. "Decentralization" does not mean that now it is the episcopal conferences, and especially their secretariats, that are to receive more "power"—the very idea is an ecclesiological perversion. It means that they are to exercise the responsibility that is theirs thanks to their episcopal authority to teach and to govern; naturally, they do so in organic unity with the primacy of the pope and of the Roman church.

The operation of the Curia is collegial, on the analogy of the collegiality of the priests under the leadership of their bishop. The prefect is only the head and representative, while the fathers in the plenary assembly bear the same responsibility for the good of the entire Church. The superiors lead the departments in a fraternal spirit, with appreciation and respect for their highly qualified collaborators. For the reform of the Curia, it is important that we should also understand ourselves as a spiritual family. Unity of spirit in care for one another, prayer and the Eucharist, retreats, and collaboration in pastoral work and in preaching give the office work a spiritual character. The great dicasteries were once called "Sacred Congregations," because they represent the Holy Roman church. This adjective was dropped, clearly because it was felt to be a decorative baroque term; nevertheless, it reminds us that the service of that which is holy obligates us to speak, think, and act in a holy manner.

The reform of the Curia and of the Church extends beyond a more efficient organization, cutting costs, restructuring, and control of expenditure. Its goal is to unite the papacy more deeply with the Church and with the bishops, and to let the pope's mission shine out brightly in the world of today and tomorrow. It can be helpful here to look at the role of the College of Cardinals and of the Curia in the context of the ecclesiological position of the Holy Roman church and of its bishop.

The Church faces a challenge from a worldwide secularism that defines the human being without God in a hitherto unknown radicality, thereby blocking his access to transcendence; and posthumanism pulls the carpet from under his feet. In the intoxication of relativism, there is no "above" and "below," neither good nor evil, and the boundary between truth and falsehood gets blurred. The Church's weakness is that it is itself infected by these grave illnesses. In order that the glory of God may once again shine out in what Jesus calls "the house of my Father" as the light for all human beings, Pope Francis is carrying out a spiritual cleansing of the temple, which is both painful and liberating. We see clearly the goal of the reform of the Church and the Curia when, like the disciples long ago, we recall "that it was written, 'Zeal for your house will consume me'" (Jn 2:17).

8.
THE MISSION OF THE POPE AND THE CHURCH TODAY

In its Decree on the Mission Activity of the Church, *Ad gentes*, the Second Vatican Council makes this lapidary affirmation: "The pilgrim Church is missionary [that is, en route as a Church that is sent] by her very nature, since it is from the mission of the Son and the mission of the Holy Spirit that she draws her origin, in accordance with the decree of God the Father" (AG 2).

"This duty is to be fulfilled by the order of bishops, under the successor of Peter" (AG 6), supported by the prayer and the collaboration of the entire Church.

The Church's mission, which is led and organized universally by the successor of Peter, is the exact opposite of a Europeanization of the Church, the seizing of the material and cultural goods of others under a religious draping (colonialism), or the economic and ideological expansion of one's own value systems in order to dominate others or force them to do what others think is good for them (neocolonialism; gender mainstreaming; the systematic destruction of natural marriage and the family; employing abortion programs as a method of birth control). The Church's mission is not only the opposite of these disgraceful and harmful activities; this mission is also the harshest criticism of such activities in the name of God. The Creator and Father of all wants to plant his love and truth in the heart of every human being and in the life of all the peoples, in order that the Church may unite all human beings in the one family of God, and that the Church of Christ may be one in the plurality of the peoples and cultures. In the Holy Spirit, who is poured out upon all flesh (Acts 2:17), they speak the one language of love. They have forgotten the language of the violence that separates and kills. Pentecost has overcome Babel.

"Missionary activity is nothing else and nothing less than an epiphany, or a manifesting of God's decree, and its fulfilment in the world and in world history, in the course of which God, by means of mission, manifestly works out the history of salvation" (AG 9).

This can liberate some persons from doubt and discouragement. Christianity not only has a future; it is also the only power through which the Western world, and finally the whole of humankind, can still hope for a future. The future of the human being is God in the temporal life that comes to an end and in the eternal life that has no end.

Saint Augustine speaks of the end without end when he concludes his grandiose theology of history in his twenty-two books about the divine citizenship. He speaks here of the final age of the world, a "Sabbath" of which:

> The end will not be an evening, but will be the eternal eighth day of the Lord, which is sanctified through Christ's Resurrection and shows in advance the rest not only of the spirit, but also of the body. Then we will rest and see, see and love, love and praise. Indeed, it will truly be without end at the end. For precisely that is our end: to come to a kingdom that comes to no end through an end.[17]

Until then, the Church fulfills its mission to be the sign and instrument of the innermost union of human beings with God and of the unity of humankind (see LG 1). It is in a special way the ministry of the pope to unite human beings in truth and justice and to lead them to unity with God because the pope is the visible principle of the unity of the Church, in which the unity of humankind and their fellowship with God is shown in advance and anticipated.

17 Augustine, *Civ.* XXII.30.

VII

The Pope—Christ's Witness to the Dignity of Every Human Being

1. THE PROPHETIC VOICE RAISED ON BEHALF OF HUMAN DIGNITY

THE ENTIRE CHURCH SHARES in the prophetic office of Jesus, its Lord and Head (LG 12): "The authority of the Magisterium extends also to the specific precepts of the *natural law,* because their observance, demanded by the Creator, is necessary for salvation. In recalling the prescriptions of the natural law, the Magisterium of the Church exercises an essential part of its prophetic office of proclaiming to men what they truly are and reminding them of what they should be before God."

The magisterium of the bishops and of the pope cannot be restricted to the faithful and complete transmission and spreading of the apostolic teaching. The doctrine of the faith must also be promoted and actualized, so that people today and tomorrow can recognize and accept the Word of God as the Word of life in the new conditions of intellectual and cultural understanding and in their existential circumstances, which are profoundly marked by technology and science. When the apostles worked as prophets, and together with other prophets (Acts 13:1–3; Eph 2:20), they did not do so in order to lift the veil from the contingent events of the future; they proclaimed to every human being that Christ is his or her absolute future, both in this life and beyond this life for all eternity. As the universal shepherd, the pope leads the flock of Christ even through turbulent times and even against headwinds. He steers the barque of Peter, trusting in the Lord even when a mighty tsunami breaks in over the Church and it seems doomed (Mt 8:24). He remains the rock on whom Christ most assuredly builds the house and people of his Church—and the gates of hell do not prevail against it. No matter what may happen, Peter strengthens the faith of the pilgrim people of God and of the Church militant in Jesus, the Christ and the Son of the living God.

When the Church resists the destructive powers of sin in itself and fights against the powers that seek to destroy it, it proclaims and bears witness to Christ, "the author of life" (Acts 3:15).

The pope, in whom the Church's mission is embodied and represented, is the witness and the guarantor that the house of our faith was built not on sand but on an unshakable rock: on Jesus Christ, the Word of God who has become flesh.

We fail to understand the pope's mission fully if we ascribe to him only a moral authority that non-Catholics too, and even non-Christians, grant him. It is beyond doubt that the pope's appeals for peace in the family of nations, for social justice, and for the rights of everyone to a share in the goods of the one earth have a significant moral weight in the ears of the governments, the United Nations, or the European institutions, and surveys repeatedly reveal that among all the political and economic leaders it is the pope who is accorded the highest credibility. However, in the struggles for political power and in the dominance of the media in the arena of public opinion, appeal is made to the pope as an authority only to the extent that this serves one's own interests. The starting point of our present reflections has to be deeper than this.

The pope's moral authority for the world's conscience is based on his religious authority for our faith in God, the Creator of the world, who is for every single person the foundation and the goal of meaning.

Every person has the religious conscience that orients us to the truth and the ethical conscience that orients us to the good. In our consciences, we are confronted with God in the Word of his revelation that is presented to us in the testimony of the Church, and with God in the natural moral law of which the supreme ecclesial authority is the ultimately binding interpreter. The revealed commandments of God in the Decalogue and the Sermon on the Mount, and the distinction between good and evil that is planted by God in every human heart (Rom 2:14–16), are likewise recalled proactively and prophetically by the Church to the conscience of the individual and to the social conscience of those who must take decisions. This means that the conscience, in its immediacy to God, does not contradict the necessity of being educated and raised up, taught and converted *ab extra* by the Church's magisterium, which is appointed by God. The conscience needs spiritual counsel and pastoral encouragement in the *forum internum*. But it is also the prophetic task of the Church to arouse the conscience of the world when self-ish nationalistic and economic interests threaten the common good, when racist ideologies or the egotism of a social class pose a threat to the equality of all human beings, or when imperialist and colonialist plans call into question the unity of the family of peoples.

One can fully understand the teaching of Vatican II about the Church as sacrament of the salvation of the world only if one looks at the concretization of this doctrine in the Pastoral Constitution *Gaudium et spes*. The Church fulfills its mission in God's plan of salvation only if it always also wants to be "the Church in the modern world." This is the modern formulation of the ancient principle *ecclesia semper reformanda*. In the draft for a work that Dietrich Bonhoeffer planned while in prison, he states: "The Church is the Church only when it exists for others."[1] And in the letter he wrote to his friend Eberhard Bethge on August 3, 1944, he affirms: "The Church must come out of its stagnation. We have to get out again into the fresh air of the intellectual confrontation with the world. We have to risk saying things that leave us open to attack, provided only that we thereby touch on essential matters."[2] In *Gaudium et spes*, the Catholic Church wants to offer an honest dialogue with everyone about the urgent challenges and problems of a world that is both global and one, and to propose collaboration in solving them.

The fact that the pope is not even mentioned in this pastoral constitution shows that the mission of the Church is not concentrated on him (in the bad sense of that word). But since the pope is the universal teacher and shepherd of the Church, it is from him that there come, again and again, the impulses, signals, and initiatives of the universal Church for the world—and without him as the principle of its unity in faith and in fellowship, the Church would be unable either to discuss or to act. This has been manifested from the social doctrine of Leo XIII onwards, via John Paul II's commitment to universal human rights, down to the encyclical *Laudato si'* of Pope Francis, which gives ecology a foundation in the theology of the creation.

1 Dietrich Bonhoeffer, *Widerstand und Ergebung*, 415.

2 Bonhoeffer, *Widerstand und Ergebung*, 555.

2.
THE HUMAN BEING IS THE PATH OF THE CHURCH

THERE CAN BE NO DOUBT THAT ONE OF THE GREAT CHALLENGES of the twenty-first century is the protection of the human being at every phase of his or her development. The Church is the only community that has always accepted this task and has emphasized in its social doctrine and its moral theology the value of the life of every single person. The ever more devastating military conflicts and crimes against humanity in every part of the world, where the dignity and the right of the human being becomes the plaything of whomever is more powerful, mean that essential factors of true human development are flouted. In his encyclical *Sollicitudo rei socialis* (1987), John Paul II made the following urgent exhortation: "The obligation to commit oneself to the development of peoples is not just an individual duty, and still less an individualistic one, as if it were possible to achieve this development through the isolated efforts of each individual. It is an imperative which obliges each and every man and woman, as well as societies and nations. In particular, it obliges the Catholic Church."[3]

The state, the nation, Europe, the United Nations—the whole world and every person are at the service of human beings, of their development, their education, their nutrition, and their property. The highly varied charitable activity of the Church belongs to its very essence, as Pope Benedict XVI emphatically declared in his first encyclical, *Deus caritas est.*

We do not adopt an attitude of passivity in face of the challenges that we must encounter. The Church, and *all* Christians—for it is here that the great ecumenical task is anchored—can give the future a specific shape by pointing to what is essential, to what is fundamental, to what is in accordance with the creation and with reason, to what is natural, and to the true human being. This is why the Church's proclamation must not weary of giving the central position, again and again, to the human being as a person in his dignity and with his rights. The ideological pluralism that wants to abandon the truth that is ultimately binding and an authority that lays down norms, and to replace these with a pseudo-tolerance, answering the question about God's existence with an aggressive atheism, is first and foremost a fight against the human being himself, who is evaluated in this system in purely innerworldly terms. All transcendence is denied: the human being is surrendered to his instincts and is therefore unconditionally free only when he creates

3 John Paul II, Encyclical Letter *Sollicitudo rei socialis* (December 30, 1987), 32.

his own self according to the measure of his desires and interests, out of an empty subjectivity. Without God, the human being is free and independent. No boundaries can stop him—not even the freedom of other persons. The loss of God reduces the human being to the biological processes, without free will, without consideration for others, and without abidingly valid ethical criteria. What is regarded today as deserving protection can be overturned tomorrow by a majority.

In principle, the only solution here is reflection on what the human being is because, as a bodily and spiritual being, he is more than the sum of his biological and chemical composition, and something completely different from an animal on two legs.

It is therefore decisively important to present the human being as a creature, as a person, and as an individual in community, with his dignity and with his rights.

A Person from the Very Beginning

In a secularized society that has surrendered to a metaphysical relativism, and thereby to the destruction of ethics, it is hard for the Christian to champion unconditionally the absolute inviolability of human life and to insist on the dignity of every human being, even of unborn and sick human beings. Human rights are not dependent on any human worldview. On the contrary, they are based on the recognition of an authority over which the human being has no control.

Recourse to the concept of person promises an unambiguous solution here. "Person" essentially means more than a psychological self-experience or a bundle of sensory stimuli; it must be seen within the ontological frame of reference. The human being is not the sum of his characteristics, experiences and moods, and biological constants. He is a center and an irreducible reality with which various characteristics are linked. Every human being is a person from the very outset and forever. The human person does not come into being with time but develops in his lifetime in accordance with his physical-social nature. The human being is not made into a person with civil rights only when these rights are formally attributed to him. The respect for every human being is an absolutely essential feature in the debate with social Darwinist approaches, and it will be the criterion of a successful, humane society in the future too. Such a society can unfold fully only if human rights and personhood are the authoritative undergirding of the evaluation of the human being.

The Church—Advocate of the Human Being

On the basis of the Christian faith, people throughout Europe, from Portugal to Russia, discovered an image of the human being that is defined by the experience of being a creature, of having come into existence thanks to the love of God, so that the human being is dependent on God. The experience of the "I" reaches its highest point when God is no longer sensed dimly as an anonymous All-One: when he comes to meet me as the fullness of all being, to whom I can say "you." The dead, deaf, and mute idols and the impassive universe are not touched by my pains, my cries, and my tears. God is a person and has a heart for us. No one could ever construct the following prayer theoretically; it presupposes the experience of God's care for us: "O God, you are my God, I seek you, my soul thirsts for you; my flesh faints for you, as in a dry and weary land where no water is. So I have looked upon you in the sanctuary, beholding your power and glory. Because your merciful love is better than life, my lips will praise you" (Ps 63:2–4).

Pope John XXIII hailed the Universal Declaration of Human Rights as an immensely important act, and this judgment has been confirmed by the popes who succeeded him. The universality of human rights, which slowly came to light and increased in strength, became a genuine field of activity for the Church, whose view of the human person as an ethically responsible agent in the world is an element of its teaching. Every single human being owes himself in his being, his understanding, and his will to God's loving care, and this means that his value and his dignity lie exclusively in this fact, which is antecedent to his existence. The Church is not merely following some political decision here, nor is it an impassive onlooker on the margin of societal developments. Thanks to its great patrimony, the Church stands in the midst of the conflicts and the creative motives of human dignity. In the study *The Church and Human Rights*, published by the Pontifical Commission on Justice and Peace in 1975, this active role is explicitly emphasized as an element of the Church's own social doctrine and is regarded as a kind of self-commitment: "the Church must first and foremost stimulate in the world the recognition, observance, protection and promotion of the rights of the human person."[4]

4 Pontifical Commission on Justice and Peace, *The Church and Human Rights* (Vatican City: Libreria editrice Vaticana, 1975), 62.

The Council and Human Rights

The elaboration of the theology of human rights is intimately connected to the Church's doctrine. The Second Vatican Council presented its own interpretation in the Pastoral Constitution *Gaudium et spes*:

> The Church, therefore, by virtue of the Gospel committed to her, proclaims the rights of man; she acknowledges and greatly esteems the dynamic movements of today by which these rights are everywhere fostered. Yet these movements must be penetrated by the spirit of the Gospel and protected against any kind of false autonomy. For we are tempted to think that our personal rights are fully ensured only when we are exempt from every requirement of divine law. But this way lies not the maintenance of the dignity of the human person, but its annihilation (GS 41).

Human rights are thus not rules constructed by a collaborative fellowship of states, even when the states formulate them in a manner resembling "statutes." They can be decoded and presented in a permanent fashion as a binding norm of society only if they are brought into connection with God. Human rights that are based on the gesture of a political ideology have temporal and ideological limits because they can at any time be interpreted and implemented differently by those in power. An anchoring in God protects them from attack and arbitrariness on the part of human beings. This means that they are adopted fully only when the human being himself is at the center, as God's creature.

The council emphatically wishes to inculcate respect for the human being, as the following impressive formulation shows: "Everyone must consider his every neighbor without exception as another self, taking into account first of all his life and the means necessary to live it with dignity" (GS 27).

The Perennially Valid Teaching of the Church

Some texts by John Paul II help us to reflect on what follows from this passage from *Gaudium et spes*: "Authentic democracy is possible only in a State ruled by law, and on the basis of the correct concept of the human person. [...] As history demonstrates, a democracy without values easily turns into open or thinly disguised totalitarianism."[5]

5 John Paul II, Encyclical Letter *Centesimus annus* (May 1, 1991), 46.

3.
HUMAN RIGHTS—A RECONCILIATION OF THE CHURCH WITH MODERNITY?

MARCELLO PERA (BORN 1943) IS ONE OF THE MOST BRILLIANT thinkers in the Italian cultural and linguistic sphere, and since the spirit transcends borders, he is also a well-known intellectual on the world stage. He understands himself as a liberal who, however, certainly remains conscious of the ties of the human being to a transempirical reality in which he is rooted. It suffices here to recall the book that he published jointly with Joseph Ratzinger, *Without Roots.*[6]

The thesis of his new book *Diritti umani e cristianesimo: La Chiesa alla prova della modernità* (2015) is both astonishing and disturbing.[7] He counters the customary view about the reconciliation between Christianity and modernity (that is to say, between the reason and human rights) since the Enlightenment philosophy by asking whether Christianity does not pay too high a price for this. This metaphor of "paying too high a price" signifies that Christianity, as a theonomous view of the human being and of the world, must not let itself be integrated into a total concept of reality that is immanent to the world and without God or is at any rate free of transcendence. In such a case, the Church could regard itself at most as a humanitarian-social institution of human beings for human beings, with some spiritual offers for those whose daily existence is shaped by rational considerations but who cannot do without a little bit of cosmic background noise and massage of the soul.

I must admit that his acute analysis of the dilemmas of the modern problems concerning human rights initially surprised me. At the end, however, I was convinced.

With regard to the connotations of concepts, each of us is marked by the period of his intellectual awakening and maturing. When I was at high school, we studied the constitution of the Federal Republic of Germany from May 23, 1949. It is historically conditioned and cannot be detached from its background—namely, the experience of the most terrible crimes against humanity that took place in the National Socialist German state. The German people gives itself this constitution in awareness of its responsibility before God and before human beings. All the human rights to life

6 Marcello Pera and Joseph Ratzinger, *Without Roots: The West, Relativism. Christianity. Islam* (New York: Basic Books, 2007).

7 Marcello Pera, *Diritti umani e cristianesimo: La Chiesa alla prova della modernità* (Venice: Marsilio, 2015).

and limb and to the fundamental needs of one's intellectual, physical, and societal existence are recognized and guaranteed by the democratic state; but they are not *granted*, still less are they attributed to the citizens through law and custom. All the basic human rights everywhere in the world have their root in the human dignity that is and must remain inviolable. They belong to every human being, irrespective of whether or not he is a citizen of this country. The rights of a German citizen are connected to human rights, but they have their origin in a different source.

We studied the German constitution in the history and social studies classes. In religion classes, we saw the explanation of the Ten Commandments as the deeper foundation of human dignity in the will of God, since God's commandments are inscribed upon the heart and the conscience of every person (Rom 2:14–15), even if he does not yet know them from the historical revelation to Israel.

When human dignity is violated, everyone can appeal not only to the universal declarations of human rights (1789 and 1948) or to its recognition in the states that are under the rule of law. One can also appeal directly to God, the Creator of the world and of the human being. *E contra*, no one can appeal to God to justify the violation of human dignity. Terrorists who think that they are accomplishing the will of God (as in pseudo-Islamic groups) are not acting on behalf of God. Their god is an idol with the grotesque face of the devil. Why is this so? Because religion is first and foremost the relation to God, with the worship of God as the source and criterion of the *verum et bonum*. It is not first of all the observance of the statutes that enshrine the commandments and prescriptions of a cultic association, when these contradict the original religious act. An ISIS fighter boasted on Facebook that he prayed to God before and after the rape of a non-Islamic woman—that is, a human being whom God created in his own image and likeness (Gn 1:28). The infringement of human rights and the blasphemy are merely the two sides of one and the same medal. One who seeks to justify his crimes against humanity by speaking of obedience to God venerates an idol and a devil—not God the Merciful, who created heaven and earth and willed the human being to be his image and likeness. Where human rights are formulated and produced with no relation of the human being to transcendence, to that which lies beyond human control, they also become banal and are capable of being manipulated. The problem is that the world is relative and needs the relationship to an absolute. If the human being's relation to transcendence is denied, it can be replaced only be some part of the world. This may be a positive law that requires sanctions, if it is to be observed; it may be the majority decision of a parliament, the administrative power of a government, or the chance decision by the majority in a panel of judges. And in that case, the rule of human beings over other persons is exercised in a dominant ideology with the instruments available in politics and the media, and with their psychological and physical means of coercion.

Human rights were never violated so frequently as after their declaration in France in 1789. This declaration rightly opposed the absolutism of the monarch and the exploitation by the aristocratic oligarchy. But it was not able to stop the Jacobin rule of terror. It has been calculated that one hundred thousand innocent victims went to the guillotine, to say nothing of the victims of other ingenious torments. The terror wreaked by virtue brought with it a totalitarianism of conviction that has accompanied the world ever since and that commits its monstrous deeds down to the present day in the programs of enforced conformity in today's mainstreaming.

The so-called modernity is confronted by the question whether ethical freedom and civic freedom exist without God or through him. If the human being were exclusively a product of the matter that plays blindly with itself, the only goal of life would lie within this world, in material goods or in their refinement in literature, art, theater, and so on. In that case, God, who would exist only as a fiction or as the legitimation of claims to rule, would be the killjoy or the enemy of my freedom to realize myself in my intellectual and sensuous well-being. But if God is, in reality, the goal that reaches beyond the brief period of life on earth and in *this* way reaches into this life, and if God is the fulfillment of the intellect and the will, he is also the content of the spirit as truth and as the goal of the will—namely, he is love in person.

This means that it may not be necessary to play down the critical remarks of the popes in the eighteenth and nineteenth centuries about the declaration of human rights that had an Enlightenment provenance and tone; one need not present them, with some contortion and embarrassment, as being slow to get aboard the train into the modern age and then claim that this tardiness was subsequently made good in the encyclical *Pacem in terris* of John XXIII (1963) and the Pastoral Constitution *Gaudium et spes* of Vatican II (1965). It is always the right and the obligation of the magisterium to react to an understanding of the reason and of human rights that is diminished by secularism, and to indicate the necessity for these rights to be founded in transcendence. It is a matter of perspective whether one thinks that the Church is limping two hundred years behind its own historical period. In that case, we would have to begin a chase to catch up, and finally the Church would sink down in exhaustion before the godless world and adore it with its last breath. But I am convinced, on the contrary, that faith has always outstripped unbelief, because the living relationship to God is the criterion of the success or failure of my existence. The Word of God makes us alive, irrespective of a person's educational achievements or of the epoch in which one lives.

The Spanish theologian Gerardo del Pozo Abejon has shown in his historical and systematic study *La Iglesia y la libertad religiosa* (2007) that the various addressees of the declarations of the magisterium, and the questions they deal with, are always a factor in the interpretation of these documents.[8] It is impossible to overlook a development of doctrine; but the outcome of this development is not a contradiction of the initial principles but a grasping of these principles on a deeper level. This is necessarily the case in the interpretation by the magisterium of the revelation of God in human words and the human intelligence, but one can demonstrate an inherently coherent development here in faithfulness to an anthropology that is always theocentric and related to the supernatural revelation and to the demand that God makes of every conscience in the natural ethical law.

When human rights are understood in an atheistic-agnostic manner as an entitlement to realize one's personal wishes at any cost, and these "rights" are employed as an attack on the Church itself, this is nothing other than an act of violence. For example, the Church teaches the ethical impermissibility of sexual acts outside of the legitimate marriage between a man and his wife. This is a sin, an action against the commandment of God, because there is no right to act against the *bonum individuale et commune* that is revealed to everyone in his or her conscience and in the Ten Commandments—that is, in both the internal and the external Word of God (Rom 2:14–29).

The peak of the self-contradiction emerges from the mists of logic when persons and institutions who explicitly deny the existence of God demand (for example) access to the Catholic priesthood, to which God alone calls out of his own free will. One who insists on a right vis-à-vis God, to whom we owe our being, our life, and all grace, and thereby imagines that he convicts God of being unjust, ought to reflect on the question: "Who are you, a man, to answer back to God?" (Rom 9:20). We have no right to grace; but it is God's grace that is the fundament of the internal and external independence of the human being in the intellectual, physical, and social existence of both state and society.

The human being as person, in the family, in his religious worship of God, in his work, and in his leisure is antecedent to the state and is above the state. The human rights, in the cultural and societal forms of life that belong to their nature, are *sui juris* and must not be restricted by the state or by individual groups; still less may they be annulled with violence. It is presumptuous for European states, under pressure from gender ideology or homosexual lobbies instead of letting themselves be guided by human reason

8 Gerardo del Pozo Abejon, *La Iglesia y la libertad religiosa* (Madrid: Biblioteca de Autores Cristianos, 2007).

or the divine revelation, to seek to define what marriage is. To tell immature children that they can choose their gender, and that this could legitimate manipulations of their internal and external sexual organs, is a disgusting crime against their dignity.

A pluralistic society is an experiment that belongs to recent times, and we still lack the experiential proof that it can succeed. A bracketing world-view that is prescribed, as in laicism or state atheism (which is nothing other than the abolition of the freedom of religion), entails graver risks than a state religion that is prescribed from above. The difference is that, in a classical Christian state religion, the ruler must take responsibility before God for the Ten Commandments and the natural moral law, whereas the worldview of the state does not transcend the intellectual horizon of its representatives and brings forth the brutal human type that we see in the emotionless apparatchik and the fanatic who commits his crimes out of conviction.

In his autobiographical work *Als wär's ein Stück von mir*, the German writer Carl Zuckmayer describes his experience of how the devil opens the gates of hell today. It was at the beginning of the Nazi rule in Vienna, in 1938:

> That evening, all hell broke loose. Hades had opened its gates and let out its lowest, its most hideous and impure spirits. The city changed into a night-mare painting by Hieronymus Bosch; lemurs and half-demons seemed to have crawled out of dirty eggs and risen up out of boggy holes in the ground. The air was filled with an unceasingly screaming, desolate, hysterical shrieking from the throats of men and women. It kept on crying by day and by night. And they all lost their faces and resembled distorted grimaces—some in fear, some in falsehood, and others in a wild triumph full of hatred. [...] What was unleashed here was the rebellion of envy, of resentment, of bitterness, of blind and wicked vengefulness—and every other voice was condemned to silence. [...] What was set free here was nothing other than the dull masses in their blind destructiveness, and their hatred was directed against everything ennobled by nature or by the spirit. It was a Witch's Sabbath of the mob and a burial of human dignity.[9]

Human rights can be given a weak, immanentist foundation or a foundation that is incontrovertibly theocentric; but they are not capable of defining the goal of the intellectual-ethical existence of the human being. They have only a protective function against the arbitrariness of those who hold power in the absolutisms and totalitarianisms in politics, finance, and the media. If freedom is the key to the modern period, then faith in the God of truth

9 Carl Zuckmayer, *Als wär's ein Stück von mir* (Frankfurt: Fischer, 1966), ch. 2.

and of love is the gate to the future, until the end and until the beginning that has no end.

Those who believe in God can collaborate with other people of good will in building up a more just world and in technological-societal progress, without making these goals an absolute. There is an eschatological reservation here, which means that paradises constructed by human beings on earth have always collapsed into a hell on earth, whereas the good that we do now will one day be transformed by the grace of God into something that is definitive and permanent.

This is the ancient teaching of the Church, which does indeed reject an unchecked and unbridled sovereignty of the people but at the same time affirms that a democracy under the rule of law is the best form of government. But a state under the rule of law, which merely displays the efficient following of procedures, is not enough. It must be understood in the substantial sense of a political society whose constitutions and laws embody the values that are in accord with the nature and the essential definition of the human being.

The modern constitutions that were written after the catastrophe of the Second World War anchor the basic rights in reverence for God and for the human being. This reverence gives democracy a solid foundation in the rule of law—in the sense set out in the last paragraph:

> Among the most important of these rights, mention must be made of the right to life, an integral part of which is the right of the child to develop in the mother's womb from the moment of conception; the right to live in a united family and in a moral environment conducive to the growth of the child's personality; the right to develop one's intelligence and freedom in seeking and knowing the truth; the right to share in the work which makes wise use of the earth's material resources, and to derive from that work the means to support oneself and one's family; and the right freely to establish a family, to have and to rear children.[10]

God Has Called the Human Being to Love

This very detailed catalogue, which is oriented to the life of a human being, also places a special accentuation on human rights that also bears in mind the corresponding obligations. The fundamental Christian view of human nature is the guide here, and John Paul II can also refer to the anthro-

10 John Paul II, *Centesimus annus*, 47.

pology he elaborated in his Apostolic Exhortation *Familiaris consortio*: God has called the human being to love.

The family thus stands at the center of Christian anthropology. It must be protected as the place where everyone is accepted in love and grows to become a person who can develop in the gift of self, in the willingness to make sacrifices, and in fitting in with others, thereby reflexively finding himself. The family is the "natural place where one becomes a human being," as Count Franz von Ballestrem put it. Christian anthropology does not wander off into a vague speculation. It has concrete guiding lines and information; we often become aware of these only when they are obscured and denied. From the Enlightenment onwards, politicians have again and again claimed to exercise the highest authority over education. One is primarily a citizen of a state and must obey obligations; it is only secondarily that one is a human being and perhaps even created by God. We can only speculate about the psychological consequences for the victims of cloning experiments.

The Church and Freedom—Answers to Pluralism

The *Compendium of the Social Doctrine of the Church,* issued by the Pontifical Council for Justice and Peace, gives the chapter about freedom the title "The Fundamental Values of Social Life." To live in society and share through one's own involvement in shaping society presupposes the freedom that allows us to collaborate in solidarity and in a free decision in the various concerns and tasks: "'Freedom is exercised in relationships between human beings. Every human person, created in the image of God, has the natural right to be recognized as a free and responsible being. All owe to each other this duty of respect. The right to the exercise of freedom, especially in moral and religious matters, is an inalienable requirement of the dignity of the human person.'"[11]

The text continues in a similar vein, affirming that the value of freedom as the expression of the uniqueness of every human person is respected when every member of society is given the possibility of fulfilling his own personal vocation.

What, then, does the Church think about the basic values of freedom and of equality (which is linked to freedom), on which the modern declarations of human rights are based? The passages mentioned above confirm the value that the Church attributes to freedom. But this concept of freedom is demanding. It is not a freedom that casts aside all rules and norms and

11 Pontifical Council for Justice and Peace, *Compendium of the Social Doctrine of the Church* (April 2, 2004), 199; quoting CCC 1738.

"imprisons itself in a kind of splendid isolation" (GS 31), for then the human being could develop into a cruel egotist who would corrupt his own self and degrade society, including politics, into the plaything of his own interests.

What we must learn is the freedom that consists in accepting the commandments that are established by God in the nature of the human being. It is only when we have learned that we are called to love that we can make the correct use of the freedom that has been bestowed on us and has been entrusted to our responsibility. Freedom does not exist when we make the wrong use of it—namely, to establish boundaries. It exists when we use it for what is good, because this makes our existence shine forth as human beings who are God's creatures.

4. THE RELEVANCE OF THE CHURCH'S SOCIAL DOCTRINE TODAY

One could summarize the entire social doctrine of the Church as follows. The nature of the human being consists of more than the state, the economic and operational processes, or a merely material security. The contribution of the Christian anthropology, and of the foundations for the dignity and the rights of the human being that it contains, is not limited to becoming aware of oneself through accepting that one is created by God. It also entails influencing society with all one's strength. In a world plagued by war, terror, dictatorship, oppression, and all the various forms of cruelty, one must be a voice that points out loudly the original dependency of the human being. This is how the Christian existence has the character of a testimony in the works of the Christian love of neighbor, care for the poorest and weakest in society, for children, sick, and elderly persons, and in championing justice where injustice reigns. Through our personal testimony, we Christians posit criteria with a "success" that can be measured visibly in the sphere of our own individual lives.

But it would be too little, if we were not to leave the purely individual sphere—if we were not to find our orientation in a larger dimension where community is formed. The perennial challenge, precisely for us as Christians, is to do everything in our power to promote peace between ethnic groups, and between states and peoples. We must hold firm to the fundamental insight, both on the individual-personal level and on the social and political level, that the demands for respect, for dignity, and for the rights of the human being cannot be reduced to an internal theme of Christian anthropology. On the contrary, these demands are the coordinates for human life as a whole. Human dignity and human rights are not *one* solution in the evaluation of life in society, alongside many other forms of evaluating the worth of a human being. They are the instruments that will help us to master the problems that face humankind as a whole.

The Human Being as Person—The Basis of Human Dignity

In his encyclical *Pacem in terris,* Pope John XXIII presented his own charter of human rights, going beyond the Universal Declaration of Human Rights by the clear accent that comes from the Christian analysis of this question. He affirms that the starting point of human dignity is the human being as person. The Church overcomes here the horizontal framework of justification, which can change quickly at any time. The pope leads the discussion to the true core of the problem: the person—the human being's personality—is equipped with reason and free will and has rights and duties that are his or hers by nature. When this is respected, it should be accepted by everyone as the common fundament of action, for then there is a genuine possibility that inequality and massive differences in the sharing of earth's resources can be overcome, and that the freedom that is valid for all human beings can become the fundamental element of every ordering of society: "Any well-regulated and productive association of men in society demands the acceptance of one fundamental principle: that each individual man is truly a person. His is a nature, that is, endowed with intelligence and free will. As such he has rights and duties, which together flow as a direct consequence from his nature. These rights and duties are universal and inviolable, and therefore altogether inalienable."[12]

The basic idea of human rights not only accords very deeply with the biblical-Christian understanding of the human being; it is also the root of every initiative to promote esteem for human life. Through the Church, these foundations are translated into the modern world. Differences of ethical origin, political affiliation, or cultural identity must not become a barrier between persons. Every form of setting up boundaries contradicts the concept of person that is clearly formulated by the Church.

The Church can contribute actively, across these religious, national, and ideological boundaries, to the formation of a consensus about the dignity and the rights of the human being that is antecedent to the law. The Christian responsibility for human rights becomes obvious in the work of information and of the formation of the public consciousness in all the questions that

12 John XXIII, Encyclical Letter *Pacem in terris* (April 11, 1963), 9.

concern the human reality in its inviolability, in influence on legal regulations for the protection of life, and in Church aid organizations that work internationally. Their contribution in emergency measures and long-term processes is not limited to material aid. The Church's involvement in poor regions that lack even the simplest necessities of life helps those concerned to rediscover their value as human beings, or perhaps to perceive this for the very first time.

In his first encyclical, *Deus caritas est,* Pope Benedict XVI elevated "the Church's charitable activity" to become the Church's program: "The Church's charitable organizations constitute an *opus proprium,* a task agreeable to her, in which she does not cooperate collaterally, but acts as a subject with direct responsibility, doing what corresponds to her nature. The Church can never be exempted from practicing charity as an organized activity of believers."[13]

Let us take up again the idea expressed above. It is truly in the love for God and for other persons that the human being grasps the definition of what he himself is.

It is then that freedom is realized in solidarity. The equality of the individual and of the peoples leads to a lasting peace; the protection of life extends to all the stages of human individual development; and justice is founded on the search for truth. It is only then that the dignity of the human being is the criterion of dealings with each other and, at the same time, the first and the unquestionable access to the essence of what the human being is.

The Gospel of Life—The Church's Path

"The Gospel of Life": this is the title of one of John Paul II's encyclicals. It is the Church's task to oppose the culture of death and the threats to the incomparable value of the human person. The Church must proclaim the greatness and the preciousness of the person and overcome the culture of death with the proclamation of the Good News. "The Gospel of God's love for man, the Gospel of the dignity of the person, and the Gospel of life are a single and indivisible Gospel. For this reason, man—living man—represents the primary and fundamental way for the Church."[14]

John Paul II affirms:

> Every individual, precisely by reason of the mystery of the Word who was made flesh, is entrusted to the maternal care of the Church. Therefore, every threat to human dignity and life must necessarily be felt in the

13 Benedict XVI, Encyclical Letter *Deus caritas est* (December 25, 2005), 29.

14 John Paul II, Encyclical Letter *Evangelium vitae* (March 25, 1995), 2.

Church's very heart; it cannot but affect her at the core of her faith in the Redemptive Incarnation of the Son of God, and engage her in her mission of proclaiming the Gospel of life in all the world and to every creature.[15]

5.
THE NEW HUMANISM: CARE FOR OUR COMMON HOME

AFTER THE ENCYCLICAL *LUMEN FIDEI* and the Apostolic Exhortation *Evangelii gaudium*, Pope Francis gave the Church, in the third year of his pontificate, the third great document of his universal magisterium, the encyclical *Laudato si'*.

The subtitle of this document, which is structured in six parts with 246 smaller sections, shows that it is not only interested in practical questions about the protection of the environment. The great theme is the responsibility of all human beings for the earth as our "common home." Ecology (from the meaning of the Greek word) means here the doctrine of the house of the human family. It contains protection of the environment but also goes far beyond this. In the contemporary ecological crisis, in which the future of humankind on this planet is at stake, all those who live on the earth must care for the broad and beautiful dwelling in which God, the Creator and Father, has given us all a place and a home.

The title is a link to the saint whose name he took when he was elected bishop of Rome. In the "Canticle of the Sun," Saint Francis addresses Our Lord and thanks him in moving words that echo the beauty of the world in the melody of faith in the Creator. "Laudato si'! Praise be to you, my Lord, through our Sister, Mother Earth, who sustains and governs us and who produces various fruits with colored flowers and herbs."[16]

To call the earth "sister" and "mother" is to express the conviction that the earth is not mere material that we use, exploit, and discard. The soil, the water, the air, and all living things have a living relationship to the human being, and they are to be respected in their own identity, because the harmony of the creation reflects the goodness of the Creator. The human body is taken from the earth and all its organically connected elements. This integrates the human being, as a living, bodily, and spiritual being, into the

15 John Paul II, *Evangelium vitae*, 3.

16 Francis, Encyclical Letter *Laudato si'* (May 24, 2015), 1.

totality of the earth. As a person and as one who belongs to a community, he is related to God, the origin and goal of the universe.

Pope Francis takes his place in the continuity of the magisterium, which, as in the social doctrine in the past and in the present, confronts the challenges of ecology, its crises and its opportunities. The Church's magisterium does not restrict itself to the exposition of the mysteries of supernatural salvation; it also derives from these mysteries insights and principles of conduct with regard to the natural moral law, in order to render a service to the common good of the family of peoples. John XXIII was the first to address not only the Catholic world, but also "all those of good will" in the exhortation to peace in his encyclical *Pacem in terris.* Paul VI explicitly took up the dramatic situation of the environment and spoke of the necessity of a radical conversion, while John Paul II coined the term "ecology of the human being" in order to highlight the inherent unity of the human person as a natural-bodily and ethical-spiritual being in the one world. This term indicates a turning to God to acknowledge the world as his creation, not as the product of a demiurge or the construction of the technical intelligence of the human being. Pope Francis often refers to his immediate predecessor, especially to the address in the German Parliament on September 22, 2011, in which Pope Benedict XVI acutely diagnosed the contemporary crisis. A turnaround from the path that leads to the self-destruction of humanity is possible if nature and human beings are no longer objectified and instrumentalized from the perspectives of economic usefulness and of the manipulation of thought and of the conscience in politics and in the media. Only then will we be liberated from the demons of a humanism without God, the false idols of self-creation and self-redemption. "In the freedom and glory of the children of God" (Rom 8:21), we now sing *laudato si'!* Praised be the Lord!

Pope Francis also praises the contributions of other churches, especially of the Ecumenical Patriarch Bartholomew of Constantinople, who has been active in promoting the common celebration by Christians of a Creation Day. The religions, with their spirituality, are also invited to take part in a serious and respectful dialogue about our shared future; and the numerous scientific and societal activities that have promoted the awareness of the threat to the environment must also play their part. However, the reference to the tradition of the teachings of the popes does not prevent Pope Francis from developing his own perspective and thus giving a completely new dynamism to the process of an ecological conversion. Saint Francis, who is (so to speak) the patron of the ecological movement and is a model not only for Christians but also for many believers of other faiths and for nonbelievers, unites two fundamental concerns of this pontificate: care for the earth as the common home of all mankind and love for the poor. The aim is to overcome the division of the world into the powerful centers and the forgotten social and existential peripheries: "I believe that Saint Francis is the example *par excellence* of care for the vulnerable and of an integral ecology lived out joyfully and authentically."[17]

If we wish to understand Saint Francis correctly as patron, and his spirituality as a paradigm, for the ecology of the creation, we must realize that he is not concerned with an external asceticism, a romanticizing of poverty, or a nostalgia for the simple life in a world without modern technology. He opposes the rationalistic and materialistic perspective that reduces the world, and thus also the human being as a part of it, to a pure object of research, of economic utilization, and to a plaything of political and ideological power interests. No: the world is a book through which God speaks to us, and in which his kindness and goodness can be perceived.[18] Thanks to the *analogia entis,* "the eternal power and divinity of its Creator, which shines out in the human spirit through the light of the reason" (see Wis 13:5; Rom 1:20), is reflected in the greatness, dignity, beauty, and perfection of every creature.

Throughout the encyclical, one notices its origin in a dialogue with theologians, philosophers, sociologists, and natural scientists. Another source is also the daily experience of life in the pope's Argentinian home country; one can feel the atmosphere of the great Latin American continent. There are frequent quotations from studies and declarations by episcopal conferences from all the continents. These are integrated into the entire picture, so that a further background experience emerges for his reflections and suggestions about the ecological turnaround, which has to be universal. This is why the pope seeks in this encyclical a dialogue with all human beings, social groupings, and religious communities. He does not want to employ his high magisterial authority in favor of one single, methodologically limited view of the environmental problems, for the experts themselves evaluate individual phenomena differently (for example, climate change, global warming, environmental pollution, nutrition and population, the rise of the sea level, the amount and quality of water for everyone).

Here, the magisterium cannot propose any definitive declarations, as it can when it expounds the revelation itself.[19] But in view of the undeniably dramatic overall situation, the pope wants to ensure the presence of ethical and societal responsibility in all the technical fields of relative autonomy, in the economy, politics, science and culture, and so on (GS 36). It is very important that the ethical responsibility and the technical knowledge are

17 Francis, *Laudato si'*, 10.

18 See Francis, *Laudato si'*, 11.

19 Francis, *Laudato si'*, 60.

linked not only in principle but also in a practical manner that is oriented to action, in order that the earth may have a future. A responsibility across the generations is needed, so that today's children and grandchildren may encounter a world worth living in. In order to meet the challenges of the ecological and anthropological crisis, we must first analyze it in a comprehensive formation of consciousness, we must understand it in terms of theology and the history of ideas, and we must discover the motivations for decisive and sustained action. What we need is a serious and unprejudiced debate by all those involved, so that we can together find a viable solution.

After listing the themes that will be elaborated in the six parts, the pope sets out continuous principles that are the axes that support the entire document and that orient his reflections to the new optics of the ecological challenge in the light of the Christian faith:

> As examples, I will point to the intimate relationship between the poor and the fragility of the planet, the conviction that everything in the world is connected, the critique of new paradigms and forms of power derived from technology, the call to seek other ways of understanding the economy and progress, the value proper to each creature, the human meaning of ecology, the need for forthright and honest debate, the serious responsibility of international and local policy, the throwaway culture and the proposal of a new lifestyle.[20]

In the first part, the pope takes up some aspects of the present-day ecological crisis.[21] Ecology is a part of the doctrine of creation, which is not set out in detail here but is presupposed, especially in the recourse to its theological elaborations in Bonaventure, a son of Saint Francis, and Thomas Aquinas, whom the philosopher Josef Pieper called *Thomas a creatore*. The human being is not the chance product of a blind and unfeeling matter that plays with itself. On the contrary, he has his origin in God's will to create, and, as a person, he is able to say "Thou" to God. The human being has a relational identity oriented to God, to whom he owes his existence through the act of creation, and who makes it possible in grace for the human being to give himself freely to God. The human being can thus recognize himself as an "I" who is sustained by God's love and can accept himself. The human being owes his existence to the goodness and love of God, and this is why love is the meaning and the logic of the creation, which is oriented to a goal—namely, the perfecting of every created spirit in the love that God himself is

20 Francis, *Laudato si'*, 15; 16.

21 Francis, *Laudato si'*, 17–61.

(see 1 Jn 4:8, 12). The history of the expansion of the material cosmos and the evolution of organic matter are studied by the empirical sciences and do not in principle contradict the origin of the finite from absolute nothing. Only one who can pose questions that go beyond the material world to reflect on the conditions that permit the being and essence of things will arrive at the certain knowledge of God as the Creator of the world. Only God, whose essence is his own being, brings about individual beings (the creatures) that, in their essence, genuinely and concretely exist in the framework of a sharing in being. As an intellectual-physical and historical-social being, the human being is a part of the world and also its partner, has a harmonious relationship to his fellow creatures in flora and fauna, although this inherent link between material nature and the life of animals and human beings was also gravely limited by sin, and waits with longing for redemption and new creation (see Rom 8:23).

In all its aspects, the creation is planned by God's love: it is his goodness that leaves its mark on all the creatures in their being and their essence. Being "good" is not an external ascription, nor is it something that one acquires for oneself (as in Pelagian thinking). It is an inherent quality in which the essential goodness of God is reflected in the world in the essence of the creatures, an essence that is a participation in God's goodness. The creatures are thus a continuous hymn of praise of God's goodness and love and point *per analogiam* to his eternal power and divinity. The human being is not "master and owner of nature" (as Descartes put it), which would be merely material for his own constructions: the human being is the image and likeness of God and is appointed to tend and cultivate the earth like a garden. Everything that is created, "each according to its kind" (Gn 1:12, 21), reflects God's perfection in the context of its own nature and cannot be reduced to a function. No creature is merely a function for some other creature. The human being cannot seek to bring the creation out of a raw condition to its perfection. He recognizes and takes hold of the perfections in nonhuman things and nonpersonal living creatures as a potential for collaborating creatively with the Creator through his or her metaphysical and instrumental reason. This is related to the common good, since the human being knows that the goods of the creation are meant for all and for all the future generations, and that through the Incarnation of the Word, through whom God created all things, in his Son Jesus Christ, the entire creation will be brought to perfection in the love of the triune God. Every dualistic antithesis between transcendence and immanence, responsibility for the world and relatedness to God, or physical and spiritual existence is made impossible through the creation and the Incarnation. This prevents both a spirituality of flight from the world and the reduction of the Christian faith and the basic ethical principles to a mere motivation for an inner-worldly humanism.

In the third part, the pope invites us to a fundamental new orientation in the way we look at the world.[22]

Scientific and technological progress, the great expansion of theoretical and practical knowledge, is to be welcomed. This progress is immensely helpful, because it makes communication easier and contributes to the overcoming of serious problems (child mortality, premature death through illnesses, famines). But one cannot fail to see the dialectic of technology, which can be misused through the immense accumulation of uncontrollable power and the manipulation of people's minds. The development of weapons has made the nuclear, biological, and chemical self-destruction of humanity a genuine possibility. The human being can be controlled totally by others; or else he abolishes himself by making himself a function of the artificial intelligence that he himself has constructed, or by submitting voluntarily to its paradigm. Financial and digital globalization can lead *both* to a more radical exploitation of the poor and the weak by the rich and the powerful, through the unbridled consumerism that plunders their resources, *and* to a new universal responsibility and a comprehensive solidarity in the human family. A narrowed-down anthropocentrism must be rejected, as must a nihilistic reduction of the human being to "an animal like every other animal" in the so-called "biocentrism."[23]

However, "there can be no ecology without an adequate anthropology," because the ecological crisis is only the manifestation of the ethical, cultural, and spiritual crisis of the modern age, which understands the human being without transcendence.[24] The consequence is that the spirit of the human being as intellect, free will, conscience, and compassion loses its support and orientation.[25] The culture of intellectual and ethical relativism, in rejecting the objective truths and the universally binding basic ethical principles, displays precisely this pathology, which generates exploitation, enslavement, human trafficking, violence, and the degradation of a human being to an object of lust.[26] If only the instrumental reason is valid, with no ethics to check it through its immovable distinction between good and evil, there is then no ethical reason to reject even cruel experiments on animals and an animal husbandry that has no respect for the intrinsic value of our

22 Francis, *Laudato si'*, 101–136.

23 Francis, *Laudato si'*, 118.

24 Francis, *Laudato si'*, 118.

25 Francis, *Laudato si'*, 119.

26 Francis, *Laudato si'*, 123.

fellow creatures. Abortion and experiments on human embryos must be absolutely rejected because the reality of human existence is the basic reason why the embryo cannot be made a means to an end. This is the fundament of the embryo as a person—a dignity that does not accrue to it because of its advanced physical, mental, and spiritual stage of development.[27]

The fourth part speaks of an ecology that is attentive to the complexity of reality.[28]

The environmental crisis forms a fatal unity with the symptoms of crisis in society and in the worlds of national and international finance and politics. And the threat to nonorganic nature also entails a threat to the historical, artistic, and cultural patrimony. Our new goal must be an integral development of the person and of society, precisely in a daily life of attentiveness that overcomes an egoistic consumerism, since the common good is the ethical compass for the ecology both of nature and of the human person. The common good can be achieved only if there is also an intergenerational justice. God has entrusted the world to everyone, not only to us in the present day: in creation, he always has in mind those, too, who belong to future generations. They are included in the blessing with which he created the human being as man and woman, in order that they might increase and have children, thereby fulfilling the responsibility that has been bestowed on them from the beginning of creation. It is in this light that we must also see the ecology of the marriage of man and woman and the family that is the fruit of the fellowship of life and of love and the bodily fellowship between man and woman. This includes the acceptance of one's own male and female bodiliness as a gift from God that reflects his goodness. The fact that disordered sexual tendencies and practices also exist does not permit us to draw the conclusion that there are more genders than do in fact exist, according to God's will, in the man and woman who exist in a complementarity where each is positively oriented to the other. It must be affirmed, against the dualistic gnosis of the past and the present (in gender ideology), that sexual difference, the existence of humankind in two genders, is an expression of God's will, and hence of his goodness. Human existence as man or as woman is not a defect from which one would need to be liberated by personally constructing one's own physical-spiritual being and joining this to one's libidinous and consumerist "I." The existence of the other human being as man or as woman can be acknowledged as the work of God the Creator, thus making possible a reciprocal enrichment and perfecting in the marital fellowship of

27 Francis, *Laudato si'*, 131, 136.

28 Francis, *Laudato si'*, 137–162.

29 Francis, *Laudato si'*, 155.

life and of love that expands through their children to become a family that takes its place in the family of humankind.[29]

The fifth part offers some guidelines for spiritual orientation and for action.[30] The theme is the dialogue about the environment in international politics, where necessary measures for the entire earth often fail because of national egotisms. We need a new politics on the national and local levels. There is a risk that politicians may encourage consumerism in the short term in order to save their seats in the next legislative period, instead of aiming at long-term solutions that grasp the problems by the root. Since "time is greater than space," it is more important to launch long-term processes of changing the world and making it better than to briefly occupy a space (of power).[31]

What we need here is an honest and unprejudiced collaboration by all those involved, by those with political and economic responsibility, the experts in the empirical sciences, and the environmental organizations with their know-how. It would be counterproductive if the old animosities of the Enlightenment and the critique of religion, and ideological hostility to the "religions," were to lead people to deprive themselves of the treasury of the spiritual experience of these religions—since the reality of the world and of the human being transcends what is empirically verifiable and can be demonstrated *more geometrico.* A genuine dialogue sets it sights on the *bonum commune* and is not obsessed with forcing everyone else to accept one's own limited view. Instead of fighting ideological wars among the various environmental movements, we should go ahead together on the "path of dialogue which demands patience, self-discipline and generosity."[32] In accordance with the eschatological reservation, "the reality is greater than the idea"—that is to say, the human idea and picture of the world, which is known completely only in God's idea of the creation.[33] "Now I know in part; then I shall understand fully, even as I have been fully understood" (1 Cor 13:12).

In the sixth and final part, the pope speaks about an ecological education and spirituality.[34]

We need a completely new orientation and a change of course for humanity as a whole. A consciousness of our common origin in God, our Creator and Father, and the insight that we belong together as brothers and sisters in

30 Francis, *Laudato si'*, 163–201.

31 Francis, *Evangelii gaudium*, 222; *Laudato si'*, 178.

32 Francis, *Laudato si'*, 201.

33 Francis, *Laudato si'*, 201; *Evangelii gaudium*, 231.

34 Francis, *Laudato si'*, 202–246.

the creation that is God's house, must bring forth new convictions, activities, and ways of life. It is not the lifestyle of using and enjoying but the lifestyle of thankfulness and of serene trust in God that has a future. Let us find our orientation in the saints, in Francis, Charles de Foucauld, and Saint Thérèse of Lisieux, and in the mysticism of Saint John of the Cross. A new style in everyday living, but also the noble gesture of humility before God and of a family intimacy with each other, of the true identification with Christ in the poor: this the path of a conversion to God the Father, who sets us free to live "a universal fraternity."[35] The Church offers us the ideal of a "civilization of love," because "social love is the key to authentic development."[36]

When the Holy Father speaks of an "ecological conversion," he obviously does not have in mind a piety directed to the environment.[37] He wants us to take seriously the ecological-societal crisis that affects the whole of humanity. This involves the willingness to encounter Christ and to draw all the necessary consequences from this for the relationship to the human beings and the world around us. The mysticism of Saint Ignatius Loyola, which has deeply marked our Holy Father all his life, is a mysticism of "finding God in all things" and situations. It is not an arbitrary option for something that might perhaps be important to me personally. It concerns the essential task of every human being, and especially of every Christian, "to be protectors of God's handiwork."[38]

This is the mysticism of a John of the Cross, where, however, the religious experience only reflects what the Christian faith in the Creator grasps and confesses intellectually and conceptually: all that is good in things and in our experience of the world is in God himself *per eminentiam,* in an infinite manner. Indeed, God himself is present in all things as the fundament that supports them.[39] This has nothing to do with pantheism and theopanism. It preserves *both* the infinite difference between God and the world *and* the mystery of the infinite closeness between God and the world. God created the world in the very same WORD in which he also assumed our flesh.[40] "Whoever confesses that Jesus is the Son of God, God abides in him, and he in God" (1 Jn 4:15).

The line of thought culminates in the Holy Father's exposition of the mystery of the Eucharist, when he speaks of the Lord's day, Sunday, as the

35 Francis, *Laudato si'*, 228.

36 Francis, *Laudato si'*, 231.

37 Francis, *Laudato si'*, 217.

38 Francis, *Laudato si'*, 217.

39 Francis, *Laudato si'*, 235.

40 Francis, *Laudato si'*, 235.

day of the transformation and salvation of the entire creation in the transfigured body of the risen Christ, the Word incarnate: "The Eucharist joins heaven and earth; it embraces and penetrates all creation."[41] It is only in the light of the Trinitarian mystery of God that we fully recognize what God is, as the origin and the goal of the entire creation. In Mary, from whom the Son of God took on human nature and united himself indissolubly to the creation, we recognize the beauty of the human vocation, the redemption and perfecting in soul and body. In the mother of Jesus, who is full of grace, we perceive the goal of the creation in the creating of the new heaven and the new earth. The cosmic dimension of redemption and grace must never be forgotten. "In the meantime, [...] we journey through this land seeking God. [...] Let us sing as we go. May our struggles and our concern for this planet never take away the joy of our hope."[42]

The Holy Father addresses this encyclical to Catholics and all those of good will, inviting them to a friendly dialogue about the ecological-social crisis that threatens our common home and asking us to take a path together in order to do justice to the worldwide challenge. It is not a matter of theoretical reflections with some practical goals; the pope is not interested in an improvement in details, but in a fundamental conversion in face of the overall situation, in which the crisis is getting worse and it is no longer possible to dodge the issue or play it down. We must recognize that we live in the same house that God has given to us all, and that we are children of the one Creator and Father in heaven.

Francis concludes his encyclical *Laduato si'* with two prayers, first "A prayer for our earth" that can be spoken by all who believe in God the Creator of the world and the Father of human beings. Even non-believers can find here an encouragement to meditate.

This is followed by "A Christian prayer in union with creation," which praises God and gives him glory in all its forms and colors, its elements and its living beings, with an eternal *Laudato si'!*

We call to God, our Lord, the Creator, the Redeemer, and the one who perfects the entire universe: "O Lord, seize us with your power and light, help us to protect all life, to prepare for a better future, for the coming of your Kingdom of justice, peace, love, and beauty. Praise be to you! Amen."[43]

41 Francis, *Laudato si'*, 236.

42 Francis, *Laudato si'*, 245.

43 Francis, *Laudato si'*, 246.

6.
THE POPE ON THE SIDE OF THE POOR

WHEN JESUS "CAME TO NAZARETH, where he had been brought up, he went to the synagogue, as was his custom, on the Sabbath day" (Lk 4:16). He was given the book of the prophet Isaiah, and he chose the following text to read aloud and to preach about: "The Spirit of the Lord God is upon me, because the Lord has anointed me to bring good tidings to the poor; he has sent me to bind up the brokenhearted, to proclaim liberty to the captives, and the opening of the prison to those who are bound; to proclaim the year of the Lord's favor" (Is 61:1–2). The apostles bring the good news of Christ for the poor and communicate freedom and the grace of God.

This is why Pope Francis, as the successor of Peter, takes his place beside the poor, from whom the Gospel of God must not be withheld:

> For the Church, the option for the poor is primarily a theological category rather than a cultural, sociological, political, or philosophical one. God shows the poor "his first mercy." This divine preference has consequences for the faith life of all Christians, since we are called to "have this mind … which was in Christ Jesus" (see Phil 2:5). Inspired by this, the Church has made an option for the poor. […] This is why I want a Church which is poor and for the poor. They have much to teach us. Not only do they share in the *sensus fidei*, but in their difficulties they know the suffering Christ. We need to let ourselves be evangelized by them. The new evangelization is an invitation to acknowledge the saving power at work in their lives and to put them at the center of the Church's pilgrim way. […] The poor person, when loved, "is esteemed as of great value," and this is what makes the authentic option for the poor differ from any other ideology, from any attempt to exploit the poor for one's own personal or political interest. Only this will ensure that "in every Christian community the poor feel at home. Would not this approach be the greatest and most effective presentation of the good news of the kingdom?"[44]

The celebrated "option for the poor" has a primarily and essentially Christological fundament. The apostle Paul says of Jesus Christ, the Son of God, who was sent by his Father "in the likeness of sinful flesh and for sin, in order to condemn sin in his flesh" (Rom 8:9): "You know the grace of our Lord Jesus Christ, that though he was rich, yet for your sake he became poor, so that by his poverty you might become rich" (2 Cor 8:9). Through his pov-

44 Francis, *Evangelii gaudium*, 198–99.

erty and self-abasement, we who are poor beggars before God, we mortals doomed to death, become sharers in his universal message of salvation and are clothed in the glory of God. The Latin American theology of liberation was inspired by the conciliar Constitution *Gaudium et spes* to widen this insight to the Church as a whole: "Theirs is a community composed of men. United in Christ, they are led by the Holy Spirit in their journey to the Kingdom of their Father and they have welcomed the news of salvation which is meant for every man. That is why this community realizes that it is truly linked with mankind and its history by the deepest of bonds" (GS 1).

The Church is authentically present where, in the mission of Jesus, "the Gospel is preached to the poor" (see Lk 7:22). On the path to this universal mission to every human being until the end of time, the Church does not allow itself to be defined by earthly splendor, wealth, and the striving for power. The Church has only one motivation: "to carry forward the work of Christ under the lead of the befriending Spirit. And Christ entered this world to give witness to the truth, to rescue and not to sit in judgment, to serve and not to be served" (GS 3).

Pope Francis takes up anew in *Evangelii gaudium* 198—"I want a Church which is poor and for the poor"—what Pope Benedict XVI had spoken of when he demanded that the Church be in a certain sense "desecularized" by means of a continuous orientation to the Gospel.

The "no" to a spiritual worldliness is contrasted with a "yes" to a truly missionary spirituality.[45] When Jesus pronounces a beatitude on "the poor in spirit" and promises them the kingdom of heaven (Mt 5:3), he is not offering a justification of a spiritualization and idealization of his Gospel that would flee from the world and shun responsibility. Spiritual poverty means a radical conformity to the mind of Christ and to the fate he met here on earth. It means that "unlike the one who thinks in earthly terms, the one who is filled with the Spirit accepts what the Spirit of God, the Spirit of Christ says to him" (see 1 Cor 2:14). A disciple of Jesus must not give his heart to deceitful wealth, to the transitoriness of power and of the prestige in the media that moves up and down in keeping with shifting public opinion. The spiritual person is liberated from slavery to false idols in order to serve others with all his material possessions and his intellectual and spiritual gifts, in order to be, like Jesus, "a human being for others" (in Dietrich Bonhoeffer's phrase). This is the true freedom "for which Christ has set us free" (Gal 5:1). This attitude of spiritual poverty as an inner freedom in Christ unites those who are married in the Lord, who rightly care for the physical wellbeing of their family, all the Christians who bear responsibility in public life, and those Christians

45 Francis, *Evangelii gaudium*, 93–97; 78–80.

who have taken a vow of poverty. This charism of freely chosen poverty is a sign that points to the comprehensive dependence of everyone on God, and to solidarity with the poor who are in material and spiritual distress. The faithful are one in Christ, across all social and ethnic boundaries. And they set their hope only on the God who is one and three, who continues his work of redemption and liberation through the Church until he himself perfects it at the end of time.

The Church and we ourselves as its members are continually tempted to present ourselves to the world as indispensable, through the activism of a solidly institutionalized spiritual-social undertaking. This is how we hope to gain prestige with the powerful and with leaders of opinion. The institutions of the Church, its cultural achievements and charitable endeavors, and the Church's property risk becoming goals that we allow to dominate us, instead of being means. This is the false spirit of worldliness, the longing to please human beings rather than God, and Pope Francis never wearies of warning us against this. Jesus promises that he will send the Counselor from the Father. The Spirit of God is "the Spirit of truth, whom the world cannot receive, because it neither sees him nor knows him; you know him, for he dwells with you, and will be in you" (Jn 14:17).

Without succumbing to the opposite extreme of a spiritualization and idealization of faith and the Church, the crisis of relativism and secularism in some parts of the Church must be overcome. The doomsday mood and inner emigration will be overcome through a new trust in the providence of God, who will make all things turn out for the best at the end. What we need is not a merely technical professionalism but the personal love for Jesus Christ and a profession of the faith that is filled with his Spirit. Although we give the outward impression of being solid in our dogmatic convictions and in our religious praxis, we secretly cling to financial security and to a feeling of power and prestige in people's eyes instead of laying down our life for others in mission. Pope Francis calls out to us: "Let us not allow ourselves to be robbed of missionary enthusiasm!"[46]

The Church that is poor in the human nature of Christ and rich in his divine nature takes the path of the Gospel. It is evangelized by Christ in the poor, and it brings to the poor the Gospel of Christ.[47] The iceberg of spiritual worldliness must melt in the fire of love for Christ in the hungry and the thirsty, and in all the works of corporal and spiritual mercy. When the Church proclaims the Gospel to those who are needy in material, human, and spiritual terms, and to all who yearn for justice, love, and eternal life

46 Francis, *Evangelii gaudium*, 80.

47 Francis, *Evangelii gaudium*, 198.

with God, it fulfills its task of making Christ present in its fellowship, as it carries out *martyria, leitourgia,* and *diakonia.*

In his Incarnation, Jesus Christ took on the poverty of creatureliness in all its facets. We must get beyond the material, economic, and political surface of poverty. As Pope Francis writes in the preface to the book *Armut: Die Herausforderung für den Glauben,* which I published together with Gustavo Gutiérrez, "poverty" is in a very genuine sense a description of our contingency. We are creatures who stand before God empty-handed. But our empty hands and our open minds are given to us by God, and they reach out to our creator. Our dependence on the Creator and Father neither humiliates nor insults us; on the contrary, we receive from him with joy and thanksgiving, in a eucharistic way, the bread that we need each day. We are created for him, and this means that our yearning for truth and love does not come to nothing. God communicates with us in his WORD, in his Son Jesus Christ, who has taken on our human existence and shares with us our human fate. He is the true bread from heaven. He gives himself to us as food and drink for eternal life. Accordingly, the transitoriness of all that is earthly does not lead us to a tragic existentialism. Rather, our existence in the world is oriented to a participation in God's truth and love in the creation, in salvation history, and in the fulfillment in his eternity. Since this participation is determined by the Logos, it is full of meaning. We do not live from pessimism, melancholy, and a longing for death à la Schopenhauer. We live from the hope that does not disappoint us, because the love of God is poured out into our hearts through the Holy Spirit who has been given to us (see Rom 5:5). Our PIN, the "personal identification number" of the Christian, is not world-weariness but *Evangelii gaudium,* "the joy of the Gospel."

Human existence in faith in Jesus Christ is always a eucharistic existence. But Christ did not take on human nature only abstractly and per se; he also took it on in the historical condition of its enslavement and distortion by sin. Paul expresses the integration of sin, with all its destructive power, into the divine-human mystery of Jesus in a formulation that bursts open every structure of human understanding: "For our sake he made him to be sin who knew no sin, so that in him we might become the righteousness of God" (2 Cor 5:21). Everything that is hatred of God and the brutal violation of human rights, enslavement and exploitation, the refusal of solidarity and fraternal love that cries out to heaven—all this is enclosed within the mystery of love and mercy, in order that we may become children of God, sisters and brothers of the Lord. The sin of the world is borne and suffered, wounded and conquered, by the Lamb of God. HE, who suffers in his own person every destructive violence, responds without violence and thus overcomes evil and suffering. His Cross becomes the sign of hope and the sacrament of the reconciliation of human beings with God and with each other. He has taken on our creaturely poverty, our fallenness in death and sin, and has filled it with the riches of his divinity. He has created us anew in order "that we might die to sin and live to righteousness" (1 Pt 2:24).

In our following of Christ, we recognize that Christianity is not an elite philanthropic worldview with a humanitarian-social praxis that is comfortably lulled in religious-sentimental experiences of one's own self. It is not a narcissistic ego trip of spiritual self-enjoyment. The internal form and the external criterion of the Christian life is not the realization of one's self with its interests and passions but the service of the kingdom of God: "Present yourselves as a living sacrifice, holy and acceptable to God, which is your spiritual worship (*logikê latreia*)" (Rom 12:1). Our faith in Christ is the beginning of a lifelong process whereby the old Adam dies and we set out every day on the path of fellowship with the risen Lord: "I have been crucified with Christ; it is no longer I who live, but Christ who lives in me; and the life I now live in the flesh I live by faith in the Son of God, who loved me and gave himself for me" (Gal 2:20). A departure from the real world into the realm of ideals; a bidding farewell to personal and public responsibility out of nostalgia for lost paradises and golden ages; a privatization of the Christian message that projects it into the sphere beyond death—all this is diametrically opposed to what God has revealed to us in the creation and in the event of Redemption, and to all that he has given us with his Son and his Spirit. For in suffering and death, Christ has overcome the world in its sin and wickedness. He came into what was his own not in order to emphasize the infinite distance between God and the world but in order to dwell among us, and to be close to us as God-with-us, and to remain always with us. "To all who received him, who believed in his name, he gave power to become children of God" (Jn 1:12).It is only thanks to Jesus Christ that we recognize, in the light of the divine vocation of the human being, the entire economic, political, and societal extent of the distress and wretchedness of people who are forced to lead a life far below the standard fit for human beings. Millions of our fellow human beings lack the bare necessities in food, clothing, and housing. They cannot afford medical care or make provision for their old age; they are denied the right to participate on equal terms in cultural life; in the political sphere, they are not acknowledged as mature and equal citizens but are degraded to objects of the claim by the powerful to have a monopoly on power, importance, and wealth at the cost of the common good. Think of the innumerable men and women who were victims of injustice and violence: in war and in genocide, through enslavement and rape, criminality and terrorism. History reads in part like the jeer of the wicked, who ask the righteous: "Where then is now your God?" (Ps 42:10).

They are our brothers and sisters, creatures of flesh and blood who have been robbed of their human dignity. When we look at this ocean of blood and tears that flows over the history of humanity, it would be impossible to resist the feeling of despair, the abyss of nihilism, or the protest against fate or against God—were it not for the fact that the God and Father of Jesus Christ has established justice for the victims of unjust violence in the Cross and Resurrection of his Son. All human beings had lost his glory, but he has manifested to them "the righteousness of God through faith in Christ Jesus for all who believe" (Rom 3:22). The judgment of the world is the victory of love over hatred.

In view of the tragic failure of the ideologies of progress in science and the economy, and of self-redemption in a capitalist or socialist paradise on earth—in short, of a "humanism without God"—the basic questions are being asked anew. Their formulation in *Gaudium et spes* has lost nothing of its actuality: "What is man? What is this sense of sorrow, of evil, of death, which continues to exist despite so much progress? What purpose have these victories purchased at so high a cost? What can man offer to society, what can he expect from it? What follows this earthly life?" (GS 10).

The Church is not setting up one more tombstone of self-redemption alongside all the explanations of the world and programs for improving the world that have been thought up by human beings. All these are condemned to perish, because faith comes from God, not from human beings. The Church bears witness in word and deed to the faith that has been given and entrusted to it through God's self-revelation. The Church believes that:

> Christ, who died and was raised up for all, can through His Spirit offer man the light and the strength to measure up to his supreme destiny. Nor has any other name under the heaven been given to man by which it is fitting for him to be saved. She likewise holds that in her most benign Lord and Master can be found the key, the focal point and the goal of man, as well as of all human history (GS 10).

In the light of Christ, therefore, the Church fulfills its mission to speak to people "in order to shed light on the mystery of man and to cooperate in finding the solution to the outstanding problems of our time" (GS 10).

When the Church proclaims the Gospel of Christ to the poor and oppressed and collaborates in building up a life in common in freedom, solidarity, and justice, acknowledging the unlimited dignity of every human being, it takes the path of Christ, who "carried out the work of redemption in poverty and persecution" (LG 8). HE was equal to God but emptied himself and took on our form of a servant (Phil 2:6); and this is why he was also exalted by God. We await from the exalted Lord, who will come as judge, that he will transform our poor body into the form of his own glorified body. The glory of God reveals itself in the Son's form of a servant. The *sacrum commercium* is the exchange of riches and poverty between God and the human being. In Jesus Christ, we see an inherent unity between the *theologia crucis* and the *theologia gloriae,* both in Christian anthropology and in ecclesiology, because Christ is for us both the crucified and the risen Lord. The God who is unknown and cannot be named has let us know him, and we are permitted to call him "Abba, Father" through the Son in the Spirit (Rom 8:15) because we are not only called the children of God but are truly so (1 Jn 3:1). This is our status, and at the same time the eschatological dynamism that determines our conduct vis-à-vis the world in relation to the mystery of the redemption and of the fellowship of life with God: "The creation itself will be set free from its bondage to decay and obtain the glorious liberty of the children of God" (Rom 8:21). The divine glory shines out on the face of the Church, so that through the Gospel all human beings may be illuminated by the light of Christ. And this is not the "deceitful riches" (Mk 4:13), the brilliance of earthly glory, the display of splendor and power. The Church follows its Lord. When it suffers and is persecuted, there shine out in the cross the glory of God, the "splendor of the Lord" (Lk 2:9), and the "fullness of his grace" (Jn 1:16).

As a visible community in this world, the Church needs material means only in order to fulfill its task "not to seek earthly glory, but to proclaim, even by its own example, humility and self-sacrifice. [... Like Christ,] the Church encompasses with love all who are afflicted with human suffering and in the poor and afflicted sees the image of its poor and suffering Founder. It does all it can to relieve their need and in them it strives to serve Christ" (LG 8). Whereas Christ, its Founder and Head, was holy and without sin, "the Church, embracing in its bosom sinners, at the same holy and always in need of being purified, always follows the way of penance and renewal" (LG 8).

This is the place to speak about liberation theology. It was born as a special response to the challenges of the poverty, exploitation, and degradation of millions of people in Latin America, a Catholic continent. Its Christological paradigm is the encounter with Jesus; it follows Jesus Christ, the merciful Samaritan. Jesus did not come on the scene as the guru of a transcendental mysticism or of an asceticism that repudiated the world. In his proclamation of the kingdom of God, with the healing of those who were blind, lame, and deaf, and in his care for the poor and rejected, we see the unity between the transcendental dimension of salvation and its immanent dimension that concerns our fellow human beings. His death on the Cross does not manifest a tragic failure. It bestows redemption from sin and injustice and reveals the new unity between the creature and God. Jesus died on the Cross in order to show God's liberating love, which transforms the world and gives everyone a hope that is real, not illusory. The death of Jesus on the Cross made the world and history a place where the new creation begins here and now. Accordingly, liberation does not come to us only in an interior spirituality and at the moment of our individual death. The end of history is the moment when salvation is perfected, when we see God in the eternal community of love with him and with all his saints. In Jesus Christ, the God-Man, a completely new, eschatological, and definitive relationship to God and to the world is realized. Christianity cannot be watered down to a feeling of dependence on the absolute (Schleiermacher), the awareness of the infinite love of a heavenly Father (Harnack), plus social involvement. The Christian existence is not the result of adding metaphysics and ethics, nor the reduction of one of these two to the other. Nor is the Christian existence a beautiful liturgy on Sunday plus social ethics for the weekdays; nor is it the traditional form plus a critique of society.

The Christian existence is born in the "encounter with Jesus" and is lived as a "risk for others." In the "Sketch of an Essay" (1944), Dietrich Bonhoeffer outlined the answer to the question: "What is Christian faith really?" It runs as follows:

> Our relationship to God is not a "religious" relationship to the highest, most powerful, best being that can be thought of—that is no genuine transcendence. Our relationship to God is a new life in "existence for others," in sharing in the existence of Jesus. The transcendent is not the infinite tasks that are out of reach, but that which is nearest, that which is given and can be reached in the particular instant. God in human form!—not, as in oriental religions, in animal forms as the terrible, the chaotic, the distant, the gruesome; but also not in the conceptual forms of the absolute, metaphysical, infinite, etc.; but also not the Greek god-human form of the "human being *per se*," but the "human being for others"!, and therefore the Crucified one. The human being who lives out of transcendence.[48]

In a lecture held in the mid-1990s in the presence of Cardinal Ratzinger, Gustavo Gutiérrez emphasized that: "It is important that ultimately, the option for the poor is an option for the God of the kingdom that Jesus proclaims to us." And he continued:

48 Dietrich Bonhoeffer, *Widerstand und Ergebung*, 414.

> The definitive reason for championing the poor and oppressed thus lies, not in the analysis of society that we employ, nor in the immediate experience that we may have of poverty, nor in our human compassion. All of these are valid reasons that indubitably play a significant role in our life and in our relationships. For Christians, however, this commitment is based fundamentally on faith in the God of Jesus Christ. It is a theocentric option and a prophetic option that has its roots in the gratuitousness of God's love and is demanded by this love.[49]

Jesus Christ died in order that the human being might experience God as salvation and as life in every sphere of one's existence. This generates the original Christological impulse of liberation theology, which can be formulated thus: it is impossible to speak of God without active, transformative, and therefore practical participation in the complex and integral liberating conduct that God initiates. Thanks to this conduct, history becomes a process in which freedom is realized. And *e contra*, the Church cannot limit itself to improving the living conditions of the poor while at the same time cheating them of God and the Gospel, for that would be an even worse discrimination and a lack of spiritual care that would cause the poor to suffer. Pope Francis argues against this idea in *Evangelii gaudium*: "The great majority of the poor have a special openness to the faith; they need God and we must not fail to offer them his friendship, his blessing, his word, the celebration of the sacraments and a journey of growth and maturity in the faith. Our preferential option for the poor must mainly be translated into a privileged and preferential religious care."[50]

If then the Church, together with the human race and in history, is at the service of this plan of Christ, it can (as Dietrich Bonhoeffer writes) be "the Church only if it exists for others."[51] This leads to an ultimate discernment of spirits, and each one is confronted by an interior choice and the discernment of spirits.

Either "the joys and the hopes, the griefs and the anxieties of the men of this age, especially those who are poor or in any way afflicted, are the joys and hopes, the griefs and anxieties of the followers of Christ" (GS 1), *or else* they are not truly disciples of Jesus. In other words: *either* the Church displays itself from this perspective as a religious fellowship that is not separated from

49 Gustavo Gutiérrez, "¿Dónde dormirán los pobres?" in *El rostro de Dios en la historia*, 9–69 (Lima: Pontificia Universidad Católica del Perú, Departamento de Teología, Instituto Bartolomé de las Casas, Centro de Estudios y Publicaciones, 1996), 18.

50 Francis, *Evangelii gaudium*, 200.

51 Dietrich Bonhoeffer, *Widerstand und Ergebung*, 415; "The Church is the Church only if it exists for others," 560.

the world and is sufficient unto itself but is instead the universal sacrament of salvation, *or else* the Church is not completely "Church" in terms of its essence and its mission.[52] As chapter IV of the Instruction *Libertatis conscientia* of the Congregation for the Doctrine of the Faith (1986) states, the Church is truly "Church" when it is faithful to its liberating mission for the integral salvation of the world, a mission that has its origin both in Jesus's message about freedom and liberation and in Jesus's deeds.[53]

Just as in the days of Bartolomé de Las Casas, about whom Gustavo Gutiérrez has written an extensive study, God is on the side of the poor. His working aims to lead them to freedom and to make it possible for them to have a share in the fulfillment of the salvation for all human beings that he has promised. From this perspective, it is absolutely clear that to speak of the "power of the poor in history" has nothing at all to do with the formulation of an ideology at the service of "perennially recurring" projects that are utopian and that generate violence.[54] The "historical power" of the poor is certainly not to be understood as the violent elimination of one societal class, ethnic group, or religion by another, as a path to removing oppression and injustice in order thus to attain the supposed paradise on earth, the classless society, or the dictatorship of opinion. Aid programs from capitalist-laicist countries are equally discriminatory when they tie development aid to the acceptance of gender ideologies and population policies that include abortion and forced sterilization, thus becoming guilty anew of the crime of colonialism.

God's love embraces even the rulers, the exploiters, the human traffickers, the drug dealers, and the Mafiosi. The threat of eternal damnation is more than just and must always be justified in keeping with a necessary theodicy. But this threat is born of the divine love that has taken upon itself in Christ the sins and crimes in order to make repentance and conversion possible. Preaching about judgment and grace frees the sinners from their own slavery: from the typical slavery of avarice, the "root of all evils" (1 Tm 6:10), from the idolization of money and power. These idols make it impossible for their worshipers ever to find peace of heart. At the end, their own greed swallows them up.

Above all, liberation theology—unlike what we hear from Marxism with its twin, capitalist liberalism—shows that Christianity is not in the least an "ideology of comfort," or "Platonism for the people" (Nietzsche), or an illu-

52 See LG and CCC 748.

53 Congregation for the Doctrine of the Faith, *Instruction on Christian Freedom and Liberation* (March 22, 1986), ch. 4.

54 Gustavo Gutiérrez, *The Power of the Poor in History* (Eugene, Ore.: Wipf & Stock, 2004).

sion and projection. On the contrary, the true theology of liberation shows that, in reality, only God, the Father of Jesus Christ, and the Gospel of grace and truth can play an authentic and lasting role for the humanization of the human person, both individually and in a societal-social perspective. As John Paul II so aptly put it in his letter to the Brazilian Bishops' Conference in 1986, the correctly understood theology of liberation "is not only opportune, but useful and necessary."[55]

This assessment by John Paul II has lost nothing of its relevance; indeed, it is more relevant than ever today, in a time when enmity and greed have become immensely powerful, in a time in which we need, as never before, the living God who has loved us unto death. In his immeasurable love, the Good Samaritan, in the fleshliness of concrete existence, bends down over the sufferers and the oppressed and those who need salvation most of all. Pope Francis put it rightly in his address in Rio de Janeiro on July 27, 2013: "We therefore need a Church that is capable of rediscovering the maternal womb of mercy. Without mercy, it is scarcely possible today to find access to a world of 'wounded' persons who need understanding, forgiveness, and love."[56] In Christ, the Son of the living God (Mt 16:16), those who are baptized in his name have themselves become "sons of the living God" (Rom 9:26) in accordance with the prophetic promise (Hos 2:1).

When we look at scripture, we see that the covenant history is a history of liberation with an ever more clearly emerging option by God for the poor, the suffering, and the exploited, so that soteriology always also entails a social ethics—social ethics as a theological discipline, that is to say, because *diakonia, caritas,* is an essential trait of the Church. "The liberating mission of the Church" has its starting point in the liberating message of Jesus and of his praxis of the kingdom of God. The Church promotes "the foundations of justice in the temporal order" and remains faithful to its prophetic-critical mission when it "condemns the forms of deviation, slavery and oppression of which people are victims."[57] But the Church also acts in accord with its mission when it also condemns the methods that avenge violence with violence, terror with terror, and the deprivation of rights with the deprivation of rights.

In all the mental and physical ills that afflict so much of humanity in unjust systems, the Church takes the preferential "option for the poor" not in order to fuel conflicts but in order to overcome barriers between social classes and to make solidarity, human dignity, and subsidiarity the uni-

55 John Paul II, "Letter to the Episcopal Conference of Brazil" (April 9, 1986).

56 Francis, "Address of Pope Francis in the Bishop's Residence" (July 28, 2013).

57 Congregation for the Doctrine of the Faith, *Instruction on Christian Freedom,* 62; 65.

versally valid principles of a social order.[58] With regard to the relationship between personal sin and structures, it must be said that there exists what John Paul II called "a structure of sin" that is the outcome of collective erroneous developments and is the expression of false mentalities; these can be called "sin" because they come, like evil desire, from the original sin, the death of the soul, and because they lead to sin.[59] This, however, does not exclude the individual's own responsibility. No one can plead in excuse that the economic and political systems compelled him to exploit other people and wreck their lives.

Processes that are alleged to be historically necessary never determine the human being in a quasi-fatalistic sense, thereby relieving him of the free use of his responsibility before God. It is not "fate" or "historical laws," ethnic, cultural, and sociological conditions, but the *providentia Dei* that determines the course of history with regard to human freedom and its perfecting in love—both in life here on earth and in view of the supernatural vocation of the human being.

The person retains priority over against the structure. This is why the liberating praxis of Christians, which is generated by our redemption from sin and by the communication to us of grace, leads to the change and the continuous improvement of the material and societal conditions of life; at the same time, it understands the personal encounter between human beings in the love of Christ as the very heart of Christian existence: "Christians working to bring about that 'civilization of love' which will include the entire ethical and social heritage of the Gospel are today faced with an unprecedented challenge. This task calls for renewed reflection on what constitutes the relationship between the supreme commandment of love and the social order considered in all its complexity."[60] This involves "an immense effort at education: education for the civilization of work, education for solidarity, access to culture for all."[61] Such an effort on the part of the entire Church is necessary for the poor in the one global world that is God's creation.

In the light of the option for the poor and for all those who look for God's salvation, we understand the Church as "a sign and instrument both of a very closely knit union with God and of the unity of the whole human race" (LG 1).

58 Congregation for the Doctrine of the Faith, *Instruction on Christian Freedom*, 68.

59 John Paul, *Sollicitudo rei socialis*, 36; Council of Trent, "Decree on Original Sin," DH 1512.

60 Congregation for the Doctrine of the Faith, *Instruction on Christian Freedom*, 81.

61 Congregation for the Doctrine of the Faith, *Instruction on Christian Freedom*, 81.

This is the universal mission of the pope and bishop of Rome, to cry out "with the boldness of Peter" (Acts 4:13) to everyone's memory and conscience that Jesus of Nazareth is the salvation of the world. This is the good news for everyone: "Blessed are the poor in spirit, for theirs is the kingdom of God" (Mt 5:3).

VIII

The Pope—Teacher of God's Truth and Guarantor of Human Freedom

1.
EVERY HUMAN LIFE HAS AN INDESTRUCTIBLE MEANING

THE FURTHER AWAY FROM CHRISTIANITY an observer stands, the smaller are the differences he perceives between the Catholic Church and the other Christian denominations. All religions look the same to an atheist. For one who is religious in the sense that he relates to an impersonal sacred mystery beyond the world that is seen, or indeed beyond the difference between being and nothing, all religions that believe in a personal God are the same; he regards their differences as concerning only the way in which the "one God," the cypher for the unutterable mystery, is revered. In the eyes of a liberal and modernistic Christian who sees Christianity only as a cultural epiphenomenon, the controversial doctrines of the churches and ecclesial communities must look rather like the expression of a narrow party spirit and of an apodictic understanding of truth. It is, however, impossible in principle for him to understand this, for just as the transcendental ego does not recognize reality, "the thing in itself," but only its phenomena, which it constitutes on the basis of its forms of perception and categories, so too the religious ego does not recognize God in the Word of his revelation, but only the human ideas about God. These ideas may perhaps reflect his mystery in various ways, but they cannot express it unambiguously in confession and in dogma. The shortest path from the phenomenalism of knowledge leads to the relativism of truth.

The relativism of the postmodern period is wrong to regard truth as in principle unknowable, for if knowledge does in fact exist, there also exists the ontological and epistemological criterion that distinguishes true from false knowledge. This also applies to the theories about truth. Similarly, concrete experience refutes the thesis that the renunciation of the knowledge of truth makes possible a tolerant living in common among persons where each possesses his or her own truth—for the vacuum that comes about through refusing to ask the fundamental questions about God, the world, and the human being will be filled by totalitarian political and ideological positions that renounce the truth and are consequently obliged to eliminate freedom too.

The human being is certainly capable of taking a realistic approach to the world and to the basic existential questions about our existence, an approach that leads to the knowledge of the truth that manifests itself to him in the being of things, and that requires him to accept the claim that the good makes. This means that the human being can deduce rationally from the existence of the world the certainty of the existence and the power of God (see Rom 1:18). He is therefore also the hearer of a revelation in which God discloses himself to him in Word and Spirit. Through the media of the creation and the Incarnation, the human being thus enters into a personal, dialogical, and sacramentally mediated fellowship of salvation with God. This knowledge is shared by all who enter into a relationship with Jesus Christ, the Son of God, who took on our humanity. This is why the confessional differences in the understanding of the historical and grace-filled mediation of truth and of life are not secondary matters, although it is also true that these questions depend on the all-encompassing mysteries of the Trinity, the Incarnation, and the deification of the human being.

The statistics of those who officially leave the Church in Germany are published every year, to the automatic accompaniment of commentaries whose tone and contents have not substantially changed in the last one hundred and forty years. The interpretation of the modern period as the outcome of an unstoppable process of secularization is thought to be confirmed, and those hostile to the Church, who make their appeal to the masses to leave the Church in the name of progress and science, celebrate the triumph of their agitation. This inglorious history began with the socialist and laicist free thinkers' movements before the First World War. It reached its intellectual and moral nadir in the German ideology of the nation and in the ideologies of Nazism and communism. At the beginning of the present century, an aggressive neo-atheism picked up where it had begun in the *Kulturkampf*.

It is of the utmost importance for the Church, for all convinced Christians, and for every "minister of the Word" (Lk 1:2) to analyze the deeper causes of the alienation from faith in Jesus Christ and in his Church that have led to this dramatic breach with one's own identity in the relationship to God that has its fundament in faith and baptism. The public distancing vis-à-vis one's own provenance and home—a distancing that is officially registered by the state authorities in Germany—is often prompted by an external circumstance ("annoyance" at something or someone) that is completely out of proportion to what membership of the Church means with regard to the eternal salvation that is mediated to believers through the Church in obedience to the commission given by Jesus. But here, as is so often the case, one must distinguish between the occasion and the cause. The process whereby the western nations have been uprooted from a bimillennial culture of the Christian understanding of the human being and of the world since the Enlightenment, via the criticism of religion and culminating in a systematic re-paganization, has penetrated very deeply, and the Church cannot counter it with a few accommodations here and there, by taking up some positive concerns and repeating them ("more women in leadership positions," "a new evaluation of sexuality," "getting our message across better," and so on).

If we accept the biblical admonition to "make a defense to anyone who asks for the meaning (*logos*) of the hope that is in you" (1 Pt 3:15) because of our faith in Jesus Christ, the Son of God and universal mediator of salvation, we must spare no effort to investigate the causes and consequences of this phenomenon of de-Christianization. Withdrawal into the milieu of a Christian remnant would contradict the essence of the Church and its mission to be the sign and instrument of God's plan of salvation. He "desires everyone to be saved and to come to the knowledge of the truth" (1 Tm 2:4).

In his confession of Christ, the pope renders a service to the whole of humanity, by reminding all that God is the foundation of the truth and of human freedom. "The Church of the living God is the pillar and bulwark of the truth" (1 Tm 3:15) because Jesus Christ has set us free from slavery and "bondage to decay" in order "to obtain the glorious liberty of the children of God" (Rom 8:21).

In his book *Desocialization: The Crisis of Post-Modernity*, Matthew Fforde presents the fruits of thirty years of precise observation and an acute historical analysis of the intellectual and cultural development in Great Britain.[1] The results and conclusions apply *mutatis mutandis* to all the western countries that have their cultural roots in the Christian culture. The spread

1 Matthew Fforde, *Desocialization: The Crisis of Post-Modernity* (Cheadle Hulme: Gabriel Communications, 2009).

of England's culture and language give it both historically and in the present day a bridging function between globalization under American leadership and continental Europe, as well as the development in Asian and African societies.

Fforde conducts a debate on a high level of reflection with all of today's relevant Christian, liberal, and anti-Christians critics of culture and of society (the old and new left wingers, liberal political correctness as a substitute for religion and an ersatz religion). Although the argumentation does not make use of theology and philosophy in the technical professional sense (as does, for example, Henri De Lubac in *The Drama of Atheist Humanism*) and proceeds historically and sociologically, it makes an important contribution to the debate about how Christianity should understand the postmodern period and react to it in the framework of the new evangelization at which the Catholic Church aims.

The Church's proclamation and pastoral work certainly have their fundament in revelation; but in the dialogue with people of today, empirical analyses of the self-understanding and the view of reality are indispensable presuppositions for hearing the Word of God, receiving it in faith, and putting it into action in a life that imitates Christ.

Fforde's central insight is the conviction that the history of the de-Christianization of Europe over the last three hundred years need not be irreversible. There is no reason for despair or apocalyptic panic, since the truth of the faith and its mediation of eternal salvation and of the success and happiness of a person's life do not depend on the number of those who confess this faith. The diaspora is the normal condition—the self-contained union of society and Christianity was the exception, historically speaking. But above all, the salt must not lose its power. And in every desert, the oasis alone is the terminal station of yearning.

The processes that have led to a secularization of consciousness and of societal life were made and directed by human beings. This is why a human being can also examine them to see whether their premises are true and their consequences promote life. Fforde's ten chapters elaborate a picture of contemporary society in its opportunities, but also in its abysses that go as far as an interior self-destruction. The postmodern period is fundamentally based on a defective anthropology that has fatal consequences, especially in a dissolution of solidarity and a desocialization. If the human being is reduced to a product of the matter that plays with itself, or to a construction of society, or becomes merely a participant in social networks, he is robbed of his subjecthood and his personality, because he is made into an object of sexual lust, of political power, or of scientific research. Fforde's statistics show the extent to which families are plagued by loneliness, isolation, inner suffering, increasing violence and brutality, egocentricity, orientation to one's own profit and to an egomaniacal self-realization, and the refusal of primary communication. He shows how the vision of a beautiful life where pleasure dominates, a life with no ethical demands, a life without orientation to the living personal God collapses like a house of cards. Whole hordes of therapists try to cure the illnesses that were created by the ideologies born of false anthropologies.

There are numerous contradictions between the positions that ultimately deny the irreducible identity of the human being, the substantiality of the soul, the form of a person's mental and physical nature and of its unfolding in history and culture. These positions cut one off from his essential relatedness to the transcendent God and thereby hand him over to the unfettered rule of humans over other humans. Despite their differences, however, they all agree in relativizing the question of truth, as I have shown in chapter 5. The denial of objective truth does not lead to freedom, because the opposite of truth is falsehood. And relativism is the foundation, not of tolerance and the free positing by the knowing subject of a relationship to the truth of reality and of being, but rather (as Pope Benedict XVI correctly said) of the dictatorship of relativism. Relativism contradicts itself when it claims an apodictically absolute validity while in the same breath denying that truth exists and can be known. Relativism is nothing other than the societal implementation of the philosophy of nothing. Relativism and nihilism are related to each other like darkness and blackness. The agenda includes a "no" to life at the beginning (abortion, preimplantation genetic diagnosis, designer babies), in the middle (making the sexual identity as man and woman a matter of indifference; the dissolution of family, relatives, and neighborhood), and at the end (euthanasia, assisted suicide), although it is always claimed that this is a matter of self-determination and the avoidance of suffering. It also includes hatred of everyone who does not succumb to this reductionist worldview and to the tendency to the homogenization of thinking, acting, feeling, and evaluating (the privatization of religion, which is made an object of contempt; the coercion to perform immoral actions even against one's own conscience). It thus also includes the undermining of democracy and of the state under the rule of law that is built upon human dignity, which is absolutely unassailable and does not depend on being granted by the state.

Fforde's response is an anthropology that indubitably draws its essential traits from the Jewish-Christian tradition but has a positive and constructive orientation that makes it possible to come together with many people of good will and of other religious-ethical traditions to form an action group. It is rationally possible to bring all the results of the modern natural and historical sciences into a synthesis with what we know from revelation; it is not necessary for a Christian today to live in *two* intellectual worlds. Besides this, however, the Christian message is the Gospel of love. Love of truth and love of the good are the core of the Christian understanding of the human being and of the world in relation to God, the Creator of the universe and the Redeemer from guilt, loneliness, and death. The human heart cannot be filled by power without service, by wealth without generosity, or by sexual pleasure without the gift of oneself. It can be filled only by accepting oneself, because each one is already accepted unconditionally by God and is loved both now and without end, beyond the end of this earthly path.

Matthew Fforde's book gives the reader insight into the hidden mechanisms and processes that do in fact determine one's daily life, even if one is not always aware of their origin and their significance.

2.
FAITH'S REASON—AND REASON'S FAITH

Pope Benedict XVI held a lecture in Regensburg that was a high point of university history in Germany. He once again set out the synthesis between faith and reason, and between freedom and love. A secular world would like to claim these four concepts for itself today and at the same time to dispute the Church's right to present itself as the basic foundation or source of a meaningful life for society. One who does not believe that Christ is the only and unsurpassable mediator of salvation praises his own openness and his capacity for tolerance, while simultaneously accusing the Church of coercing consciences and of intellectual imperialism. It seems that the tolerance that a pluralistic worldview absolutizes in this way does not extend all that far when it is a matter of the Christian with his or her fundamental decision of faith.

Behind this there often lies the idea that the human being can attain a deeper knowledge only one-dimensionally, in a purely inner-worldly way. That which is not visible is pushed down into the realm of psychology or of the construction of myths, as a subjectively influenced pattern of coping with an intolerable reality. In other words, its de facto existence is denied. This means that there is no claim to truth, no ultimate criterion, no God. But how can a person with an agnostic attitude utter such an apodictic verdict?

This is the genesis of the dictatorship of relativism of which Cardinal Ratzinger spoke at the opening of the conclave from which he emerged as Benedict XVI. The denial of transcendence entails dangers that can be documented in the events and tendencies in history: when the human being was made an ideal, this led—and leads—to totalitarianism and dictatorship, and the power of the one who is stronger destroys the Christian image of the human being. No one has ever displayed more authoritarianism than the relativistic liberalism of the nineteenth century with its raging against the Church. No other movement was more hostile to human beings than the atheism of the twentieth century with the pseudo-religious habitus of the "new human being." The nomenclature of the "superman" brought millions of murders, with death and devastation, upon the entire world. In the name of freedom, war was waged against the Church and the faith.

Relativism with regard to truth is not only a philosophical line of thought. It leads inevitably to intolerance vis-à-vis God. At most, the central affirmations about God—Jesus—Christ—Church are regarded as the subculture of a religiously motivated group. God becomes an "ideal" that is employed to edify people or to teach them. Jesus Christ becomes a special "case" who could serve as an example for the morality of society, and the Church is a free association—in the manner of a club—for people who have the same subjective religious views.

These are the reasons why religious themes are taboo in the public sphere and the Christian message and the Church have been expelled from political discourse. It is said that the Church represents religiously motivated persons who have no claim at all to take part in dialogue and in constructing the world. They are tied to a limited cultural paradigm that is not universally binding and that belongs in the realm of individual and collective subjectivity.

This evaluation of the faith is not without its consequences for theology's self-understanding. Is it still a genuine involvement with God that employs the reason, or is it now merely a program that attracts a few adherents?

It is intolerable for liberalism, as an active form of pluralism, if God has in fact revealed himself to the human being—for one would then have to admit that the human being, far from being the measure of all things, owes his or her existence to God's love, which gives the gift of freedom. The hedonistic liberalism that absolutizes pleasure and profit forms a contrast to the eucharistic human being who owes his existence to God and who is redeemed to the glorious liberty of the children of God.

Can a World without God Succeed?

This is not a purely theoretical question. It must be posed under the premise that God exists and that we are driving him out of what belongs to him. What is involved here is thus not the *question* whether God exists; what is at stake is the sheer *denial* of his presence. One who acknowledges God as the mainstay of his own life is often laughed at, not because there would be no God to whom one could turn but because there is a conscious desire to expel God from reality. A progressive reason declares itself to be God and suggests that the human being is self-sufficient.

Our confession of faith itself contains the seed of an encounter with God that is oriented to the human reason. Reason and rationality are not concepts incompatible with faith, no matter how often the pluralistic and relativistic modern age may make this accusation. As rational beings, we are designed in such a way that we do not conceal God from the reason. It was he who created the reason, and he is the LOGOS that encompasses all things and alone can lead us to experience and to knowledge. The human being thinks about himself and the world, and thereby about the transcendental cause that allows everything to come into existence. The human being uses his reason. How can the reason think of itself without any relation to God? Pluralism and secularism serve the person who would like to live without God in order that no rules may be imposed on him—although these rules arise from human existence itself. A discussion without this point of reference unhinges the human being, since there is no longer any basis that can show him who he really is. Without the liberating rule of Jesus Christ, that which constitutes the human being becomes a farce. It cannot endure, and it terrorizes those who cannot put up resistance, as so many examples demonstrate: the millions of abortions that are propagated in a perverted manner as a woman's human right to self-determination; the research into embryos that uses them and then discards them; and euthanasia, the murder of old and incurably ill persons, which can take the form of forcing one who does not want to be a burden on society to kill himself.

It is precisely for this reason that the world needs a reason that is not deaf to the divine. In Jesus Christ, the divine Logos has taken on human form. This is the faith that teaches the reason to understand, the reason that comes to faith, and the freedom that acts in accord with the conscience.

3. THE TRUTH OF GOD IS THE BASIS OF HUMAN FREEDOM

ABOVE THE DOOR TO THE AUDITORIUM in the University of Freiburg, where I studied, are engraved the words of a logion that is ascribed to the Johannine Jesus: "The truth will make you free" (Jn 8:32).

This is a glorious profession of adherence to the western intellectual tradition out of which the universities emerged in the Middle Ages. It alludes to the program of the unity of faith and reason, of the knowledge of God and the knowledge of the world. In this unity the identity of the Christian human being is based and develops. God establishes and guarantees the dignity and the greatness of the human being: "We know that in everything God works for good with those who love him, who are called according to his purpose. For those whom he foreknew he also predestined to be conformed to the image of his Son, in order that he might be the firstborn among many brethren" (Rom 8:28–29). The truth of the human being before God is the fundament of his freedom in God, and the goal of freedom is love. The identity of the human being does not consist in a static and autarchic self-possession, nor is it realized as a circling around oneself and in oneself. Personhood means transcending oneself towards other persons. It is in love that the personhood of the human being is realized: first in the relationship to other human beings, and then in all things and above all things in God, who reveals his being as love in the fellowship of the Father and the Son (see 1 Jn 4:8, 16).

In their reciprocal relatedness, truth and freedom constitute the intellectual-ethical nature of the human being and his relatedness to transcendence. God in his own nature is spirit and truth, love and freedom. In his intellectual being and in the realization of his freedom, the human person shares in God's own being. In his reason and his freedom, he is oriented to God, his Creator. The human being—precisely in his mortality and in the insubordination of his arrogant reason against his Creator—finds the ideal expression of his deepest striving in the words of Saint Augustine: "And yet he wishes to praise you, God, the human being who is himself a particle of your creation. You prompt us to praise you with joy, because you have created us with an orientation to yourself (*ad te*), and our heart is restless until it rests in you."[2]

In theology and philosophy, in the sciences of history and of society, of culture and nature, thinking strives upwards towards the knowledge of the truth and finds its crowning in freedom. There are not two self-contained worlds, hermetically sealed off against each other, that the human being inhabits in accordance with his choice. Or, to put it in classical terminology, there is no double truth. What is correct in philosophy cannot be false in theology, and vice versa. The empirical scientific theories about the origin of the cosmos and of life cannot contradict faith's confession that God has brought into existence out of nothing, in accordance with his truth and his freedom, everything that exists and that works outside himself—provided that this confession is given a correct theological exposition.

Materialistic monism, with the thesis that everything is matter, wishes to confront us with the alternative either that the human being is the chance

2 Augustine, *Conf.* 1.1.

product of an evolution of life, or else that he owes his personhood to an immediate creative act. This is only an apparent contradiction. The conditions of the material development of our species and of our individual existence explain our bodily form. But they give no answer to the question of what our nature is—a nature that does not exist concretely without its intellectual form with the reason and the will. The spirit knows itself in the acts of thinking and willing, and only the spirit is capable of making matter, as that which is other than itself, the object of empirical research. These are not mutually exclusive answers to one and the same question, but rather two answers to two different questions that are, however, compatible in the complex reason of the human being.

This has consequences. The human being is not the object but first and foremost the subject of philosophy, science, and politics. No other human being assigns him his meaning and his goal, nor does any other human being deny him these: they are implanted in him by his Creator, and in their unconditional character they form the basis of all ethics. A pan-naturalistic mysticism that is meant to make nihilism bearable suggests that the human being is a part of the world, in the sense that he finds the meaning of his intellectual existence in the evolution of the organic and animal living beings. But blind nature cannot bring forth from itself a being endowed with a mind. A human being who denies the essential difference between himself and an animal is actually *confirming* this difference. In pantheistic and naturalistic nihilism, the question of truth and freedom is irrelevant, because being is merely an appearance, truth merely a fiction, and freedom merely an illusion; there is no escape from the wheel of determinism. It is impossible to answer the question "What is the human being?" by having my ashes scattered at sea or in the wood and thus letting my mortal remains sink down as fertilizer into the material cycle of the "dying and coming to life" of organic nature, so that even then I would be making myself useful. The soul of the human being is endowed with intellect and will. Unlike the animals, it is oriented to truth and love, so that its goal and content can only be the personal fellowship with God—not the dissolution of the intellectual person into the biochemical processes of material nature. This is what we mean when we speak of the immortality of the soul and the hope of the resurrection of the flesh in Christ. The question of the difference between merely organic life and intellectual life demonstrates the categorical and essential difference between subintellectual and intellectual-personal life—as indeed does the denial of this difference. We discover the meaning of human existence above ourselves, not below ourselves.

From the eighteenth century onwards, there has existed a remarkable limitation on the knowledge of truth, which runs counter to the history of freedom. Metaphysical agnosticism absolutizes itself in a paradoxical manner, rejecting as impossible a self-revelation of God in history before it has even taken account of the facts. But can one demonstrate *more geometrico* that the human reason is in principle *incapax infiniti*? How can one exclude a priori the possibility that even a finite created reason can be elevated by God to share in his own reason through the mediation of his Word made flesh? The reason is essentially oriented to the truth. The dynamic of freedom brings it to unite with the good in love.

In his drama *Nathan the Wise* (1779), Gotthold Ephraim Lessing (1729–1781) did not in the least demonstrate irrefutably that there can be no certain knowledge of revelation, and that accordingly the only use for the religions could be moral and humanitarian (in other words, functional). All he did was illustrate his own agnostic position, not demonstrate it in a rationally conclusive way. Nor did Immanuel Kant (1724–1804) succeed in refuting once for all the possibility of metaphysics. All he did was to conceptualize the impossibility of bridging the gulf between rationalism and empiricism, which, however, are only elements that have broken out of an original synthesis. Feuerbach saw faith in a reality of God and in the mysteries of revealed faith as a projection that alienates the human being from what he truly is—namely, a higher animal. However, he failed to see that the events of the historical revelation are not deduced idealistically from the individual and collective consciousness of believers. This means that his thesis that God and the contents of the Christian faith are only projections, and that theology can be reduced to anthropology, begs the question: what was to be demonstrated sounds so convincing only because it is already presupposed. Auguste Comte's (1798–1857) law of three stages is nothing other than a subjective schema that he wants to impose upon the history of ideas, without taking account of the spontaneity of philosophical knowledge, which is qualitatively different from the knowledge of empirical objects. Marx and Lenin are equally wrong in seeing religion as the opium of the people and for the people. On the contrary, religion as the worship of God the Creator and father of all human beings proves to be the deepest source of the *humanitas* that respects every human being without exception. In my neighbor, I recognize my brother and my sister, in whose fears and distresses Christ himself encounters me. Jesus will say at the Last Judgment: "As you did it to one of the least of these my brethren, you did it to me" (Mt 25:40).

In his intellectual-physical nature, the human being knows that he is oriented to the truth of reality (see GS 14) and to that which is good per se. His bodiliness means that he belongs to the physical and organic world, but in his interior dimension, in which he knows himself and is intellectually and spiritually at home in himself, he transcends the totality of things, as the Second Vatican Council so clearly analyzed in the Pastoral Constitution *Gaudium et spes* (GS 14). The instrumental reason has helped the human being to investigate the material world through the empirical sciences and technology, and to make the world highly useful for his own ends. Nevertheless:

> He has always searched for more penetrating truths, and finds them. For his intelligence is not confined to observable data alone, but can with genuine certitude attain to reality itself as knowable, though in consequence of sin that certitude is partly obscured and weakened. The intellectual nature of the human person is perfected by wisdom and needs to be, for wisdom gently attracts the mind of man to a quest and a love for what is true and good. Steeped in wisdom, man passes through visible realities to those which are unseen (GS 15).

It is only with the aid of the reason and the ethical principles of freedom and of responsibility for our salvation and for the common good—principles that are inherent in the reason—that we can also humanize the achievements of the natural sciences and technology and make them serve us. This does not mean a technical mastery of the potentially destructive and even suicidal consequences of the developments in medicine, global communications, weapons systems, and so on. It means an orientation of the conscience to the good and to the truth. It is in morality that the reason crosses the threshold of the realm of freedom.

The great theme of modern philosophy is freedom as the ethical autonomy of the subject. An antithesis to the theological concept of freedom arises only when freedom is understood in a purely formal sense as self-determination, devoid of any link to the content and the goal of the free will. There is no rivalry between divine and human freedom: they encounter each other in the love that God is and that he has for us, and in which he raises up our freedom to himself. Freedom belongs to the creaturely nature of the human being and is the peak of what it means to be the image of God—and hence of the inalienable dignity of the human being. Freedom is not restricted and limited through the good that God is in his nature, the goodness that he has ascribed to everything created (Gn 1:31). On the contrary, this good brings human freedom to its flowering. In the freedom led by grace, the free will unites to God. The human being comes to perfection when he cooperates in love with the will of God. A freedom without love, an autonomy without a transcendental relatedness to God, inevitably meant the collapse of the modern history of freedom into nihilism and contempt for human beings.

The Second Vatican Council praised the high appreciation that freedom enjoys in the modern period. But freedom goes off the rails if it is understood only as the justification for doing whatever pleases us as individuals or as a society, whatever is useful and gives pleasure, or promotes a ruthless self-realization. Truth is not my own property. It leads me out, beyond my bourgeois possessiveness and mediocre striving for enjoyment, into the wide spaces of responsibility for others. One who acts only in accordance with his own interests or declares that these interests are his right and his truth becomes their servant. An old proverb says: "He who wants to be his own teacher is the pupil of a fool. And one who only wants to be his own master becomes the servant of his passions." No matter how they might want to justify themselves with their al dente truths and philosophies, it remains objectively true that warmongers, arms smugglers, drug dealers, terrorists, abusers of children, rapists, thieves, liars, adulterers and destroyers of families, cynics and the frivolous, idlers and exploiters, and all who act against the commandments of God (the Decalogue) that communicate salvation, are unable to inherit the kingdom of God, as Paul writes to the Galatians (Gal 5:19). Those who do such things tell themselves that they are freed from the shackles of a morality that knows nothing of the world, but they are in fact slaves of their irrational behavior. They lack the truth that makes them free to give their lives a higher meaning through the service of others. But the apostle calls out to us: "For freedom Christ has set us free; stand fast therefore, and do not submit again to a yoke of slavery" (Gal 5:1). To live in accordance with God means living rationally (see Rom 12:1–2). What was proclaimed to the Jews as a divine law was written by God on the hearts of the Gentiles, so that they can distinguish good from evil in their consciences (Rom 2:14).

The Christian faith does not alienate us from life, and a fortiori not from the modern culture that is built upon the principles of *humanitas.* But it enables us to resist the tendencies of this culture to self-destruction. In his first encyclical, *Redemptor hominis,* John Paul II explained as follows the connection between the Church's mission and the contemporary challenges:

> Since man is the way for the Church, the way for her daily life and experience, for her mission and toil, the Church of today must be aware in an always new manner of man's "situation." This means that she must be aware of his possibilities, which keep returning to their proper bearings and thus revealing themselves. She must likewise be aware of the threats to man and of all that seems to oppose the endeavor "to make human life ever more

3 John Paul II, *Redemptor hominis*, 14.

> human" and make every element of this life correspond to man's true dignity—in a word, she must be aware of *all that is opposed* to that process.[3]

In the encounter with the God of grace and truth, the human being is given the supreme encouragement to grasp the true freedom that aims at a fellowship of life in love. In the encounter with Jesus Christ, who proclaimed the kingdom of God with "power and Spirit" and brought about this kingdom through his Cross and his Resurrection, God reveals himself as the origin and the goal of every human being: "Only in the mystery of the incarnate Word does the mystery of man take on light" (GS 22). Belief in the transcendent God ("Glory to God in the highest") and responsibility for the immanent world ("Peace on earth") are intimately united in Christ, the God-Man. The hope that the victims of injustice and violence will receive justice in eternal life obligates Christians to serve the poor and to commit themselves to peace and justice in this present world. Love for God with all one's heart and love for one's neighbor as oneself is the heart of the Christian existence. The God of truth guarantees and supports human freedom, which is perfected in love.

The ruthless ideologies of National Socialism and communism, in their hatred of human beings, presented themselves as the goal of history; but they have taught us *e contrario* that the opposite of truth is not the humble search for truth but rather the falsehood with which the one who opposes God seeks "to suppress the truth through injustice" (see Rom 1:18). The search for truth and the love of truth unite people even when their faiths are different. The truth that enlightens our understanding and the truth in us that warms our heart make us peaceful and friendly in our dealings with each other. Even if I do not see the source of the light that shines upon me, because I have the sun at my back, the shadow that lies before me is nevertheless a testimony to the existence of the source of light behind me. A Christian who has recognized God in the light of Christ as the truth knows that he is united to those who would only have to turn around in order to leave the shadow behind them and be able to pray: "God, with you is the fountain of life; in your light do we see light" (Ps 36:9). There is a unity between the witnesses to the revealed truth and those who look for the truth in the traces, images, and parables of the creation; and both of these groups oppose those who hate "the true light that has come into the world" (Jn 1:9). Truth unites, but falsehood separates. The Christian testimony to the truth is humble and welcoming, because the Christian knows that he has received the light of the truth from the infinite reason of God. But the ideologue proudly and fanatically insists on the constellation of his ideas, which he takes only from the small light of the finite reason. The deliberate falsehood and the organized disinformation in the totalitarian ideologies undermine the trust that is necessary in every society.

Falsehood is generated by the hatred that is the driving force of all wars and hostilities; and the antithesis of freedom is coercion, oppression, and hatred. Freedom is never lessened by obedience to the commandments of God, since it is precisely these commandments that make freedom possible. This is the truth that sets people free. It is in my openness to the good that I find the freedom I seek. I experience liberation from my egocentricity when I make the gift of my person to God and to my neighbor in love. In every truth that I recognize, I implicitly recognize God; and in every good deed that I do, I am aiming at the goodness of God, which draws me on. Freedom is possible only because there is the truth that makes known to us the supreme meaning of existence. The Church, which proclaims God's endless goodness and his love of humankind (see Ti 3:4), is thus the advocate of the human being, of his inalienable dignity, and of his rights in the face all the totalitarian ideologies that destroy freedom and truth.

Freedom presupposes the internal and external possibility of living in accord with one's own conscience, of doing the good for its own sake, and of resisting immoral commands or demands. The German experience, first with the ideology of the authoritarian state at the time of the *Kulturkampf* (which saw society as constructed on the basis of the state—rather than the state as constructed by the free initiative of the citizens) and then with two godless dictatorships that were hostile to humankind in Nazi Germany and in communist East Germany, necessarily makes us skeptical about every form of state omnipotence and every institution set up by human beings. The state is *relatively* necessary for the common good, but it must never claim absoluteness in its legislative, executive, and judicial power with regard to the intellectual life and the moral conscience of the citizens. The democratic state is not above the conscience of its citizens, nor above the natural moral law—unlike the absolute prince of earlier times under the doctrine *cuius regio, eius religio.* The difference between a free democracy and an ideological "people's democracy" is that the former is based on the unconditional recognition of human dignity and of human rights, which are under no circumstances subordinate to the will of the majority. Democracy never simply means that "the majority decides" even about morality and the conscience. Democracy means, instead, that the parliamentary majority and minority agree in respecting the inviolability of the dignity and the natural rights and duties of the human being. Positive legislation is relative and never absolute, for that would be the end of democracy under the rule of law. The human being is essentially more than a citizen. The state is for human beings, never vice versa. The state must order the temporal concerns of its citizens and of society and must guarantee that the basic human rights will be observed. It must not let itself be made into the instrument of the claim of an ideology to absolute power. There are grave dangers lurking in this field today. From the other perspective, individual societal groups cannot take possession of the state in order to promote a dominant ideology through the potential offered by education in schools and universities, and by the dissemination of information and the formation of opinion in the media. A mainstreaming directed by the state and by an ideology not only reveals the old authoritarian and totalitarian way of thinking. It also contradicts the human right to accurate information and to the formation of one's own opinion. Those who quite rightly oppose an ideology that is momentarily dominant in the media, the parliaments, and legislation (abortion as a human right, the redefinition of marriage as any kind of sexual partnership, etc.) must not face discrimination and the limitation of their civil freedoms.

Since we are social beings, religious freedom can never be interpreted in an exclusively individual sense. It necessarily has a social component. This is why one of the inalienable human rights is the freedom to join with others in a fellowship with a common confession of their basic intellectual and moral principles, with public worship in common, and with a constitution of their fellowship for which they themselves are responsible. This entails the right of a religious fellowship to regulate its internal matters personally, provided only that the natural moral law is respected; and this is not a concession by the state but has its fundament in human rights themselves. The Church and the fellowships based on a religion or a worldview must not be excluded from participation in public life on equal terms. Our democratic state recognizes them, first of all, as corporations under public law and uses tax money to support their activities for the common good (for example, kindergartens, schools, hospitals, and youth work). The modern democratic state, which is in accord with the intellectual and sociological developments of the present day and has therefore abandoned every form of authoritarian-state paternalism, cannot declare the Church, or Jewish, Islamic, and other established religious communities, to be a state religion. Nor, on the other hand, can it declare atheistic and political associations to be a state ideology and concede to those who think differently merely the status of a tolerated minority. The axiom that "religion is a private matter" leads to a systematic exclusion of Christianity from the public sphere that fundamentally contradicts both individual and the societal human rights. A state without the public presence of the religious confessions of its citizens would not possess a legitimation in secular natural law. It would be perverted into a dictatorship of opinion.

The contemporary structural transformation of Europe challenges us to examine anew the various traditions that have defined the relationship between the state and the Church or the non-Christian religious fellowships. A typical characteristic of ideological narrowness is the denial of historical facts. Europe does not exist as a historical and cultural reality without its roots in the Christian anthropology. Without Christianity, it would be only a geographical concept. The program of the de-Christianization of Europe in the Jacobins of the French Revolution, in Nazi Germany, and in the Soviet Union profoundly shattered the moral foundations of entire societies. A European Union that would put its hope in capital and finance alone, and would systematically marginalize Christianity, would be doomed to perish. Our task, on the basis of the equal participation of all the citizens, is to discover a constructive relationship of the state to the religious fellowships and to the communities based on a worldview. The secularity of the state—that is to say, its justification in natural law (which is in accordance with the Catholic tradition)—needs a positive new definition, for otherwise society will deprive itself of the intellectual, moral, humanitarian, and charitable resources that derive from the religious predisposition of the human being and from the historical religions. The moral principles and the citizens' praxis of solidarity can certainly not be enforced legalistically through state laws and the corresponding sanctions; the human conscience must be formed in moral-philosophical terms ("the categorical imperative") and religiously ("I am the Lord, your God. You must ...") in such a way that it acknowledges the basic moral law, which states that the good is to be done for its own sake, and the evil must be unconditionally avoided.

In the present context, let us look once again briefly at the Pastoral Constitution on The Church in the Modern World. The council explicitly addresses all of humanity, even the atheists, in order to offer a sincere dialogue to all those of good will about the great topics of peace and war, in a situation where today's weapons make possible the destruction of all humankind, and about the immense possibilities of science and technology to make possible for humanity a future in dignity. And no one is permitted to look away when the number of those who hunger, who are deprived of their rights, and who are enslaved increases; when the drama of the refugees penetrates the "European house"; and the globalization of opportunities and of risks has become the greatest challenge for the one world. In today's world, the Church is not a lobby that is active only on behalf of the interests of its own societal group. Everything that is stated in *Gaudium et spes* about the dignity of the human being, about human society, and about the ultimate meaning of human activity "lays the foundation for the relationship between the Church and the world and provides the basis for dialogue between them" (GS 40). The Church offers not only dialogue but also collaboration in "fostering that brotherhood of all men that corresponds" to the lofty and divine vocation of the human being (GS 3). The conciliar fathers then take up the hermeneutic of suspicion against the Church that persists in the heart of the anticlerical rage and seduces the masses down to the present day: "Inspired by no earthly ambition, the Church seeks but a solitary goal: to carry forward the work of Christ under the lead of the befriending Spirit. And Christ entered this world to give witness to the truth, to rescue and not to sit in judgment, to serve and not to be served" (GS 3).

The Declaration *Dignitatis humanae* of the Second Vatican Council is very important for the definition of the relationship between the Church and the non-confessional state with its neutral worldview. The Church knows and proclaims "the principle of religious freedom as befitting the dignity of man and as being in accord with divine revelation" (DH 12). The exercise of religious freedom is bound to the natural moral law and must respect the legitimate public order and legitimate authority (see DH 7). Since violations of human rights are a contradiction of the natural moral law, they can never be justified in religious terms—that is, by appealing to God. For God is the author of the moral law and the judge of our good and evil acts. The only possible foundation of a democratic society under the rule of law is the dignity of the human being, which is bestowed on him by the Creator, not by other persons. This dignity is inherent in his intellectual-ethical nature and constitutes the mystery and the uniqueness of his person.

The freedom of the person is not called into question by the confession of the truth of God in Jesus Christ—namely, the confession that the human person is capable of the truth—for this affirms the supreme vocation of the human being (see GS 10). It is the relativizing of truth that is the greatest threat to freedom. But only the truth can make us free, "because the creation itself will be set free from its bondage to decay and obtain the glorious liberty of the children of God" (Rom 8:21).

IX

The Pope—The Church's Pastor on Its Path to God

"The Roman Pontiff and the bishops are authentic teachers, that is, teachers endowed with the authority of Christ, who preach the faith to the people entrusted to them, the faith to be believed and to be put into practice."[1] The Council of Trent understands the justification of the sinner as the complete remission of original sin and of personal sins, and thus the full union of life with God in love. For "God's love has been poured into our hearts through the Holy Spirit who has been given to us" (Rom 5:5). God dwells in us, and we are his sons and daughters in Christ. "This is why the human being receives in justification itself, forgiveness of sins through Jesus Christ whose member he becomes. At the same time, all this is infused into him: faith, hope, and love. For if hope and love are not joined to faith, faith does not unite a person fully with Christ. Nor does it make one a living member of his body."[2]

1. THROUGH FAITH WE HAVE PEACE WITH GOD (ROM 5:1)

Pope Francis's Encyclical *Lumen fidei*

A PAPAL ENCYCLICAL IS NOT MEANT to be read in haste: it is to be studied with care. But the human being is also a social being, and this is true precisely when he "hears the Word of God in the human mouth of his preachers" (see 1 Thes 2:13). This makes it completely

1 CCC 2034.

2 DH 1530–31.

appropriate to come together in an auditorium for a thorough study of this first encyclical by the new pope. For the "faith without which it is impossible to please God" (Heb 11:6) is an absolutely key concept for the entire Christian existence. Faith comes from hearing with the ears (*fides ex auditu*) and makes it possible to see the glory of God with the eyes and indeed to touch the "Word of life" (1 Jn 1:1) with the hands. Faith communicates salvation and divine life. "For God so loved the world that he gave his only-begotten Son, that whoever believes in him should not perish, but have eternal life" (Jn 3:16). Faith gives us intellectual and moral orientation in the world. Jesus reveals himself as the light of the world: "He who follows me will not walk in darkness, but will have the light of life" (Jn 8:12). Faith, united to baptism in the name of the Father and of the Son and of the Holy Spirit (Mt 28:19), leads us into the fellowship of life with the triune God and makes us members of the body of Christ and stones in the temple of the Holy Spirit (see Eph 4:4). Paul sums up in the following words the entire movement of human existence towards the triune God: "Since we are justified by faith, we have peace with God through our Lord Jesus Christ. Through him we have obtained access to this grace in which we stand, and we rejoice in our hope of sharing the glory of God. [...] And hope does not disappoint us, because God's love has been poured into our hearts through the Holy Spirit who has been given to us" (Rom 5:1–3, 5).

Pope Benedict XVI took the three theological virtues of faith, hope, and love, through which we are comprehensively and dynamically related to the God of love, as the theme of a sequence of three encyclicals. We recall *Deus caritas est* and *Spe salvi,* which met with a very positive response. The work on the completion of this trilogy was already far advanced on February 11, when he declared his abdication, and he handed over to his successor the draft that was fairly fully elaborated. Pope Francis decided to make a final redaction now, in the middle of the Year of Faith and as its high point, so to speak. His first encyclical, *Lumen fidei,* thus appeared on the Solemnity of the Apostles Peter and Paul, the founders and patrons of the Roman church.

It is a beautiful sign of the continuity in the Petrine ministry when, despite all the obvious differences in their life experience, their intellectual formation, and the emphases they make, the Holy Father thanks his predecessor for the work already carried out: "As his brother in Christ I have taken up his fine work and added a few contributions of my own."[3]

There is no point in a literary-critical exercise that would attribute particular sections of the text to one or other of the authors. In its final form, the

3 Francis, Encyclical Letter *Lumen fidei* (June 29, 2013), 7.

encyclical *Lumen fidei* is a coherent document of the magisterium of Pope Francis. Besides this, the substance of which the encyclical speaks is not the intellectual property of any one human author. Christ himself is the "author and perfecter of our faith" (Heb 12:2), which is professed by the Church and is lived in its fellowship.

The encyclical presupposes that the great decisions of the magisterium in the following areas are already known: faith and grace, faith and justification, faith and works, faith and reason, faith and baptism, faith as a personal act (*fides qua creditur*) and as the Church's confession (*fides quae creditur*), faith and the communication of faith in the dogmatic, liturgical, and catechetical tradition of the Church. We recall the rejection of Pelagianism and Semi-Pelagianism, and the debate about the *sola fide* of the Reformation and about the assurance of salvation, with the response in the Decree on Justification by the Council of Trent. We should also mention, precisely on the topic of faith and justification, the 1999 Augsburg Declaration, which has brought about a great ecumenical rapprochement in this old controversial theme. A common testimony to the faith that brings salvation is urgent and necessary today, "that the world may believe that the Father has sent the Son" (Jn 17:21), for "he is truly the Savior of the world" (Jn 4:42), as the non-Jewish Samaritans recognize and profess. We likewise recall the debate with rationalism and traditionalism in the nineteenth century, to which the Catholic view of the organic connection and the distinction between faith and reason was the answer. The Dogmatic Constitution *Dei Filius* of the First Vatican Council about the Catholic faith is important in this context; it was taken up anew thematically by John Paul II in the encyclical *Fides et ratio.* We arrive directly at the high point of the contemporary consciousness of this problem when we see how revelation and faith are understood as a personal encounter and a dialogical fellowship between God and the human being, in the summary account of the concept of faith that is given by the Dogmatic Constitution on Divine Revelation, *Dei Verbum.* In the context of revelation as God's self-communication in his incarnate Word and in the Holy Spirit as grace, truth, and the life of the human being, the Second Vatican Council understands faith as the total response made by the human being to the Word of God that takes hold of us in every dimension of our creaturely existence, sheltering us and embracing us:

> "The obedience of faith" (Rom 16:26; see 1:5; 2 Cor 10:5–6) "is to be given to God who reveals, an obedience by which man commits his whole self freely to God, offering the full submission of intellect and will to God who reveals," and freely assenting to the truth revealed by Him. To make this act of faith, the grace of God and the interior help of the Holy Spirit must

> precede and assist, moving the heart and turning it to God, opening the eyes of the mind and giving "joy and ease to everyone in assenting to the truth and believing it" (DV 5).

In terms of its literary genre, the encyclical most closely resembles a patristic sermon that is wholly nourished by the biblical message but takes up in a concrete and pastoral way the contemporary dogmatic and spiritual questions, as well as the moral and societal issues. It is not a professional theological dissertation about faith and consciously avoids, where possible, academic terminology; it does not enter into theological debates. In the Year of Faith, the pope presents his encyclical to all the faithful in the service of the new evangelization. It is precisely the Christians in countries with an ancient Christian tradition who must once again become fully aware of the unsurpassable and perennial newness of the Gospel of Jesus Christ. The intention is not to ensure that the *Church* still has a future, humanly speaking. What the pope wants to affirm is that without the light of faith in Jesus Christ, there is no shining and happy future for *humanity.* For hope is not a vague unease or a human program of world improvement that is always doomed to failure; our hope is Jesus Christ in person. We remember *Abraham, the father of faith,* who has a large space in the encyclical, in keeping with Paul's words:

> In hope he believed against hope. [...] He grew strong in his faith as he gave glory to God, fully convinced that God was able to do what he had promised. That is why his faith was reckoned to him as righteousness. But the words, "it was reckoned to him," were written not for his sake alone, but for ours also. It will be reckoned to us who believe in him that raised from the dead Jesus our Lord (Rom 4:18, 20–24).

The Year of Faith began with the commemoration of the fiftieth anniversary of the opening of the Second Vatican Council. The echo of *Lumen gentium* in *Lumen fidei* is thus no accident. The Dogmatic Constitution on the Church calls Christ the light of the peoples: "Because this is so, this Sacred synod gathered together in the Holy Spirit eagerly desires, by proclaiming the Gospel to every creature, to bring the light of Christ to all men, a light brightly visible on the countenance of the Church" (LG 1). For the Church is not just any old religious community created and organized by human beings. It is the sacrament of the salvation of the world, established by God and effective in the Holy Spirit, in Jesus Christ, the *Verbum incarnatum* (GS 48; LG 8).

The new pope's preaching typically eschews digressions and is not slowed down by learned footnotes, but it is certainly conscious of the problems and goes deep, in order to address people and, indeed, to rouse them, to encourage them, and to fill them with confidence. One can thus see the four main parts of the encyclical as extensive catecheses, like those held at the World Youth Days.

In his daily sermons and meditations, the Holy Father is capable of putting words to what many people deeply feel; and many who often were skeptical and sometimes even aggressive feel that he is indeed speaking to them. His gestures, which are sometimes interpreted in a merely banal and sensational manner, are the profound expression of his uncompromising love of the poor Christ and of Christ in the poor. One is reminded here of the opening words of the Pastoral Constitution on the Church in the Modern World, in its celebrated introduction:

> The joys and the hopes, the griefs and the anxieties of the men of this age, especially those who are poor or in any way afflicted, these are the joys and hopes, the griefs and anxieties of the followers of Christ. Indeed, nothing genuinely human fails to raise an echo in their hearts. For theirs is a community composed of men. United in Christ, they are led by the Holy Spirit in their journey to the Kingdom of their Father and they have welcomed the news of salvation which is meant for every man. That is why this community realizes that it is truly linked with mankind and its history by the deepest of bonds (GS 1).

But just as Pope Francis is united to the sufferings and cares of people today, so too he radiates the certainty of the faith that Christ, who died for all and rose from the dead, gives everyone light and strength through his Spirit so that each may follow his supreme calling. This is his conviction, and the motive force of his pastoral activity. The Church "holds that in her most benign Lord and Master can be found the key, the focal point and the goal of man, as well as of all human history" (GS 10). This also shows us what we might call Francis's program from the beginning of his pontificate: namely, to let the light of the faith shine out brightly as the path to happiness and salvation.

What is the theme of this encyclical? Let me quote the words of the council, which are identical with the goal of Pope Francis's first encyclical: "Under the light of Christ, the image of the unseen God, the firstborn of every creature, the council [and our Holy Father today] wishes to speak to all men in order to shed light on the mystery of man and to cooperate in finding the solution to the outstanding problems of our time" (GS 10).

The encyclical takes up this theme with the *cantus firmus* that resounds throughout the text: the light of faith is kindled by God's self-revelation in Jesus Christ. "We have beheld his glory, glory as of the only-begotten Son of the Father" (Jn 1:14). Christ is "the true light that enlightens every man" (Jn 1:9). In the light of the Holy Spirit, whose love is poured out into our hearts, we grasp the depths of the reality that lies behind the external phenomenon, because everything came into being through the Word who is God. Reality in nature, history, and society becomes transparent to the transcendent God. The pagan world in which the light of Christ shone out through the Church's proclamation venerated the *Sol invictus,* the "unconquered sun," whose light did indeed win the victory over the darkness every day but shed no light on the gloom of death. But Christ is the true sun whose light never dies; he has overcome the darkness once and for all. When Martha mourns her dead brother Lazarus, Jesus says to her: "Did I not tell you that if you would believe, you would see the glory of God?" (Jn 11:40). Those who have the light of faith know the totality of reality; "they see with a light that illumes their entire journey, for it comes from the risen Christ, the morning star which never sets."[4]

Faith illuminates "*every aspect* of human existence," in living and dying, in joy and suffering, in grief and hope.[5] "Our faith" in the God who is transcendent but has taken upon himself our humanity even unto death on the Cross, "far from divorcing us from reality, [...] enables us to grasp reality's deepest meaning and to see how much God loves this world and is constantly guiding it toward himself."[6]

At the very beginning of the encyclical, the pope takes up the decisive objection to faith, which separates many persons—precisely those whose origin lies in the Christian cultural sphere—both intellectually and emotionally from their roots and brings them into a tragic identity conflict. We can see here that although the encyclical is not written in the style of an academic discourse, it does not give a merely descriptive account of faith. It is absolutely conscious of the problem involved, but it enters sympathetically into the situation of the modern and postmodern human being and takes him or her seriously as a brother and sister in search of the truth that has been lost.

For is not faith a deceptive light, an illusion? This was how the critique of religion in the history of ideas, politics, and the depth psychology of the nineteenth and twentieth centuries sought to unmask Christianity. Or did not the Enlightenment of the eighteenth century declassify the light of faith as a preliminary stage to the mature, free-thinking, and self-determining reason of the modern period? Did it not thereby consign to the past the pre-Enlightenment "dark Middle Ages" (a metaphor for historical Christianity)

4 Francis, *Lumen fidei*, 1.

5 Francis, *Lumen fidei*, 4.

6 Francis, *Lumen fidei*, 18.

as an epoch of clerical paternalism and of the deceit practiced by priests to promote an infantile belief in miracles and fairytales, as the vulgar Enlightenment rhetoric asserted? Has not the autonomous reason borne the torch of progress through technology and science in order to prepare a bright and shining future for humankind? Let us have done with the hope in redemption from on high and after death! Instead, let us trust in our own strength, which creates paradise here on earth! These are the slogans of faith in progress, which still ring in our ears. And it is from this historical period that the feeling of superiority comes to those who believe in progress, a feeling that can escalate into a war against Christianity as the enemy of Enlightenment and autonomy—while on the other side, we see the inferiority complex in believers in God who have been talked into believing that they must always prove that they are in step with the times. (The slogan that is meant to reconcile the Enlightenment and Christianity runs: If you have to be Catholic, then at least be critical of Rome!)

The Church is very far from belittling the successes of the reason in science, technology, medicine, global communication, sociology, and international law, to which believing Christian natural scientists and sociologists have made important contributions. Similarly, the Church refrains from exploiting the gross errors of the ideologies and political programs of self-redemption in the twentieth century in order to compel people to believe. The greatest damage is done to the true faith in the sovereign God when he is given the function of a stopgap in intellectual questions or in the promotion of moral goals, as if faith would begin to function only when the reason could get no further.

We do not believe in God because we need him. We believe in God because he loves us.

The words: "We know and believe the love God has for us" (1 Jn 4:16) proclaim the innermost essence of faith in God the Father and his Son in the Spirit and bear witness to the exact opposition of the derivation of religion (as a relatedness to God) from the fear of death or of the forces of nature, or from the inability to explain these forces and bring them under control. This position argues that the modern natural sciences and technology have relegated belief in the existence and activity of God to the realm of fables and myths.

The creation, redemption, and perfecting of the world and of the human being are the free revelation of his goodness, which neither gains nor loses anything in his care for us but flows from his love in what Saint Thomas calls a "light that cannot ever be drunk to the full."[7] Faith and reason are

7 See Josef Pieper, *Unaustrinkbares Licht: Das negative Element in der Weltsicht des Thomas von Aquin*, 2nd ed. (Munich; Kösel, 1963), 73–79.

intimately linked, because faith and morality will always belong to a person who sees the entire world and the immanence and contingency in which he or she lives through faith in the light of God, to whom the human being has a personal relationship. Faith in God integrates the multiplicity of human thoughts and actions in the unity of the person and brings about a relational and dialogical human identity. And faith both lays the foundations of the unity of the human race through grace and nature and sustains this unity. This is why the pope writes at the beginning of the encyclical, not in the manner of a schoolmaster who levels accusations, but in convincing and attractive words:

> There is an urgent need, then, to see once again that faith is a light, for once the flame of faith dies out, all other lights begin to dim. The light of faith is unique, since it is capable of illuminating *every aspect* of human existence. A light this powerful cannot come from ourselves, but from a more primordial source: in a word, it must come from God. Faith is born of an encounter with the living God, who calls us and reveals his love, a love which precedes us and upon which we can lean for security and for building our lives. Transformed by this love, we gain fresh vision, new eyes to see; we realize that it contains a great promise of fulfillment and that a vision of the future opens up before us. Faith, received from God as a supernatural gift, becomes a light for our way, guiding our journey through time. On the one hand, it is a light coming from the past, the light of the foundational memory of the life of Jesus which revealed his perfectly trustworthy love, a love capable of triumphing over death. Yet since Christ has risen and draws us beyond death, faith is also a light coming from the future and opening before us vast horizons which guide us beyond our isolated selves toward the breadth of communion. We come to see that faith does not dwell in shadow and gloom; it is a light for our darkness.[8]

It is precisely this that the encyclical *Lumen fidei* wishes to recall to our mind: the light that comes from faith, from God's self-revelation in Jesus Christ and in his Spirit, illuminates the depths of reality, and helps us to recognize that it bears, inscribed upon itself, the indelible signs of God's salvific acts. Thanks to the light that comes from God, faith can indeed illuminate the "entire journey," "*every aspect* of human existence."[9] "Far from divorcing us from reality," our faith "enables us to grasp reality's deepest meaning and

8 Francis, *Lumen fidei*, 4.

9 Francis, *Lumen fidei*, 1; 4.

to see how much God loves this world and is constantly guiding it toward himself."[10]

At the origin of everything stands God. Believing in him means acknowledging this fact. This enlarges the understanding and the heart of the human being, opening up to him new horizons, bringing him closer to other people, and opening the gates onto a new way of life that corresponds to the sublimity of his calling. Indeed, we must admit that whenever we fail to live the faith in God because of our thoughtlessness, our inactivity, or our lack of love, we are failing to contribute to the construction of a more humane world. When we act in this way, we bear witness against God and disfigure the face of the Church.

Our great resource lies in the living faith in God, to which his only-begotten Son, Jesus Christ, gives us access through his Spirit. It is on this that the success or failure of every reform depends—and not only in the Church, for here is a gift that the Church cannot hang onto for itself alone. Faith and the life of grace that God makes possible for us are truly a treasury of the good and the true for all human beings, because all are called to live in friendship with God and to experience the horizons of freedom that open up for the one who lets God take him by the hand.

Faith in the God whom Jesus Christ reveals to us is the true rock on which the human being can build his own life and the life of the world. Faith is a gift that can "never be taken for granted," but "needs to be nourished and reinforced" continuously.[11] Thanks to faith, we are able to recognize that "a great love" is offered to us every day, a love that transforms us, indicates the path into the future, and allows the "wings of hope" to grow.[12] Thanks to the faith that endows us with a confidence that sustains us and that nourishes this confidence in us, we can look to the future with realism, without letting our hope be taken away from us, as Pope Francis never tires of repeating. "Thus wonderfully interwoven, faith, hope, and charity are the driving force of the Christian life" of a human being who is open for the gifts of God.[13]

All this is emphasized by the encyclical *Lumen fidei,* which has four parts that we could see as the four panels of one great painting. Each of the four chapters is headed by a scriptural text. These texts construct the unity of the text and show that these are catecheses of the faith.

10 Francis, *Lumen fidei*, 18.

11 Francis, *Lumen fidei*, 6.

12 Francis, *Lumen fidei*, 7.

13 Francis, *Lumen fidei*, 7.

1.

"We have accepted love in faith" (see 1 Jn 4:16). Here, we enter into the history of the faith of Abraham and of Israel down to the fullness of revelation and to salvation through faith in Jesus Christ in the *communio* of the Church.

2.

"If you do not believe, you do not understand" (see Is 7:9). This is about being and remaining in God's truth through faith. Faith leads to the knowledge of God in his truth and love. Faith is hearing the Word, seeing the light of God, and grasping, touching, and embracing the Word of God in its bodily form, in the Word that became flesh and has made its dwelling among us, the Word that remains with us and goes ahead of us as the Good Shepherd. Faith is related to God, whom human reason, which investigates the world and shapes society, seeks in his transcendence and in his immanence. Theology, not in isolation but in union with philosophy and the empirical sciences, serves the Church and the whole of humanity in the search for truth, which has its goal in the knowledge of God in his creation and in his historical self-revelation in grace and truth.

3.

"I hand on to you what I have received" (see 1 Cor 15:3). In accordance with the nature of the fellowship that unites one generation to another, faith is mediated through tradition. The Church is the subject of revelation and of its historical mediation above all in the Word and the sacraments of God. Faith also means entering fully into the Church's fellowship of prayer. One cannot separate participation in the liturgy from living according to the precepts and commandments. The tradition of the one, holy, catholic, and apostolic Church also guarantees the unity and integrity of the faith through which we know God, and through which we receive life and salvation.

4.

"God prepares a city for them" (see Heb 11:26). Faith is not a private matter, a private conviction that does not concern anyone else. Of its very nature, Christian faith is related to the common good. Responsibility for the world and the creative shaping of the world on the basis of the Christian anthropology have their origin in the positive character of existence and are always oriented to the revealing verdict by God: "And God saw everything that he had made, and behold, it was very good" (Gn 1:31). The positive character of the creation, which is the analogy to the essential goodness and truth of

God, categorically excludes every Manichaean dualism and pessimism as a kind of primal heresy. Faith is a light for marriage and the family. Faith makes possible a meaningful life in society and also discloses the principles of our social doctrine, the personal dignity of every human being, solidarity, and the promotion of freedom. Faith also shows us the closeness of Christ to the suffering and the dying and can identify and fight against negative developments in society.

Let Me Take up Some Important Points in Greater Detail

The first part outlines the path from the faith of Abraham, as a man who in the voice of God "recognizes a profound call which was always present at the core of his being," to the faith of the people of Israel, who oscillate between the "temptation of unbelief" and the adoration of the idols that are a work of human hands, and "the grateful remembrance of God's mighty deeds and the progressive fulfillment of his promises."[14] The interesting point here is that the antithesis of the biblical concept of faith is not unbelief as the denial of a supernatural knowledge, but the worship of idols. The idols are absolutized, finite things and values that ensnare people among the varied things they offer them and make them captive in a labyrinth of many paths from which there is no way out. Faith in God, the Creator of the world and the sovereign Lord of the calling, the election, and the covenant, leads the people into freedom, on the path to that freedom into which God himself leads the people as the Lord and Shepherd. From the perspective of "faith in the one God, the almighty Father, the Creator of heaven and of earth," polytheism is only one historical variety of atheism, whereas faith in the biblical sense signifies the dependence of the human being on God (*fides*) and the reliable faithfulness of God (*fides*) vis-à-vis the human being. God's call and election are followed by the fulfillment of his promise in the act whereby he sets the people free. This leads to Israel's profession of faith in the form of a narrative of God's saving deeds, which are recalled in worship in order that, by means of the *memoria*, the children and grandchildren and all future generations may receive a share in God's salvific activity in the past, the present, and the future, thereby becoming heirs to his promise, which is fulfilled again and again.[15] In a similar way, our baptismal confession of faith and our creed do not contain a list of supernaturally communicated, ahistorical truths. We believe *Deum esse, in Deo,* and *Deo,* who has communicated

14 Francis, *Lumen fidei,* 11; 13; 12.

15 Francis, *Lumen fidei,* 12.

himself to us in the Creation, the Incarnation, and the sending of the Spirit in the history of salvation as the way, the truth, and the life.

Finally, the story of Jesus offers the compendium of salvation, in which all the trajectories of Israel's salvation history come together and coalesce: "He becomes the definitive 'Yes' to all the promises, the ultimate basis of our 'Amen' to God (cf. 2 Cor 1:20)."[16]

With Jesus Christ, we can definitively say that we have "known and received in faith the love that God has for us" (1 Jn 4:16), because he "is the complete manifestation of God's reliability."[17] With him, faith reaches its perfection. "Christ's death discloses the utter reliability of God's love above all in the light of his resurrection."[18] This faith invites us to acknowledge that God has not remained in the distant heights of his heaven: he has revealed himself in Jesus Christ, who died and rose again, and who remains present among us.

When we follow Jesus, the entire existence of the human person is transformed thanks to faith. The believer is a new creation, a child of God and a fellow-heir of Christ, the crucified and risen Lord and the Son of God. The "I," the person of the believer, is opened to receive the original love that is bestowed in faith and expands to embrace "an ecclesial existence."[19] By opening us for fellowship with our brothers and sisters, faith wishes not to reduce us to "a mere cog in a great machine" but to help Christians "to come into their own in the highest degree."[20] "For those who have been transformed in this way, a new way of seeing opens up," and faith becomes the true "light" that invites them to let themselves be transformed again and again by God's call.[21]

In the second part of the encyclical, the emphasis lies on the question of truth, which is "central to faith."[22] Faith thus concerns the knowledge of truth too, since faith is an act of knowledge: "Faith without truth does not save. [...] It remains a beautiful story [...], or it is reduced to a lofty sentiment."[23] We live today in a crisis of truth that can easily turn into a dictatorship of one worldview that posits itself as an absolute—namely, into the dictatorship

16 Francis, *Lumen fidei*, 15.

17 Francis, *Lumen fidei*, 15.

18 Francis, *Lumen fidei*, 17.

19 Francis, *Lumen fidei*, 21; 22.

20 Francis, *Lumen fidei*, 22.

21 Francis, *Lumen fidei*, 22.

22 Francis, *Lumen fidei*, 23.

23 Francis, *Lumen fidei*, 24.

of relativism. It seems that objective criteria for an intersubjective, universal communication exist only in technology and the experimental sciences, as well as in the digital world of cyber communication. In that case, the specific truth of the individual subject would consist solely of one's authentic self-perception. Recourse to the truth that is universally applicable, binding, and unifying—the truth that is God and that is revealed to us in Jesus Christ—is suspected of intolerance and of moral constraint ("I'm not letting anyone else tell me what I have to believe").

According to Ludwig Wittgenstein, faith is something like the experience of being in love, in the sense that it can lay claim to validity for my own self, but not to an objective validity. Love, however, is not only an emotion in the sense of being affected by something that is aesthetically attractive. Love is the gift made by the will to the truth or to the moral responsibility for a person, for one's family and children, or the laying-down of the life of the Good Shepherd. Love and truth coincide in God, so that faith in God unites the communication of his truth to the making present of his love. Faith is a freely given response that unites one to the others in the Church who believe. Truth not only affects my feelings, which I cannot share with anyone else. Truth challenges me to assume responsibility. It obligates me vis-à-vis everyone else in the practical love for my neighbor as for myself, and in the horizon of the love for God, the love to which we owe everything—what we are, what we do, and what we shall become.

The question of the truth and the active endeavor in searching for the truth are indispensable. Similarly, we cannot exclude a priori the contributions to the search for truth in the great religious traditions, especially where these concern the fundamental truths of human existence. This is why faith does not shut itself up in a circle of like-minded persons. It unites people in their religious and philosophical search and in the question of the truth that obligates each one immediately in his or her conscience, even when the content of the question of truth is in fact defined differently.

What then is the contribution that faith in Jesus Christ can offer here? Faith opens us up for the love that comes from God and transforms the way we look at things, "because "love itself brings enlightenment."[24] It may indeed seem to the modern human being that the question of love has nothing to do with the question of the truth that he knows and confesses, but one "cannot truthfully recite the words of the creed without being changed," because faith prompts us to a constant conversion and forbids us to settle down into a comfortable sedateness.[25]

24 Francis, *Lumen fidei*, 26.

25 Francis, *Lumen fidei*, 45.

Love is authentic when it is linked to the truth, and the truth entices us with the power of love: "This discovery of love as a source of knowledge, which is part of the primordial experience of every man, finds authoritative expression in the biblical understanding of faith."[26] This is perhaps one of the most important and beautiful aspects of the encyclical.

Since faith is related to knowledge and is linked to truth, Thomas Aquinas can speak of the *oculata fides* ("the faith that has eyes"), of faith as an act that concerns "seeing."[27] Faith concerns hearing, but it is also "a process of gazing" that seeks and recognizes the truth, a process in which "faith and reason each strengthen the other."[28] Saint Augustine discovered long ago that "all things have a certain transparency" and thus "reflect God's goodness."[29] Faith thus helps us to investigate the foundations of reality in their depth.

We can thus understand the level on which the light of faith "can illumine the questions of our own time about truth"—that is to say, the great questions that arise in the human heart in face of the totality of reality, with its beauties, but also its dramas.[30] This is because truth—and here, faith comes into play—is linked to love and comes from love. Truth need not make us afraid, because it does not impose itself with violence but seeks truly to convince us *fortiter ac suaviter,* "powerfully and gently."

This is why the encyclical maintains that "faith broadens the horizons of reason to shed greater light on the world which discloses itself to scientific investigation."[31] This applies both to scientific research and to the searching by every genuinely religious person, because faith reveals to us that the one who begins to seek the truth and the good is already drawing closer to God and is already supported by his help, even without being conscious of this.[32]

I should like to draw attention only to a few important aspects in the third and fourth parts of the encyclical. First of all, let me point out briefly how faith arises. Faith is an event that touches the person in his or her innermost core. The human being is not an isolated and isolating "I" standing over against God; the human being is integrated into a fellowship. This is why "faith is passed on, we might say, by contact, from one person to another, just as one candle is lighted from another."[33]

26 Francis, *Lumen fidei*, 28.

27 Francis, *Lumen fidei*, 30.

28 Francis, *Lumen fidei*, 30; 32.

29 Francis, *Lumen fidei*, 33.

30 Francis, *Lumen fidei*, 34.

31 Francis, *Lumen fidei*, 34.

32 See Francis, *Lumen fidei*, 35.

33 Francis, *Lumen fidei*, 37.

The Church is the place *in which* this movement of the person, which has its origin in lived faith, has its foundation; it is also the place *from which* this movement is impelled forward without ceasing. The Church opens us for God and for the others, so that there arises a new worldview, a special way of looking at the world. The Church, as Romano Guardini so beautifully put it, "is the bearer within history of the plenary gaze of Christ on the world."[34]

The Church is the place in which faith comes into being and in which faith becomes an experience that one can communicate to others and to which one can bear testimony in a comprehensible and trustworthy manner. For "what is communicated in the Church [...] is the new light born of an encounter with the true God."[35] This is a completely different concept of the living tradition as a process that is inseparable from its content—namely, the whole of revelation itself in the life of the Church. What has this rich and profound understanding of the apostolic and ecclesial tradition in common with the reduction of the Church's teaching, in the circles around Marcel Lefebvre, to the opposition to the nineteenth-century liberalism that was hostile to revelation, and to modernism with its subjectivist limitation of the reception of tradition? In Lefebvre's party, the concept of tradition is reduced to the mechanical handing on of supernatural information. It is not elaborated on the basis of the relationship and fellowship with the God who communicates himself as truth and life in the history of his people.

This encounter with the living God enables the Church to bear credible witness to him. The instruments and the efficacious signs of this encounter are "the sacraments, celebrated in the Church's liturgy."[36] This is why the encyclical emphasizes that faith has a sacramental structure.

This makes it easy to understand the movement that is characteristic of faith: it begins with the visible and material in order to open us "to the mystery of the eternal."[37] The believer is taken up with his entire existence into this movement into the truth, which he recognizes and confesses.[38] Accordingly, one "cannot truthfully recite the words of the creed without being changed."[39] Faith impels us to a constant conversion and forbids us from lulling ourselves into a self-satisfied coziness.

34 Romano Guardini, "Vom Wesen katholischer Weltanschauung," in *Unterscheidung des Christlichen: Gesammelte Studien 1923–1963*, ed. Hans Waltmann (Mainz: Matthias-Grunewald-Verlag, 1963), 24, quoted in Francis, *Lumen fidei*, 22.

35 Francis, *Lumen fidei*, 40.

36 Francis, *Lumen fidei*, 40.

37 Francis, *Lumen fidei*, 40.

38 See Francis, *Lumen fidei*, 45.

39 Francis, *Lumen fidei*, 45.

Secondly, I wish to quote from words that we find in the third part of the encyclical. They come from a sermon by Pope Leo the Great: "If faith is not one, it is not faith."[40] We live in a world that is divided and split, despite all the tendencies to globalization. In the many different "worlds," people are indeed linked to each other, but they often lead isolated lives and are all too often in conflict with each other. This is why the unity of the faith is a precious good to which the pope and his brothers in the episcopal ministry bear witness, a good that they nurture and protect. This unity is the harbinger of a unity that ought to be a gift for the whole world.

This is no monolithic unity but a unity in rich and living variety. God himself is one and, at the same time, triune. The testimony to unity belongs to the mission of the Church, which the Second Vatican Council called the "sign and instrument" of the unity that comes from God (LG 1). This unity is destined to embrace the whole of humanity.

This unity is rightly called "catholic," because its foundations are in the truth that it must serve, the truth that is the criterion on which it will be judged. It is capable of "assimilating everything that it meets in the various settings in which it becomes present and in the diverse cultures which it encounters," because this unity is based in the truth.[41] Accordingly, it takes nothing away but rather enriches us with the gifts that come from the generosity of the divine heart and of every single human being.

This unity in truth, to which God the Father leads us, can also help us to discover the true root of brotherhood.[42] Without truth and without God, it is impossible for the dream of universal brotherhood, which stands at the beginning of the modern age, to be realized. The only outcome will be a repetition of the sad experience of Babel. If it lacks "a reference to a common Father as its ultimate foundation," brotherhood "cannot endure."[43] This is shown very clearly by the history of the last two centuries.

Finally, let me take up one aspect of the fourth part of the encyclical. It is true that genuine faith is filled with joy and "enhances our lives."[44] This, by the way, is an idea that links Pope Francis closely to Benedict XVI. At the same time, the light of faith does not allow us to "forget the sufferings of the world."[45] It opens us to embrace "a history of goodness which touches

40 Francis, *Lumen fidei*, 47.

41 Francis, *Lumen fidei*, 48.

42 See Francis, *Lumen fidei*, 53.

43 Francis, *Lumen fidei*, 54.

44 Francis, *Lumen fidei*, 53.

45 Francis, *Lumen fidei*, 57.

46 Francis, *Lumen fidei*, 57.

every story of suffering and opens up a ray of light."[46] Only the light that comes from God, the incarnate God who suffered death and conquered it, can offer a credible hope in face of the manifold suffering that weighs down upon human life.

Let me sum up. The encyclical wishes to confirm in a new way that faith in Jesus Christ is a good for the human being—and for all human beings. Faith:

> ...is a common good. Its light does not simply brighten the interior of the Church, nor does it serve solely to build an eternal city in the hereafter; it helps us build our societies in such a way that they can journey toward a future of hope. [...] The hands of faith are raised up to heaven, even as they go about building in charity a city based on relationships in which the love of God is laid as a foundation.[47]

The Holy Father writes, looking to Mary: "Blessed is she who believed" (see Lk 1:45). Here we see once again that faith is not an intellectual system or a bundle of moral principles and imperatives but rather the relationship between persons and God. The history of faith began with *Abraham, the father of faith,* and it reaches its fulfillment in *Mary, the mother of faith,* who bore us Christ: "a light for revelation to the Gentiles, and for glory to your people Israel" (Lk 2:32). Mary is the mother of faith and the mother of the community of faith, the Church of Jesus Christ. This is why the pope turns to Mary at the close of the encyclical and prays:

> Mother, help our faith! Open our ears to hear God's word and to recognize his voice and call. Awaken in us a desire to follow in his footsteps, to go forth from our land and to receive his promise. Help us to be touched by his love, that we may touch him in faith. Help us to entrust ourselves fully to him and to believe in his love, especially at times of trial, beneath the shadow of the cross, when our faith is called to mature. Sow in our faith the joy of the Risen One. Remind us that those who believe are never alone. Teach us to see all things with the eyes of Jesus, that he may be light for our path. And may this light of faith always increase in us, until the dawn of that undying day which is Christ himself, your Son, our Lord![48]

47 Francis, *Lumen fidei*, 51.

48 Francis, *Lumen fidei*, 60.

2.
IN HOPE OF GOD'S GLORY (ROM 5:3)

OUR FAITH LIVES FROM HOPE in redemption in Jesus Christ. In a special way, Advent displays to our eyes the urgent signs of the Christ who is to come. We wait expectantly for the Savior of the world, who takes a concrete form at Christmas in Jesus Christ, the incarnate Son of God.

This hope in which we live is not a laborious effort to envisage an uncertain future. Rather, it is a certainty, "a trustworthy hope, by virtue of which we can face our present."[49]

God has given us in faith the certainty of his presence and the ability to tackle the future with the strength of the faith that is salvation and hope.

"*SPE SALVI facti sumus*"—"We were saved in hope," Paul tells the Romans and us (Rom 8:24). According to the Christian faith, "redemption," salvation, is not something that simply exists. Redemption exists for us in such a way that hope was given us, a reliable hope that allows us to master our present day. The present day, even when it is arduous, can be lived and accepted if it leads to a goal, and if we can be certain of this goal—if this goal is so great that it justifies the effort of the path. This immediately prompts the question: What then is this hope that permits us to say that we are redeemed through this hope and because this hope exists? What kind of certainty is involved here?

The concept of hope, as "a key word in biblical faith," is interchangeable with faith.[50] Faith always entails the manifestation of hope in the coming of the Lord at the end of time, as well as hope in God's abiding and loving care for us in the course of our lives. This is not only the hope of improved living circumstances but the fundamental hope of redemption. Pope Benedict has given a vivid testimony to the power of the hope that is based on faith to change everything.[51] This is the story of the slave girl Bakhita, who finds in Christ Jesus the Lord who gives her life its true meaning because he redeems and liberates her and gives her hope:

> Yet at this point a question arises: in what does this hope consist which, as hope, is "redemption"? The essence of the answer is given in the phrase from the *Letter to the Ephesians* quoted above: the Ephesians, before their encounter with Christ, were without hope because they were "without God in the world." To come to know God—the true God—means to receive

49 Benedict XVI, Encyclical Letter *Spe salvi* (November 30, 2007), 1.

50 Benedict XVI, *Spe salvi*, 2.

51 Benedict XVI, *Spe salvi*, 3.

hope. We who have always lived with the Christian concept of God, and have grown accustomed to it, have almost ceased to notice that we possess the hope that ensues from a real encounter with this God. The example of a saint of our time can to some degree help us understand what it means to have a real encounter with this God for the first time. I am thinking of the African Josephine Bakhita, canonized by Pope John Paul II. She was born around 1869—she herself did not know the precise date—in Darfur in Sudan. At the age of nine, she was kidnapped by slave-traders, beaten till she bled, and sold five times in the slave-markets of Sudan. Eventually she found herself working as a slave for the mother and the wife of a general, and there she was flogged every day till she bled; as a result of this she bore 144 scars throughout her life. Finally, in 1882, she was bought by an Italian merchant for the Italian consul Callisto Legnani, who returned to Italy as the Mahdists advanced. Here, after the terrifying "masters" who had owned her up to that point, Bakhita came to know a totally different kind of "master"—in Venetian dialect, which she was now learning, she used the name *paron* for the living God, the God of Jesus Christ. Up to that time she had known only masters who despised and maltreated her, or at best considered her a useful slave. Now, however, she heard that there is a *paron* above all masters, the Lord of all lords, and that this Lord is good, goodness in person. She came to know that this Lord even knew her, that he had created her—that he actually loved her. She too was loved, and by none other than the supreme *Paron*, before whom all other masters are themselves no more than lowly servants. She was known and loved and she was awaited. What is more, this master had himself accepted the destiny of being flogged and now he was waiting for her "at the Father's right hand." Now she had "hope"—no longer simply the modest hope of finding masters who would be less cruel, but the great hope: "I am definitively loved and whatever happens to me—I am awaited by this Love. And so my life is good." Through the knowledge of this hope she was "redeemed," no longer a slave, but a free child of God. She understood what Paul meant when he reminded the Ephesians that previously they were without hope and without God in the world—without hope *because* without God. Hence, when she was about to be taken back to Sudan, Bakhita refused; she did not wish to be separated again from her *Paron*. On 9 January 1890, she was baptized and confirmed and received her first Holy Communion from the hands of the Patriarch of Venice. On 8 December 1896, in Verona, she took her vows in the Congregation of the Canossian Sisters and from that time onwards, besides her work in the sacristy and in the porter's lodge at the convent, she made several journeys round Italy to promote the missions: the liberation that she had received through the encounter with the God

> of Jesus Christ, she felt she had to extend, it had to be handed on to others, to the greatest possible number of people. The hope born in her which had "redeemed" her she could not keep to herself; this hope had to reach many, to reach everybody.[52]

What does this hope consist in? Is it a liberation from political rule, a call for boundless autonomy, or the human yearning that is prompted by the chaos of anarchy? Does it involve the rejection of existing societal, political, or ethical obligations? And do not all these forms lead to egotism, to the self-importance of self-appointed "liberators" and "redeemers"?

The message of the faith that bestows hope is different because what Jesus Christ did is something completely different. He himself died on the Cross for us and has brought us into the encounter with the Lord of all lords, the living God, the God of hope and of life. His death is hope. Because this death was stronger than slavery, oppression, and suffering, it has changed the world and given it a new form, the form of love.

A God who died on the Cross for us is not a mere element of the cosmos that is subject to the laws of matter. He himself rules over the stars and the universe. And the inexorable power of matter is no longer the last word. We encounter a person, a love, the will to redeem. And this gives hope even to the isolated, to the dying, and to the despised.

Eternal Life?

At the same time, life itself acquires a new dimension here and now. It is detached from the narrowness of earthly limitations. We are familiar with the dilemma: on the one hand, we do not want to die, but we do not want to go on living forever. But what is "eternal life"?

> On the one hand, we do not want to die; above all, those who love us do not want us to die. Yet on the other hand, neither do we want to continue living indefinitely, nor was the earth created with that in view. So what do we really want? Our paradoxical attitude gives rise to a deeper question: what in fact is "life"? And what does "eternity" really mean? There are moments when it suddenly seems clear to us: yes, this is what true "life" is—this is what it should be like. Besides, what we call "life" in our everyday language is not real "life" at all. Saint Augustine, in the extended letter on prayer which he addressed to Proba, a wealthy Roman widow and mother of three consuls, once wrote this: ultimately we want only one thing—"the

52 Benedict XVI, *Spe salvi*, 3.

> blessed life," the life which is simply life, simply "happiness." In the final analysis, there is nothing else that we ask for in prayer. Our journey has no other goal—it is about this alone.[53]

It is about this alone: that we recognize in God the goal our life, "plunging into the ocean of infinite love, a moment in which time—the before and after—no longer exists."[54] It is the return to God, who welcomes us with joy, as the evangelist John describes it: "I will see you again and your hearts will rejoice, and no one will take your joy from you" (Jn 16:22).

The theme of the papal visit to Bavaria in 2006 was: "The one who believes is never alone." This expresses the perception of redemption, of true life, in community. We are not isolated individuals, and redemption does not mean emphasizing the precedence of one person over another.

Salvation in Christ concerns everyone. He makes the offer of salvation and proclaims his message through the Church. And the Church is the worldwide community of believers. Its visible manifestation already leads people to unity.

The Church is an instrument in the hands of Christ and points to the "blessed" life that transcends the present world. And it is the image of the unity that is perfected by God in eternity.

Modern Forms of Redemption

When "God" is dragged down by the human being into the purely inner-worldly sphere—that is, when he is reduced to a useful function and his existence is denied—a perceptible emptiness spreads in the human being himself. The philosopher Kant was willing to concede validity to Christianity only as an ethical postulate, and all that he left of God was the idea of the totality of being. He held that only the moral foundations can be justified in inner-worldly terms and can be made the criterion of a successful life in common. A catalogue, a rulebook, of ethical-moral laws would bring about the kingdom of God on earth, provided that everyone observed the categorical imperative ("Act only according to that maxim whereby you can, at the same time, will that it should become a universal law").

God himself, in the sense of the supernatural self-revelation and as an external lawgiver, is not necessary here. He prevents the enlightened human being from coming to himself and keeps him prisoner in his own immaturity.

53 Benedict XVI, *Spe salvi*, 11.

54 Benedict XVI, *Spe salvi*, 12.

Every hope in salvation and redemption that genuinely leads the human being to life gives way here to a construction of ethical autonomy and of the establishing of a society that continuously perfects itself.

The political "theories of redemption" in Engels and Marx are even clearer. It is in industrial progress that the human being, the worker, comes to be what he is meant to be. The "kingdom of God" is established within the world. In the exact process of historical necessity, the worker becomes the ideal of a society that is oriented to economic processes. Property is transferred to the state, the ruling class is expropriated, political power is overthrown—the revolution has brought redemption and liberation. But at what price? The reduction of the human being to a segment in economic process is inhuman, for, according to this system, if he is to become a human being, he must submit to the mechanisms of production.

But the true kingdom of God is a gift. It is always more than we deserve. Human ideologies were and are oriented to personal advantage, even when they promise freedom, self-determination, and success. But one who is "God's fellow worker" attempts to open up for God the path into the world. Life becomes hopeless if the goal is only what is attainable. Human kingdoms have forgotten who the human being is—namely, a creature of God who has been created in view of perfection. It is not the human being but God alone who fulfills this hope. The newly gained freedom, which strode ahead into the future without any rules, brought ruin, servitude, oppression, and the unchecked domination of the party. What then was wrong in the politically motivated visions of a Marx, which seem so harmless when expressed in a literary form?

> He forgot that man always remains man. He forgot man and he forgot man's freedom. He forgot that freedom always remains freedom for evil. He thought that once the economy had been put right, everything would automatically be put right. His real error is materialism: man, in fact, is not merely the product of economic conditions, and it is not possible to redeem him purely from the outside by creating a favorable economic environment.[55]

We know many forms of hope. Every day is filled with them, and every situation in life knows a different hope. When one is young, one is marked by the hope for fulfillment in work, for love, and for a family. But one soon realizes that this can be experienced in its true significance only if hope reaches

55 Benedict XVI, *Spe salvi*, 21.

out towards something that is higher than what is finite and that is exempt from temporal limitations—something that transcends the human being.

It is in this reference to a personal God that family, work, education, and active involvement in Church and in society become means to change the world.

The little hopes of daily life that keep us going along the path need the great hope that transcends everything. And this hope can only be God himself, who encompasses the totality of things, who can bestow gifts on us, who loves us and redeems us and thereby gives us hope of the true life.

Prayer as a School of Hope

One primary place where we learn to hope is prayer. If there is no longer anyone who listens to me, if there is no longer anyone to whom I can speak—in this forsakenness, I always have God. The person who prays is never alone.

But praying does not mean seeking one's own advantage. It does not take us out of history, and it does not isolate us from others. Praying aright is a process of inner purification that makes us capable of a relationship with God and, precisely thereby, capable of a relationship with other people.

Praying aright is a personal encounter of my "I" with the living God, which flows into the communal prayer of the Church, into the Lord's Prayer, the Hail Mary, and the prayers of the liturgy.

This is how we can truly speak with God, and this is how God speaks with us. This encounter generates the purification that permits us to be persons of hope—hope that keeps the world open for God.

Action and Suffering as a School of Hope

"All serious and upright human conduct is hope in action."[56] We strive to achieve the fulfillment of our goals and our hopes, and we make our contribution to making the world a little more human, so that, in this way, doors can be opened onto a future full of hope.

If we no longer hope, or concentrate on purely worldly forces, we soon have no hope. It is only the great trust that despite so many failures my life is sheltered in the hand of God, who gives it meaning, the courage to act, and the strength to continue on my way, that teaches us the hope in which we are saved.

56 Benedict XVI, *Spe salvi*, 35.

But suffering too belongs to our life and is a place where we learn hope. Unjust suffering, one's own finitude, and the torments that many people are forced to endure: all these are transformed into joy, because God sets us free and changes fear and grief into serenity and joy. He is a God of consolation, the one who is literally "with" (*cum*) the one who is "alone" (*solus*). With this hope, we are led out of the suffering that can take so many different forms.

The Judgment—Training in Hope

The third place where we learn hope, according to Benedict XVI, is the Judgment. The middle section of the Nicene Creed, which deals with the mystery of the eternal birth from the Father and the temporal birth from the Virgin Mary, via the Cross and the Resurrection, to his return, closes with the words: "He will come again in glory to judge the living and the dead." The look ahead to the Judgment has always served Christianity as the criterion of the present life, as a challenge to the conscience, and as a sign of hope in the justice of God. It is not a scenario of fear but "an image that evokes responsibility."[57]

This look ahead gives Christianity its power in the present day as well as trust in God's justice. Righteousness exists, redress exists, justice exists, and the flesh will be raised to life again. This is why the belief in the Last Judgment is first and foremost hope in the God who turns everything to the good.

Our hope and redemption is not just any "god" who is hidden from our eyes but rather the God of Jesus Christ, who has bestowed his face on us, who has brought us peace and salvation at Christmas.

We take our place before Christ alongside Mary. She is the star of hope, because she opened the door for God—the door to her own heart and to the entire world. She said "yes" to hope, to the hope in view of which we are saved:

> So we cry to her: Holy Mary, you belonged to the humble and great souls of Israel who, like Simeon, were "looking for the consolation of Israel" (Lk 2:25) and hoping, like Anna, "for the redemption of Jerusalem" (Lk 2:38). Your life was thoroughly imbued with the sacred scriptures of Israel which spoke of hope, of the promise made to Abraham and his descendants (see Lk 1:55). In this way we can appreciate the holy fear that overcame you when the angel of the Lord appeared to you and told you that you would give birth to the One who was the hope of Israel, the One awaited by the world. Through you, through your "yes," the hope of the ages became real-

57 Benedict XVI, *Spe salvi*, 44.

ity, entering this world and its history. You bowed low before the greatness of this task and gave your consent: "Behold, I am the handmaid of the Lord; let it be to me according to your word" (Lk 1:38). When you hastened with holy joy across the mountains of Judea to see your cousin Elizabeth, you became the image of the Church to come, which carries the hope of the world in her womb across the mountains of history. But alongside the joy which, with your Magnificat, you proclaimed in word and song for all the centuries to hear, you also knew the dark sayings of the prophets about the suffering of the servant of God in this world. Shining over his birth in the stable at Bethlehem, there were angels in splendor who brought the good news to the shepherds, but at the same time the lowliness of God in this world was all too palpable. The old man Simeon spoke to you of the sword which would pierce your soul (see Lk 2:35), of the sign of contradiction that your Son would be in this world. Then, when Jesus began his public ministry, you had to step aside, so that a new family could grow, the family which it was his mission to establish and which would be made up of those who heard his word and kept it (see Lk 11:27f.).[58]

3.
THE LOVE OF GOD IS POURED OUT INTO OUR HEARTS (ROM 5:5)

THE HISTORY OF THE TWENTIETH CENTURY was written by demagogues and despots who wanted to impose their will ruthlessly on the world at the cost of the happiness of millions of other people. Stalin, Hitler, Pol Pot, and Mao Zedong saw their own ideas as the salvation of the world. The future of the human race was to be shaped in their image and likeness. Still today, we experience how the will to dominate and worldwide terrorism, sometimes even in the name of God, declare hatred and violence to be the instruments that will bring about a better future world. And all this was only the beginning of processes that led millions of people in Germany, Russia, and the whole of Europe and Asia into the abyss of hell on earth.

In contrast to this, Christianity is the religion of the Spirit and of love. The love that God bestows on us in an overflowing measure, the love to which our answer is the gift of self to God and to our fellow human beings, is the fulfillment of the existence of the human being. This is the supernatural fulfillment of the human being who is created with an orientation to God.

58 Benedict XVI, *Spe salvi*, 50.

The essence of Christianity consists not in the perfection of natural morality and of the knowledge of created things, nor in the striving for happiness in the world where one lives, but in being raised up by God's grace, in being the child of God, in the indwelling of the three divine persons in the soul, and ultimately in eternal life in fellowship with God. This is how the Council of Trent describes the essence of the justification of the sinner:

> The effective cause of justification is the merciful God [...] and the formal cause is the righteousness of God—not the righteousness through which he is righteous, but that whereby he makes us righteous (that is to say, through the mercy that the Son of God merited for us in his suffering on the cross). This righteousness is bestowed on us by him, and we are renewed within our spirit. We are not only counted as righteous: we are in truth called righteous and are so, by receiving within ourselves righteousness—each one receiving the righteousness that is his own—according to the measure that the Holy Spirit distributes to the individuals as he wills, and according to the preparation and collaboration of each one.[59]

Our theological and spiritual task, precisely in 2016, the Holy Year of Mercy, is not the speculative task of identifying the qualities of God's mercy and righteousness in the context of a philosophical doctrine of God, but rather the task of understanding them in their salvation-historical and soteriological sense as God's self-communication in grace and truth. The imitation of Christ, our being conformed to his death and his Resurrection, means that we make our own the divine life that is bestowed on us. The infused theological virtues of faith, hope, and love have a power here to shape our entire life. The faith that justifies us is far more than a mere trust in the divine mercy. It is a new existence and a life with Jesus Christ, since grace would remain purely external if it was not also a favorable disposition of God towards us. The grace of God is given to us so that we may make it internally our own. It transforms us into a new life and makes possible and promotes a life in accordance with the precepts of God. Grace justifies us because we have, in reality, been transformed by God from the status of a sinner into the status of one who is justified. In the eternal Son of the Father, we are sons and daughters of God through the grace of Christ.[60] Or, as the encyclical *Deus caritas est* puts it, "Since God has first loved us, love is now

59 Council of Trent, "Decree on Justification," ch. 7, DH 1529.

60 Council of Trent, "Decree on Justification," can. 11; 12, DH 1561; 1562.

61 Benedict XVI, *Deus caritas est*, 1.

no longer a mere 'command'; it is the response to the gift of love with which God draws near to us."[61]

The love of God and the love of neighbor are the very core of the Christian faith in the creative, redemptive, and perfecting power of God the Father, the Son, and the Holy Spirit.

Love and hate—it is between these two alternatives that the fate of the world and of every single human being will be played out.

This was the theme of the first encyclical of Pope Benedict XVI. The message of the mercy of God, which embraces everyone, and of his unconditional readiness to forgive, which Pope Francis has made the great theme of his own pontificate, follows directly from the encyclical *Deus caritas est.*

The Unity of Love in Creation and Salvation History

Love can be misunderstood as nothing more than a moral appeal, a summons to do good that has no practical consequences, while the real world goes untroubled on its way of hatred and egotism, of self-seeking, a way that is oriented to selfishness and ruthless self-realization. But one can also ask why the twentieth century produced not only monsters but also people like Mahatma Gandhi, Dietrich Bonhoeffer, Frère Roger Schutz, Maximilian Kolbe, or saints like Mother Teresa and Pope John Paul II.

Christians are persons who have believed in love. The Christian existence is realized in the encounter with the person of Jesus of Nazareth, in whom all of God's promises have become real and effective. In him, love of God and love of neighbor are intimately united, as was already indicated in the history of the revelation and of the faith of the chosen people of Israel.

This is why the confession of God in the testimony that "God is love, and he who abides in love abides in God, and God abides in him" (1 Jn 4:16) is the only safe path into the bright future, both in the temporal dimension of history and in the perfecting of the human being in the eternal love of God. In the first part of his encyclical, Pope Benedict elaborates the unity of love in creation and salvation history; in the second part, he speaks in practical terms about *caritas,* the action in love on the part of the Church as a fellowship of love. The interpretation of what love is has decisive consequences for our knowledge of God and for the image we have of the human being.

We speak of love in all successful human relationships that have something to do with meaning and fulfillment. We speak of love between siblings, between parents and children, and among friends; but there is also the love of one's work, of art, music, and science.

But the highest perspective in which we speak of love, in every culture and especially in the sphere of the biblical revelation, is the spiritual and bodily fellowship of husband and wife in marriage. Because of the inner unity of the human being in spirit and matter, in soul and body, one cannot separate the *erôs* of bodily desire, the *philia* of the soul, and the *agapê* of the heart, the love that receives and that makes the gift of itself, the love that lives from grace and bestows itself on others. It is important that all the egotistic emotions that ultimately make the human being the slave of his own ego or of the commercialized pleasure industry should be purified. The goal is the integration of body and soul and openness to one's neighbor in the gift of self. In the Creator's plan, the human being is constituted in such a way that he can succeed only by making the gift of himself to his beloved fellow human being and by being integrated with the other person into a fellowship of love.

This is also the answer to the objection by the philosopher Friedrich Nietzsche to Christianity (which he doubtless interpreted in the sense of a gnostic dualism, not in terms of the Incarnation), that it had given eros poison to drink. Eros did not die as a result, but people had been given a bad conscience, and their biological and natural instincts had been declared to be vices. But one cannot contrapose *logos* and *bios* as two completely separate spheres.

A hostility to the body that sees the human being as a pure spirit beyond the biological conditions of his existence *and* a consumerism that makes the body an idol and wishes to shake off spirit and ethos as a superstructure that is alien to the real world *both* destroy love. True love desires eternity: "only you, and forever." This is why monogamous marriage is in accordance with the faith in the one God that became the kernel of the identity of God's people Israel.

We see thus that the newness of the biblical faith in Israel and in the Church lies in the indissoluble union of the image of God and the image of the human being. What then is this completely new dimension of the biblical faith in God?

Let us leave aside the often-strange approaches to the understanding of the divine in the polytheistic religions and look at the summit of Greek philosophy: how did Aristotle understand the divine? He knows only one god, whom human thinking can reach. All that exists loves god and aspires to him, but he himself does not love. He needs love.

Judaism and Christianity likewise acknowledge God as the highest being. But the wholly new element is that God, the Creator of the world and the one who has chosen Israel as his people, is a loving and forgiving God. And indeed, eros can be discerned in his love of his people. He is a jealous God. He is full of wrath at the obstinacy, the indifference, and the withdrawal of love with which the Israelites (and we ourselves today) seek to punish him. But his passionate love even to this stubborn and sinful people is greater. Just as a bridegroom loves his bride and is consumed by longing for her and even responds to her infidelity with a still greater love, so God loves his bride Israel.

In the New Testament, we do not simply find new ideas. The new element consists in the person of Christ, the incarnate reason and love of God. In his passionate love of human beings, he goes unto the Cross. When we look at his injured body and his pierced heart, we sense what it means to say that God is love and that his mercy is inexhaustible. The love of God in Christ is realistic and is present in the celebration of the Eucharist, where we do not receive in a merely static manner Christ's self-giving love. Rather, we are caught up into this love. Just as Jesus lived completely for us, so, too, we ourselves can be Christians only by opening ourselves and giving ourselves to other people, with him.

This mystical union with Jesus in self-sacrifice and in receiving Communion, as a fellowship of life with him and with the members of his body, our brothers and sisters, "is social in character," as Pope Benedict says.[62]

Unity in Christ

It would be completely wrong to split up the Christian existence into three different complexes—namely, the confession of the faith, morality and ethics, and, finally, worship and liturgy. In Christ, the love of God and of neighbor, orthodoxy and orthopraxis are two sides of the same coin. In our own reflections and in dialogue with others, however, we are constantly confronted by two objections: Is it possible to love God, when we do not see him? And can one command love? "You are to love God and your neighbor!" It is indeed true that God is not visible to our bodily eyes: "No one has ever seen God; the only-begotten Son, who is in the bosom of the Father, he has made him known" (Jn 1:18).

When Philip asks: "Lord, show us the Father," Jesus replies: "He who has seen me has seen the Father" (Jn 14:8–9). And indeed, we have seen the Word of life with our own eyes, we have heard it with our own ears, and we have touched it with our own hands. And through Christ, we have fellowship with the Father (1 Jn 1:1–3). The disciples saw the love of God with their own eyes when Jesus healed the sick, reintegrated into the fellowship those who had been expelled, gave back her dead son alive to a grieving mother, preached the good news to the poor, and consoled the mourners. And he remains with us, fulfilling the request of the Emmaus disciples, through his Word and the

62 Benedict XVI, *Deus caritas est*, 14.

sacraments, the Eucharist, the prayer that he hears, and through the love that we experience and that we can give to others.

If love is more than a feeling and means allowing oneself to be drawn into the history of God's love with human beings, we also learn to see with the eyes of God those whom we dislike, those who are annoying and boring, and even our enemy. It then becomes possible to fulfill the commandment of love. We triumph over our inability to love. The one who is justified by faith lives in hope and is filled with the love that is poured out into his heart in the Holy Spirit (see Rom 5:5). We are only handing on what we ourselves have received. Love grows through love. Love can never remain merely a religious obligation. Love makes us sensitive to God and to our neighbor.

"If I give away all I have, and if I deliver my body to be burned, but have not love, I gain nothing" (1 Cor 13:3).

Caritas and *diakonia*: The Church is a Fellowship in the Love of God

God, who opens up his Trinitarian life to embrace us human beings, is love; out of love, God creates the world and calls us as his beloved sons and daughters. In the Incarnation, the Son becomes one of us. He shows that love is more than a nonbinding feeling: love is the active gift of self. The Spirit of the Father and the Son is poured out into the hearts of all human beings, of the entire Church, and of ourselves personally, so that, freed of all arrogance, we can perform the slave's task of washing other people's feet, like Jesus himself (see Jn 13). Because the Holy Spirit lives in the heart of the Church, everything it does is the expression and the communication of God's love in the world. And this is why *leitourgia, martyria,* and *diakonia* are inseparable.

Diakona, as the *caritas Christi,* is an expression of the nature of the Church. We read in the Acts of the Apostles: "All who believed were together and had all things in common; and they sold their possessions and goods and distributed them to all, as any had need" (Acts 2:44–45).

As the Church grew in size, it became necessary to organize *caritas* on the levels of the parish community, the local church, the diocese, and today, a fortiori, on the national and international levels. Just as revelation is universal, so too love is universal. *Caritas* is an essential expression of the Catholic dimension both of salvation and of the Church itself.

There are many examples from the age of the church fathers that show that the pagans regarded the care of the poor and distressed by Christians and by the Church as a special characteristic of Christians. When he was six years old, Emperor Julian the Apostate experienced the murder of his father and his relatives by members of the imperial family who claimed to be Christians. This made him a fervent hater of Christianity. When he sought to establish his Neopaganism, he set up pagan charitable organizations to counter the Church—precisely because Christianity had become so popular through its praxis of love of neighbor.

This means that organized *caritas* is not only an activity of humanitarian benevolence that could equally well be entrusted to the state or to other organizations. It belongs to the essence of the Church and is an inalienable expression of what the Church is.[63] The Church is God's family in a world in which everyone in need is my brother and sister, in whom Christ himself comes to meet me.

Preserving the Humane and Overcoming the Inhumane with Christ

Pope Benedict also speaks of the great societal upheavals in nineteenth- and twentieth-century Europe that were launched by the industrial and scientific revolutions. Belief in progress had developed in the aftermath of the eighteenth-century Enlightenment, and this made its greatest historical impact on the history of ideas in liberal capitalism and in socialist Marxism.

Capitalism is interested in the profit of those who are efficient at the cost of the great majority. It regards the Christian social doctrine, which is built upon solidarity and social justice, as the fruit of an unworldly ethic that is outcompeted by the harsh laws of the market. Marxism holds that the antithesis between capital and work can be overcome through the forcible establishing of a classless society. Christian charitable activity is denounced as a stabilization of the unjust social order and as an easing of the consciences of the powerful.

Despite their strong political differences, both systems have one thing in common: namely, their inhumanity. The redemption from all the ills of mankind is to be achieved through the violent suppression or destruction of the other social class, or in an educational dictatorship that employs political means and the media to attain the intellectual conformity of all the citizens in the final classless or unthinking state of a self-redemption with an inner-worldly goal.

Christian social doctrine is not oriented to counterproductive utopias. It presupposes that justice and solidarity in society can be established, at least approximately, by means of rational action on the basis of the legal order. The

63 Benedict XVI, *Deus caritas est*, 25.

Church, as the sacrament of salvation, has no directly political task. It cannot take the place of the state, which has the duty of organizing a just social order. The state must steer the political confrontations between the groups in society, while involving all the citizens. "Justice is both the aim and the intrinsic criterion of all politics."[64] The state is incapable of letting people experience love in the love of God and of neighbor, and of giving them insight into the absolute dignity of the human being who is made in the image and likeness of God and whose vocation is to become God's child—but Christians as individuals and the Church as a fellowship are called to do this.

The laity have the important task of collaborating in their work and in politics in the construction of just structures. Since justice and solidarity can be identified by the human reason that we all share, collaboration with people who have other religious positions, or a purely humanist worldview, is both possible and necessary. This also entails a positive cooperation of the charitable organizations of the Church with organizations of the state and NGOs.

No matter how good the social order may be, it will never be able to remove all human suffering from the world. This is where the charitable activity of every Christian and the organized aid relief of the ecclesial institutions have their place. Their concrete charitable activity makes it possible for people to experience God's love for human beings in their intellectual-religious, mental, and bodily distress.

Those who are active in the Christian name should help others to experience that no matter how great earthly fragility and transience may be, the dignity of the human person can never be lost, since it has its origin and its goal in the love of God.

Love of Neighbor

We need to make the specific profile of the Church's charitable activity clearer. In response to its denunciation by Marxism, we must emphasize that the charitable motivation is free of any ideology and has no ulterior motive. For why do we give aid, like the Good Samaritan, to the man who had fallen into the hands of robbers? Our immediate reaction is surely not to reflect on an improved surveillance by the police! As human beings, we have a compassion that springs from our spiritual nature created by God, and it is this that moves us concretely, here and now, to help this specific person. As Christians, we say: "The love of Christ urges us on" (2 Cor 5:14).

64 Benedict XVI, *Deus caritas est*, 28.

We have no hidden motives when we help our neighbor. We do so simply because he is our neighbor. We do not instrumentalize the practical love of neighbor and turn it into a means of proselytism. The experienced Christian knows when he should speak about God and when he should be silent about God. The wordless example is sometimes the best testimony to the love of God, which can also lead to faith in God and to the experience of the love of Christ in the fellowship of his Church.

The best defense of God and of the human being consists precisely in love.[65] The Church as a whole is the subject of the charitable action, just as it also remains the subject of the confession of the faith and of the celebration of the sacraments.

One who carries out the Church's service of love professionally must take care to avoid two contrasting risks. There is the temptation to succumb to ideologies that lead one astray by pretending to solve all problems if the human being takes into his own hands what God's governance of the world has not resolved up to now. But there is also the danger of resignation, because we always have poor and suffering persons among us. One can have the impression that all the donations and practical endeavors are being poured into a bottomless vat. All that we do for our neighbor requires prayer—for prayer protects us against both blind activism and a fanatical attempt to improve the world. Otherwise, we may succumb to an arrogant totalitarian stance that can even engage in terrorism in the name of God, or else we may withdraw sulking into the snail shell of our own little happiness. "An authentically religious attitude prevents man from presuming to judge God, accusing him of allowing poverty and failing to have compassion for his creatures. When people claim to build a case against God in defense of man, on whom can they depend when human activity proves powerless?"[66]

In the powerless of his Cross, Jesus cried out his distress in death and his abandonment in prayer to God. His voice was heard by the Father, and he was justified in the Resurrection. With him, we, too, die into the hope that eternal life in the love of the triune God gives us.

In this hour of history, when humanity once again stands at a parting of the ways, we, too, must decide between love and hate, between life and death. We are convinced that the deepest reasons for secularism, or for the inner distance that many people take vis-à-vis the Christian tradition, are not intellectual difficulties about this or that doctrine of the Church's faith but rather a lack of trust in the power of God's love to transform the world and give hope.

65 Benedict XVI, *Deus caritas est*, 31c.

66 Benedict XVI, *Deus caritas est*, 37.

Pope Benedict XVI sums up as follows:

> Love is the light—and in the end, the only light—that can always illuminate a world grown dim and give us the courage needed to keep living and working. Love is possible, and we are able to practice it because we are created in the image of God. To experience love and in this way to cause the light of God to enter into the world—this is the invitation I would like to extend with the present Encyclical."[67]

"Whoever confesses that Jesus is the Son of God, God abides in him, and he in God. So we know and believe the love God has for us. God is love, and he who abides in love abides in God, and God abides in him" (1 Jn 4:15–16).

Christianity will grow in strength among us, and faith will once again be experienced as a gift, if we grasp that God is love.

This is also the great concern of Pope Francis, who never wearies of proclaiming the message of the love and goodness of Jesus Christ and the justice and mercy of God to a world that has little hope and is torn apart by fanaticism.

He thereby fulfills the charge that was given to him in Saint Peter by Jesus at the Last Supper: "Strengthen your brethren!" This commission can be carried out only in the power of Jesus's promise: "I have prayed for you, that your faith may not fail" (Lk 22:32).

This is the mission of the pope of Rome who is the pastor of the universal Church.

67 Benedict XVI, *Deus caritas est*, 39.

X

The Mission of the Pope in God's Universal Salvific Will

1. WITNESS TO THE GOSPEL OF JESUS CHRIST, THE SON OF GOD

THE HIGHEST RESPONSIBILITY with which God entrusts a human being on earth is the mission of the bishop of Rome. Like Simon Peter at the beginning of the Church, the pope today is to "strengthen the brethren" (Lk 22:32) in faith in "the Gospel of Jesus Christ, the Son of God" (Mk 1:1). The successors of Saint Peter have been carrying out their salvation-historical mission from Rome for the past two thousand years. With Peter, the entire Church confesses, until he returns at the end of the world:

Tu es Christus, filius Dei vivi
You are the Christ, the Son of the living God

"Filled with the Holy Spirit" (Acts 4:8), Peter declared before the powerful men of the world, the Sanhedrin, that Jesus "is the stone which was rejected by you builders, but which has become the cornerstone. And there is salvation in no one else, for there is no other name under heaven given among men by which we may be saved" (Acts 4:11–12).

To be Peter's successor thus means bearing witness before all human beings to Jesus as the divine bringer of salvation and presenting them with the Church's confession of faith in the authority of Christ. The teaching of the Church that the pope champions is not the outcome of an academic reflection but is first of all testimony to a person in whom the entire truth of God for the world is revealed and who gives everyone support and hope. Every mortal human being owes his life to God—his Creator, his origin, and his goal.

There is only one rescue from the wretchedness of our existence—namely, the inexhaustible love of God for us in Jesus Christ. "For God so loved the world that he gave his only Son, that whoever believes in him should not perish but have eternal life" (Jn 3:16). By confessing on behalf of the assembly of all the believers that Jesus Christ is the Lord of the world and the Head of the Church, Peter also serves, in his successors, their unity in faith and their fellowship in the love of God. This is why the risen Jesus appointed him their universal shepherd. The pope fulfills the task given by Christ, not in his own authority, but in the authority bestowed on him by the Lord of the Church. According to Saint Augustine, the apostle Peter is the personification, as it were the personal principle, of the universality and the unity of the Church. In the person of the pope, Jesus has charged the entire Church to proclaim the Gospel to everyone, to forgive sins, and to open the door to eternal life with the keys of the kingdom of heaven that have been handed over to him.[1]

The Church does not spread human opinions about God, the human being, and the world. The ground and the purpose of its existence is to proclaim the "Gospel of God" and the "good news about Jesus Christ, our Lord" (Rom 1:1, 4). It is in Christ that the entire happiness and salvation of the whole of humanity and of each individual lie. The Church does not presume to offer theories that explain the world nor programs of self-redemption. Instead, it keeps to the tradition of the apostles, "who from the beginning were eyewitnesses and ministers of the word" (Lk 1:2). This is why the pope and the Church's bishops guarantee that what we believe in is the Word of God, not mere human inference. Saint Paul formulated this paradigmatically: "My speech and my message were not in plausible words of wisdom, but in demonstration of the Spirit and of power, that your faith might not rest in the wisdom of men but in the power of God" (1 Cor 2:4–5).

"Peter, apostle of Jesus Christ" (1 Pt 1:1) remains always, in the bishop of Rome, the most important "witness of the sufferings of Christ and of the glory that is to be revealed" (see 1 Pt 5:1). Peter (Cephas) and the apostles as witnesses are essential elements in the earliest kerygma, which Paul received from the Church in Jerusalem: "I delivered to you [...] that Christ died for our sins in accordance with the scriptures, that he was buried, that he was raised on the third day in accordance with the scriptures, and that he appeared to *Cephas*, then to the Twelve" (1 Cor 15:3–5; italics added).

1 Augustine, *Serm.* 295.

On this rock the Lord built his Church, which defies the storms of the ages and stands firm against all the powers of evil and death. As Peter's successor, the pope confesses with the entire Church that the mystery of the human being is illuminated only in the light of Christ, and that a humane solution to the great challenges facing humanity can be found only with Christ. We need a new humanism in the spirit of Jesus of Nazareth. For Christians believe that "Christ, who died and was raised up for all, can through His Spirit offer man the light and the strength to measure up to his supreme destiny. [...] She likewise holds that in her most benign Lord and Master can be found the key, the focal point, and the goal of man, as well as of all human history" (GS 10).

The Petrine ministry has its foundations in the commission given by Jesus, and it is exercised in the power of his Spirit. The unshakable testimony to Jesus, the bringer of God's salvation, is the mission of the papacy in Rome in the history of the world. And this papacy was founded by Christ.

2.
THE VOICE OF A NEW CALLER IN THE WILDERNESS

As the successor of Saint Peter, the bishop of Rome reminds people in every time and place that they can place their hope, in living and in dying, only in God, the Father of Jesus Christ. All the programs of human self-redemption were and are doomed to failure. Not one single individual can pull himself by his own hair out of the swamp of transience—whether with philosophical speculations, or mythical gnosis and the utopias of a home-made "New Age," or with unscrupulous potentates and romantic social engineers, or by means of the social utopias of a classless society as in Marxism-Leninism, or with hoarding gigantic sums of money and gold as in the liberal capitalism that is reflected in the global ranking of narcissistic billionaires, or with the attempt to go back once more into the natural cycle of life through reincarnation, thereby defying the personal dignity of the immortality of the soul. The Lord says to everyone who puts his hope in the means and goods of this transient world, instead of in the eternal God, "Fool! This night your soul is required of you. [...] So is he who lays up treasure for himself, and is not rich toward God" (Lk 12:20–21).

With the prophetic power of John the Baptist, the successor of Peter becomes the precursor of a new coming of God in the hearts and the lives of many people. The words of the prophet Isaiah apply to him too: "A voice cries: In the wilderness prepare the way of the Lord, make straight in the desert a highway for our God" (Is 40:3; Mt 3:3).

The ideological ravines, the towering mountains of egotism in families, and the hostilities between states that destroy everything are to be overcome: "The crooked shall be made straight, and the rough ways shall be made smooth; and all flesh shall see the salvation of God" (Lk 3:4–6).

Like John the Baptist, Peter's successor, too, says that he must not be confused with the Messiah. Only Jesus of Nazareth is the definitive mediator of the whole of the salvation that comes from God. When the tax collectors and soldiers ask him: "What shall we do?", he says: "He who has two coats, let him share with him who has none; and he who has food, let him do likewise. [...] Rob no one by violence or false accusation, and be content with your wages" (Lk 3:10–14).

It is impossible to overlook the contemporary relevance of these words when Pope Francis denounces the machinations of organized crime, when he appeals for social justice and for the nonviolent resolution of pseudoreligious, political, and economic conflicts, or when he stirs up people's hearts and weeps because of the misery of the refugees in Africa and the children who drown in the Mediterranean. He recalls the words of Jesus not only to weary agnostics, but also to Christians who have doubts: "Let not your hearts be troubled; believe in God, believe also in me. In my Father's house there are many rooms" (Jn 14:1–2). And he does not shun the enemies of the Church and the brothers and sisters who have gone astray in various ways from the good path of their life, from the path of God.

3.
A FISHER OF MEN FOR CHRIST

The pope is certainly familiar with the disappointment of many popes, bishops, and priests in the last few centuries in the face of their apparently fruitless endeavors to combat the maelstrom of secularism, of a world without God. But as the successor of Peter, he remains obedient to the Lord when he, too, utters the apostle's words: "Master, we toiled all night and took nothing! But at your word I will let down the nets" (Lk 5:5). And at the close of this story, the disciples who worked with Peter are "astonished" at the immense number of fish that are caught in the net of the kingdom of heaven. This is why Jesus says anew to Peter in his successors in the episcopal see of Rome: "Do not be afraid; henceforth you will be catching men" (Lk 5:10).

This is the special charism of the present pontificate. Pope Francis is, so to speak, the voice of a new caller in the wilderness. The Church speaks on behalf of the poor and the sick, the handicapped and the homeless, and those who are cast aside as useless and worthless; on behalf of the children abandoned by their parents and of young people who suffer neglect; on behalf of the unborn children in their mothers' wombs and of the dignity of old people who are ill and dying; on behalf of the material and spiritual peripheries, of those who have no religious and moral orientation; and of all "who sit in darkness and in the shadow of death, to guide our feet on the way of peace" (Lk 1:79).

With his keys, the pope opens the gates to the kingdom of God. Popular art depicts Peter as the stern heavenly gatekeeper who controls admission to the kingdom of heaven and prevents some people from entering—but this is not in the least the case. He fulfills his mission in precisely the opposite way, by inviting everyone in friendly and cordial words to take part in the heavenly wedding feast, because God has a place in his house for every single human being. Jesus tells his servant: "Go out quickly to the streets and lanes of the city, and bring in the poor and maimed and blind and lame. [...] Go out to the highways and hedges and compel people to come in, that my house may be filled" (Lk 14:21–23; Mt 22:2–10).

Pope Gregory the Great understood himself as the "servant of the servants of God," but not in order to cloak the absolutism of Enlightenment despots in the manner of the Prussian King Frederick II (r. 1740–1786), who gave himself the title "first servant of my state." The successor of Peter and Vicar of Christ correctly exercises the authority bestowed on him by God for the salvation of humankind when he imitates the Son of man, who "came not to be served but to serve, and to give his life as a ransom for many" (Mt 20:28).

It is not Sisyphus (the myth of everlasting failure) but Christ (the good news of hope) who leads to peace of heart and to the success of our lifework in God's eternity. The apostles were dragged before a court of this world and condemned "because of a good deed done to a cripple" (Acts 4:9). The violent of this world will one day be called to account before the judgment seat of God because of their "evil deeds to good people" and of all the disasters that human beings have brought upon other human beings in this world.

4. PREACHER OF DIVINE MERCY

THE CHURCH OF CHRIST ON EARTH, with the pope at its head, bears witness to "the tender mercy of our God" (Lk 1:78) for all human beings and to the certainty that all are called to know that they are brothers and sisters in the family of God, because we are all sons and daughters of the heavenly Father.

In the Holy Year of Mercy in 2016, Pope Francis wanted to communicate the love of God that includes each and every one. It is the love of God and of one's neighbor that builds bridges and brings down the strongest walls of hostility.

By reminding the disciples of Jesus and everyone in the human family of their responsibility before God and of the Gospel of the grace and truth of Christ, the pope of Rome is carrying out his mission to make the voice of Christ the conscience of the world. He does not have recourse to the instruments of worldly power in order to ensure that things will be better next time around. He offers divine instruments of salvation that bring us a rescue that lasts forever.

These are the miracles that accompany the apostles' preaching. Those who had come to faith in Christ through the apostles "even carried out the sick into the streets, and laid them on beds and pallets, that as Peter came by, at least *his shadow* might fall on some of them" (Acts 5:15; italics added). Peter said to a wretched man who was lame from birth and who had only asked for alms that would help him in the immediate future: "'I have no silver and gold, but I give you what I have; in the name of Jesus Christ of Nazareth, rise and walk.' And he took him by the right hand and raised him up. [...] And all the people saw him walking and praising God" (Acts 3:6–7). The sick man experiences through the healing of his body the working of God and the imperishable salvation of God that is bestowed on him. Through Christ, the Head of the Church, and through the Church's sacramental means of grace, one enters into the fellowship of life with God.

The sacraments are nothing other than the social media of communication with God in the "Facebook" of Jesus and his worldwide "followers" who are the fish in Peter's net. The boundaries of finitude are left behind, the shackles of misery and illness are burst asunder, and sin and evil are destroyed. "Behold, the dwelling of God is with men [...], and death shall be no more, neither shall there be mourning nor crying nor pain any more" (Rv 21:3–4).

The Church continues the mission of Jesus for the salvation of the world until his message reaches everyone. Everyone must get the chance to attain life in fullness through faith. This is what Jesus, the Good Shepherd who lays down his life for his sheep, says: "The thief comes only to steal and kill and destroy; I came that they may have life, and have it abundantly" (Jn 10:10). The Messiah of the Jews, who apparently suffered defeat on the Cross, sends his apostles out in the world, with Peter at their head. The Lord who is risen from the dead meets the disciples, who still doubt, with the words of divine sovereignty: "All authority in heaven and on earth has been given to me. Go therefore and make disciples of all nations, baptizing them in the name of the Father and of the Son and of the Holy Spirit, teaching them to observe all that I have commanded you; and behold, I am with you always, to the close of the age" (Mt 28:19–20).

5.
THE KEYS TO THE KINGDOM OF HEAVEN IN THE HANDS OF THE POPE

FROM THE PERSPECTIVE BOTH OF SALVATION history and of world history, it is impossible to refuse the following insight: the hands of the pope with the keys to the kingdom of heaven are more important than the fists of earthly potentates on the handles of their swords—today, this means their thumb on the nuclear button, which would open the gates of hell on earth. This metaphor expresses the fact that the Church, imitating Christ, is sent to build up rather than to tear down, to give people hope rather than to leave them alone in their solitude and despair. Christ gave the apostle Paul a ministry that leads to life and to righteousness (see 2 Cor 3:9).

"The Son of the living God" put "the keys of the kingdom of heaven" into the hands of the apostle Simon Peter and, in him, of his successors, the bishops of the holy Roman church (Mt 16:19). The kingdom of heaven is the kingdom of God that HE proclaimed to be a reality close at hand. But he not only proclaimed it. In his person and in the story of his life until his death on the Cross and his Resurrection from the dead, he realized it. In his person, God is really and physically present in the world. He who is the eternal Son of God in the Trinity became like us through the Incarnation in time. As God, he is our Lord; as man, he made himself our brother. Through him we have access to the heavenly Father in the Spirit whom we received in baptism and confirmation.

Everyone who adheres to the confession of Peter and of the Church that Jesus is "the Christ, the Son of the living God" (Mt 16:16) has access to the house and the people of God. Through the preaching of the Gospel and the sacramental mediation of salvation, the believer enters through wide-open gates into the eternal kingdom of the Father, which has no boundaries and no end. The kingdom of God is not of this world, and it is not organized according to the style of dominion in this world (Jn 18:36). The kingdom into which God leads us is his own realm "of righteousness and peace and joy in the Holy Spirit" (Rom 14:17). Where God rules and his will is done (Mt 6:10), the kingdom of God is already truly and effectively among us in Christ (Lk 17:21).

In his own person, Jesus Christ is the hidden kingdom of God that is already present on earth and that will be revealed to all human beings at the end of time, "so that God may be everything to everyone" (1 Cor 15:28). We have already been genuinely "transferred to the kingdom of his beloved Son" (Col 1:13) through baptism. Christ is always "the Head of the body, which is the Church" (Col 1:18), from whom all grace flows. At the same time, the visible, societally structured Church on earth is the instrument that HE uses in order to communicate his grace to the members of his body.

The Church is the "one and total Christ, as Head and body."[2] He leads the people of God to eternal perfecting in the fellowship with God the Father and the Son and the Holy Spirit. The Church in its entirety, as the work of God and "as a people made one with the unity of the Father, the Son, and the Holy Spirit,"[3] differs essentially in its origin, its being, its constitution, and its mission from all the organizations that have been founded by human beings.

6.
THE CHURCH IN GOD'S PLAN OF SALVATION

HUMAN UNDERTAKINGS SERVE AIMS AND GOALS with a limitation in time. Rulers found splendid kingdoms that blossom and then crumble into dust. Alexander the Great, Julius Caesar, Genghis Khan, Napoleon Bonaparte are the objects of learned historical studies, and they can give powerful wings to our imagination through films that tell their stories. Captains of industry and media moguls dominate the market for a time and then decline into the reminiscences of a family saga. But no one will expect them to answer the question of why we are here on earth and how we can make something useful out of the brief duration of our lives, irrespectively of whether we work industriously with our talents or are lazy and bury them (Mt 25:14–30; Lk 19:12–27).

God, on the other hand, builds us a house for eternity, "and of his kingdom there will be no end" (Lk 1:33). The works of the divine providence realize God's "eternal plan" for our salvation, in order that we may be "conformed to the image of his Son" (Rom 8:28–29). The power of death and the wickedness of sin do not triumph over the house and people of God, because they were set up by God in order to overcome the transience of the world and the destructive might of evil.

The ultimate goal of every spiritual creature can consist only in the perfected and perfecting knowledge and love of God.[4] The Church, the fellow-

2 Augustine, *Serm.* 341.1.1.

3 Cyprian of Carthage, *Domin. or.* 23, quoted in LG 4.

4 Thomas Aquinas, *S.th.* I–II a8.

ship of the believers, is established in God's eternal plan of salvation. In the course of history, it entered into the world through Christ as a powerful sign of eternal salvation (Eph 3:10). The crucified and risen Lord is the Head of his body, the Church. The mediator of creation is also the mediator of salvation and the Head of the body, his Church (Eph 1:23).

7.
THE CHURCH'S MINISTRY OF SALVATION FOR HUMANKIND

As the sacrament of the kingdom of God, the Church serves as an instrument, so that the rule of God on earth may spread more and more until it is perfected in the return of Christ at the close of history (Mt 28:16–20):

> While helping the world and receiving many benefits from it, the Church has a single intention: that God's kingdom may come, and that the salvation of the whole human race may come to pass. For every benefit which the People of God during its earthly pilgrimage can offer to the human family stems from the fact that the Church is "the universal sacrament of salvation," simultaneously manifesting and exercising the mystery of God's love. For God's Word, by whom all things were made, was Himself made flesh so that as perfect man He might save all men and sum up all things in Himself. The Lord is the goal of human history, the focal point of the longings of history, the center of the human race, the joy of every heart, and the answer to all its yearnings (GS 45).

8.
THE MESSAGE OF CHRIST—HOLDING UP A MIRROR TO THE CONSCIENCE OF THE WORLD

Peter, the rock of the Church's faith in Christ, bears witness to this truth until the close of human history, and this means that the pope addresses the conscience of the Church and of humankind. The Church, which exercises its service of humanity in the person of the pope as its highest teacher, confirms that freedom of religion is a fundamental human right. This means, first of all, that one may join an existing religious community of one's free choice, without coercion from the state or from society. On a deeper level, the freedom of the religious act consists in opening oneself with all one's understanding and all one's strength to the mystery that shows itself in its traces, images, and parables in this world to be our first origin and our ultimate goal, the mystery that we revere and adore in love and devotion. At the same time, this freedom underscores the right and the obligation of everyone to obey in faith the truth of God that has been recognized in Christ, in a freedom that is enlightened and guided by grace. This is why the magisterium of the Catholic Church stated at the Second Vatican Council, in the Declaration on Religious Freedom:

> The right to religious freedom has its foundation not in the subjective disposition of the person, but in his very nature. In consequence, the right to this immunity continues to exist even in those who do not live up to their obligation of seeking the truth and adhering to it, and the exercise of this right is not to be impeded, provided that just public order be observed. Further light is shed on the subject if one considers that the highest norm of human life is the divine law—eternal, objective, and universal—whereby God orders, directs, and governs the entire universe and all the ways of the human community by a plan conceived in wisdom and love. Man has been made by God to participate in this law, with the result that, under the gentle disposition of divine Providence, he can come to perceive ever more fully the truth that is unchanging. [...] Truth, however, is to be sought after in a manner proper to the dignity of the human person and his social nature. The inquiry is to be free, carried on with the aid of teaching or instruction, communication and dialogue, in the course of which men explain to one another the truth they have discovered, or think they have discovered, in order thus to assist one another in the quest for truth. Moreover, as the truth is discovered, it is by a personal assent that men are to adhere to it (DH 2–3).

The pope is both the guarantor and the interpreter of the right to religious freedom that is inherent in the free intellectual nature of the human being. He is likewise the guarantor and the interpreter of the truth of God that has in fact been revealed in Christ. This shows the baselessness of the deceptive alternative between an absolutism and a relativism in the question of truth. Every human being is oriented to the truth that of its nature transcends him, and all ought to be bonded together in the love of truth. The radical doubt about the capacity of the human reason to grasp the truth cuts the human being into two and subjects it to the rule of subjectivism, which absolutizes itself and thus perverts philosophy (which ought to mean the "love of wisdom") into an ideology. An ideological absolutism or totalitarianism is always relativistic, because when the political or ideological leaders are changed, the adherents of the ideology cross over opportunistically to the new position and revere the new idol with the same blind devotion, thus making a mockery of every free use of the reason. Relativism is absolutist when it claims that there is no truth and that God cannot reveal himself in one single human individual such as Jesus Christ—and that even if he wished to do so, he could not create in the human being the intellectual conditions that would elevate the finite spirit to receive the divine truth. It is as if those who hold this position had "never even heard that there is a Holy Spirit" (Acts 19:2).

It is true that the dialectical relationship between finite reason and divine truth cannot be abolished by that which is finite. But since the God who is three and one is, in his being and his life, the unity of immediacy and mediation, he can give us a share, through the Incarnation of the Logos and the pouring out of the Holy Spirit into our hearts, in his self-knowledge in the Son and his self-affirmation in the Spirit: "Through [Christ] we have obtained access to this grace in which we stand, and we rejoice in our hope of sharing the glory of God, [...] because God's love has been poured into our hearts through the Holy Spirit who has been given to us" (Rom 5:2, 5).

Jesus tells the Samaritan woman at Jacob's well, who wavers unclearly between Judaism and paganism: "The hour is coming, and now is, when the true worshipers will worship the Father in spirit and truth" (Jn 4:23).

The Church's magisterium does not force the truth of revelation on anyone, because its very nature means that it can be received only with free consent and that it comes to fulfillment in love. The Second Vatican Council presented the truth of the Gospel in the form of the confession of faith:

> God Himself has made known to mankind the way in which men are to serve Him, and thus be saved in Christ and come to blessedness. We believe that this one true religion subsists in the Catholic and Apostolic Church, to which Jesus the Lord committed the duty of spreading it abroad among all men. [...] On their part, all men are bound to seek the truth especially in what concerns God and His Church, and to embrace the truth they come to know, and to hold fast to it (DH 1).

9. THE MORAL AUTHORITY OF THE POPE IN THE FAMILY OF PEOPLES

There can be no doubt that Holy See has enjoyed a higher moral authority in the world community than the most important representatives of politics, precisely in the pontificates from Leo XIII down to Pope Francis.

The Church understands itself as the sign and instrument, not only of the supernatural fellowship with God but also of the natural unity of humankind in peace and justice (see LG 1).

The Church has also had an empirically observable effect on intellectual and cultural history and on the history of the world down to the most recent times. Let me mention only a few examples: Catholic social teaching; the message about the dignity of the human person; or Pope Francis's recent encyclical *Laudato si'* about an ecology based on the theology of creation. The theological and the empirical approaches can enrich each other here.

Through the authentic interpretation of the natural moral law and the preservation of the principles of a social and just societal order, the pope is the highest advocate of human beings in their personal dignity and freedom. And, by the way, the theme of human rights did not begin with the United Nations in 1948. It was proclaimed as long ago as 1537 by Pope Paul III, when he condemned the enslaving of the Indio population in the Spanish colonies in America. Against the background of the justification of human rights and international law already in the natural moral law (and not only in the supernatural revelation), as the school of Salamanca argued, the bull *Sublimis Deus* (May 2, 1537) and the breve *Pastorale officium* (May 29, 1537) emphasize that the Indios, the inhabitants of the New World, are beings endowed with reason and an immortal soul and are thus human beings like everyone else, even if they are as yet outside the bosom of the Mother Church.[5] The consequence is freedom of religion, the freedom to be baptized and to accept the faith without any coercion.

If the peaceful Christianization of the peoples, in accordance with Jesus's words "Make disciples of all nations" (Mt 28:19), is to be just, this requires that they be invited through preaching and a good example to accept faith in Christ in full freedom and thereby to become members of his body, the Church.

The Second Vatican Council likewise justified human rights and religious freedom by appealing to natural law and forbidding the state to intervene in any way in the freedom of conscience. It thus also takes a stance against the ideological liberalism of the nineteenth century, which contradicted its own principles by finding its political form in the omnipotent state: the council affirms that the supernatural perfecting of freedom lies in obedience to the God who reveals himself. The Church is the advocate of reason, in which the human being recognizes the basic principles of morality that have their origin in the goodness of God, thanks to which the world and human beings exist. And this is why the pope, as the representative of the Church in

5 DH 1495.

the name and with the authority of Christ, rightly enjoys the highest moral authority in the states and the international organizations. This authority, however, is always oriented to the higher goal of the common good of the family of peoples, and this is why the Church's preaching and pastoral care are addressed not only to its own members but also to "all persons of good will," who are the objects of God's grace and his universal saving will (see Lk 2:14; 1 Tm 2:4). *Diakonia* and *caritas* are essential activities of the Church.

10.
THE CHURCH'S COLLABORATION FOR THE COMMON GOOD

THE CHURCH IS ITSELF AN INTERTWINING OF THE DIVINE calling and the earthly and manifest signs of its realization of this calling. In the same way, its supernatural mission and its commission to contribute to the good of society are not merely juxtaposed dualistically and disjunctively. Eternal salvation and earthly well-being are related to each other because both of them correspond to the dignity of the human being and to the unity of his earthly and heavenly calling:

> Pursuing the saving purpose which is proper to her, the Church does not only communicate divine life to man, but in some way casts the reflected light of that life over the entire earth, most of all by its healing and elevating impact on the dignity of the person, by the way in which it strengthens the seams of human society and imbues the everyday activity of men with a deeper meaning and importance. Thus, through her individual members and her whole community, the Church believes she can contribute greatly toward making the family of man and its history more human (GS 40).

Avoiding the extremes of an idealist flight from the world and a materialistic worldliness, the concrete location of Christianity is a "Christian humanism"—that is to say, the synthesis between faith and reason. The unity of creation and redemption, of the religious mission and the task in the world, is the inner relatedness, indeed "the marriage of grace and nature."[6]

6 See Matthias Joseph Scheeben, *Handbuch der katholische Dogmatik*, vol. 3 (Freiburg: Herder, 1933) 900, 902.

11.
THE MEANING OF THE PRIMACY OF THE CHURCH OF ROME AND OF ITS BISHOP

THE UNIVERSAL FELLOWSHIP OF THE BELIEVERS with their shepherds, the bishops of the local churches, encompasses both space and time in their unity with God and with the totality of the faithful. This fellowship is "summed up" corporately in the bishop of Rome. The visible gathering together of the faithful is represented in his person. The risen Lord charged Simon Peter with a task that must be accomplished by the bishops of Rome until the end of time: "Pasture *my* lambs and sheep!" (Jn 21:15, 16, 18). The pope and the bishops in fellowship with him guide the Church, God's "people and the sheep of his pasture" (Ps 100:3), on the path to fellowship with God in eternal life (see 1 Jn 1:3).

Paul, together with his fellow apostle Timothy who was his successor in the apostolic ministry, presented to the believers in Colossae the meaning of this apostolic ministry and of the mission of the Church:

> I became a minister of the Church according to the divine office which was given to me for you, to make the word of God fully known, the mystery hidden for ages and generations but now made manifest to his saints. To them God chose to make known how great among the Gentiles are the riches of the glory of this mystery, which is Christ in you, the hope of glory (Col 1:25-27).

What then is the meaning of the primacy of the pope, the bishop of the *ecclesia principalis* at Rome, in the fellowship of the local churches that are headed by their own bishops—that is to say, the *communio ecclesiarum* (LG 23)—and represent the universal Church in their organic totality?

The highest authority of the Church declared definitively at the First and Second Vatican Councils "the teaching about the institution, the perpetuity, the meaning and reason for the sacred primacy of the Roman Pontiff" on the basis of the fact that:

> Jesus Christ, the eternal Shepherd, established His holy Church, having sent forth the apostles as He Himself had been sent by the Father (Jn 20:21); and He willed that their successors, namely the bishops, should be shepherds in His Church even to the consummation of the world. And in order that the episcopate itself might be *one and undivided,* He placed Blessed Peter over the other apostles, and instituted in him a permanent and visible source and foundation of unity of faith and communion (LG 18; italics added).

12.
THE POPE AS SUCCESSOR OF PETER AND VICAR OF CHRIST

THE DOCTRINE OF THE PRIMACY OF THE BISHOP of Rome can be understood correctly only in connection with "the doctrine concerning bishops, the successors of the apostles, who together with the successor of Peter, the Vicar of Christ, the visible Head of the whole Church, govern the house of the living God" (LG 18). Every pope has received his office directly from Christ, the Head of the Church, and exercises it in his name; and this is why he is very rightly called the "Vicar of Christ." Some find this title offensive, and it requires a little explanation. Every Christian is spiritually a "vicar" of Christ in relation to his fellow Christian and to everyone who seeks salvation and help. In the first place, this is the role of a mother and father vis-à-vis their children whom God has given and entrusted to them. When they accept and educate their children, Christian parents are practicing the common priesthood of the entire Church.[7]

The authority bestowed on them to build up the Church makes the priests "vicars" of Christ for their parishes, and the bishops for their dioceses, since they act in the person of Christ, the Head of the Church, in their preaching, their sacramental ministry, and their pastoral guidance (LG 21). The apostles are "ambassadors for Christ, God making his appeal through us" (2 Cor 5:20).

The Roman bishop is the Vicar of Christ as the universal shepherd for the entire Church, since it was to him that the risen Lord at the Sea of Tiberias gave the charge to tend and feed it. He does this as the successor of Simon, the son of Jona (John), as Peter, the rock on whom the Lord built his Church and continues to build it, and as the one who holds the keys of the kingdom of heaven in his hand. It is objectively wrong to hold that initially the pope modestly called himself *Vicarius Petri,* and that only his exaggerated claims to dominion led him to call himself *Vicarius Christi.* "Vicar of Peter" means the same as "successor of Peter," whereas the term "Vicar of Christ" affirms that the one who sits on the *cathedra Petri* exercises his ministry as teacher and pastor not in the name of Peter but with the authority of Christ. The latter title designates the direct relationship to Christ, while the former title refers to the historical succession that goes back to Simon as the first "Peter" on whom Christ built and builds his Church, which acknowledges Peter's presence today in the church of Rome. Cyprian of Carthage

7 1 Pt 2:5, 9; Eph 6:1–4; Col 3:5–4:1.

calls Bishop Stephen of Rome the *vicarius et successor* of his predecessor Cornelius, and it becomes customary from the fifth century onwards to call the pope *Vicarius Christi.*[8] *Vicarius est qui vices gerit alterius,* "a vicar is one who acts in the place and in the name of another."[9] For it is not the church of Simon from Bethsaida, nor do the sheep belong to the son of John: it is the flock of Christ, the Son of God, that the pope guides as the successor to the office of Saint Peter and the one who holds Peter's authority.

Saint Bonaventure (1221–1274) explains the role of the pope in the ecclesial hierarchy, the structure of the spiritual ministries:

> The further the fullness of authority descends, the broader it becomes. The further it ascends, the more concentrated it becomes. This is why there are more bishops, fewer archbishops, very few patriarchs, and only one father of fathers, who is rightly called "pope." He is, so to speak, the one, first, and highest spiritual father of the fathers, and indeed of all the believers. It is he who holds the first place in sacred rule, as the only bridegroom, the undivided head, high priest, Vicar of Christ, source, origin, and criterion of all ecclesial governance. From him, as the summit, the authority flows down to the lowest members of the Church, in accordance with the special dignity in the ordered structure of the holy Church.[10]

13. THEOLOGY AND SPIRITUALITY OF THE EXERCISE OF PRIMACY

A MISSION THAT IS SO EXCEPTIONAL, and so decisive for the salvation of human beings, demands both from the one who sits on the *cathedra Petri* and from all the members of the Church a continuous spiritual and theological study, in depth, of the essence and the form of the papacy in the context of the episcopate and of the fellowship of the entire Church. The program of a constant reform of the Church in its head and members is the very opposite of a banalization of the Cross and a weak secularization of the Church. The more deeply the Church is rooted in the mystery of the crucified and risen Lord, the closer it is to those who give God the glory at the proper time and confess that HE alone is the origin and the goal of our life.

8 Cyprian of Carthage, *Ep.* 68.5.

9 Gelasius I, *Ep.* 27.5. See Josef Hergenröther, *Anti-Janus*, 61, 70.

10 Bonaventure, *Breviloquium* VI.12; see also Hugh of Saint Victor, *De sacramentis* 43.

This is inseparable from a critical and unceasing reflection on the tension between the divine commission and human weakness, a tension that will last until the end of the world. We are accompanied by God's promise, on the one hand, and the possibility of human failure, on the other.

The word "critical" in the last paragraph does not mean a carping and destructive distance, a sensational protest, or an inner emigration. We need a spiritual sense of judgment and a differentiating perspective on a divine institution that can indeed be obscured and discredited by the weakness and sin of its office-bearers, but that can never be extinguished. Criticism without love corrodes. But love without criticism is nothing other than a repellent flattery. The supreme ministry that Jesus entrusted to Simon Peter and his successors is exercised precisely by men who do not shine in their radiant dignity but always remain in the shadow of the Lord, whom they follow. The great Dominican Melchor Cano (1509–1560) stated something that the opportunists and courtiers in every age are unwilling to hear: "Peter does not depend on our lies and flatteries. It is precisely those who blindly and uncritically defend every decision of the pope that make the greatest contribution to undermining the authority of the Holy See. They do not strengthen its foundations, but rather destroy them."[11]

The celebrated *Consilium de emendanda ecclesia* was a memorandum drawn up by a commission of cardinals headed by Gasparo Contarini (1483–1542) and discussed frankly in the presence of Pope Paul III on March 9, 1537. It was an unsparing account of the defects and deficiencies of the Church that had led to the outbreak of the ecclesiastical revolution in 1517, and it was an important milestone on the path to the Council of Trent and the Catholic reform in the sixteenth and seventeenth centuries. The leading church historian Hubert Jedin (1900–1980) comments on this text:

> Frankness in the presence of the Vicar of Christ with his threefold crown is even harder and rarer than frankness before the thrones of kings. Even the historian almost holds his breath when he reads in this document that was meant for the eyes of the pope the terrible accusation that the root of all the ills lies in the exaggeration of the papal theory. This text affirms that flatterers have convinced some popes that their will is law, that they are the lords of all benefices and therefore are entitled to do as they like with the

11 Melchor Cano, *De locis theologicis* (Salamanca: Mathias Gastius, 1563) V, cap. 5 ad 4; see Albert Lang, *Die Loci theologici des Melchior Cano und die Methode des dogmatischen Beweises: Ein Beitrag zur theologischen Methodologie und ihrer Geschichte* (Munich: Kösel and Pustet, 1925), 135–146; John Jay Hughes, *Pontiffs: Popes Who Shaped History* (Huntington, Ind.: Our Sunday Visitor, 1994), 11.

benefices without ever committing simony. This view was the Trojan horse out of which numerous abuses broke into the Church.[12]

We recognize on the face of the Church the reflection of the glory of God, so that all may acknowledge: "Christ is the light of the peoples" (LG 1). The Church is the light *only* from the light that points us to the triune God. In a similar way, the moon reflects the rays of the sun and does not shine with its own power—yet it gives us orientation in the dark. The Church imitates its Lord, who took on the form of a slave in his Incarnation (Phil 2:6), so that we can say:

> The Church, "like a stranger in a foreign land, presses forward amid the persecutions of the world and the consolations of God," announcing the cross and death of the Lord until He comes (see 1 Cor 11:26). By the power of the risen Lord it is given strength that it might, in patience and in love, overcome its sorrows and its challenges, both within itself and from without, and that it might reveal to the world, faithfully though darkly, the mystery of its Lord until, in the end, it will be manifested in full light (LG 8).[13]

We need a theology and a spirituality of the Roman primacy and, by analogy, of all the ecclesial offices and ministries, that discern what is essential in their authority and their mission from all the secondary overlays. This theology and spirituality will allow the Spirit of Christ to impact both personally and existentially the exercise of these various ministries.

When we speak here of the theology and spirituality of the papacy, these are not matters of abstract theories and devout and sentimental effusions. The concept of "theology" here refers to the Logos, the Word of God, to whom the Church owes its existence and in whose light the Church understands its own being ever more fully. "Spirituality" here means the exercise of the Petrine ministry in the Holy *Pneuma*, the Spirit of God, for when the "Spirit of truth" comes as the "Paraclete" (Jn 16:7, 13), he will lead the disciples into all the truth. And the truth of the truth is the light of the world in the Word that has become flesh (Jn 1:9; 8:12).

12 Hubert Jedin, *Geschichte des Konzils von Trient,* vol 1, *Der Kampf um das Konzil,* 3rd ed. (Freiburg: Verlag Herder, 1977), 339–40.

13 Includes note on quotation: "S. Augustinus, Civ. Dei, XVIII, 51, 2."

14. AN ECUMENICALLY ACCEPTABLE FORM OF THE PAPACY?

THE PAPAL PRIMACY CAN BE EXERCISED only in the total devotedness of the pope to Christ. He must continuously point to Christ, in whom alone salvation can be found (see Acts 4:12). He binds the believers to Christ, in whom the Church is both the invisible fellowship of grace with God and at the same time the visible gathering of the baptized, including the sinners. This fellowship is practiced in the doctrine of the faith, in the spiritual and sacramental life, and in the divinely given constitution of the Church (see Acts 2:42).

This is the ecumenical form of the papacy, which also addresses an invitation to non-Catholic Christians on the path to the full unity of all the baptized in the one flock of Christ. Pope John Paul II spoke of this in his encyclical *Ut unum sint* (1995), number 95:

> As Bishop of Rome I am fully aware [...] that Christ ardently desires the full and visible communion of all those Communities in which, by virtue of God's faithfulness, his Spirit dwells. I am convinced that I have a particular responsibility in this regard, above all in acknowledging the ecumenical aspirations of the majority of the Christian Communities and in heeding the request made of me to find a way of exercising the primacy which, while in no way renouncing what is essential to its mission, is nevertheless open to a new situation.[14]

What then is the essential element of the papal primacy that was intended by the divine founder of the Church, as this primacy has unfolded in dogmatic theology, canon law, and the pastoral dimension in the history of the Church—as opposed to historically conditioned and therefore secondary matters that have arisen in the vicissitudes of world history? What is the new situation of the world, today and in each new period of history, that demands the unanimity of all Christians in their confession of Jesus Christ, the Redeemer and liberator of all human beings, when the successor of Peter speaks the one confession of Christ in the name of everyone, so that all the believers are united in Christ as the Head and Lord of the Church, his body?[15]

14 John Paul II, Encyclical Letter *Ut unum* sint (May 25, 1995), 95. See Lino Piano, *Le prerogative del primato papale alla luce dell'Enciclica "Ut unum sint": Rivolti ecclesiali e ecumenici, Annotazioni storiche a 500 anni dalla riforma luterana 1517–2017* (Turin: Elledici, 2016).

15 See the fundamental studies by Leo Scheffczyk, *Das Unwandelbare im Petrusamt* (Berlin: Morus-Verl, 1971); "Das Petrusamt in der Kirche: Übergeordnet—eingefügt," in *Glaube als*

15.
SUMMING UP THE THEOLOGY OF THE PRIMACY

THE UNITY OF THE CHURCH is not the result of skilled diplomatic mediation between various opinions about God and his revelation in salvation history. It is the divine gift that incessantly unites the members of the body of Christ with their Head, and with each other in Christ. The Church is thus a Head and a body. Jesus Christ gave Simon Peter the task of uniting the Church in the confession of him who is the Son of the living God.

Peter speaks *daily* through the mouth of the entire Church in his successors, the bishops of Rome, the confession of the truth: "You are the Christ, the Son of the living God."[16]

In order that the episcopate and the entire Church might remain one and undivided in the faith and in the fellowship with Christ, "He placed Blessed Peter over the other apostles, and instituted in him a permanent and visible source and foundation of unity of faith and communion" (LG 18).

The risen Lord promised the apostles and their successors, and thus the entire Church, that they would have his Holy Spirit and his genuine and effective presence until his return at the end of the world (Mt 28:20). This means that the promise to Peter and to all who would be his vicars in his episcopal see in Rome likewise holds good until the close of history.

"What Peter believed about Christ is valid forever. What Christ instituted in Peter is likewise valid forever."[17]

Peter is the rock on whom the Lord built his Church. And the promise that it would always exist and remain in the truth of the Gospel of the love of the triune God was given to Simon Peter for the Church of all the ages. Accordingly, when his successor, the bishop of Rome, reminds the one, holy, catholic, and apostolic Church that it is, in Christ, the sacrament of the salvation of the world, he is carrying out the task that was given to him in Saint Peter at the Last Supper: "Strengthen your brethren!" And this mission

---

Lebensinterpretation: Gesammelte Schriften zur Theologie (Einsiedeln: Johannes Verl, 1980), 394–412; Karl Lehmann, ed., *Das Petrusamt: Geschichtliche Stationen seines Verständnisses und gegenwärtige Positionen* (Munich: Schnell and Steiner, 1982); Jean-Marie Tillard, *L'évêque de Rome* (Paris: Cerf, 1984); Michele Maccarrone, ed., *Il Primato del vescovo di Roma nel primo Millennio: Ricerche e testimonianze* (Vatican City: Libreria editrice Vaticana, 1991–1997); *Il Primato del successore di Pietro: Atti del simposio teologico 1996* (Vatican City: Libreria editrice Vaticana, 1998). The article "Primauté du Pape" in DThC 13 (Paris 1936), 247–391, remains unsurpassed in its presentation of all the historical and theological sources. See also Alfonso Carrasco Rouco, *Le primat de l'évêque de Rome: Étude sur la cohérenc ecclésiologique et canonique du primat de juridiction* (Fribourg: Editions Universitaires, 1990).

16 Leo I, *Serm.* 3.3 on the Feast of Peter and Paul.

17 Leo I, *Serm.* 3.2 on the Feast of Peter and Paul.

can be accomplished only with the aid of the Lord who says to him: "I have prayed for you, that your faith may not fail" (Lk 22:32).

His faith is the faith of the entire Church in Jesus, the Messiah, the Son of the living God (Mt 16:18).

This is the mission of the Roman pope, who is the shepherd of the universal Church.

Bibliography

Unless otherwise noted, Vatican documents available at www.vatican.va

Abejon, Gerardo del Pozo. *La Iglesia y la libertad religiosa.* Madrid: Biblioteca de Autores Cristianos, 2007.

Batiffol, Pierre. *L'Eglise naissante et le Catholicisme.* Paris: Lecoffre, 1909. Translated by Henri L. Brianceau as *Primitive Catholicism.* New York: Longmans, Green, and Co., 1911. Reprint, Forgotten Books, 2015.

_____. *Cathedra Petri: Études d'histoire ancienne de l'Église.* Paris: Cerf, 1938.

Baumann, Richard. *Was Christus dem Petrus verheißt: Eine Entdeckung im Urtext von Matthäus 16.* Stein am Rhein: Christiana Verlag, 1988.

Beck, Hans Georg. *Kirche und theologische Literatur im Byzantinischen Reich.* Munich: Beck 1959.

Benedict XVI. *Deus caritas est.* Encyclical Letter. December 25, 2005.

_____. *Spe salvi.* Encyclical Letter. November 30, 2007.

Betti, Umberto. *La dottrina sull'episcopato del Concilio Vaticano II: Il capitolo III della Costituzione dommatica* Lumen gentium. Rome: Pontificium athenaeum Antonianum, 1984.

Blumenberg, Hans. *Die Legitimität der Neuzeit.* Frankfurt: Suhrkamp, 1966.

Bonhoeffer, Dietrich. *Sanctorum Communio: Eine dogmatische Untersuchung zur Soziologie der Kirche.* Vol. 1 of *Dietrich Bonhoeffer Werke.* Munich: Chr. Kaiser, 1986. Translated by Clifford Green as *Sanctorum Communio: A Theological Study of the Sociology of the Church.* Minneapolis: Fortress Press, 2009. First published in 1930.

_____. *Ökumene, Universität, Pfarramt 1931–1932.* Vol. 11 of *Dietrich Bonhoeffer Werke.* Gutersloh: Chr. Kaiser, 1994. Translated by Isabel Best, Nicholas S. Humphrey, Marion Pauck, Anne Schmidt-Lange, and Douglas W. Stott as *Ecumenical, Academic, and Pastoral Work: 1931–1932.* Minneapolis: Fortress Press, 2012.

_____. *Widerstand und Ergebung: Briefe und Aufzeichnungen aus der Haft.* Vol. 8 of *Dietrich Bonhoeffer Werke.* Munich: Chr. Kaiser, 1970. Translated by Isabel Best, Lisa E. Dahill, Reinhard Krauss, Nancy Lukens, Barbara Rumscheidt, and Martin Rumscheidt as *Letters and Papers from Prison.* Minneapolis: Fortress Press, 2015. First published in 1951.

Borutta, Manuel. *Antikatholizismus: Deutschland und Italien im Zeitalter der europäischen Kulturkämpfe.* Göttingen: Vandenhoeck and Ruprecht, 2010.

Bouyer, Louis. *L'Église de Dieu, corps du Christ et temple de l'Esprit.* Paris: Cerf, 1970. Translated by Charles Underhill Quinn as *The Church of God: Body of Christ and Temple of the Spirit.* San Francisco: Ignatius Press, 2011.

Brandenburg, Albert and Hans Jörg Urban. *Petrus und Papst: Evangelium, Einheit der Kirche, Papstdienst.* 2 vols. Münster: Aschendorff, 1977–1978.

Brandmüller, Walter. *Das Konzil von Konstanz (1414–1418).* 2 vols. Paderborn: Schöningh, 1991–1998.

_____. *Licht und Schatten: Kirchengeschichte zwischen Glaube, Fakten und Legenden.* Augsburg: Sankt-Ulrich-Verl, 2007.

Brecht, Martin. *Die Erhaltung der Kirche.* Vol. 3 of *Martin Luther.* Stuttgart: Calwer Verlag, 1987. Translated by James Schaaf as *Martin Luther, Volume III: The Preservation of the Church, 1532–1546.* Minneapolis: Fortress Press, 1993.

Camelot, Pierre-Thomas. *Ephesus und Chalcedon.* Mainz: Matthias-Grünewald, 1963.

Cano, Melchor. *De Locis Theologicis.* Salamanca: Mathias Gastius, 1563.

Carrasco Rouco, Alfonso. *Le primat de l'évêque de Rome: Étude sur la cohérenc ecclésiologique et canonique du primat de juridiction.* Fribourg: Editions Universitaires, 1990.

de Las Casas, Bartolomé. *Kurzgefasster Bericht von der Verwüstung der westindischen Länder.* Translated by Hans Magnus Enzensberger. Frankfurt: Insel, 1981. Originally published as *Brevísima relación de la destrucción de las Indias.* Seville: Sebastian Trugillo, 1552.

Caspar, Erich. *Geschichte des Papsttums von den Anfängen bis zur Höhe der Weltherrschaft.* 2 vols. Tubingen: J. C. B. Mohr, 1930–1933. Reprint, Munster: Stenderhoff, 1985.

Congregation for the Doctrine of the Faith. "Instruction on Christian Freedom and Liberation." March 22, 1986.

Clarke, Graeme W., trans. *The Letters of Cyprian of Carthage.* 4 vols. Ancient Christian Writers 43, 44, 46, 47. New York: Newman Press, 1983–1989. [Note: this translation follows the CSEL numbering of the *Letters* used in this work. Some earlier translations rely on a different numbering system.]

von Döllinger, Ignaz. *Kirche und Kirchen, Papsttum und Kirchenstaat: Historisch-politische Betrachtungen.* Munich: J. G. Cotta, 1861.

_____. *Das Papsttum.* Darmstadt: WBG, 1969.

Duchesne, Louis. *Églises séparées.* Paris: Albert Fontemoing, 1905. Translated as *The Church Separated from Rome.* London: Kegan Paul, Trench, Trübner, 1907.

Dvornik, Franz. *Byzance et la primauté romaine*. Paris: Cerf, 1964. Translated as *Byzantium and the Roman Primacy*. New York: Fordham University Press, 1966.

Elsner, Heinrich. *Umfassende Geschichte des Kaisers Napoleon*. vol. 4. Stuttgart: Leipzig Rieger, 1837.

Feuerbach, Ludwig. *Das Wesen des Christentums*. Leipzig: Wigan, 1840. Translated by Marian Evans as *The Essence of Christianity*. London: J. Chapman, 1854. Reprint, Cambridge: Cambridge University Press, 2011.

Fiedrowicz, Michael. *Theologie der Kirchenväter: Grundlagen frühchristlicher Glaubensreflexion*. Freiburg: Herder, 2007.

Fforde, Matthew. *Desocialization: The Crisis of Post-Modernity*. Cheadle-Hulme: Gabriel Communications, 2009

Franzen, August and Remigius Baumer. *Papstgeschichte: Das Petrusamt in seiner Idee und in seiner geschichtlichen Verwirklichung in der Kirche*. Freiburg: Herder, 1974.

Francis. "Address of Pope Francis in the Bishop's Residence." Speech delivered at the Meeting with the Bishops of Brazil, Rio de Janeiro. July 28, 2013.

_____. *Lumen fidei*. Encyclical Letter. June 29, 2013.

_____. *Evangelii gaudium*. Apostolic Exhortation. November 24, 2013.

_____. *Laudato si'*. Encyclical Letter. May 24, 2015.

Fuhrmann, Horst. *Die Päpste: Von Petrus zu Johannes Paul II*. 3rd ed. Munich: C. H. Beck, 1998.

_____. *Die Päpste: Von Petrus zu Benedikt XVI*. 4th ed. Munich: C. H. Beck, 2012.

Gnilka, Christian, Stefan Heid, and Rainer Rieser. *La morte e il sepolcro di Pietro*. Vatican City: Libreria editrice Vaticana, 2014.

Gnilka, Joachim. *Petrus und Rom: Das Petrusbild in den ersten zwei Jahrhunderten*. Freiburg: Herder, 2002.

Goethe, Johann Wolfgang von. *Faust: Der Tragödie Erster Teil*. Stuttgart: J. G. Cotta, 1833.

Granfield, Patrick. *The Papacy in Transition*. New York: Doubleday and Co., 1980.

Greschat, Martin, ed. *Das Papsttum*. 2 vols. Stuttgart: W. Kohlhammer, 1984–1985.

Gutiérrez, Gustavo. *Beber en su proprio pozo: En el itinerario espiritual de un pueblo*. Lima: Centro de Estudios y Publicaciones, 1983. Translated by Matthew J. O'Connell as *We Drink from Our Own Wells: The Spiritual Journey of a People*. Maryknoll, N.Y.: Orbis Books, 1984.

_____. *Dios o el oro en las Indias, Siglo XVI*. Lima: Centro de Estudios y Publicaciones, 1989.

_____. *El rostro de Dios en la historia*. Lima: Pontificia Universidad Católica del Perú, Departamento de Teología, Instituto Bartolomé de las Casas, Centro de Estudios y Publicaciones, 1996.

_____. *The Power of the Poor in History*. Eugene, Ore.: Wipf and Stock, 2004.

Haller, Johannes. *Das Papsttum: Idee und Wirklichkeit*. 5 vols. Stuttgart: Port Verlag, 1950–53.

Harnack, Adolf von. *Das Wesen des Christentums: 16 Vorlesungen für Studierende aller Fakultäten im Wintersemester 1899/1900*. Leipzig: Hinrich, 1900. Translated by Thomas Bailey Saunders as *What is Christianity? Lectures Delivered during the Winter Term, 1899–1900*. London: Williams and Norgate, 1908.

Herbers, Klaus. *Geschichte des Papsttums im Mittelalter.* Darmstadt: WBG, 2012.

Hergenröther, Josef. *Anti-Janus: Eine historisch-theologische Kritik der Schrift "Der Papst und das Konzil" von Janus.* Freiburg: Herder, 1870.

Horn, Stefan Otto. *Petrou Kathedra: Der Bischof von Rom und die Synoden von Ephesus (449) und Chalcedon.* Paderborn: Bonifatius-Druckerei, 1982.

______. "Das Verhältnis von Primat und Episkopat im ersten Jahrtausend: Eine geschichtlich-theologische Studie." In *Il primato del successore di Pietro: Atti del simposio teologisco, Roma, Dicembre 1996*, 194–213. Vatican City: Libreria editrice Vaticana, 1998.

Hughes, John Jay. *Pontiffs: Popes Who Shaped History*. Huntington, Ind.: Our Sunday Visitor, 1994.

Hünermann, William. *Brennendes Feuer: Papst Pius X*. Innsbruck: Tyrolia, 1954.

Jedin, Hubert. *Der Kampf und das Konzil.* Vol. 1 of *Geschichte des Konzils von Trient*. 3rd ed. Freiburg: Herder, 1977. Translated by Ernest Graf as *A History of the Council of Trent, Volume I: The Struggle for the Council.* St. Louis: Herder, 1961.

John XXIII. *Pacem in terris*. Encyclical Letter. April 11, 1963.

John Paul II. *Redemptor hominis*. Encyclical Letter. March 4, 1979.

______. "Letter to the Episcopal Conference of Brazil." April 9, 1986.

______. *Sollicitudo rei socialis*. Encyclical Letter. December 30, 1987.

______. *Centesimus annus*. Encyclical Letter. May 1, 1991.

______. *Evangelium vitae*. Encyclical Letter. March 25, 1995.

______. *Ut unum sint*. Encyclical Letter. May 25, 1995.

______. *Apostolos suos*. Apostolic Letter *motu proprio*. May 21, 1998.

Katholischer Katechismus der Bistümer Deutschlands. Freiburg: Herder, 1955.

Knoch, Otto. "Petrus im Neuen Testament." In *Il primato del vescovo di Roma nel primo millennio: Ricerche e testimonianze: Atti del simposio storico-teologico,* edited by Michele Maccarone, 1–52. Vatican City: Libreria editrice Vaticana, 1991.

Kirch, Konrad. *Enchiridion fontium historiae ecclesiasticae antiquae*. Barcelona: Herder, 1965.

Kreuzer, Georg. *Die Honoriusfrage im Mittelalter und der Neuzeit.* Stuttgart: Hiersemann, 1975.

Lang, Albert. *Die Loci theologici des Melchior Cano und die Methode des dogmatischen Beweises: Ein Beitrag zur theologischen Methodologie und ihrer Geschichte.* Munich: Kösel and Pustet, 1925.

Lehmann, Karl, ed. *Das Petrusamt: Geschichtliche Stationen seines Verständnisses und gegenwärtige Positionen.* Munich: Schnell and Steiner, 1982.

Lessing, Gotthold Ephraim. *Nathan der Weise: Ein dramatisches Gedicht in fünf Aufzügen.* Berlin: C. F. Voss, 1979. Translated by Ronald Schechter as *Nathan the Wise.* Boston, Mass.: Bedford Saint Martin's, 2004.

Löser, Werner, ed. *Die Römisch-Katholische Kirche.* Frankfurt: Evangelisches Verlagswerk, 1986.

De Lubac, Henri. *Die Kirche: Eine Betrachtung.* Translated by Hans Urs von Balthasar. Einsiedeln: Johannes Verlag, 1968. Originally published as *Méditation sur* l'Eglise. Paris: Aubier, 1953.

Ludwig, Joseph. *Die Primatsworte Mt 16,18.19 in der altkirchlichen Exegese.* Münster: Aschendorff, 1952.

Luther, Martin. *Wider das Papsttum zu Rom vom Teufel gestiftet.* In *Schriften, 1543–1546,* edited by O. Clemen, 195–299. Volume 54 of *Weimarer* Ausgabe. Weimar: Böhlau, 1968.

Maccarrone, Michele, ed. *Il Primato del vescovo di Roma nel primo millennio: Ricerche e testimonianze: Atti del simposio storico-teologico.* Vatican City: Libreria editrice Vaticana, 1991–1997.

Marschall, Werner. *Karthago und Rom: Die Stellung der nordafrikanischen Kirche zum Apostolischen Stuhl.* Stuttgart: Hiersemann, 1971.

McPartlan, Paul. *A Service of Love: Papal Primacy, the Eucharist, and Church Unity.* Washington, D.C.: The Catholic University of America Press, 2016.

Menke, Karl-Heinz. *Sakramentalität: Wesen und Wunde des Katholizismus.* Regensburg: Pustet, 2012.

Michl, Anton. "Der Kampf um das politische oder petrinische Prinzip der Kirchenführing." In *Entscheidung um Chalkedon,* edited by Alois Grillmeier and Heinrich Bacht, 5th ed., 491–562. Vol. 2 of *Das Konzil von Chalkedon: Geschichte und Gegenwart.* Würzburg: Echter-Verlag, 1979.

Mirbt, Carl and Kurt Aland. *Quellen zur Geschichte des Papsttums und des römischen Katholizismus,* 6th ed. Tübingen: J. C. B. Mohr, 1972.

Mikrut, Jan, ed. *La Chiesa cattolica e il Comunismo in Europa centro-orientale e in Unione Sovietica.* Verona: Gabrielli, 2016.

Möhler, Johann Adam. *Die Einheit in der Kirche: Oder das Prinzip des Katholizismus: Dargestellt im Geiste der Kirchenväter der drei ersten Jahrhunderte.* Edited by J. R. Geisleman. Cologne: Hegner, 1957. Translated by Peter C. Erb as *The Unity of the Church, or, the Principle of Catholicism: Presented in the Spirit of the Church Fathers of the First Three Centuries* (Washington D.C.: The Catholic University of America Press, 1996). First published in 1825.

_____. *Athanasius der Grosse und die Kirche seiner Zeit, besonders im Kampfe mit dem Arianismus.* Frankfurt: Minerva, 1972. First published in 1827.

———. *Symbolik: Oder Darstellung der dogmatischen Gegensätze des Katholiken und der Protestanten nach ihren öffentlichen Bekenntnisschriften.* Edited by J. R. Geisleman. Cologne: Hegner, 1958. Translated by James Burton Robertson as *Symbolism: An Exposition of the Doctrinal Differences between Catholics and Protestants as Evidenced by Their Symbolical Writings.* New York: Crossroads Publishing, 1997. First published in 1832.

Müller, Gerhard Ludwig. *Gemeinschaft und Verehrung der Heiligen: Geschicthlich-systematische Grundlegung der Hagiologie.* Freiburg: Herder, 1986.

———. *Katholische Dogmatik: Für Studium und Praxis der Theologie.* Freiburg: Herder, 1995. A portion of this text has been translated by William Hadfield Burkhardt as *Catholic Dogmatics for the Study and Practice of Theology*, vol. 1. New York: Crossroads Publishing, 2017.

———. *John Henry Newman.* Augsburg: Sankt Ulrich, 2010.

Müller, Gerhard Ludwig and Gustavo Gutiérrez. *Armut: Die Herausforderung für den Glauben.* Munich: Kösel, 2014.

Newman, John Henry. *An Essay on the Development of Christian Doctrine.* London: Toovey, 1846.

———. "Biglietto Speech." In *Addresses to Cardinal Newman with His Replies etc., 1879–1881*, edited by W. P. Neville, 61–71. New York: Longmans, Green, and Co., 1905.

Obrist, Franz. *Echtheitsfragen und Deutung der Primatsstelle Mt 16,18f. in der deutschen protestantischen Theologie der letzten dreißig Jahre.* Münster: Aschendorff, 1961.

Pastor, Ludwig von. *Geschichte der Päpste seit dem Ausgang des Mittelalters.* 16 vols. Freiburg: Herder, 1886–1933.

Pascal, Blaise. *Pensées.* Paris: Guillaume Desprez, 1670.

Pera, Marcello. *Diritti umani e cristianesimo: La Chiesa alla prova della modernità.* Venice: Marsilio, 2015.

Pera, Marcello and Joseph Ratzinger. *Senza Radici: Europa, relativismo, cristianesimo, islam.* Milan: Mondadori, 2004. Translated by Michael Moore as *Without Roots: The West, Relativism, Christianity, Islam.* New York: Basic Books, 2007.

Piano, Lino. *Le prerogative del primato papale alla luce dell'Enciclica "Ut unum sint": Risvolti ecclesiali e ecumenici, Annotazioni storiche a 500 anni dalla riforma luterana 1517–2017.* Turin: Elledici, 2016.

Pius XI. *Mit brennender Sorge.* Encyclical Letter. March 14, 1937.

Pontifical Biblical Commission. *The Jewish People and Their Sacred Scriptures in the Christian Bible.* Vatican City: Libreria editrice Vaticana, 2001.

Pontifical Commission on Justice and Peace. *The Church and Human Rights.* Working Paper. Vatican City: Libreria editrice Vaticana, 1975.

Pontifical Council for Justice and Peace. *Compendium of the Social Doctrine of the Church.* June 29, 2004.

Il primato del successore di Pietro: Atti del simposio teologisco, Roma, Dicembre 1996. Vatican City: Libreria editrice Vaticana, 1998.

Raem, Heinz-Albert. *Pius XI. und der Nationalsozialismus: Die Enzyklika "Mit brennender Sorge" vom 14. März 1937*. Paderborn: Schöningh, 1979.

Rahner, Hugo. *Kirche und Staat im frühen Christentum: Dokumente aus acht Jahrhunderten und ihre Deutung*. Munich: Kösel, 1961.

Rahner, Karl and Joseph Ratzinger. *Episkopat und Primat*. Freiburg: Herder, 1961. Translated by Kenneth Barker, Patrick Kearns, Robert Ochs and Richard Strachan as *The Episcopate and the Primacy*. New York: Herder and Herder, 1962.

Ranke, Leopold von. *Die römischen Päpste: In den letzten vier Jahrhunderten*. 6th ed. Leipzig: Dunker and Humblot, 1874.

Ratzinger, Joseph. *Introduction to Christianity*. Translated by J. R. Foster. London: Burns and Oates, 1969. Originally published as *Einführung in das Christentum: Bekenntnis—Taufe—Nachfolge*. Munich: Kösel, 1968.

_____. *Kirche—Zeichen unter den Völkern*. Volume 8 of *Joseph Ratzinger: Gesammelte Schriften*. Freiburg: Herder, 2010.

Richter, Friedrich. *Martin Luther und Ignatius von Loyola: Repräsentanten zweier Geisteswelten*. Stuttgart: Schloz, 1954.

Rousselot, Pierre. "Les yeux de la foi." *Recherches de science religieuse* 1 (1910): 241–259, 444–475. Translated by Joseph Donceel as *The Eyes of Faith*. New York: Fordham University Press, 1990.

Schatz, Klaus. *Der päpstliche Primat: Seine Geschichte von den Ursprüngen bis zur Gegenwart*. Würzburg: Echter, 1990.

Scheeben, Matthias Joseph. *Handbuch der katholischen* Dogmatik. Vol. 3. Freiburg: Herder, 1933. First published in 1873.

Scheffczyk, Leo. *Katholische Glaubenswelt: Wahrheit und Gestalt. With an Interivew with Benedict XVI and an Introduction by Johannes Nebel*. Paderborn: Schöningh, 2008.

_____. "Das Petrusamt in der Kirche: Übergeordnet--eingefügt." In *Glaube als Lebensinterpretation: Gesammelte Schriften zur Theologie*, edited by Leo Scheffczyk, 394–412. Einsiedeln: Johannes Verl, 1980.

_____. *Das Unwandelbare im Petrusamt*. Berlin: Morus-Verl, 1971.

Schlier, Heinrich. *Das Ende der Zeit*. Volume 3 of *Exegetische Aufsätze und Vorträge*. Freiburg: Herder, 1971.

Schneller, Hermann. *Der katholische Glaube: Gott—Christus—Kirche*. 5th ed. Munich: Kösel, 1962.

Schwaiger, Georg. *Papsttum und Päpste im 20. Jahrhundert von Leo XIII. zu Johannes Paul II*. Munich: Beck, 1999.

_____. *Päpstlicher Primat und Autorität der Allgemeinen Konzilien im Spiegel der Geschichte*. Munich: Schöningh, 1977.

Scola, Angelo. *Chi è la Chiesa? Una chiave antropologica e sacramentale per l'ecclesiologia*. Brescia: Queriniana, 2005.

Seppelt, Franz Xaver. *Geschichte der Päpste*. 5 vols. Munich: Kösel, 1954–1956.

Strauss, David Friedrich. *Das Leben Jesu: kritisch bearbeitet*. Tübingen: C. F. Osiander, 1835.

Tillard, Jean-Marie. *L'évêque de Rome*. Paris: Cerf, 1984.

Wermelinger, Otto. *Rom und Pelagius: Die theologische Position der Römischen Bischöfe im pelagianischen Streit in den Jahren* 411–432. Stuttgart: Hiersemann, 1975.

Winkler, Gerhard B. *Das Papsttum: Entwicklung der Amtsgewalt von der Antike bis zur Gegenwart*. Innsbruck: Tyrolia, 2002.

Zuckmayer, Carl. *Als wär's ein Stück von mir*. Frankfurt: Fischer, 1966.

Index

C

D

N

O

P

U

V

W

X

Z

Scripture Index

OLD TESTAMENT

NEW TESTAMENT

Mark

Luke

John

2 Corinthians

Galatians

Ephesians

Philippians

Colossians

1 Thessalonians

2 Thessalonians

1 Timothy

2 Timothy

Titus

Hebrews

1 Peter